Large-Scale Models
for Policy Evaluation

Wiley Series on Systems Engineering and Analysis
HAROLD CHESTNUT, Editor

Large-Scale Models for Policy Evaluation

Peter W. House

Visiting Scholar
ITS
University of California
Berkeley

and

John McLeod

Consultant
Editor Emeritus, *Simulation*
Editor, *Simulation in the Service of Society*
Associate Editor, *Behavioral Science*

A WILEY-INTERSCIENCE PUBLICATION

JOHN WILEY & SONS, New York • London • Sydney • Toronto

Library of Congress Cataloging in Publication Data:

House, Peter William, 1937-
   Large-scale models for policy evaluation.

   (Wiley series on systems engineering and analysis)
   "A Wiley-Interscience publication."
   Includes index.
   1. Social sciences—Mathematical models. 2. Public administration—Mathematical models. 3. Environmental policy—Mathematical models. 4. Policy sciences.
I. McLeod, John, 1911-   joint author. II. Title.

H61.H75   300'.1'51   76-57255
ISBN 0-471-41555-3

Printed in the United States of America

10 9 8 7 6 5 4 3 2 1

To the contributors to this book, and to
all contributors to the art and science of
simulation who have made it possible

SYSTEMS ENGINEERING AND ANALYSIS SERIES

In a society which is producing more people, more materials, more things, and more information than ever before, systems engineering is indispensable in meeting the challenge of complexity. This series of books is an attempt to bring together in a complementary as well as unified fashion the many specialties of the subject, such as modeling and simulation, computing, control, probability and statistics, optimization, reliability, and economics, and to emphasize the interrelationships among them.

The aim is to make the series as comprehensive as possible without dwelling on the myriad details of each specialty and at the same time to provide a broad basic framework on which to build these details. The design of these books will be fundamental in nature to meet the needs of students and engineers and to insure they remain of lasting interest and importance.

Preface

This work reports on the creation of computer software (or algorithms) to enrich man's decision-making ability. We have examined a small subset of this ability, the use of large-scale computer models for public policy purposes. Our examination has been further restricted to those large-scale models that are concerned with social science issues (primarily environmental) rather than models of physical or natural phenomena. All the models we discuss were designed primarily for policy purposes rather than for research or pedagogy. These models are considered from the point of view of theory and methodology, data adequacy, capability of programming, validation, and finally, utility and transferability.

This book is written to give policymakers and members of their staffs information needed for developing large-scale models that can be used for comparing and evaluating alternative policies and strategies in long-range planning.

Several different points of view are presented concerning the feasibility and efficacy of large-scale models. One group appears to favor the creation of more than a mere extension of human capabilities. At times these people appear to promise the prognostic capability of the mythical crystal ball. At the other extreme are modern-day "Luddites" who hold that it is impossible to build, validate, or productively employ large-scale models. Somewhere in between these extremes are a great number of people who are faced with the realization that complex decisions made in a complex world require the use of *all* available aids, including sophisticated computer algorithms.

There are also numerous authors (Boulding, Fuller, and Commoner, to name a few) who have argued that it is not useful to carry on analysis of the social system without taking a holistic approach. Then there are those who question whether it is necessary or even possible to construct a computer model with such grandiose goals. Alonso, for example, argues that the cumulative error introduced by sequential data errors will produce enough noise in the simulation to invalidate the results. Lee argues for the use of partial models and reasons that, on the basis of past results, comprehensive models are not feasible. Brewer is disappointed with these same past experiences and argues for a testing facility for models. Finally, Drake, in his work for the Department of Transportation, finds there has to be considerably more attention paid to the administration of contracts that are let to procure these models.

It is likely some truth exists in each of the sweeping allegations. However, the fears seem to be overreactions, particularly when they claim that large-scale models cannot (or even should not) be built. In the course of this study, a more positive viewpoint has been taken from some of the recent modeling and related studies supported by the Environmental Protection Agency and the National Science Foundation. In addition to addressing the question of the place of large-scale models in the policy arena, especially at the federal level, the study also reports on the current state of affairs in large-scale modeling in general. In the Introduction we give a capsule version of the most important points and developments; then, in later chapters, we go into greater detail concerning the models, how they are built, and how they are or should be used.

It would be almost impossible to credit those who have helped with this work. There have been some forty reviewers, many of whose efforts are included herein. As usual, we hope that there has not been an inordinate amount of damage done to their concepts because only portions of the total studies were selected for inclusion. Where noted, the basics are theirs; the subsequent interpretations are ours.

The research reported in this book was accomplished under unusual circumstances and at a unique period. When begun, Dennis Meadows had just recently presented his treatise on the Limits to Growth at the Smithsonian Institute in Washington, D.C. Its effect is hard to describe, but it appeared to polarize defenders and detractors into factions arguing the validity of the findings. One of the groups formed was a Committee on Forecasting Models (under the now defunct Office of Science and Technology). The climate created by this activity permitted one of the most detailed analyses of large-scale models undertaken, and a portion of it is reported here. The participating actors are numerous. They start with the policymakers who had the vision to recognize the need for large-scale systems and the courage to pursue the unpopular research to test the feasibility of creating them. Most memorable are Robert Fri, the Deputy Administrator of the Environmental Protection Agency, who first asked for the systems, and Dr. Stanley Greenfield, who made the program possible under his Office of Research and Development and who took a deep personal interest in the results. The researchers who worked on the specific system literally number in the hundreds. At the Environmental Protection Agency, however, the core research groups were small. Dr. Philip Patterson, in one fashion or another, contributed to all the models. Mr. Edward Williams co-authored SOS and was heavily involved with SEAS and GEM. Mr. Gene Tyndall was one of the early developers of SEAS. Mr. Sam Ratick has been with SEAS from the very beginning and has often proved invaluable. Finally, Mr. Al Pines took over the responsibility for the spatial modeling.

Zeroing in on the direct production of this book would also require a long list of supporters and colleagues who have helped to make it better. Dr. Will Steger, Dr. Hal Carpenter, and Dr. Bruce Goeller are notable in this regard. Ms. Carol Swinburn is responsible for putting an earlier draft of this manuscript into readable form and for the earlier editing and typing. A later version was completely retyped by Ms. Mary Bogdan. Her ability to decipher our scrawl and to make sense out of pieces of cut and paste manuscript never ceased to amaze me. The present version was completed in California with both Suzette McLeod and Laura Steinman putting the much revised manuscript into final form.

It should be noted that the responsibility for this book lies with the authors. Although much of the original research was done at EPA, this book was written by the two of us in our private capacity. No official support or endorsement by the Environmental Protection Agency or any other agency of the Federal Government is intended or should be inferred. At the time of the final writing of the manuscript, John McLeod is in La Jolla, California, and Peter House is on leave in Berkeley, California at the Institute of Transportation Studies, University of California, Berkeley. The latter would like to thank Professor William Garrison and his staff for the time and assistance required to finish this work.

PETER W. HOUSE
JOHN McLEOD

Berkeley, California
La Jolla, California
November 1976

Contents

Large-Scale Models
for Policy Evaluation

1

Summary and Conclusions

1.1 About This Book

1.1.1 Background

In the chapters that follow, the authors attempt to cover, by description and example, all important aspects of computer modeling and simulation applicable to the development and use of policy models.

The book begins with a summary and an abbreviated version of our conclusions. This should clue the reader to whether this book is for him.

Because simulation is a relatively new field of endeavor (particularly in aiding the formulation of public policy) and because it is more an art than a science, it is strongly influenced by subjective points of view. To reflect this subjectivity, we quote extensively those people with pertinent experience. Consequently, contrasting opinions concerning the most basic questions (the adequacy of data to support policy models, for example) are included.

The authors planned it that way. There is no one correct way to develop a model to support a particular simulation study. Therefore, in an effort to minimize the intrusion of our own bias, we give the point of view of a number of selected authorities. Of course, the selection of quotations introduces our bias to a degree, but we have tried to strike a representative balance.

1.1.2 Chapter Contents

In this chapter, we describe some subjects covered in the other chapters and appendices, explain some pertinent concepts, comment on lessons learned, and propose the directions our efforts should take if we are to improve simulation technology and make the results more politically useful.

Chapter 2 clarifies our subject by explaining some of the terminology. The chapter concludes with brief comments on outstanding technical problems that will be discussed at greater length in subsequent chapters.

1

Data is defined to include the numbers and information used to (1) construct a computer model and (2) run simulation experiments to study some system of interest. The significance of data gathering will be recognized. This important subject has so many ramifications, so many sources where data may be obtained, and so many innovative ways of generating or synthesizing required data, that we devote the entire third chapter to that important subject.

Once we have adequate data, how should we proceed to develop the desired model? Authorities differ in minor ways, but there are certain basic steps that must be taken and a logical order that is generally agreed upon. Chapter 4, therefore, presents and discusses methodology.

Having built a model, how do we know that the results of the simulation experiments are correct? Chapter 5 addresses matters of verification (checking to be sure the computer model does function as intended) and validation (assuring the model represents the simuland to the extent required for the study being undertaken). Validation is a task that can often be accomplished only imperfectly. This problem is treated at some length in Chapter 5.

Documentation should begin with the collection of data and proceed through every step of the modeling, simulation, analysis, and implementation process. Because a large part of the documentation should be completed before the model is actually used for other than trial simulation runs, Chapter 6 discusses this important aspect of the overall simulation process.

Simulationists who have progressed this far with their project are now ready to reap the benefits of their labors. They can now *use* the model to run the simulation experiments for which it was developed.

The simulationists undoubtedly will derive great pleasure from this. Unfortunately, they may ultimately generate only long columns of numbers that are impressive but meaningless to other people. On the other hand, they may generate sets of beautiful, squiggly lines. These too are somewhat esoteric, but often are easier to explain. However, suppose no one wishes to listen? If the results of the analysis of data in the printouts or graphs are not implemented, then our simulationists have been playing (very expensive) games with themselves. Because this happens all too often, Chapter 7 discusses implementation, which is the object of it all.

If implementation does take place, the policies developed as a result of a simulation study are usually implemented only by the agency for which the study was made. Would it not be desirable for a successful model to be transferred by others at another location for use? Certainly, but few models are. The reasons and some possible solutions are also considered in Chapter 7.

Chapter 8 is devoted almost exclusively to excerpts from writings that seem particularly pertinent. The reader can gain an excellent overall perspective of the state of the art of computer modeling and simulation by reading this chapter alone. The authors quoted have "been there."

Appendix I presents brief descriptions of models currently important or interesting. They are presented in different formats to illustrate various ways of documentation.

Appendix II gives more details concerning some of the models briefly described in Appendix I. In no case, however, is sufficient information given to allow readers to "repeat the experiments." That would mean publishing complete documentation, and few people would care to read it even if they could lift the voluminous material. However, sources where complete information may be obtained are given in most cases.

Appendix III identifies more possible sources of data than it would have been practical to include in Chapter 3.

1.1.3   Credits

The authors have drawn on the works of others throughout this book for the reasons previously mentioned; we wish to present the various aspects of simulation from differing points of view. Short quotations are included in the text. Most of the longer quotations are given in Chapter 8 or in the Appendices to avoid major digressions from the sequence in which basic material is presented.

We have tried to give proper credit to other authors in all cases. If we have failed in any instance, it is either because the actual source was unknown to us, or because we were misinformed. We sincerely hope we have slighted no one.

1.2   Concepts

1.2.1   Policymaking

Although defining policymaking is difficult, it is possible to bound the process generally by describing policymaking in terms of level and scope.

It is important to acknowledge the obvious differences in levels wherein public policy is made and to illustrate the differences in the scope of problems. In recognizing these differences, we mention the levels of policymaking and point out the similarities in process so that the principles suggested here can apply to all policymaking that fits our description. It should also be recognized that such a discussion is, of necessity, oversimplified. However, since we are not specifying particular policy problems or case studies, generalizations are necessary.

Our hypothesis, then, is that for our purposes, policymaking can be defined as actions determined by elected officials or their immediate staff that should be taken in response to perceived problems at all levels of government.

The consistent need to decide on a course of action or no action without sufficient information or time to consider all ramifications of possible decisions is a situation familiar to policymaking in the public sector as well as in management decision making in industry.

1.2.2 Policymakers

Within the scope of this book, the term "policymaking" is restricted to the public sector. At this level of description, the policymaker will be recognized as the person or group of persons (e.g., his immediate staff) who makes the principal decisions that guide the public sector. Within our institutional form, these persons are elected (and/or appointed or confirmed) by a constituency whose desires they presumably serve; thus they are responsible to the constituency for their actions.

To discharge their duties, policymakers operate with a staff that normally is divided along functional lines and is specialized to carry out the specific portions of the policy program. Figure 1-1 illustrates in simplified fashion the paradigm of the policymaker. It also points out one of the anomalies of the departmental system that helps explain some of the difficulties involved in modeling for policy uses. Although one description of the policymaker's role in this nation is that of a translator for implementing the public will, the existence and roles of the media and professional societies (as spokesman for the public) define a direct link often bypassing the policy level. It is the existence of this "shunt route" which lies at the root of one of the basic modeling problems for policymakers (namely, the requirement to satisfy not only the needs of the policymakers, but also the demands of the professional community). Because policymakers change as a function of elections, and one's professional career is predicated on peer group status, the modeling community usually tends to be more loyal to the demands of the professional community than to the needs of the policymaker.

1.2.3 Scope of Policy Problems

Concomitant with the highest level of policymaking is a set of problems that model builders, political scientists, and public administrators often ignore, except in a theoretical sense. Nevertheless, political figures make critical decisions on courses of action that involve huge investments of

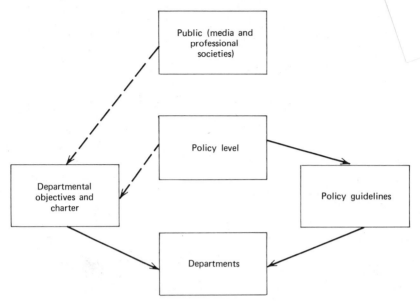

Figure 1-1.   Policy and the organizational structure.

funds and time. The breadth of these issues is often overlooked because of the nature of the political process, but positions are taken and policies are made anyway.

Consider briefly policymaking in industry compared to policymaking in the public sector. The overall objective of any industrial concern is to maximize profit. This desire is shared by the president of the company, by the board of directors who elect him, and by the stockholders who elect them. It is also often shared by the labor force. This means that it is possible to state an overall goal or an "objective function" that is generally consistent for all concerned. It is relatively explicit and the measures of effectiveness are fairly well understood.

By way of contrast, consider the sociopolitical arena. There is no question that business-economic objectives are better defined and accepted than are the goals available to the political decision maker. The personal goal of the president of a corporation, in oversimplified terms, is to remain the president. He generally does this by making a profit and maximizing the growth of this company over both the long and short run.

An elected (or appointed) public official also has the personal goal of remaining in office, but what he must do to achieve this is less clear. To remain in office, he must balance his goal of staying in office with the values and desires of his constituency. Goals of the constituency are often diverse and at times contradictory, yet they are the group from which all his power legally derives.

Moreover, the political candidate must play adversary politics in order to be elected to office. He continually attempts to shift the objectives of his constituency and convince them that he can maximize the benefits to be derived by setting new goals. If the goals of the candidate and of his constituency are perceived by the latter to be nearly equal, then he is likely to be elected. If his adversary can appear to create or enlarge any gap between the politician and his constituency, that may be enough to cause a candidate to lose an election or to force an incumbent out of office. The validity of this analysis becomes more obvious as elections approach.

Certainly it would be a misstatement to assert that all policy models should be aimed at maximizing the potential number of votes for the politician. However, conceptualizing the politician's duty as "satisfying a constituency," rather than as a more readily definable discipline or functional standard (such as efficiency or cost-benefit ratios, and so on) may help to modify the rigidity of the model in the area of normative solutions to include structuring designs that are broader in scope—though admittedly more difficult to quantify.

This oversimplified yet illustrative analogy enables one to see the scope of problems with which the elected policymaker is concerned. The key variables, values and desires of the constituency, should always be the basis for public policy analysis.

We thus see that policymaking varies by level and by problem scope. Yet we know that decisions on public policy are made continually without recourse to analytical methods. To the extent that models can be helpful to the process (and the thrust of this book is that they can be), analytical tools such as simulation should be developed and applied as an integral part of the policy formulating process.

1.3 Needs of Policymakers

One of the basic problems associated with modeling for the policymaker is the difficulty of developing a clear definition of user needs that can be agreed upon by both the model builder and the policymaker. Generally speaking, there appears to be little interaction between the policymaker and the model builder during the initial and design periods of the model. Yet there is often a feeling on the part of the model builder that he understands the problem and certainly has mastered the analytical technique to be used. Consequently, there follows much discussion by way of briefing or "educating" the policymaker as to what is "good" for him. Seldom, however, are there any meetings in which the focus is inverted and the designer himself is educated. It is not surprising, then, that the potential users of these models often feel alienated from the modeler and that the resulting products are not really tailored to the policymakers' needs.

1.3.1   Communication

Interviews and questionnaires offer a technique for establishing better communications between the policymaker and the modeler. This method, which was pursued within the Environmental Protection Agency, involved the use of questionnaires in a highly personalized and ongoing interview process. That approach is described in Section 4.3.4.

There are other ways of improving communications to determine the needs of the policymaker. However, the most effective approaches have one characteristic in common: they get the policymaker involved in the modeling process from the beginning.

A psychologically good method for doing this is to ask advice. In addition to asking what the policymaker's problems are, and how he expects to use the model to help solve them, he should be consulted about the inputs and system interactions that he believes are important. What data does he have and what sources can he suggest? The more numerous his inputs, the more he will feel that it is *his* model. If the modeler can imbue that feeling, he will go far toward eliminating the communication problem.

It is also helpful to erect and operate a simple model as soon as possible. Ask what the policymaker thinks of it, and, if possible, get him to do some hands-on experiments. If he likes the outcome, he will be sold. If he does not, the sooner the model designer finds out, the better. It is relatively easy to change a simple preliminary model. If it is changed in accordance with the policymaker's suggestions, his proprietary interest in the model should be strengthened.

1.3.2   Modeling and the Environment

The use of models is a professional discipline as well as a method used to study the environment and to aid policy and decision makers. This was made clear recently when the former Office of Science and Technology set up a Committee on Forecasting Models. This group held a few formal meetings, but it quickly became evident that, although each of the federal agency representatives had the credentials to sit on the committee, there was little common ground for communication.

This revelation led to the decision to develop a publication entitled *A Guide to Models in Governmental Planning and Operations* (Mathematica, 1974). This publication describes the current status of models in selected functional areas, including transportation, environment, health, and others. Because it was an aim of the committee to broaden the use of models in all government sectors (federal, state, and local), the publication also includes expository material that can serve as an introduction to models for the full range of users. Thus the product of this effort can be considered a guide to model use enabling the reader to follow a path from general model principles to specific model application.

Although many of the techniques discussed in the *Guide* could be utilized to study environmental problems, none describes the whole picture; none is truly "comprehensive."

Comprehensive Models. A comprehensive model is a complete treatment of a large number of pertinent components and relationships that make up the empirical world, whether the final product is the result of a holistic or a partial model approach. As with a holistic model, the comprehensive model is capable of application to various specific areas at different levels of aggregation.

A consideration of the policymaker's needs suggests a need for comprehensive models. Even here, though, it is unclear what "comprehensive" means. The following is just a sampling of some of the proposals and designs sent to EPA that were reported to be comprehensive: (1) an ecological model that included a part of a detailed description of the natural subsystems (the human linkages), but reduced these and their activities to six equations; (2) an engineering model that evaluated a single industry; (3) river basin models that detailed source, flow, and pollution loadings for a river but treated all emission sources as loaded parameters; and (4) social science models that were designed to simulate the migration, land use, and traffic patterns of urban locales, but included no environmental factors.

There are those who believe that everything should be included in a model that deals with the environment. The attempt to meet such criteria in operation is overwhelmingly difficult. The dangers take the appearance of polar extremes. The first of these poles can be characterized by a model that is very broad in scope and includes the whole world described by what the designers believe to be relevant variables. These models generally suffer because they are so aggregated that their usefulness is questionable except for pedagogic purposes. At the other extreme are models that bite off a large segment of the world (a whole nation, state, or the like) and attempt to define *all* of the relevant subsystems in a way that is amenable to the model construction. Few of these models are ever successfully programmed, much less used in policy formulation. Thus, even within the modeling profession, the word "comprehensive" means something different to each modeler.

Decision versus Policymaking Models. Just what is a policy model? (Based on Mathematica, 1974.) If one were to attend a number of the professional meetings held each year or read the articles written by modeling practitioners, it would become apparent that almost all feel their creations are "policy" models. In fact, the great majority of the models known in the public sector were claimed at one time or another to be of this type. From one point of view, many of these models are probably related to policy scheme. To leave "policy" at this vague point, however, equates it to the term "decision."

Logically, all models can be handled as a subset of decision models. Further, the methodologies used to address policy questions can be viewed synonymously with those used for any others. It is our contention that this logic set is the principal reason for the dearth of models in this area. Although the techniques may indeed be similar or analogous, the problems themselves are so unique that many analysts who propose to build "policy models" appear to fall short of the goal. Therefore, the problem can be said to be one not of technique necessarily, but of content. Having understood the problems, it is possible that one may wish to develop or expand techniques, but such steps are presently only conjecture. What is worse is that the models that purport to be of policy scope are being used to assist in the optimization of the administration of a program or a policy *after* it has been decided to implement it.

Most decisions to fund model development (or model application) in the governmental sector are executed by people who make, or help make, policy. Consequently, it pays for those who wish to build models to profess an ability and willingness to make models useful to such people.

An Assistant Secretary of Transportation lucidly stated this problem (Cherrington, 1969). His essential point was that systems analysis, with its "bag" of models, causes policymakers considerable frustration because analysts constantly demand time to develop, complete, and test a variety of models before policy choices should be made. On the other hand, policy decisions arise and often must be made immediately. Utility of models is rarely the principal goal of the analysts.

In reality, researchers do not interact with the policymaker himself and only to some limited extent with his staff or with a particular department.

The researcher's goals and desires may not agree with those at the policy level, and the resulting lack of specificity relegates models to art forms developed by modelers who merely guess at what the client really needs. A typical process is one in which, once the contract work statement is approved, the "client" is no longer the policymaker but one of the staff assigned to monitor the effort. The staff monitor may indeed be technically competent, but the policymaker loses interest if his own needs are slighted. This process, having been repeated time and time again in government, has helped cause staffs to become cynical and to question seriously the utility of all models.

For purposes of the policy-model designer, the most important basic goals of the elected official would seem to be the following: first, to satisfy the needs, interests, and goals of his constituency; second, to satisfy his own personal needs in terms of pursuing the programs and ideals that motivate his political life; and third, to be able to select from a full range of possible policy decisions those most effective in meeting the above two needs.

Within this context, the ultimate policymaking model might allow the policymaker to project the effectiveness of various policy alternatives based upon their ability to achieve both his personal goals and their potential effects upon societal values and thus public opinion. The official who understands which of the issues are really the most relevant and which should be given the greatest weight will maximize his vote-getting potential. And the official who can weigh beforehand various policy alternatives in terms of their efficacy toward achieving societal goals will be able to make more effective decisions and be able to judge their developing impact more accurately in terms of his original needs.

1.3.3 Feasibility of Comprehensive Models

Before discussing how the task of developing the kind of comprehensive model policymakers need is undertaken, and what the components of the research design should be, it is crucial to note that not everyone agrees that achieving such a goal is feasible. The avowed need for comprehensiveness—regardless of how right it appears in the case of environmental issues—was, within the last decade or more, argued heavily with respect to the analysis of urban-regional problems. In general, the attempts to build comprehensive, general models of the urban area met with little success in proportion to the amount of rhetoric (and in some cases, funds) expended in that direction.

As a backlash against those who would build holistically, there have appeared warnings of some of the dangers; several of these are summarized in the following paragraphs and are covered in more detail in Chapter 8.

In "Requiem for Large-Scale Models" (see Section 8.11), Douglas Lee lists "Seven Sins of Large-Scale Models" and then offers three guidelines for model building. Another severe critic of simulation, Brewer (1973), emphasizes some points similar to those covered by Lee. However, because the author does not summarize them in a form suitable for quotation, we will simply set down some of his more pertinent points as we understand them:

- At the date of writing, the author knew of no simulation models that had been useful for the formulation of urban policy. He sees this as a failure to suit the model to the needs of the policymaker rather than as a shortcoming in modeling technology.
- Problems also arose from the different perspectives of those involved: the salesmen, the model developers, the academic consultants, the users, and the managers.
- A misunderstanding and/or misrepresentation of the difficulties involved caused trouble. The simuland was not understood well enough, nor were the problems of managing such a demanding undertaking.
- Simulation salesmen did not understand (or ignored) the potential backlash of overselling. The result was a loss of credibility in simulation and enmity on the part of decision makers.
- Models may be built for ulterior reasons:
  To rationalize a decision already made.
  To delay having to make a difficult decision.
  To "make work" in a project.
  To justify investments in computing equipment.
  To create an illusion of progress.

Still another author (Drake, 1973; see Section 8.2), examines the question, "Why do many computer-based transportation models fail?"

Drake discusses several hypotheses related to modeling, and offers 11 factors that he believes will increase the usefulness of models. He also reports on a survey of more than 20 modeling projects and offers many concrete suggestions for improvement.

Each of these authors certainly makes numerous valid points. It was the recognition of difficulties which they have delineated that prompted many of them to follow a research strategy which attempted to balance ambitious goals with achievable but less grandiose intervening subtasks. This effort has been conducted by reviews of the current state of the art, by aggressive, creative design, and by the cynicism that often comes with experience.

To summarize, the problems described by the critics just cited and the ameliorating actions they suggest can be restated under three general headings:

1. Data: reducing the labor and difficulties of collection and preparation.
2. Theory: tackling questions of its existence and/or adequacy.
3. Implementation: alleviating problems attendant on constructing the models and improving their utility, including their use and transfer.

Each of these topics is addressed in some detail in this book.

It was realized that an undertaking of the magnitude required to deal with problems we have outlined would be a massive task and that, although each of the issues was to be faced squarely and analyzed to the fullest extent possible, several dead ends or blind alleys would almost certainly appear and lead to frustration. Also, because current knowledge was not adequate, judgment would have to supplement available data and existing technology.

Finally, although this book draws heavily on research at EPA and although one of the prime objectives of one of the Agency's Divisions (Environmental Studies Division) was to create a general, comprehensive man-machine system to be used by policy-level decision makers for strategic purposes, we do not presume that this effort completely covers the field of large-scale policy modeling. Certainly, other research exists that might have been cited. However, the examples chosen were felt to be sufficient to illustrate our case.

1.4 Lessons Learned

Several of the complaints against the past large models can be summarized by saying that the models have been oversold and underdelivered. For example, one critic previously mentioned (Brewer, 1973) has written:

Caveat emptor is an ill-suited bromide for technically unsophisticated public officials when the disease is a sophisticated problem solution, for a price . . . Public officials may be led to expect too much, from social science research in general and from simulation activities in particular, in the way of answers to a class of difficult questions that are not scientific in the commonly accepted sense. Unfortunately, they are political questions, such as "What should the goals of the city be?", "What should politicians do about them?", "To whom should it be done?" In the absence of information on the limits and the possibilities of present-day social science, expectations become inflated. Prediction is expected even where the crudest understanding has not yet been reached. This particular misconception is widespread and not limited to any special group of individuals.

The same study suggests that some model promoters are hucksters of the worst sort and infers that there is something unclean about these activities. We agree with the principle that one should not have to sell an idea if it is needed or valid. Unfortunately, the real world is seldom so astute as the one found in texts, and when resources are limited, a certain amount of salesmanship is inevitable. This is particularly true when such models may cost many millions of dollars—sums not usually available for social science-oriented research.

By the time this book is published, readers and authors alike will hopefully have learned additional lessons. However, we believe that those learned to date can serve as a bench-mark, a point of departure to survey new territory. So let us consider where we currently seem to be on our way toward our goal of making policy models more helpful to policymakers.

We begin with some comments on what the research undertaken to supply material for this book indicates to us concerning models in general and policy models in particular.

1.4.1 Capabilities

Policy models can:

- Be developed, even within the very real constraints of available data and current technology.
- Be validated, with respect to the assumptions upon which their development was based.
- Be useful, within the constraints of appropriate application.

Considering the qualifying phrases attached to the three foregoing assertions, those assertions probably cannot be seriously questioned; but they have been, are, and will be challenged. Some of the challenges are logically and/or scientifically sound. Others are much more emotional. Often critics seem to feel that professionally unqualified upstarts are poaching on their established disciplinary preserves.

To acknowledge the very real shortcomings of computer modeling and simulation, and to spike the guns of the detractors, we agree to the following.

1.4.2 Limitations

Policy models (and simulation in general) cannot:

- Predict the future (except to a limited extent under special conditions; see Section 5.3).

- Produce reliable output from unreliable data (for more on this, and prediction; see Section 8.1).
- Be validated except in a limited sense (see Section 5.2).
- Transcend stupidity.

1.4.3 *Alternatives*

Now let us consider the alternatives to modeling. What are they? It can be that there are no alternatives to the use of models by policymakers. The claim is that all decisions must be based on the decision maker's paradigm, his own mental model of the relevant facts and their interaction. This may be true, but it certainly does not mean there are no alternatives to *computer* modeling. Among the alternatives are:

- Basing decisions on the knowledge and experience of the decision maker and his advisors. When such knowledge and experience have contributed to the development of mental models, and these models influence decisions subliminally, the decisions are said to be based on intuition. Perhaps the imperfection of such models and the fact that their help is invoked subconsciously accounts for the "Counter-Intuitive Behavior of Social Systems" (Forrester, January 1971).
- Basing decisions on "expert opinion." Such opinions may be gathered in many ways, but one such method is the Delphi technique developed by Olaf Helmer and Norman Dalkey at the Rand Corporation. (For an update see Linstone and Turoff, 1975, and for a discussion of its weaknesses, see Sackman, 1975.)

Pure input-output and cross-impact analysis techniques may also be used. These are basic cause-and-effect matrices that may or may not involve the use of computers. While such matrices are certainly models of a sort, they are usually static (although they can be computerized and made dynamic in a sense) and reflect data and relationships at a given time or during a certain period. True, they can be used to examine possibilities at other times, including the future, by making assumptions concerning the inputs at another time; but they are ill-adapted to the "march through time" that dynamic models based on differential equations do so well.

There are also various techniques of mathematical analysis that can be helpful to the decision maker, and although details are beyond the scope of this book, they should be considered items in the policymaker's armament.

It is not the authors' contention that computer modeling is the only alternative. On the contrary, we believe the task of the policymaker is so difficult that he should make use of every tool at his disposal. We do believe, however, that computer modeling, as it is treated in this book, is not only one of the most powerful tools available, but one that can coordinate the application of all others.

For instance, a Delphi-like technique might be used to help "quantify unquantifiables" and "get a handle on fuzzy" relationships. The input-output and cross-impact matrices can strengthen the modeler's concept of the interrelations in the model as well as supply infomation needed to establish initial values for the model variables. Then mathematical techniques can be used to check the simulation experiments and, while it is not done to the extent it should be, establish confidence limits on the results.

For other thoughts on alternatives to modeling see Section 8.5.3.

1.5 Directions for Progress

Simulationists have a long way to go, but the directions are obvious and the tasks that must be undertaken are clear. These are considered in some detail in subsequent sections (see especially Section 2.3).

Here we simply list the principal areas in which more effort must be expended if we are to progress in our attempts to make computer modeling and simulation a more effective methodology for policymaking. We *must*:

- Learn to quantify data heretofore considered unquantifiable; a prime example is "Quality of Life" (see Section 2.3.1).
- Learn how to handle the unpredictable (see Section 2.3.2).
- Learn how better to determine the relative importance of characteristics of the system to be modeled (see Sections 2.3.3 and 2.3.4).
- Learn how to recognize and compensate for the inevitable biases that creep (or are pushed) into our models, our simulation experiments, and our analysis of the results (see Section 2.3.5).
- Ensure that models are not used for purposes beyond their capability (see Section 2.3.6).
- Establish (flexible) standards for meanings of terms, documentation, and methodology (see Section 2.3.7).
- Educate the modeler concerning policymaking and policymakers, that is, concerning the environment in which the model is to be used (see Section 4.3.4).
- Educate the potential user as to the capabilities and limitations of models (see Section 4.3.3).
- Avoid overselling (see Section 4.4).

The foregoing looks like a big order—and it is. However, as we are progressing into an era where we are becoming concerned with problems that are multidisciplinary in scope and impact (i.e., the environment, energy, raw materials, etc.), the models being used for some of these policy issues are broader in scope and forecast further into the future (ERDA talks of the year 2000) than has usually been done in the past. In short, necessity has pushed us into a world of large-scale policy models and has consequently formed many challenges for the modeling profession. All of this is healthy; it is a sign that modeling is growing up. No longer is it merely the toy of the intellectual dilettante, but now the tool of modern-day policy analysts.

2

Introduction

2.1 Background

An introductory story about a man who lived his life eccentrically will illustrate the follies of the incremental approach in the decision-making process. First of all, his house was always completely shut up: the doors were closed, the windows shuttered, and the curtains drawn. His first daily contact with the outside world was when he left his house each morning.

This seclusion from the outside world meant that each morning the gentleman chose his clothing based entirely upon random process of selecting whatever he encountered first in his closet or whatever struck his fancy. This process resulted in several departures from the house in wool suits on 90 degree days and, alternately, linen departures in sub zero weather.

It took the gentleman quite some time to change his ways even though his selections often resulted in ridiculous matches between weather and attire. It seems his father's people had always done it in the fashion he followed, and he felt a need to continue the policy.

One day, after almost freezing to death because of the chance occurrence of choosing a lightweight garment in the midst of the coldest spell of the season, he decided to bend tradition slightly. The following morning he chose a wool garment to meet the freezing cold.

The choice, of course, was a correct one, and the random game he had been playing changed; he now had the correct clothing on when he went outside more times than not. The selection process now progressed to where he was absolutely wrong only at the major turning points in the weather. That is, he missed all of the seasonal change guesses and was never prepared for rain. To increase his number of correct guesses, he devised a scheme to average the weather and his clothing choices over several days. The system he finally chose showed considerable improvement, although he still did very poorly at the turning points.

He was so pleased with his success that he felt he had to tell his neighbors. The neighbors listened to his presentation in silent amazement. They were impressed with the eruditeness of his methodology, but puzzled as to why the process was needed. One of them did deduce the problem and suggested our friend look out of the window each morning to check on the weather before selecting his clothes.

Our friend was abashed. He quietly went home to ponder his new wisdom. Having committed himself to experimentation, however, he merely added the checking of the weather to his system. Lo and behold, his success soared with this new process. Unfortunately, he still had a single consistent problem, and he returned to seek further consultation from his neighbors.

It appeared now there was little random error in our friend's choice. He anticipated the turning points in the weather well, but he still was not able to foresee changes in the weather from one decision period to the next. If it was not raining when he checked in the morning and had not rained for the sample period, he would often get caught in the rain, snow, or hail. On the other hand, if it was raining, he was often in a quandary to explain it in light of his data from the previous days if it had showed no rain. At this point, somebody suggested that he make use of radio forecasts.

Regardless of our personal opinions of the weather forecaster, it is certain that his skills could help our decision-making friend. The story itself certainly is ridiculous. Who would ever make decisions in the fashion discussed above? No one, of course.

On the other hand, suppose we change the item of a wardrobe to a budget, the clothes to the expenditures required each year by a government, the man to the public decision maker, and the weather to the business, political, and social cycles and vagaries of our social system. In this case, maybe the story is not so silly.

Lindbloom made famous the process he referred to as incremental decision making or "muddling through." In brief, the process faces each decision in isolation and in turn without conscious referral to other decisions or to previous experience of future consequences. Each decision is made, therefore, symptomatically. It is not clear if those who followed his analysis actually advocated the methodology; but there appears to be unanimous agreement that the process as described too often represented public decision making. Does this sound familiar?

Let us continue. In recent years, following the advent of the computer and the science (or art) of computer programming, the software and modeling communities began to approach the public decision maker with "predictive" models. These models were designed to replicate from some point in the past, up to the point in which the decision maker was interested, and then to the project beyond. This process was touted as "useful" for the policymaker *to extrapolate the experience of the past to help him make his present decisions.*

Does this still sound familiar?

Our mythical friend is, of course, very silly, and the analogy might appear overly long to make a seemingly obvious point. Although the world is complex, there are portions of it which are sufficiently systematic to not impose a large burden on our individual and collective daily existences. Furthermore, it would appear logical that any device which could add rigor and scope to the analysis and understanding of this order would be embraced wholeheartedly. Computer models would appear to serve this purpose, yet they are not so avidly espoused. The question is, Why? This question is a focal point of this book. Specifically, we are interested in large-scale or general models that can be used for a variety of purposes.

To be strictly fair in our discussion of the lack of widespread model acceptance, there are people who simply do not believe building of these models is possible. One segment of this group has looked at the performance of those who have, in the past, claimed the ability to build such models (or systems). Others have looked at the state of our knowledge on cause-and-effect relationships, the data available, and the limitations of the computer, both in terms of hardware and software. They have reached the conclusion that such grand endeavors are quixotic. There is a second segment of this group that has a much less clearly defined scientific basis for their reticence; on the basis of gut feelings for realities of the policy area (or because of some deeply felt psychological repulsion), they merely condemn such endeavors.

The set of arguments used by the first segment of skeptics is very important and has incited healthy debate in the professional societies. Topics such as validity, model documentation and use, data standards, manipulation algorithms, new software languages, and hardware configurations are being discussed with increasing frequency. In addition to these, the whole area of theory building in the social sciences has been undergoing a revolution as the conceptualizations of society's operation are continually reformulated and described with precision so that they can be programmed on a computer. The earliest of these attempts were highly formalistic in the mathematical sense and, because of limitations imposed by the rigor, often were too elegant and abstract for good mapping of model and reality. At the other extreme, because a clever programmer can code nearly anything that can be described, computer algorithms of unbelievable complexity and unguaranteed accuracy were being derived. What was called for was some wedding of these two potential extremes: elegance and reality.

Let us turn our attention to the environment, which, by its nature, appeared to call for the existence of large-scale policy models. Demands for protection of our environment appeared on the national scene with unexpected force; within a short period, large numbers of people from all levels of the public and private sectors were mobilized for the effort.

At the federal government level, this resulted in the organization of two new institutions, the Environmental Protection Agency (EPA) and the Council on Environmental Quality (CEQ). Intense organizational activity took place throughout the spectrum of the scientific, administrative, and technical communities. Physicists, chemists, physicians, engineers, and social scientists joined with lawyers, managers, computer specialists, and laboratory technicians as part of the range of specialists who had, and still have, a specific interest in environmental matters. Each of these professionals brought his own particular perspectives, value systems, and techniques to bear on this issue.

In contrast to this professional specialization, the environmental issue addressed has been described by one writer (Commoner, 1972) as:

. . . a system comprising the earth's living things and the thin skin of air, water, and soil which is their habitat. This system, the ecosphere, is the product of the joint, interdigitated evolution of living things and of the physical and chemical constituents of the earth's surface . . .

The basic functional element of the ecosphere is the ecological cycle, in which each separate element influences the behavior of the rest of the cycle, and is in turn influenced by it. For example, in surface water, fish excrete organic waste which is converted by bacteria to inorganic products; the latter are in turn nutrients for algal growth; the algae are eaten by the fish, and the cycle is complete. Such a cyclical process accomplishes the self-purification of the environmental system in that wastes produced in one step in the cycle become the necessary raw materials for the next . . . However, if stressed by an external agency, such a cycle may exceed the limits of its self-governing processes and eventually collapse . . .

Because the turnover rate of an ecosystem is inherently limited, there is a corresponding limit to the rate of production of any of its constituents. Different segments of the global ecosystem (e.g., soil, fresh water, marine ecosystems) operate at different intrinsic-turnover rates and therefore differ in the limits of their productivity. On purely theoretical grounds it is self-evident that any economic system which is impelled to grow by constantly increasing the rate at which it extracts wealth from the ecosystem must eventually drive the ecosystem to a state of collapse.

The system described obviously does not map very well on a discipline-by-discipline view of society.

With this in mind, it is evident that our approach to environmental problems should go beyond the prejudices of any specific profession. A former Administrator of the EPA (Fri, 1973) enunciated the necessary strategy in an address to the National Conference on Managing the Environment. A pertinent section from his address follows.

We cannot create new air, land, or water, so we must husband these resources. Surprisingly, we are just now relearning the husbandry our forebears knew so well.

But can we manage our environment wisely? To be sure, we have set the stage for control of the more obvious kinds of air and water pollution, but we have only begun to consider the subtler interactions between man and his environment. We are only now beginning to understand the complex web of forces that determines the quality of our life-forces such as land and energy use, transportation, economic growth, urbanization, population, and the advancing juggernaut of technology.

Managing the environment as a system is complicated. However, it is no secret to the well-informed that we have information to develop a system solution to a great many of our ecological problems now. We do not need any fabulous breakthroughs or quantum leaps to at least get started on the design of an environmentally integrated society.

The more difficult question is: "Who is going to apply all of this sophisticated knowledge?" In solving environmental problems, the burden will fall, as it often does now, on the shoulders of state and local governments. Systems thinking does not change the reality that these levels of government remain closest to the problems and are most able to determine what should be done and what is possible.

For let there be no mistake about it—getting control of air and water pollution will be simple compared to solving the higher problems of an advanced technological society. We must go beyond enforcement, important as that is, and focus more sharply on land use, transportation controls, energy planning and an assessment of technology itself.

Nor is it a task for lawyers or scientists or public servants acting alone; it demands cooperation, breadth of mind and openness to change.

The greening of America will be largely up to the creative leadership of public health and pollution control departments, mayors, council members, regional planners and county officials, working with citizen groups to devise action plans for the integrated environs of tomorrow.

The society of the future will be more orderly and efficient than the one we have known. We will enjoy longer lives and better health. We will waste fewer resources. We will not be so obsessed by quantity in lieu of quality.

2.2 Terminology

In this book we offer a distillation of a potpourri of ideas and methods, some adopted from others and some worked out by the authors and applicable to the development of models and simulations for strategic analysis and policy evaluation. Because any new art or science typically generates new words and/or assigns new meanings to old ones, we will define some terms here and others as they are used.

The methods described and the definitions given may not be unanimously acceptable to other simulationists, but we believe they have great merit. We hope that our colleagues will agree, but agreement is less important than consistency. Therefore, while adhering to the following definitions, we will remain alert for any signs of a growing consensus in favor of other nomenclature. If and when they appear, we will change. Certainly, agreement on definitions is necessary if computer modeling and simulation are to become more science than art.

Whereas the terms "modeling" and "simulation" have been widely used interchangeably, we believe a distinction exists and should be clarified.

Modeling is the process of developing a model. While realizing there are many kinds of models, we limit our discussion in this book to models developed by programming a digital computer to mimic the dynamic behavior of some real or postulated system of interest in all respects pertinent to a particular study.

Simulating is the act of using a model to perform experiments in lieu of performing them on the system modeled. Even though there are other ways of simulating—some better suited for certain purposes—all the simulations discussed in this book used digital computer models with or without human interaction.

The foregoing give rise to related terms, which we also define with respect to their usage in this book.

Model, the end result of modeling; for our purposes, a computer program. Digital computer programs may exist as punch-card decks, printed listings, programs on punched paper or magnetic tape or in computer memories.

Simulation, the result of performing experiments with a model on a computer.

Simulationist, one who simulates—a person.

Simulator, that which simulates—a machine.

Simuland, the real or postulated system that is simulated.

System, a group of interrelated entities, which may themselves be systems.

Mechanization, adapting a machine to perform a task; used herein to signify programming a computer to process the information that constitutes a model.

Implementation, the putting into effect of plans or policies; in this book, plans or policies formulated with the aid of simulation (not to be confused with mechanization).

Verification, the process of ensuring that the computer model runs as intended, that is, that the mechanization is correct. This includes, but is not limited to, "debugging" the program.

Validation, the procedure required to assure that the model mimics all pertinent characteristics of the simuland as accurately as necessary for the study at hand. Not to be confused with verification.

Conceptualization, formulating ideas, preparing a verbal description of the simuland, and writing a precise definition of the problem to be investigated.

Formalization, preparation of a diagram indicating the interrelation of state variables and other elements of the simulation, writing the equations that describe the interactions, and preparing the computer program—the model.

Exogenous variable, a variable the value of which is determined by factors external to the simuland. Such variables are usually set by the operator and may or may not be changed during a simulation run.

Endogenous variable, a variable whose initial value may change during a simulation run as a result of interaction with other variables.

State variable (called "levels" in system dynamics), one of the important endogenous variables whose values collectively completely describe the state of the simulated system at any given time.

Parameter, a measure of a system that is determined by the characteristics of the simuland and remains constant during any specific run.

2.3 Toward A Better Simulation Technology

Critics of simulation are not without ammunition. Simulation is a versatile and, when properly applied, extemely useful tool, but its very versatility makes it vulnerable to attack when it is misused. A knife, too, is a useful tool; however, if one tried to use a machete to perform an appendectomy, would critics then condemn knives? Yet when simulations are unable to predict the future, simulation as a technique is more likely to be condemned than the person who said, or implied, or thought that simulation could do the impossible. Only under very special circumstances can simulation be used for prediction, and even then, the predictions should be carefully qualified. That is a far cry from "predicting the future."

In Section 1.5 we listed nine areas where we feel further work is required. Let us now consider some of these again and suggest how our efforts might be directed to solve, or at least alleviate, most of those technical problems. (Those areas related to administration are addressed in Chapter 4.)

2.3.1 Data

There are at least three problems associated with obtaining adequate data for policy (and other) models:

1. Availability.
2. Reliability.
3. Quantification.

Because these problems, individually and collectively, are so important—and because so much has and must be done to cope with them—we have devoted all of Chapter 3 to the subject, making use of the difficulties attendant upon "getting a handle on" the "Quality of Life" to illustrate the difficulty of measuring and assigning numbers to other "unquantifiable" quantities.

In this section, therefore, we will proceed at once to the problem of modeling possibilities.

2.3.2 *Modeling Despite Unpredictables*

With respect to the kind of modeling we are interested in, unpredictables are of two kinds: trends, and discontinuities. In a model, an unpredicted change in a trend has the effect of altering rates. A discontinuity, such as a technological breakthrough on the one hand or a major catastrophe on the other, changes rates in a stepwise fashion, or possibly may require changes in the basic causal diagram (see Section 4.2.1).

In either case, the method for handling unpredictables is the same as other "what-if" studies. The investigator should make "worst case," "best case," and "best guess" runs to create an "envelope" of possible outcomes. Statistical analysis can then be used to assign probabilities to the results. Because these probabilities are functions of the probabilities upon which assumptions concerning "best" and "worst" were based, some way of establishing these extreme situations must be found.

History might help. What are the highest and lowest values some variable has attained in the past? Statistically, what is the probability that it will again attain the values used in the simulations?

If this approach is inappropriate or inadequate, we must resort to "expert opinion," either the modeler's or the decision maker's. Hopefully it can be a combination of the two. Failing that, a form of the Delphi technique (see Section 1.4.3) may be invoked. If properly designed, such a study can begin to yield probabilities and confidence factors.

A simulation involving possible trend shifts or discontinuities that require changes in the basic assumptions used as the foundation of the simulation is useful for exploring possibilities, but its ability to forecast is certainly contingent upon many "ifs." Nevertheless, such simulations suggest the need for, and can contribute to, the design of contingency plans.

2.3.3 Sensitivity

It has been said that a better part of wisdom is knowing what one can ignore. This truism applies particularly to model building. Too much detail makes a model difficult to program, expensive to run, and, in the extreme, as difficult to understand as the simuland.

However, too little detail might mean that something important is being left out. So how does one know?

There are formal mathematical methods of sensitivity testing that are helpful in reducing the number of variables considered. There are also less rigorous methods that simply amount to making small changes in individual parameters and variables and then noting the effect on the model outputs. If the changes in the outputs are within the "noise level" of the simulation results, the parameter or variable under investigation may be considered relatively unimportant and so be deleted from the model. Other statistical methods are available to help evaluate the importance of individual variables (i.e., regression techniques). In most cases, theoretical analysis of the problem gives some clues to the requisite variables and, at least, provides a starting configuration.

The determination of the noise level and what is relatively unimportant are matters that the modeler must decide. This is no place for amateurs. Computers are impartial; they amplify incompetence just as they do proficiency.

2.3.4 Aggregation

Much that we have said about determining what to include or leave out of models applies to aggregation—the grouping of diverse entities under one heading (grouping men, women, young, old, representatives of different ethnic groups, different cultures, and different nationalities together as "people"). This might be acceptable in some "broad-brush" treatments of global problems, as in *World Dynamics* (Forrester, 1971), but such aggregation would be intolerable in models for which demography is important.

We can say very simply that the amount of aggregation is strictly a matter of what question the simulation study is meant to explore. Again, the modeler's judgement is invoked; it has to be good.

2.3.5 Biases

All models involve biases; some are acceptable, some unavoidable. A model developed to explore interactions in a given culture should not be expected to take into account the fact that people from other cultures with different value systems would disagree. This is obvious. What is not so obvious are the biases that influence the development of a model which stem from skewed data sources, the modeler's judgment, and the user's opinions.

The only thing to do about such biases is to recognize that they are inevitable, try to evaluate their effects, and then compensate for them. This is primarily the modeler's responsibility. However, because he usually cannot recognize his own biases, some of the problem devolves on the user.

As honest and as objective as a modeler tries to be, his bias will be reflected in his model. For example, the data sources he chooses to use, the aspects he considers important, and even interpretation of the potential user's requirements may determine significant details of his model.

A way to alleviate this problem is for the modeler and the potential user to work together on the project from its inception to the analysis of the results. Because the modeler and the user will almost certainly have different biases, they will (hopefully) tend to offset each other.

2.3.6 Each According to Its Ability

The problem that has discredited modeling and simulation more than any other is misapplication. In some cases, this has been the result of overselling. In others, it has been a simple lack of understanding of what a specific model is capable of. A screwdriver should not be used to drive nails or cut wood, yet people continue to expect simulations to do things they were not designed to do. It must be realized that the reasons for simulating, designing models, and experimenting form a broad continuum from the very simple to the extremely complex. An article, "Simulation Today— from Fuzz to Fact" (McLeod, March 1973), puts it this way:

. . . if your reason for simulation is that you need reliable, quantitative "answers" to specific questions, you will be working at one extreme — and the most difficult — end of the spectrum. The requirements for your data, your computer model and your simulation experiments will be quite different from those that would be imposed if you wished only to explore some fuzzy hypothesis.

Let's examine the spectrum in more detail, beginning with the vague simulations, which we can arbitrarily place at the left-hand end. Here our knowledge of the real (or hypothesized) system, the simuland, is minimal. Data pertaining to the elements of the system are not available or are suspect, and the relationships among the elements—how a change in one affects the others—can only be assumed.

Hopeless? Not at all. In fact, under these circumstances simulation can be most useful. But don't expect any "answers." Answers can be obtained only at the extreme opposite end of the spectrum—and that's a long way off!

Let me repeat that, in a different way. The naive are apt to expect too much from simulation, and that fact has given and is still giving simulation a bad reputation in some circles: Only under very special circumstances, which we will approach as we work our way across the spectrum from left to right, will simulation give reliable "answers."

Now, back to the left-hand end of the continuum: How can any simulation so vague as that suggested above be useful? Well, at the very least it will be an "aid to cogitation," a mechanized way of toying with ideas. Further, if more than one person is involved, the model will serve as an explicit base for discussion. At least everyone will have a common reference, and that can certainly preclude a lot of misunderstanding.

Finally, just the attempt to develop a model with inadequate information will point up the most important of the inadequacies. Thus it will narrow the field of research necessary to improve the model, and in that way allow one to move in the continuum toward more credible simulations. Certainly the foregoing points alone are sufficient to justify fuzzy simulations.

If information concerning the simuland is more nearly complete and/or more reliable, there are more reasons to simulate. Experiments can be designed to determine the sensitivity of the simuland to changes in input data and in the assumptions on which the model is based. This might allow simplification of the model, because factors having negligible influence on aspects of interest can be ignored. But, more importantly, it will yield information concerning "pressure points" in the simuland, those places where the ratio of input energy to output change is greatest. Note that to be useful for the foregoing purposes, the data and assumptions need not be good enough to yield quantitative results. The reason for running this kind of simulation lies somewhere between the two ends of the spectrum, where qualitative results are all that are expected. Such models are "valid" for specific kinds of simulation experiments only—and great care must always be exercised to assure that no model is used for purposes beyond its capability.

The foregoing is probably the most important statement that can be made about simulation. Failure to heed this admonition has not only made trouble for individual investigators, but has in some cases laid the whole practice of simulation open to attack.

Now let us consider the extreme right-hand of the spectrum where the reason for simulation is to obtain answers. Now we're playing in a different league! Data must be complete and accurate, interactions among elements of the simuland must be rigorously described mathematically, the model must be correctly mechanized on the computer, and the simulation investigation must be carefully planned according to the best principles of experimental design.

Furthermore, there is no reason that a large-scale model should be a general one. For example, the model or collection of models built and used for Project Independence (PIES) (Section AI-6) is an example of an extremely large model that was designed for a single purpose. However, in today's world where increasing reliance is placed on computer models and data bases for use in analyzing policy questions, the time required to tailor-make models is usually excessive. Therefore, the users of such systems habitually turn to existing systems to jury rig them to suit their need of the moment. Many times, this is satisfactory. More often it is not. The pressures for such widespread use of a system are particularly noticeable within a specific agency that has a system like SEAS (Sections AI, AII-4). The number of questions the political policy level asks the average bureaucrat-technician outstrips his ability to respond. The development of a tool like SEAS often results from a request for aid, and because the system survives at the pleasure of the agency, a frenetic desire is made to meet the request. In some ways, this feature is little different from any client relationship in or outside the government. Recognizing this pent-up potential demand places two interesting pressures on the builders. There is a constant need to prevent the model from being used before it has been checked out, and there is an analogous need to keep the model from being used for purposes for which it was not designed.

2.3.7   Standards

If simulation is to progress from the present state of the art to a science, some standards must be established. The standards currently in greatest need of attention are terminology and documentation. We touched on the matter of terminology in Section 2.2. More is being done along these lines by the Society for Computer Simulation, which has an active Standards Committee that has prepared an eight-page report (Society for Computer Simulation, 1976) on the subject.

The need for uniform documentation, like the need to standardize terminology, stems from a need to improve communications among modelers. The development and use of a standard format for documenting models would do much to assure that the documentation is adequate and understandable to other modelers. This subject is discussed at length in Chapter 6.

2.4   A Rationale

It would not be difficult to demonstrate that the decision making, at the federal level at least, has expanded to include not only the more traditional areas organized along sectoral lines (such as Agriculture, Commerce, and Interior), but has included a greater emphasis on issues that are trans-sectoral (such as ERDA and the EPA). It is immaterial just how unique this phenomenon is. The substantial argument is that these agencies appear to be the creatures of perceived "crisis"; no existing structure could deal with the vital issues. What is significant for us here is that the conceptualization that required the reorganization also called for more holistic and longer-run analysis than were heretofore deemed proper. Even the 1975 Budget of the President contained a forecast to 1980. Several other macro-economists who previously had only done quarterly forecasting models now will prepare projections from the year 1985 to beyond 2000.

In brief, it is clear the demand for broad-scope forecasting models is upon us. Unfortunately, specifying a need or desire for such systems does not guarantee they will be forthcoming. In fact, as we will see from excerpts reported in this book, there are several professionals who assert that such models cannot reasonably be built. An investigation of the reports in which those statements are made reveals they are based on analyses of models often a decade or more old. The works of Brewer and Lee (Sections 1.3.3, 1.4, and 8.11) are cases in point.

It is still too soon to see whether the problems that plagued us during those early days are with us today. There are several reasons to believe, however, that they might not be. For example, several of the models built more than a decade ago were mechanized on computers that are primitive by today's terms. Also, the software that is now available is richer and more flexible. Systems analysis has become a widespread methodology; theoretical constructs are better, and data sources are more plentiful. All of these factors help build better models. A danger might be that our expectations have grown, so that the problem is relatively no different than it was when we first attempted to build large-scale models.

Furthermore, although communications are pretty dismal in the area of models and modeling technology, they are better now that the need for big systems is being taken more seriously by those who make policy and allocate funds. In 1975 alone, there were four major model assessment efforts produced that are not fully reported in this book. They are, however, covered in the Bibliography (Beller, 1975; Moore 1975; Chestnut, 1975; Library of Congress, 1975).

Obviously, not all of the work produced during this time period is directly applicable or of high quality; however, its existence does give one a reasonable indication of the interest level in the utility and technical capabilities of large systems. Furthermore, this information will reach those who would use such systems in a more timely fashion. Therefore the potential effectiveness of large systems, using information that is closer to the state of the art, is subject to reappraisal. This book is aligned to that spirit.

3

Data

One of the most persistent deficiencies pointed out by model builders, and their detractors, is the usual inadequacy of the data required for building models, particularly large-scale models.

William Thomson, Lord Kelvin (Kelvin, 1891–94), remarked:

When you can measure what you are speaking about, and express it in numbers, you know something about it; but when you cannot measure it, when you cannot express it in numbers, your knowledge is of a meager and unsatisfactory kind: it may be the beginning of knowledge, but you have scarcely, in your thoughts, advanced to the stage of science.

In this chapter, we consider general approaches to the problem of obtaining numbers, that is, adequate data; specific sources are given in Appendix III. In a broad sense this data may fall into three categories based on the source.

Primary data is searched for by the modeler to satisfy specific requirements of the model under consideration.

Secondary data is that which has been gathered for some other purpose or purposes, but which is available to support the model development.

Synthetic data is generated rather than collected. This might be necessary because the data is not otherwise available; or synthesizing it might be faster, more productive, or more economical than obtaining data by other means. We will describe two methods of generating synthetic data in Section 3.3: describing a typical city, and simulating a data base.

3.1 Primary Data

Because the kind and amount of primary data required for the development of a particular model depend on the purpose and intended use of the model, no specific instructions can be given for its collection. However, two generalities are in order.

First, the availability of secondary data and the advisability of synthesizing data should be considered because of the probable high cost, in time and money, of collecting primary data for a single purpose. Second, the use of a very simple model—the simplest that can be designed with relatively easy to obtain data—should be designed and used as a tool to determine the requirements for additional data.

The latter point deserves some explanation. Even the attempt to build a simple model will give a first approximation of the kind, quantity, and quality of the data needed to improve the model to the degree necessary for the purpose intended. Properly interpreted, this information can preclude wasteful attempts to gather more data and/or more accurate data than is actually required.

3.2   Secondary Data

During the past few years, an extensive effort has been made at all levels of government to collect and catalog data for policy purposes. This new data (plus the more familiar information collected by surveys and censuses of the government departments and professional societies) was intended to support comprehensive management information systems. However, this wealth of data makes a rich lode for those designing models, thus making the need to collect primary material less compelling.

3.2.1   *Integrated Municipal Information Systems (IMIS)*

The first approach to the use of secondary data is to gather all required information from local sources using local records. Because this is, in general, the rationale behind the Urban Information Systems Inter-Agency Committee (UISIAC) project (which has received heavy funding from Federal and other government levels), it is appropriate that we explain the background and operation of the UISIAC project.

In the words of UISIAC Chairman (Knisely, 1973),

UISIAC was formed in 1968 by representatives of several Federal departments concerned with the fact that the Federal government was paying too little attention to information technology at the local general purpose government level. [The Committee] felt that information flows are the sinews of government, and that the individual attempts on the part of cities across the nation were not utilizing to the fullest the information technologies developed in defense and space work. . . . It was agreed that . . . funds should be made available for a research and development program which would assist selected cities to develop full or partial Integrated Municipal Information Systems (IMIS).

The balance of this discussion is from an article which appeared in *Nation's Cities* (Wright, 1972).

There are many facets to IMIS. In fact, IMIS is really a body of concepts which is still in the process of evolving and being tested. No city in the United States yet* has an IMIS. Six UISIAC cities are involved in a research effort to determine the validity of these concepts and their value in actual practice. However, with the project moving into its third year, there is every indication that the basic concepts are valid.

The systems evolving in the six UISIAC cities are being developed in a modular fashion—that is, each segment is comprised of a group of interrelated parts which can operate efficiently as an entity. As each module is completed, it will, in effect, be regarded as a "product" which will be made available in various forms to all other American cities at minimal cost. The UISIAC chart, Figure 3-1, illustrates one method of grouping functional activities common to local governments.

A subobjective of this ambitious project is to make data available for modeling and other analytical purposes. To the extent that local data is available and up to date, there is little question that such data should be used in any models of the area constructed or used. Unfortunately, it is becoming increasingly apparent that the collection, organization, and up-dating of such information is very costly, and even though the resulting benefits may be quite substantial, the process is beyond the financial means of most localities. Thus, it is fortunate that there are other sources of secondary data.

A recent model developed by the Department of Transportation has suggested the efficacy of using "default" values gathered from average or secondary sources where primary data is not available (Zimmerman, 1973):

To make data preparation easier, some data items are input for groups of communities with similar characteristics, rather than for individual communities. Data items of this nature include construction costs, dislocation rates, capacities, speed limits, etc. The model is completely flexible on community type aggregations, but most of the "default" data items have a CBD (Central Business District), central city, suburb and non-CBD commercial-industrial breakdown.

Though these default data items, obtained from national compilations, allow CAPM's (Community Aggregate Planning Model) operation with little information preparation by the local agency, a more accurate use of the model would entail local derivation of such data as the ones mentioned above, signal spacing on arterials, ramp spacing on freeways, and the travel distribution equations, etc.

The use of such techniques allows central model design, data collection, and fine model tuning to be done by localities. The extent of such

*Note that this is excerpted from an article written in 1972.

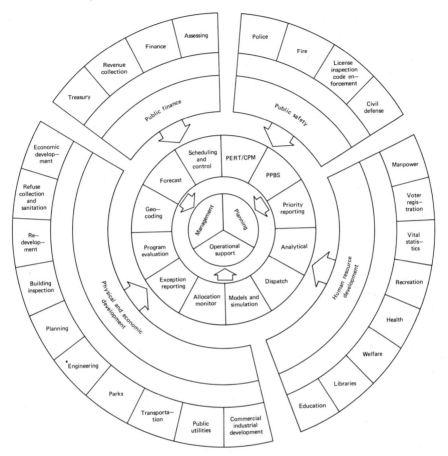

Figure 3-1. The UISIAC MIS chart.

fine tuning is a function of the use of the model and the resources available.

The Federal Government census began with a constitutional requirement to count the populace and mushroomed with numerous additional agency and Congressional mandates. Now, it is the largest data-gathering institution in the world. Not only is there a tremendous amount of data collected annually, but most is of high quality and is collected with some consistency and organization.

Unfortunately, the availability of the information is not widely known. We are not speaking of the U.S. Census of Population reports, which have a great deal of visibility and use, but of the various yearly surveys and reports issued by individual agencies for more limited purposes.

Many of these reports do not receive widespread publicity and are little used.

This amounts to a waste in the Federal system and has prompted the following recommendation (Data, 1972) by the Working Committee on Data at an NSF-RANN-sponsored workshop investigating the research and new techniques needed to plan the nation's physical environment:

(1) All funding agencies should employ a bonus as part of each research grant to encourage researchers to produce comparable or compatible data.

(2) Access to data by public and citizens cannot be stressed too strongly. There are three aspects of particular concern: (1) making known the data which are available, (2) providing direct man/machine interface without need for highly technical computer language, and (3) developing data needed by all citizens to plead their cases, and not limiting data to the concerns of powerful interest groups or strata of population. All funding institutions should consider these three concerns when making research grants.

In addition to the data which is collected for other specific purposes, there appears to be a growing awareness of the need for either centralized collection or specification of information for policy and research purposes. Legislation to establish a National Environmental Data System (NEDS) and the Earth Resources Observation System (EROS) program suffice as examples of this trend.

3.2.2   *National Environment Data Systems (NEDS)*

Congressman John D. Dingell (D. Mass.) has twice introduced legislation in the House of Representatives to establish a National Environmental Data System in concert with policies established in the National Environmental Policy Act of 1969. In the 93rd Congress, the legislation (HR 4732), "National Environmental Data System and Environmental Centers Act of 1973," established a National Environmental Data System which, as set forth in Section 102 of the bill, is intended to:

Include an appropriate network of new and existing information processing or computer faciles both private and public in various areas of the United States, which, through a system of interconnections, are in communication with a central facility for input, access, and general management . . . The purpose of the Data System is to serve as the central national coordinating facility for the selection, storage, analysis, retrieval, and dissemination of information, knowledge, and data relating to the environment so as to provide information needed to support environmental decisions in a timely manner and in a usable form. Such information . . . shall be collected and received . . . from all Federal agencies, private institutions, universities, and colleges, State and local governments, individuals, and any other source of reliable information, knowledge, and data. Information . . . shall also be sought from international sources . . .

Section 103 of H.R. 4732 establishes that the information in the Data System will, generally, be available free of charge to those institutions in a position to feed in data and, at a cost, to others desiring it.

3.2.3   Earth Resources Observation System (EROS)

There is now another valuable source of data, that from the Earth Resources Technology Satellite (ERTS), administered under the EROS program of the U.S. Geological Survey, Department of the Interior, in cooperation with NASA and many other federal, state, and local government offices and private industry. The first ERTS was launched July 23, 1972.

The EROS Program was "established to employ remote sensing data acquired by aircraft and spacecraft in research on applications to resource and land-use inventory and management." Results suggest that the EROS program is proving useful in a wide spectrum of activities, including crop inventory, land use planning, oil, mineral, and water prospecting, new map preparation, census taking, and pollution regulation. In an issue of *Science,* Abelson (1973) explains that:

Most of the data from the satellite have come from a multispectral scanner subsystem that views an area 185 by 185 km in four wavelength bands. . . . The images obtained in the various wavelength regions are transmitted directly to earth when the satellite is over the United States. At other times, the images are stored on magnetic tapes for readout when in range of U.S. stations.

Of greatest interest for our purposes is a data facility that has been established at Sioux Falls, South Dakota, from which ERTS imagery is redistributed by the Interior Department. Users throughout the world may purchase the data at nominal cost. The EROS program has also established a number of "Browse Files." At these facilities, the prospective user of ERTS data may view the projected image of each scene viewed by ERTS sensors. This material is provided by NASA on 16 mm film, and is viewed in an enlarging viewer at 1:1,000,000 scale. NASA, the Department of Agriculture, the Department of Commerce, and several state government agencies maintain browse file facilities as well. Special training courses in the use of ERTS data are also being conducted by EROS.

Both the NEDS and the ERTS data, when added to the already rich lode of information currently available, could be used to supply much of the data needed for a local or metropolitian land use model. The use of such readily available secondary sources could reduce significantly the collection time and cost, thereby making large-scale models more feasible for local communities.

3.2.4 *Strategic Environmental Assessment System (SEAS)*

To be really useful to the model builder or user, the data sources must be clearly understood. There can be no ambiguity in what the data is and how and where it can be obtained. The work done on the data base for the Strategic Environmental Assessment System (SEAS) (Sections AI-1, AII-4) in EPA provides a ready and abundant source material on the use of secondary data sources. Because of the anticipated need for great amounts of data and the concomitant concern for its availability on an annual basis, an EPA contractor for the SEAS Information System, IBM, held a discussion with representatives of each of the Federal agencies. The results of this survey are reported in some detail in Appendix III-1.

All of the data described is available at little or no cost. The use of secondary data sources does not, however, mean that there will not be trouble gathering data for a particular comprehensive model. What it does suggest, on the other hand, is that for some applications, a great deal of the data is available for general model use.

3.3 Synthesized Data

Even with the considerable supply of primary and secondary data for models, there is seldom enough information of sufficient quality for many modeling efforts. Techniques are being developed to help mitigate these problems. Many of these techniques were devised to alleviate the very real difficulty encountered when attempting to transfer models produced for a specific location, or use, to different uses or locations (see Chapter 7).

There remain at least two other concepts which can be used to approximate the information necessary to model an area. These are simulating a data base and describing a "typical" city. Each of these is, by definition, less precise than the IMIS or some other sources of secondary data, but the relative difference in cost and time may make one or more of them acceptable. Their specific and relative utility will depend on numerous factors, however, including the model to be used, the problem addressed, the time available, the level of detail, and accuracy required. Each of these techniques will be illustrated by liberal reference to other research.

This does not suggest, however, that the example used is the only approach possible or even that the particular approach is especially good or bad.

Whether one's predilection when building models is to start with theory and then search for relevant data, start with the data and through analysis develop a theory, or some combination of the above, the fact remains that there is a positive, although not specifically understood, relationship between such factors as the scale and level of aggregation, or grain, of a model and the amount of data required. In general, the larger the model the more data required. Usually, the greater the data requirements, the more expensive the model is to build, debug, and use. The latter statement is especially true if the largeness referred to is coupled with increasing functional relationships rather than just more numbers for a single kind of data (e.g., number of people rather than the characteristics of a population and their resulting behavior).

Part of the introduction to a report (Voorhees, 1973) covered in Section AIII-2 contains some important points for our current discussion:

One outstanding feature which runs throughout all [large-scale modeling] efforts is the level of resources typically devoted to the collection of data and preparation of this data for use in analysis. It has been the experience of this consultant, for example, that a minimum of 20 percent of the cost of applying land use models will be directly associated with data collection, while in the case of standard travel analyses, 45 percent to 50 percent of the cost is likely to be incurred before any real analytical efforts can be made. The nature of these data requirements severely limits the range of situations to which models may be applied. Only when a major study is undertaken, or when there is clearly an on-going need for analytical capability, will the level of resources available be adequate to support an application of models requiring large input data bases.

In contrast to the situation in which the application of models may be financially feasible is the typical situation in which models might be most useful: public decision makers often have questions about the possible results of one or another course of action, questions which arise in the ongoing formulation and application of policy. An immediate solution is desired, and it therefore is assumed that accuracy or certainty in prediction may be sacrificed in order to achieve a quick decision. Models, as currently designed, provide little assistance in this incremental decision making context.

Because availability of data is a key determinant of model cost, it is suggested that this availability be considered more seriously when the proposed model is to be transferable to other users.

Although the techniques of synthesizing a data base for a model are applicable to the data needs for all kinds and models, let us assume that the data base we wish to develop is for a particular city or metropolitan area.

3.3.1 Simulated Data Bases

The basic hypothesis of a data synthesizing technique (the Simulation City Approach) is that it is possible to approximate the detailed input data base required for complex planning models, given only a relatively gross description of a specific metropolitan area and general knowledge of urban composition patterns. This approximation leads to a substantial reduction in the costs associated with data preparation; thus a decision maker is given the opportunity to ask a range of questions at substantially reduced cost in time and money.

The approach is based upon the principle that there is a sufficient body of knowledge about the structure and operating character of the system of activities comprising a metropolitan area to permit the simulation of a considerable portion of the detailed description of an area. Based on a knowledge of the principal industry and median income in an area, for example, one may infer a great deal about the socioeconomic character of the area. To make this inference, one needs knowledge of the whole country's current character and of the body of research available in urban economics. Similarly, a knowledge of total population will allow one to make a reasonable assumption about the amount of urban-developed land. While such a simulation cannot replicate the actual real-world situation, it will possess a sufficient resemblance to the real world to induce the same decisions that would be made using a "perfect" model. To draw an analogy, the dimensions of a building plan are not usually specified in fractions of an inch; decisions regarding the allocation of space may be made on a coarser basis.

This kind of city model is a means of approximating the description of a metropolitan area required for input to one or more planning models. Details of how this might be accomplished are given in Appendix III-2.

3.3.2 Typical Cities

In recent years, a statistical technique known as factor (or principal component) analysis has been increasingly employed. This technique has numerous uses, but one of particular interest to the model builder is that it can be used to construct average or "typical" societal systems. The technique in essence requires the specification of various items as descriptors of the reference area (e.g., a city) and the use of these descriptors to segregate a discrete number of such areas. Each of the cluster areas created is internally similar, but distinct from each of the other clusters. Further analysis of each cluster enables one to choose a "most representative" area from among the clusters, or to devise an average area from within each cluster.

As in the case of the simulation of a data base, the approach is less accurate than designing a data base for a specific locale. It may, however, be all that is necessary, even in the case of a specific area, when only an approximate solution is required.

In Appendix III-3 we report excerpts from two studies (Pidot, 1973; Berry, 1973) that built such classification schedules, although only the first discusses the feasibility of applying the technique to a specific model.

3.4 Summary

In summary, all of these methods are potentially adequate for answering many policy questions. Admittedly, none of these methods is normally sufficient for most research scientists who require a considerable higher degree of detail and accuracy. Because most decisions have a sense of urgency (whereas science is not supposed to), the questions of time required and cost involved in collecting the data must always be weighed against the value of information that might be generated for the policymaker. In the main, however, it can be argued that data is not a serious restriction to the construction of large-scale models for policy purposes, particularly at the level of strategic policy analysis.

4

Methodology

The development of useful models, and their successful application, does not depend upon technology alone. The technology must be implemented in a suitable administrative environment. We intend to cover both aspects in this chapter; however, because the administrative climate should exist or be created before model development begins, we consider that aspect of the process first.

4.1 Administration of Simulation Projects

There are numerous possible subjects that could be covered under this heading. Here we concern ourselves with the problem of the sponsor's best strategy.

In the main, two administrative approaches seem to be of interest to sponsors. The first concerns use of a team versus a single builder. This category includes such topics as the composition of the team (single versus several companies). The second is building the model in-house versus building it under contract or grant. In practice, one finds that most models are actually a mix of these extremes. Because of changes in program emphasis, shifts in internal manpower, differences in contractor/grantee style, and capabilities (not to mention personality complications among those involved), little can be done to recommend administrative practices except to describe techniques used with various models.

If we rank the models described in Appendix II in degree of in-house involvement, we find that the STAR San Diego and Harris (HPMP) (see Sections AII-1 and AII-2) efforts have had little more sponsor involvement than is normally expected in responsible contract or grant management. In these cases, most work by the government was devoted to helping define the scope of the project, and reading and commenting on the progress reports, and listening and reacting to briefings.

At the other extreme lies the SEAS project (see Sections AI-1 and AII-4). SEAS is a system conceived in the Environmental Protection Agency. The basic design was generated internally. The in-house team, with assistance from other sections of EPA, kept reasonably tight control over the system. During the test model phase, biweekly meetings were called at which all of those with responsibility for the models were expected to report on their progress. These reports were subject to review by other participants. The reports were supplemented by design papers focusing on specific parts of the system. These also were subject to general review before being programmed. The design and mechanization of SEAS, therefore, was open and evolutionary (at least in detail); changes or additions to the system were made by consensus of the experts building the model. The constraints were defined by the in-house group with an eye toward eventual widespread internal use of SEAS in the formulation of EPA policy.

Between the above extremes lie GEM (see Sections AI-4 and AII-5) and SOS (see Sections AI-5 and AII-7), each of which was, both by design and circumstance, handled differently. Because the RIVER BASIN MODEL (the core of GEM) was already in existence, those who worked on GEM had a constraint placed upon them that was not present to the same extent in the development of the other models.

Even though the SEAS system and the HPMP made use of existing models, these were not seen as constraints. In fact, these projects were designed to discover and test existing partial models and build only those that were needed. In the case of GEM, the overall design of the system was conceived in-house and the model designed and programmed on a task-by-task basis with close interaction between the in-house and contractor builders. Furthermore, model development and production were sequential and theoretically permitted evolution of the basic structure.

SOS was developed under an entirely different type of management. Here, it was decided to delineate completely the theoretical portion of the model and to design and program a test of the resulting construct using close in-house/contractor cooperation. With the test model and an analysis of its results, a contract was then let to refine and expand the original model for policy use.

We have described several approaches, but because of numerous variables, only a few of which have been noted here, it is impossible to analyze the approaches to mechanizing these models in a comparative sense. We therefore cannot say that one strategy is preferable to another in the building of policy models. Nevertheless, it is possible to make some general statements.

4.1.1   Administrative Difficulties

Within the Federal Government, it has historically been very difficult to isolate a group of analysts who would be dedicated to large-scale models, particularly if such models will take a long time to complete. The reasons for the difficulty of administering the development of large-scale models are legion and varied. One problem is assembling a large number of first-rate modeling professionals in one government agency and keeping them together. This is difficult for several reasons, not the least of which is that the required skills are not necessarily seen as useful by most bureaucratic administrators. Furthermore, even after such a group has been organized, there is likely to be pressure from the agency to commandeer the personnel to "stamp out brush fires," unless the agency is truly dedicated to the modeling effort or has sufficient personnel to meet both requirements.

Again, it is difficult and often impossible for the professional to put in the great amount of time needed to become fully informed of all the models available or details of a single model. There is a positive relationship between such difficulty and the size and number of models being designed or used.

Another consideration is that if an agency chooses to remain relatively uninvolved in the development of a model, it will have a problem understanding and believing in the model. This is also a direct function of the complexity and size of the model.

One possibility for overcoming the usual lack of broad-gauged in-house expertise is to create a core team of model designers and then supplement their talents by adding professionals in specific disciplines on an as-needed basis. However, getting a person assigned to a task when he is needed and then depending on his professional integrity alone to ensure quality often proves less than satisfactory because of the number of competing demands on the time of most individuals, and because of the lack of a clear reward structure. Unless the person is directly tied to the project and can obtain rewards from its success, a piecemeal or ad hoc input is usually all that can be expected, and even then this input should be regarded with suspicion.

Finally, one of the major constraints to building models (especially when one uses interdisciplinary teams) is the amazing lack of communication among the builders. This problem became very apparent in the EPA and in other agencies as well. Consequently, the EPA commissioned a study to investigate the frame of reference and methodologies used by various disciplines to model within their spheres of interest.

Several chapters of the resulting report (Mathematica, 1974) describe the use of models in a variety of social-urban fields. Each chapter is basically self-contained, but relies on the prior reading of the primer. In addition, each author presents information on models that complement the material in the primer.

In sum, the report is an attempt to present to a nontechnical, government-oriented audience an overview of what models are and how they have been used in a number of important social-urban areas. It represents a source from which government officials and others can obtain an understanding of the modeling approach to decision making.

4.1.2   The Planning Team and Its Objective

Benyon (1972) has discussed the concept of a modeling team and its formation and gives a potpourri of general hints. These guidelines are presented as the consensus of a group of researchers:

An initial planning team should be formed by attaching to a core of computer scientists, mathematicians, etc., one expert for each main discipline, or group of closely related disciplines, considered to be highly relevant to the particular project. An upper limit of 15 members is suggested. Many more than this number could ultimately participate in the project either as consultants or as members of separate teams developing various parts of the model.

A short educational course (a day or so) would often be desirable to ensure that all members understand the nature and the purpose of models. The course would preferably include computer demonstrations of a model in action. For many environmental projects it would be appropriate to demonstrate World 2, a simple model of world population, resources and pollution (Forrester, 1971).

The objective of the initial planning team would be to decide how best to break the complete modeling task into more manageable sub-tasks and then to set up an organization of modeling teams appropriate to these sub-tasks.

4.1.3   A Hierarchy of Models and Modeling Teams

A different approach to the formation of modeling teams is proposed by Clymer (1969):

The sub-task should be related to the practical arrangement of a model, not as one monolithic whole, but as a number of separate but interlocking models. One of these would be an overall model simulating the dynamics of the whole system as its different parts interact with one another. Supporting this model in various ways would be a number of sub-models (in some cases themselves supported by sub-models, etc.) each simulating in detail the behaviour of one particular section or aspects of the complete system. The support could, in each case, take one of a number of forms:

(1)   The complete sub-model could be included in full as part of the main model.

(2)   At the opposite extreme, a sub-model could be used merely to confirm that certain effects are negligible for the purposes of the project and need not be represented at all in the overall model.
(3)   Some of the intermediate possibilities are:
    (a)   the sub-model could be operated independently to determine the value of a constant used in the main model;
    (b)   the sub-model could be operated independently until sufficient understanding has been obtained to enable a simplified version to be formulated for inclusion in the main model. The simplification would be achieved by such steps as aggregation of variables, neglect of short time-lags in series with much longer time-lags, etc.;
    (c)   the complete sub-model could be used, but instead of being included directly in the main model, its outputs for a wide variety of inputs could be . . . tabulated and just these tables included in the overall model.

Which of these various methods is the appropriate one for any particular sub-model depends, firstly, on just how sensitive the behaviour of the whole system is to the behaviour of that part and, secondly, on how complex is the behaviour of that part.

Small teams of specialists would be set up to formulate and validate each of the sub-models, with a main team to look after the overall model and supervise the work of the specialist teams. Thus, there would be a hierarchy of modeling teams corresponding to the hierarchy of models.

These hierarchies would be planned with care since they influence the way the whole project is carried out. This is why the initial planning phase is being discussed in detail.

4.1.4   Roughing Out Model Plans

The final ideas on the subject are based on two other publications (Forrester, 1968; Goodman, 1971) and cited by Benyon (1972):

The initial planning team would begin their task by defining the boundary of the system to be considered and by identifying the main questions or types of questions needing to be answered. They should seek suggestions from various quarters to determine what are the most pertinent questions. They may not be able to anticipate all the questions that will eventually be asked, but they must decide on the classes of questions or it will not be possible to make sensible decisions on what features of the real system to include or not include in the model.

They should then be in a position to see which are the key variables whose values at any given time collectively define the state of the system in all relevant aspects. These are the "state variables" whose changes over time have to be modeled.

The planning team would then endeavour to map out the major paths of cause and effect by which interactions occur between one variable and another. In particular, they would look for any closed paths of "feedback loops" that might be present in the pattern of cause-and-effect relationships. This is a very important step because it is these feedback loops that are responsible for the difficulty of understanding the behaviour of the whole system even when the behaviour of its component parts is understood. It is largely this feature of systems that makes the "systems approach" necessary.

An example of such a feedback loop in an environmental situation might be that as pollution increases, public awareness of the need for some action increases; this in turn leads the public to approve more money be' made available for remedial measures, and these measures eventually react on pollution. However, because of the time delays in each part of the loop, and because of other things going on at the same time (such as growing population and industry contributing further sources of pollution), it may be difficult to see whether pollution will, in fact, increase or decrease.

The planning team may need to go through the steps outlined above several times, progressively refining their ideas. If, for instance, it were to become apparent that part of an important feedback loop lay outside the system as originally defined, then it would be desirable that they redefine the system boundary to bring in the whole loop. Eventually, however, their picture of the system would become clear enough to proceed to the next important step: the actual division of the model into sub-models.

There are a number of factors that could assist the planning team in deciding which parts or aspects to include in particular submodels:

(1) *Time scale and space scale.* Generally it is undesirable to attempt representing very small scale and very large scale phenomena in the same sub-model.

(2) *Spatial location.* It may be appropriate to have different sub-models for different regions of space.

(3) *Functional level.* For example, in an ecological system, it might be useful to have a different sub-model for each trophic level.

(4) *Accessibility for measurement.* All variables crossing boundaries (i.e., variables that are inputs and outputs of submodels) ideally would be recorded or measured because this facilitates independent validation of each sub-model.

(5) *Degree of coupling.* Parts of the system that are very strongly cross coupled usually should be kept together within the same sub-model.

(6) *Available expertise.* The content of each sub-model should be challenging and yet within the areas of competence and interest for the people available to work on it.

To carry out their work properly, the initial planning team would have to analyze the system in some depth. However, they obviously would not be able to anticipate all the features that may be brought to light later by the specialist teams. They would therefore need to strike a balance between (a) ensuring that the teams have clearly defined tasks with no gaps or overlaps and (b) providing flexibility to cope with the unexpected.

The initial planning should be carried out with care and patience and would necessitate frequent meetings of the planning team over a period of several months, although many of these would be very informal meetings requiring only a few to attend. To give the team some initial momentum, a few of its members would do some preliminary work and at the first full meeting put forward a suggested outline model (or, perhaps, a number of competing or complementary models).

4.2   Developing a Simulation Model

Nonbelievers sometimes justify their skepticism of modeling and simulation results on the grounds that the technology has no firm foundation in theory. If by "theory" we mean "a coherent group of general propositions used as principles of explanation for a class of phenomena," and if we seek to find a single theory to support model construction or simulation practices, it is true that such a theory does not exist. However, there are applicable theories in mathematics, cybernetics, and information processing that can be and are combined by an established—if not rigorous—methodology. It is this methodology that we discuss in the following section.

Simulation methodology is not rigorous in the sense that every step must be followed according to a precise procedure. However, there *are* a finite number of basic steps that a simulationist ignores at his peril.

In the sections that follow we go from the general to the specific; first we give the basic steps that should be considered when undertaking any simulation project. Next we describe a particular methodology pioneered by Professor Jay Forrester and employed afterward at various centers throughout the world.

4.2.1   A General Approach

Seventeen steps are basic to the development and execution of a useful simulation. The peculiarities of a specific project may dictate that some steps be skipped or the order be changed, but all should be seriously considered before and during the course of the project.

1.   Specify the objective of the project, document, and consult.
2.   Describe the simuland in words, document, and consult.
3.   Determine what is important, document, and consult.
4.   Construct an influence diagram, document, and consult.
5.   Determine data requirements, document, and consult.
6.   Collect data, document, and consult.
7.   Describe the influence diagram actions and interactions mathematically, document, and consult.
8.   Write the computer program, document, and consult.
9.   Mechanize the model, document, and consult.
10.   Verify the mechanization, document, and consult.
11.   Validate the model, document, and consult.
12.   Design the simulation experiment, document, and consult.
13.   Make the simulation runs, document, and consult.

14. Analyze the results, document, and consult.
15. Formulate recommendations, document, and consult.
16. Complete documentation and consult.
17. Cooperate with implementation, document, and consult.

Let us consider what is meant by the concurrent responsibility to document each step and the responsibility to consult concomitantly with others concerned, *especially the decision maker who will be responsible for implementation.*

Specify the objective. Certainly, there must be a reason for launching every project; however, that reason is often not precisely stated, and in too many cases it is little more than a vague idea in someone's mind. The first item on our list makes it plain that the purpose should be concisely stated, put in writing, and discussed with the project sponsor, colleagues, and potential implementer of the results.

Describe the simuland. At this point, we prepare a verbal (natural language) and/or graphic (block diagram) description of the real-world system to be simulated. This description should be documented and discussed in consultation, as all steps should be. Because documentation and consultation apply to all steps, we do not repeat this admonition again. It should be remembered, however, that documentation and consultation are actions that should be carried on in parallel with each step throughout the program. Projects have died from "too little, too late."

Determine what is important. We emphasize that model building and simulation are iterative processes. The first time this item is encountered in the procedure, it may be possible only to guess what is important. Later, as model development progresses, the model itself will begin to reveal what is important. Then, "go back to Step 3."

Construct an influence diagram. It is a truism that "everything influences everything." At this step, the problem is to determine what influences what, to the extent that the influence is important to the study being undertaken.

This diagram might best be constructed graphically as a schematic of the elements of factors previously determined to be important. The elements then may be interconnected by the way they influence one another.

Determine the data requirements. This is the "how much" step of the process. What numbers describe each element in the diagram? How much does each element affect all the others? What is the magnitude of the time delays? The last question introduces the time element and requirement for historical data that will also be needed later for validation.

Collect data. This step will probably begin with a literature search. It is also the step most likely to be discouraging—so much so that many people give up, saying there is insufficient data for constructing the desired model. Indeed, this is often the case, and some go so far as to state that for this reason it is impossible to construct *any* large-scale societal model. The authors claim that, whereas the collection of adequate data often presents an obstacle, it is not an insurmountable one. Chapter 3 and Appendix III are devoted to possible solutions to the data problem.

In any case, if all the required data cannot be obtained at this point, "educated guesses" can be made for the most likely values.

Describe mathematically the influence diagram interactions. This is a reasonably straightforward step of translating natural-language and graphical statements into mathematical language to produce a mathematical model.

Write the computer program. In this step, the mathematical model is described in computer language, a series of instructions to the computer that will result in the computer's "solving" the set of mathematical equations constituting the mathematical model. For dynamic models, these solutions must be made iteratively by using the results of the previous solution to increment the values of variables for the current solution. In the case of "continuous" models, the solutions are automatically repeated at predetermined increments of time; incremental solutions of "discrete" models are triggered by "events."

Mechanize the model. This step involves setting up the computer and peripheral equipment (card readers, disks, tapes, print mechanisms, or whatever is required to run the program), inputting the program, and preparing for test runs.

Verify the mechanization. This is the step that verifies the fact that the computer program causes the computer to replicate properly the mathematical model. More on this subject appears in Chapter 5.

Validate the model. This step reaches back through verification and the mathematical model to ensure that the computer replicates satisfactorily the simuland. Procedures for accomplishing this are discussed in Chapter 5.

Design the simulation experiment. Experimental design has been well described and explained in many books; for this reason, we make no attempt to cover it here. However, we do wish to emphasize the importance of planning the simulation experiment in such a way that the results will be meaningful, that the output will be amenable to analysis, and, if possible, that a probability factor can accompany the analysis.

Make the simulation runs. This is simply a matter of following the steps in the experimental design.

Analyze the results. The method of analysis depends on all the preceding steps and especially the objective of the project, the experimental design, and *all* assumptions made. Hopefully, each step will have been and will be documented.

Formulate recommendations. Some believe making recommendations to be beyond the scope of responsibility of the simulationist; the authors consider this to be a matter of degree. Certainly, no simulationist should go to a policymaker and say, "You ought to . . ." At the other extreme, however, the simulationist should not hand over a large quantity of computer output without explanation. The proper course of action lies between these extremes: He should turn over key results in an easily understood form—graphs are often best—with an explanation of how results are obtained, the assumptions upon which they are based, and the confidence that is warranted. He then should stand by to offer further explanation.

Complete documentation. We have said that documentation should begin with project inception and should be updated at each step. Even if this has been done, a final wrap-up is in order. This should result in a comprehensive but readable report that can serve as a basis for publishable documentation as described in Chapter 6.

Cooperate with implementation. If the recommended consultation at each step was possible and was carried out, this step should present no difficulties. If the decision maker has actually become involved in the ongoing process, it will be practically automatic. If such cooperation has not been previously established, it may be difficult or impossible at this point for the simulationist to involve himself with implementation.

Personal tact and diplomacy, which should have been exercised all along, will be essential. Implementation is discussed further in Chapter 7.

4.3 Actual Experiences

There are great differences in opinion between those who would (or would not) design and those who actually have built large models. Rather than dwell on the philosophy of model building, we need more work reporting the experiences of modelers or teams of modelers as they construct their systems.

The following description of an actual experience is narrated by one of the authors in the first person. (See Sections 8.6 and 8.7 for discussions of building man-machine simulations in the urban and water resource fields.)

These excerpts agree with others on several points; the differences often are a function of the model situation or the personalities involved.

4.3.1   The SEAS Experience

SEAS was designed for a very broad variety of purposes by technical or policy staffs, or by the builders themselves to support policy analysis. The following brief narrative describes the development of SEAS.

The 1972 request that the EPA Office of Research and Development develop an ability to forecast future pollution problems was subsequently broadened to include a comprehensive assessment of the impact of present and proposed guidelines and standards on the environmental quality of the nation. The early stages of the model development were to discover what could really be done to meet such a charge, given the data availability and the quality of information on the various functional relationships. Obviously, development of such a potentially broad-based system could not be accomplished without wide agency support.

4.3.2   Create A Proper Design

Since we have just said that the builder of a large-scale model is apt to find himself with a dearth of information as he goes about the process of model development, the question arises of how one can decide on the correct design when the building materials and the final goal are often vague. Because it is necessary to make sure that all of the modules are of the same grain (one module cannot handle variables of different taxonomic size unless there is a transformation function embedded in the program), it is best to design the model in stages. SEAS, for example (see Sections AI-1 and AII-4), went through three building stages and is presently being carried through implementation. The first stage, that of the Test Model, was intended for trying out the overall concept of the model. In many ways, it was the most ambitious of the stages, for it attempted to cover the broadest scope. On the other hand, it was the most inexpensive to build because the plan was not to create any new algorithms or data, but merely to tie together what was currently available. More than that, no attempts were made to make the results useful for policy, and so the documentation could be limited to the needs of those designing the model, and the grain could be quite coarse. In short, the payoff from this exercise was to be found largely in what it taught the builders about what it would be possible to use or modify from "off-the-shelf" and what would require more research.

The second stage, the Prototype, saw the direction change from pure research to narrowing the scope to create a model that would eventually be useful for personnel at the policy level. This would involve preparing documentation that would be available to all users and structuring the output toward specific policy uses. This stage was first marked by considerable effort in calibrating reams of government data to mesh with a single operating system. Census data, OBERS, USDA land use and crop projections, and numerous other data collections (see Section AIII-1) were collated, assumptions were evaluated, and then procedures were designed to enable these disparate sources to be used.

The second chore was to design a computer program that was sufficiently flexible and modular to allow us to readily add or subtract individual variable values, as well as whole modules. This process required considerable reprogramming of all of the modules and other routines that had been brought over almost in toto from elsewhere. Although the design required that we scrap a large portion of the Test Model program, it was felt that later expansion would make this worthwhile. Finally, this whole program had to be designed to allow any combination of modules to be run efficiently.

An auxiliary part of the plan was to design the computer output. The goal was simple: to make available to the user the maximum information in the most concise form. On the other hand, no analyst worth his pay would accept the output of a model without including the ability to query the model for considerable detail in the area of interest. The output forms presently available from SEAS fill a good size workbook (one approximately one to two inches thick) and are so structured that the user can call for those outputs he desires at the beginning of a model run.

The areas selected for modeling and the resultant algorithms had to be designed, discussed, programmed, and tested. Methods had to be developed to allow the widest possible exposure of the designs to ensure they were based on the latest state of the art. Meetings had to be arranged constantly between individual module builders to ensure the use of the same taxonomies, and to ensure that they would be compatible with the final model.

Finally, because the Prototype was never expected to be used for policy purposes, a balance had to be struck between keeping the policymakers interested in the project and getting their inputs and preventing them from using the outputs of the system prematurely.

The final stage, Phase III, was that in which all the lessons learned in building the Prototype were to be employed to produce a usable policy model. This particular stage is characterized by a number of features.

First, the overall program developed for the Prototype did not turn out to be sufficiently general, so considerable reprogramming was undertaken to improve flexibility and allow more detail.

Second, SEAS was used in three major efforts during this stage, and information requirements actually drove the work.

On the positive side, large amounts of new data became available. Because these data were to be collected for SEAS, it was possible to prepare specifications before collection was accomplished. This meant that for the first time many assumptions related to collecting, preparing, and presenting the data were known in advance and could be specified.

On the negative side, much of the data available to the Prototype, and the algorithms constructed to handle it, were scrapped.

Third, even though SEAS was quite comprehensive, potential users and fellow analysts continually demonstrated desires to expand it. Because of the time delay necessary to build and test new modules, the model had to be designed in such a way that a heavy research program could proceed while the system was being prepared for policy use.

In summary, the SEAS experience showed an absolute requirement for a strong design at the beginning of each stage. Even though the realities of resource constraints may have forced us to retrench once in a while, the "moving target" and politically active nature of developing large-scale models demands a definitive structure, even if it is only used as a guideline.

4.3.3 Seeking Support

The strategy chosen to secure the necessary support for SEAS was two-pronged. On the one hand, a very intensive educational program was started to engender understanding and support for the program. Numerous educational techniques were used, including briefings and overview publications. It was hoped this extensive front-end effort would enable various EPA administrative offices to understand the intent of the system and hence to support the development effort.

In reality, the education program often engendered the opposite effect. The project apparently was interpreted by many as a threat, and the result was an aggressive backlash which almost killed the endeavor. The technical advice and support of the various offices of the Agency were often not forthcoming and had to be extracted by administrative fiat. Such aggression did not endear the project staff and their products to those who were thus commandeered. This situation caused many nontechnical problems for the designers of the system.

Whether responding to either a proposal or an executive decision, or attempting to sell a modeling project, the very first step is to make sure that someone really wants the project to come into being and wants to use the final results. Large models are generally expensive and usually take a long time to complete. Consequently, even if one is fortunate enough to start out with complete agreement on the need for the project, there are sure to be times along the way when the project will come under attack.

To prepare for this inevitability, it is necessary to have a precise idea of what the project should model. A communications system allowing frequent interaction between the builders and client is also needed so that the final goals can evolve naturally. It is clear that most modeling projects are only sketchily conceptualized. This danger of insufficient conceptualization is very pronounced with large-scale, general models. Furthermore, it is almost impossible to imagine how insufficient conceptualization could be avoided in the preparatory stages; problems that require large-scale models are likely not to be well understood. At the beginning of the effort, it is also uncertain whether there are adequate data available, how new data will be collected to fill the gaps, or what surrogates will be necessary. Finally, unless there is a predisposition on the part of the client or builder, it is not evident what modeling methodology should be used.

Given these facts, great care must be exercised to develop a method for keeping the client informed as the model evolves. One persistent problem of many large-scale models is the failure to keep lines of communication open. This leads to a scenario where the client has a picture of what he expects a model to be and what he hopes it will do. The actual builders normally find the original conceptualization too ambitious, and because of resource limitations, they are forced to constrain various parts of the model. If such changes are accomplished incrementally, in collaboration with the client, the client can direct the inevitable mid-course corrections. Instead, the builders usually continue to make trade-offs based on some set of standards they believe important. It would be highly fortuitous if these standards were the same as those of the client. Consequently, at some stage in the development, the builders appear before the client for a briefing. Often, this appearance happens when there is a need for additional funds. Assuming that the client expects what he said he wanted in the first place, this meeting is apt to be one of shock. If the builder is a good salesman and has the confidence of the client, he will convince him that the result is what the client really wanted, or at least that it is the best he is able to get, given the resource constraints. If the project has been expensive but necessary, the mid-course correction will take the form of additional funds to expand a section or so of the model. Because the overall model has to be balanced, this mid-course correction usually costs more than it would have if communication lines had been kept open from the beginning.

4.3.4   *Education by Questionnaire*

Policymakers and modelers need to be educated concerning each other's perspective and objectives. In Section 1.3.1, we mentioned a method based upon interviews and questionnaires intended primarily to educate the modeler concerning the policymaker and the policymaking process. Then we went on to suggest how the policymaker might be educated about modeling through personal involvement in the process. Now let us return to an EPA approach to the problem of educating the modeler.

The purpose of the project was to design a strategic policy assessment system tailored to the needs of agency administrators. We hoped that the policymakers would be able to use our modeling skills to push the state of the art in the direction of their needs, even where such directions might be contrary to the instincts and training of the modelers.

To begin this process (which was expected to be, and was, lengthy) the questionnaire discussed in the following paragraphs was constructed. In many instances, the approach is quite naive, but it is useful in bounding the discussion. We repeat most of the questions here and, rather than report the outcomes of our meetings (which were for internal use), we discuss the rationale behind the queries and what we learned in a general sense from the process.

About the Policymaker

1.   Have you had any training or education in the use of computers? If yes, what type?

2.   What is your personal opinion of the use (or misuse) of computers in policy situations?

3.   Have you ever had an experience where you made a decision with the assistance of a model? If so, what do you feel should have been improved in the process?

4.   Do you have any analytical training or education? What kind and at what level? From what disciplinary point of view? (i.e., engineering, social science, natural science, etc.) Do you apply this skill in typical policy situations?

The overall purpose of these initial questions is to identify a policymaker's frame of reference. Often, models have little relation to the vocabulary and training of the potential user, particularly if he/she is a policymaker. Several years ago, for example, a study of liberal arts, legal, and social science professions noted that usually only economists were trained to interpret graphics. Consequently, the presentation of information in the form of histograms and graphs added little to the comprehension of the information presented; in fact, the results suggested that the graphs added a degree of confusion.

Furthermore, we experienced an era when we tried to do something about the real need for large masses of data to be used for decision making. Computer packages were developed to provide manipulative capabilities, such as statistical routines and canned analytical algorithms. These packages, however, were well beyond the understanding of many policymakers. Although the policymaker was told that information was kept in some standard form and that it was possible to carry out all sorts of sophisticated statistical operations on it, his training might not actually allow him to accomplish these tasks. To complicate matters, most policymakers have not been personally involved with an interactive man-machine system. Therefore, they have no idea what is expected from machines or from the system.

These points serve to illustrate reasons for filling the literature and the software industry with so-called management information systems. To the extent that the policymaker has no formal analytical training, he may find the use of computers or modeling ego-threatening. Furthermore, if he has no computer training or understanding, he might expect a great deal more or a great deal less than the computer operation can perform. Only if he possesses some degree of training, education, and/or experience in the use of computers in management does an opportunity exist for meaningful dialog on the capabilities *and* limitations of models with respect to his real problems.

In short, the modeler needs educating too. An understanding of the background and training of the policymaker may tell him what kind of assumptions he can make in terms of model input and output. This understanding will also indicate how much work he needs to do to preprocess data (or outputs) for the policymaker's use. In fact, given the demanding schedule of most policymakers, it is unrealistic to assume they will have time to reeducate and strengthen themselves in analytical or technological capabilities.

On the Policymaking Process

1.   In the context of your role in this organization, how do you best characterize your responsibilities in policymaking terms?

2.   How do you usually make a policy decision? Do you utilize a staff of advisors, a few principal ones, or mostly rely on your own judgment?

3.   How would you like to see policymaking done, ideally? Why?

4.   How and in what form do you prefer to receive policy-oriented

information: By memo? By report? By problem statements with alternatives? Why?

It would seem from many so-called policy model descriptions or other model documentation that few model builders have a clear understanding of how policy is really made. In fact, it may be the case that nobody really understands this very complex process. Nevertheless, it is imperative that the model builder understand, not how decision making is done in some abstract fashion, but how the particular policymaker, for whom he is interested in building a model, conceives of and carries out his policymaking duties. He must also understand the specific requirements and resources available to him. However, it is likely this very complex and individualistic process is little understood by the policymaker himself, simply because he carries it out almost intuitively.

The use of computer models requires more than pure intuition (though just knowing what the policymaker means by "intuition" could be useful). Nevertheless, the process must be reduced to an explicit form if the model is to be used. Interestingly enough, discussion of the foregoing questions will provide a much needed education for many model builders who may think that they understand policy matters and policymaking.

On the Use of Models in Policymaking

1. Models and simulations can be perceived as information-organizing devices that can be used by policymakers to help solve complex problems. They can also be conceived of as an "advisor" who can be consulted on specific types of questions and whose advice can be weighed by the policymaker along with that from other sources. Do you feel comfortable with either of these statements? One more than the other? Why?

2. If a "true" policy model were successfully built, how would you want to use it? For periodic reports, or forecasts? For predicting the impact of past or current decisions? For frequent use in assisting in day-to-day policymaking? What kinds of outputs would you prefer—charts, graphs, numbers, memos, or others?

3. Would you prefer to interact directly with such a model or delegate its use to your immediate staff for formulating policy advice? Why?

4. It is asserted that modeler decision making should take full advantage of sophisticated information systems and hardware. Such a viewpoint suggests either (a) a specially designed "situation room" (see section 7.2.3) with full information displays and/or (b) immediate access to the system. Which would you prefer?

5. Do you face any policy questions on a continuing basis which a specific policy model might be able to assist in answering?

6. What kinds of questions might other high-level administrators face

that are different from those you mentioned? How about the regional administrators?

7.   Would you prefer a model that would provide quick summaries of real-world data, or would you prefer a system that enables you to project the probable impact of various policy choices over time?

These questions are aimed toward understanding (before any real modeling interaction occurs) what the policymaker would hope to get from a model and how he might expect to use it if he should get a model designed to meet his own needs.

Listening to the policymakers who are having models designed and built for them can be a disheartening exercise for model developers. The expectations of policymakers usually far outstrip the current state of the art. Early specification of these expectations can help the model builder to know whether he is supposed to push the art of modeling significantly and/or to gather new data, or whether the policy problems can be simplified and handled with available tools. In either case, the understanding that can be gained from the foregoing questions will help pinpoint the model builder's own work in terms of time, manpower, and available resources.

These most important questions seek to answer exactly how the policymaker expects to use the model when it is complete. There are obvious but important options for use which ought to be discussed, if only in a general sense, at the outset. Some of these options are:

a.   a "situation room," continuously available for policy use;
b.   intermittent use for "status of the system" reports;
c.   personal use by interaction with a terminal or video display unit;
d.   use by policy and support staffs; or
e.   combinations of the above uses.

Preliminary Results. Since the questionnaire has been used in EPA, we should comment on its utility. During the interview process, the questions were not strictly adhered to. However, they provide an opening for discussions of the real policymaking issues and needs. The interviewees were told that the questions might or might not seem pertinent in their particular areas. They were assured, however, that the information was needed. The purpose was to define the needs within EPA as rapidly as possible in order to ensure the highest grade of model and to reduce the necessary expenditure of funds by eliminating needless trial and error. For instance, the original design of the policy assessment system was to construct an interactive capability that would allow manipulation of the model results by a variety of policy-level users.

However, such a design does not currently appear to meet the perceived immediate needs of the highest policy-level personnel. Given current operating procedures, they would rather receive periodic reports on the state and future of the environment.

It is suggested that similar interviews take place as a matter of course between policy-level people and model builders directly, with no department heads in between. It helps the model builder understand explicitly what the final policy-level user of the model will need, without the filter provided by the functional disciplines of the departments. This point is important because functional and administrative spheres of influence can, in an organizational sense, constrain the comprehensiveness and resultant utility of the model. The model builder must be relatively free to develop the tool for the policymaker as he understands the need for it. Continuous interviews are critical because needs can and do change over time, and the model must be flexible enough to accommodate the changing requirements.

4.3.5   Time-Money Skeptics

There are few champions of computer models, fewer still of large scale general purpose, and almost none if the models are going to be expensive and take a long time to build. Consequently, a mandate to build a large-scale model that would be expensive and take three years would not appear to lead to a task destined for success. The first requirement, as noted earlier, was the requirement that a policymaker desire a system be built. This commitment on his part requires that he protect the system during its very early days. The project is particularly sensitive during this period of time because the system is a net expense item, draining the budget and having no immediate payoff to an agency. Because there are never enough resources available to do all the things required of a government unit, any single project that is drawing a large block of funds and using several professionals will surely be a potential target in a budget battle.

There are several ways to combat this attack on the model builders' resources. One is to tie the model to a crisis and build the eventual need for it up to a point that will overcome resistance. A similar strategy is to have a policymaker use his personal power to protect the model. This technique is noted above; but in the world of politics where the power base shifts readily, to depend on such power is risky unless the system itself is doing something to demonstrate its utility.

One way to reduce the risk of cancellation is to partition the development of the system into research projects that can be used for more than one purpose. For example, it is necessary to decide what data would be necessary to load the model. Often this same data is needed by others in the agency for their own purposes, and therefore the cost of development of the project can be shared. This approach reduces the direct cost of the system. This is particularly important because the whole idea behind research in the federal agencies is utility, both of research in general and of models in particular. The joint effort approach lends ammunition to gain support in the constant battle to do "relevant" research projects.

In addition to keeping the net cost of the individual model projects as low as possible, there is a need to demonstrate to various skeptics in an agency that a model's development is proceeding as the project plan has promised. This latter requirement can be fulfilled by arranging for reviews of the status of the model. There should be several reviews, each hopefully successful and each demonstrating enough success to allow the policymakers who were supporting the model development to approve the next stage of the project. The purpose of the reviews, therefore, is not only to provide pacing guidelines for the builders and to brief the potential users, but to provide bureaucratic ammunition for the model supporters at the policy level as well.

4.3.6 *Institutionalizing the System*

One of the more interesting questions associated with a large system like SEAS is what to do with it once it is built. For one thing, the existence of such a system means there is a large data base to be updated periodically. Although basic research may be required to collect the data, there will also be a large task that consists of calibrating the data each year that is taken from other sources. An ideal situation would be to require EPA to produce the data findings of their other studies in a format and with assumptions compatible with SEAS. Such a practice would mean SEAS could be used either as large information retrieval system or as a forecasting system, and thereby serve as a repository of data for the agency, as well as a policy tool.

To survive over the long run, the SEAS system must be tied to a project or series of projects that are mandated as agency output. One such project is the requirement for a periodic report on the state of the environment and on the cost to clean up the air and water. Other similar reports would further legitimize the system and allow it to be utilized for various other purposes. Furthermore, it is only through such use that the system will be improved.

The latter point brings up the question of when SEAS stops being a research project and becomes a tool for policy uses. If the decision is to be made by someone who is a researcher by inclination and interested in developing analytical tools for policy use, the answer is "never." It is clear that it will always be possible to improve SEAS with better data, and so its continued use will ensure such growth. Equally important is the research that improves the scope of the model. For example, the model has a test-level stocks module that is useful not only for policy analyses of natural resource-based pollution, but can give important help in bounding the INFORUM I/O model that currently runs open loop. Because the SEAS model is designed to investigate problems and relationships in the long run, the demand questions become less important and the assumption of supply availability (a feature of short-term models) less tenable.

A final point in the problem of institutionalization is that of personnel. It is clear that SEAS is not a stand-alone model and was never designed for that use. In fact, the original design concept required that the system be exercised either directly by or under the control of a core group of interdisciplinary analysts. If it took a very large number of specialists to actually build the model, it is logical to stress the fact that it will take an equally broad-based group to use it. Constraining the use of the system to a demand basis without the existence or knowledge of a first-rate analysis team presages its demise; forecasts that are released without proper analysis are not only sure to be incorrect—and likely to be discovered as such—but almost certainly the errors will be blamed on the system. Good analysts who are familiar enough with the model to recognize its weaknesses and take them into consideration, can prevent such errors. In brief, the team using it is at least as important as SEAS.

The concluding remarks might be best summed by reminding the potential developer of a large-scale model that the largest single determinant of model success might well be found in the area of politics and not in the area of technical feasibility. Having sufficient theory and data are necessary but not sufficient conditions for producing a working model. The correct environment, a top notch professional team, and opportunity likely will prove to be the more difficult ingredients to find and hold.

4.4   A Large Land Use Project

The following is a paper by one of the members of a land use project at Oak Ridge Laboratories. His problems and suggestions stem from experience in building a model and a desire to improve the modeling art. As with other works, we shall present the essence of his report by quoting liberally concerning RESA (Regional Environmental Systems Analysis) (Voelker, 1975).

Technical Problems
Systematic design procedures were of little help in anticipating technical problems, and the records of subsequent years reveal we continued to underestimate

the problems of model building. As unforeseen problems surfaced, we were forced to extend time estimates and constrain the scope of the model.

Perceptual Problems

There was, however, another class of problems affecting the utility of models which stemmed from the perceptions and backgrounds of the people involved. These problems were exemplified by RESA's attempts to transfer technology.

As the RESA project approached its conclusion, and whereas our planner contacts have learned to build computer data bases and make interpretative uses of the data very well, their initial lack of background and experience precluded their acceptance of computer models as a part of their work-a-day world.

Problem Genesis

Apparently the process of peer review and self-evaluation, which refines and strengthens traditional science, has not been operative in land use modeling.

There are really two aspects of the review process, and both have failed to reveal much of the first-generation model-builders' experience. The first stems from the science of land use, that is, the process of hypothesis development and testing that leads to improved theory. Theory available to land use modelers is woefully inadequate, and large simulation models are extremely poor tools for promoting the science of land use.

The second review failure relates to the technology of land use modeling which is opposed to the science of land use. Technology normally tests the validity and usefulness of new procedures; however, it has failed to pinpoint model inadequacies and misrepresentations by modelers, because the effort needed to do this is nearly equivalent to implementation of the original model. Poor documentation only serves to obscure the model further. Self-criticism has not been effective in advancing model technology.

Pitfalls

CAN A MODEL SATISFY EVERYONE?

In this typology, the two major groups of model builders and model users are further divided into designers and technicians, planners and decision makers, respectively.

The simple fact is that no one model can satisfy all interested parties. A gap will always exist between the modeler's intended application of the model, the planner's ability to use it, and the decision maker's expectation of it. Any particular model is most likely to reflect the interests of its designers and not its users.

WHO SHOULD RUN MODELS AND HOW SHOULD THE OUTPUT BE PRESENTED?

If we assume that the ultimate beneficiary of a land use model is the decision maker, then there is a wide range of involvements possible between the decision maker and the model. At one extreme is the concept touted mainly by technicians, that is, direct communication between the decision maker and the model. This concept is reflected in the large number of projects attempting to tie decision makers directly to computers through CRTs, cable television, and leased lines.

At the other extreme is the relationship that interposes a person between the decision maker and the computer. The computer output, interpreted and transformed, would be supplied to the decision maker along with his normal informational input. With this alternative, the computer would be essentially invisible to the decision maker.

What does the experience of our project reveal about this spectrum of relationships? The thrust of the RESA land use model design has always been toward interactive software, and we have gained considerable experience in encouraging local politicians and planners to interact with our on-line computer models. Several conclusions have grown out of this experience. First, the language and hardware limitations of computers impose such severe hardships on the uninitiated user that they preclude the acceptance of computer technology. Communication with a computer is still much too artificial to appeal to other than the highly motivated person willing to learn a new language. Second, our experience with actual decision makers showed that they were not satisfied with the fixed set of answers briefly available from a computer. They soon asked questions beyond the capability of any model.

Because model output always will have to be supplemented with additional information for real-world decisions, and because the function of data synthesis is already performed by the staff of decision makers, our opinion is that land use models need not be made directly accessible to decision makers.

IS IT POSSIBLE TO OVERCOME THE LACK OF LAND USE THEORY
IN BUILDING LAND USE MODELS?

More resources than are now allocated should be assigned to the extremely important design function of clarifying and testing the hypotheses underlying our models. If done properly, this step can guide the modeling teams' efforts in performing subsequent quantification tasks. It can bracket the expectations of model accuracy and detail, and it can create a base for documentation to be delivered to the next generation of model builders.

MUST A SIMULATION MODEL BE A GIANT COMPUTER PROGRAM?

This problem may be overcome by structuring a land use model with independent subprograms operating together in such a way as to minimize the problems stemming from a single large program.

Our experience with subprogram organization shows that the resultant model has both strengths and weaknesses. The approach lengthens the time to run one model iteration from hours (including setup time) to days. Furthermore, the risk of user-induced error is greater because of increased handling of data by the user.

4.5   Model Delivery

As noted in the summary, several of the complaints against the large models of the past could be summarized by saying that the models have been oversold and underdelivered. It was also alleged in that same section that a certain amount of early discussions, because it concerns issues that are unknown or unknowable at the outset, have to be taken on faith. This situation leads to instances where the allegation of "overselling" can be put forth. Oversold models are, by definition, those that fail in some manner or other. It would be difficult to honestly believe that funding agencies would deliberately engage in an activity that they knew beforehand would fail. Possibly, the allegations are in the domain of Monday morning quarterbacking rather than sage reflection.

Let us continue to investigate the concept of overselling. This term implies that either the builder has promised to deliver a system that will perform in a certain fashion by a certain date, or that the buyer believes he will so deliver, or some combination of the above, and that the builder has not delivered as expected. From our investigation of both sides of the contracting procedure, it is clear to us there are numerous situations that result in a delivery gap besides the one suggested by the term overselling.

Many contracts let by government agencies are not well specified and do not elicit very clear proposals in return. Verbal discussions among the involved parties sometimes result in a better definition of the final product, but more often, the hoped-for meeting of the minds never comes about. This tendency would seem to be most prevalent in agencies where the funding-to-man ratio is very high or where the in-house staff is required to carry out other duties in addition to grant and contract management.

Lack of definition is an especially acute problem where large-scale models are concerned because mere specification of the problem to be modeled is a significant research task. Often this dilemma is handled by having a feasibility study as the first phase of the contract. The success of this technique is directly proportional to how the contract funds are justified from within the agency. If the original idea is sold before the feasibility study, then the odds are that the model will be funded in a fashion similar to what was described to the policymaker by the staff who had the responsibility for justifying the funds allocation. In essence, the staff is often locked-in to the idea because their credibility (not that of the contractor) is on the line; it is usually their specification of the design that causes the needed funds to be allocated. Contractor failure in these cases is not differentiated from the failure of the concept, and so there is a strong bias for the study to find that the original idea is "feasible."

To decide whether the model should be funded depends on numerous factors within the agency in question: budget priorities, the attitude of the next layer of management, and current interests of the organization. Very seldom is the decision to fund the model really based on the feasibility study alone (which we have just argued is apt to be suspect). Strong pressure of the type noted could easily lead to model concepts that cannot be built for the funds or time programmed. In the end, the result is another model oversold (or over-hoped for).

Moving on from misconceptions developed at the birth of the contract, there are at least two other possible breakdowns in communication. The first is that the model designer finds some of the theories he postulated are wrong, some of the algorithms he thought were available are not, or some of the data he expected to be adequate are not right or ready. Research proves the original proposal to have been overly ambitious for these reasons rather than because of design planning. All of these problems have actually occurred, and have been cited at one time or another as reasons for model failures.

Another communication breakdown is as pervasive, but almost never mentioned. It concerns the agency commitment, or lack thereof, to the original concept of the model requirement. Politics and policies are fluid, and often these large-scale decision efforts are expected to respond with similar flexibility. When the nature of the model design precludes flexibility, the effort becomes unpopular and the model likely useless if and when it is finally delivered. Furthermore, a change in the original design adds to the cost, and often results in a product that is inferior to that initially planned. This phenomenon, well known to the builders of custom houses, kitchens, recreation rooms, and the like, haunts the builders of models also. Specifically, as the buyer begins to understand what his purchase really is going to look like or do (as it moves from the concept or blueprint stage to completion), he begins to request changes or additions. It is very difficult for the builder to operate in this arena of shifting expectations, so there is often a feeling of disappointment on the part of the client whose desires and expectations are moving ahead faster than the product.

Before we leave this topic of selling, we should look at the interesting dichotomy that occurs when one tries to sell the idea of a model for policy use. There is often a built-in conflict between the person to whom the model must initially be sold and the person who will ultimately use it. As a general rule, large-scale policy models have to be sold to policymakers. Unfortunately, the top administrators are usually not going to use them directly; this job usually falls to their staffs. Such a situation is tailormade for conflict. A competitive, negative response from the policy staff user can almost be assumed if they have skills similar to those of the consultants; they will see the models as potential "turf raiding" or, worse, as a threat to their jobs. However, selling the staff first is frustrating, because the policymaker himself usually likes to retain the credit for originating ideas that are as bold and as visible as most large-scale modeling efforts are.

Satisfying both needs is a real challenge. Probably one successful strategy is to work closely with the policy-level administrator to obtain funding legitimacy. If the model can survive the original onslaught from the staff level, then it should be pretty well left alone until the time comes to test it. It therefore makes sense, under this scenario, to force a confrontation with the staff level early when the model is in a honeymoon stage with the administrator who wanted it. This is also advisable because during the concept and design state, it is most difficult to prove a model cannot be built. It is equally difficult to prove it can be, but the burden of proof will be on the attacker rather than on the defender during that stage. This advantage quickly dissipates, however.

In the long run, the way to success is basically simple: *deliver the model as promised*. Keep the policymaker constantly informed so there are no surprises and there is no delivery gap. During the building time, get to the staff for help and advice. These are the people for whom the model is really built. If the model inputs and its flexibility are tailored to them, the format of the output can be policymaker determined. In short: Deliver that which is promised to the policy-level administrator so that his faith is protected. Deliver the content to the technical level staff. In some cases, one may have the pleasure of being able to combine these two groups and talk concept and content to both. but this occurrence is apt to be rare.

5

Verification and Validation

In 1953, the Simulation Council, antecedent of the Society for Computer Simulation (SCS), held a meeting to consider the theme, "How Do You Know You're Right?" The meeting covered verification and validation without distinction. The terms were used interchangeably if at all. Computer modeling and simulation have come a long way in the years since that meeting and, as indicated in Section 2.2 on terminology, we now use "verification" to mean determining that the computer program runs as intended and "validation" to mean that the model represents reality to a degree suitable for the particular simulation study of concern. However, the question "How Do You Know You're Right?" is still with us, and will be, ad infinitum.

5.1 Verification

In computer modeling, there are three facets to the problem of ensuring that the computer program "runs as intended":

1. ensuring that the program, as written, accurately describes the model as designed;
2. ensuring that the program is properly mechanized on the computer;
3. ensuring that the program as mechanized runs as expected.

These are by no means simple problems, except in the case of very simple models. As the models become more complicated, checking and "debugging" become increasingly difficult in relation to some power of the number of computer instructions; these, however, are all technical problems that are adequately covered by numerous books on programming. In this book, we are more concerned with the design of models, their validation, and their use. We are also very much interested in how to increase the implementation of the simulation results.

66

5.2 Validation

There is, of course, no reason to believe that a verified model is capable of reproducing reality, even those aspects of reality pertinent to the purpose the model was designed to serve. Its capability in this respect is a matter of model validity.

5.3 Difficulties

Let us approach the question of validation in down-to-earth business terms by considering what a business man would be willing to spend to build a forecasting model. The business man cannot afford to discount a "hoped-for" infinite return as the result of an unknown expenditure for a near-perfect model today. Our business world exists in the present, so the businessman will be satisfied to buy a somewhat less than perfect model for a known cost (provided we and he understand the model's limitations). He therefore must obtain some indication of the model quality and capacity from the model builders. In discussing the imperfections of their simulations, modelers are wont to make such statements as "The order of magnitude is correct," "The slope is right," or "The rate of change is reasonable." These statements sound erudite and make the user comfortable and confident. Very seldom, however, can the builder give convincing empirical evidence of the model's performance.

The question has now shifted from perfect validity to probable accuracy. However, despite first appearances, we have not progressed by abandoning the first question for refuge in the second. It is very difficult to prove the probable accuracy of specific model predictions. We must know the future to prove the accuracy of predictions concerning it.

What is really possible? How accurate must our models be? At first, it would seem we should strive to make them perfect replicas of reality; but is this really desirable? Such models would be as difficult to understand as the system modeled. In any case, perfection is unattainable. In the present state of the modeling art, we are only beginning to classify our tools and to test possibilities for replicating the past and projecting trends into the future. In this section, we explore whether we can realistically expect to overcome the technical difficulties of model construction and then build demonstrably "valid" models.

Confining this discussion to the field of large-scale models in the social sciences, we repeat that complete validation of such models is currently impossible.

One argument against the possibility of absolute validation for social science models can be drawn from the field of physics. It rests on a well-known theorem that has been used repeatedly to give warnings concerning the veracity of measurements made by a sensor, or set of sensors, implanted in any system. It states that the measurement instrument, by its very intrusion, changes the system itself. This theorem is, in the physical sciences, associated with the Heisenberg Uncertainty Principle. If we take liberties with the original purpose and content of that principle, and gloss over some of its more important fine points, we find that when applied to the social sciences, this theorem suggests that our perceptions of reality are similarly likely to be distorted. Consequently, a model that replicates these perceptions would by definition be a replication not of reality, but of our perceptions of it. This may appear to be a highly academic argument, but the ivory-tower glow disappears when we remember that the models we are discussing are intended, and currently are used, to formulate public and private policy.

Where the basic data were gathered in such a fashion that the observations have distorted the model of the system, the theory and models derived from these data are questionable. It should come as no surprise that models based on misconceptions of reality will show unrealistic behavior when compared with real-world system performance.

The well-known Hawthorne experiment, conducted around workers in a manufacturing plant, demonstrated the problems of attempting to measure "what is," and the study, although carefully done, could have resulted in data sets that would have produced completely erroneous models. The results of the Hawthorne experiment have been used to demonstrate numerous points, but for our purpose here, the most significant is that the largest single factor in worker performance was the experimenters' interest in the workers and not the working conditions as had been postulated in the original study design.

Similar results have been shown in studies using questionnaires, where attitudes of people as reported to an interviewer may not represent their real feelings at all. Nonrepresentation can be caused by a variety of factors, among which is a desire to please the questioner.

While it is true that implementation of results derived from a model based on perceived rather than actual facts could change reality in a fashion similar to a deliberate policy choice (although hopefully to a lesser degree), we should be able to compensate for the difference as we factor out all but the policy-induced effects from analyzed results.

The problem becomes infinitely more complex when we are confronted with using a model that forecasts the future to aid a decision maker who would make policy to alter the future. In this case, very little is known about the possible impact of the policy, and thus the scientist's desire to create a controlled environment is perplexing. We suggest that the real weakness is in the attempts to validate models. Validation requires an available standard for comparison.

To demonstrate the foregoing point, let us imagine the existence of a truly valid model that has the confidence of the builder, his peers, and the user. The model, in this case, is to be used to forecast the future state of the nation for decision makers in the public sector, and the results will be presented to the policymaker on an annual basis. The purpose is to provide the policymaker with some feeling for the probable future as he prepares his policy choices for the coming year.

Our policymaker also might wish to study several possible alternate decisions and use the model to predict the probable outcomes. If the model is sensitive to the variables he chooses to change, then it will react and produce a modified forecast of the future, thus demonstrating the effects of his policy choices.

Now, let us examine some of the weaknesses of these projections. If, for argument's sake, the model is designed to forecast ten years into the future and if it responds noticeably to policy changes in the one-year period, then does it not appear likely that similar decisions made for the ensuing nine periods would cause equally noticeable changes in the model response, and that some of these changes would be cumulative in effect? In brief, changes in the assumptions may so change the relationships in the model that the output is not valid. The introduction of policy inputs (and other assumptions) throughout the ten cycles may make the exercise so conjectural and the paths of the outputs so untraceable as to render questionable the utility of the original forecast over the ten-year period. There is no easy solution for this paradox. But is a solution necessary? Modeling is self-defeating if changes are made to avoid an undesirable prediction, because that prediction is less likely to come true. On the other hand, if changes are made to realize a desirable future, the model can be self-fulfilling. Thus, if there is a solution to the paradox, it is to construct models that can be updated in order to continually take ongoing changes into account. We have emphasized two points concerning validity which we will now present as generalized hypotheses.

The first hypothesis is that we are able to construct models that have validity in the formal sense (historical validity), given adequate data. However, such models will be crystal ball illuminations of the future because they do not inherently handle the unexpected "turning points" of the system. What is needed then, if this hypothesis is valid, is more intensive research on these turning points. Possibly this can be done by further study in the area of futures forecasting.

The second hypothesis is that the real world is so complex that attempts to completely validate forecasting models are futile. The arguments given rest on the assumption that historically validated projections which are looked at in retrospect by rational policymakers will provide the basis for new policies. The resulting policy changes make for a new alternative future, thereby rendering the original model projection "invalid."

Those who espouse futures research cannot make deterministic predictions because there are many possible paths from the present to the future, and simple extrapolation portrays only one of these. What is really needed is an envelope of all potential paths to alternative futures arranged so that each is associated with a probability of occurrence. This methodology would allow the user to be aware of the risks associated with the future he believes is most likely to occur, given his personal hunches and prejudices.

From the standpoint of validation, this method of improving modeling practice can strengthen the user's confidence in the use of simulation results.

The alternative futures concept has plausible validity but creates practical difficulties that may prove to be inherently insoluble. The future that will actually occur is only one in a whole range of possibilities, and the probability associated with a specific model run is at best a guess as to which is the most likely. There is no reason to suppose the most likely future will be the real one, and thus the use of historical validation seems futile. If, in any run of a simulation, a model successfully predicts the present from past data, then it should be considered formally valid. However, the numerous projections using this base model while changing the assumptions to produce alternative futures cannot all be valid because they all predict what the world will be like in the future. They are valid only in the sense that they portray the future, *given known changes in the original assumptions*.

To summarize, the outlook for validation of models that relate to the social sciences is as follows:

1. Historical validation gives one a comfortable feeling about the capability of the model to forecast the future, but little real assurance that the forecast is an improvement over one arrived at less rigorously. The longer the time gap between "today" and "tomorrow," the more sophisticated the analysis needed for forecasting. Fortunately, good policymakers realize they are not making each decision to hold for all time. They can and should change policies often enough to satisfy pressures and adjust for new developments. Hence, based on this argument, all that is necessary to validate a policy model is to ensure that its replication is satisfac-

tory and its ability to forecase the future adequate for the study of the probable effects of each policy shift.

2. Most of the statistical techniques used for validation include standard sampling theory, which tests to see whether the model prediction represents reality. Not only does this require a definition of reality after the fact, but also carries with it all the problems of other forms of historical validation.

3. There is no agreement as to the meaning of absolute prediction. Some model builders are reduced to claiming that the explicit nature of models in itself represents an improvement over the mental models used by managers and decision makers. However, the decision-making process is so complex, as are most of the decisions themselves, that such a statement is little more than wishful thinking.

4. Only recently have we settled on some tentative indicators concerning the economic, social, and environmental factors that describe our society. If we have only now begun to measure the performance of our system in the broadest sociopolitical terms, then we are faced with the very real fact that it will be some time before we can say for certain what our indicators really measure. To the extent that monitoring current conditions is still in its infancy, there is some question as to whether we have a realistic standard against which to gauge our model projections of the future.

The final two difficulties are concerned with the concept of the complexity of the model.

5. One type of complexity concerns the holism of a model. It has been argued with increasing frequency that models should be very straightforward and composed of a limited number of parameters. These arguments are based on the belief that the fewer the number of variables, the more transparent the model and the easier it will be to demonstrate validity.

On the other hand, it has been argued (particularly in view of the revived interest in the environment) that simple, transparent models do not explain enough and that we really need richer, more complex models to support a relative evaluation of the tradeoffs available to decision and policymakers. However, the more complex the model, the more difficult it is to apply standard validation techniques. This is one reason two models are needed, a basic or skeletal one for transparency and a fleshed-out, holistic one for more detailed studies.

6. Finally, with respect to the problem of validation, the natural and physical sciences can usually depend upon the reproducibility of the system under study (i.e., there are recognized laws of nature which the scientist can discover and depend on). The social scientist does not possess such luxuries. Either he does not understand the natural laws

governing society to the extent that they exist, or the human animals go about introducing change in his system of interest almost as soon as he "understands" it.

Quo Vademus? The aspects we have described thus far suggest a bleak and discouraging future for the complete validation of our models. In fact, it might almost appear expedient to abandon attempts at validation, and look only at the usefulness of models for aiding the policymaker.

Numerous compelling arguments that support modeling have appeared in the literature, so, even if we are unable to validate them, we shall not present an apology here. Instead, like good modelers, we shall extrapolate some present trends. Computers are coming into use in more and more sectors of our society. As experience increases and technology improves, the time cannot be far distant when the impact of computers will bring about societal changes as great as those from the Industrial Revolution.

Computers are remarkable for their ability to store and organize large amounts of information. It is inevitable that such data will be used to project the assumptions based on our present state of knowledge into the future. After all, it is in this manner that the human mind traditionally makes decisions, and certainly man will use in similar fashion the tool which extends his mental processes. The real question, therefore, is not whether he should place confidence in such devices, but how effective they are when compared to other available tools.

Now we view the problem of validity from a different perspective. Models should be tested not against reality but against alternative methods for measuring reality (mental models) and their successors.

Research along this line has not yet been done and will be difficult to carry out. However, the case can be made that standard validation tests that some would require of models are significantly more rigorous than those we require of alternatives, or of the policymaker himself. In the latter case, his decisions are subjected only to ex post facto validation when he or his organization must suffer the consequences of his invalid projections.

Both in the case of the mental model and the computer model used to help make policy, a concerted effort on the part of the policymaker to act as if the model were true causes "self-fulfilling prophecy." The introduction of such purposeful behavior in the midst of any attempt to validate either the mental or the computer model scientifically makes for serious difficulties. However, the fact remains that the computer model is normally the only one required to prove its credibility in any rigorous fashion before it is used to guide policymaking.

5.4   Toward Solutions

The difficulties discussed in the preceding section seem to indicate that complete validation of all useful models is certainly not possible.

There can be no question, however, that to the extent that models can be validated, they should be. For this reason, much has been written on the subject, even though proving absolute validity can be accomplished only in very special cases and then only after answering the question, "valid for what?"

In spite of the difficulties noted, there will always be some cry for validation. If models are to be validated to the fullest extent possible, several approaches to the problem must be considered. Some are discussed by the authors quoted in Chapter 8 and others in the quotation which follows.

How Validation Should be Carried Out (Biggs and Cawthorne, 1962)

The most rigorous method of validation is detailed comparison of model outputs against historical or experimentally measured outputs of the real system when the model is presented with the same inputs as occurred in the real system. To be effective this method must be applied to small sections of each model or sub-model, rather than to the model as a whole. Otherwise, when it comes to correcting the discrepancies that are sure to be present at first, it will be difficult to know which equation or numerical value, amongst a bewildering array, requires amendment. If the model is validated by comparing the behavior of each small section with the behavior of each corresponding section of the real system, then there will be no possibility of juggling the model of one part to overcome what is really a deficiency in the model of some other part. The possibility of artificiality in the model will thereby be minimized.

Indeed, the aim of the modeling teams, throughout their work of formulation and validation, must be to produce models that not only behave in a similar manner to the real system, but do so for the correct reasons, that is, as a consequence of similar mechanisms. Otherwise the final model will be of little value other than as a representation of just those particular sets of observed data with which it has been forced to agree. Such a model would have doubtful utility when it came to extrapolating to the very different regimes that might exist in the future. There are, of course, always risks in attempting to extrapolate, but there is no better way of extrapolating than through use of a model embodying all of the known or suspected internal mechanisms of significance in the system. In other words, curve fitting alone is not enough for prediction: the model should have physical, biological or social plausibility.

It is highly desirable that representatives of planning authorities and political bodies be in close contact with the modeling teams during the validation phase. Only by seeing for themselves the degree of agreement with observed data and the degree of realism of each assumption will these people come to have the confidence in the model that will be necessary if they are to accept and act upon its predictions.

The Parameter Estimation Problem

When validating each small section of the model as discussed above, it is desirable that the inputs and outputs of the corresponding section of the real system be recorded from that system while the whole of it is in operation in its normal working environment. This will help to ensure that the complete omission of an input to one section of the model from some other section does show up as a discrepancy in this type of validation test. It will, in particular, guard against the possibility of a coefficient or parameter in the equations taking on a different value in the actual working environment to that which may have been estimated originally from partial system tests or laboratory experiments where it may have been difficult to simulate the working environment.

The recorded inputs and outputs, particularly when obtained under these actual working conditions, are likely to be contaminated to a considerable extent by measurement errors. Generally, these errors can be assumed to have the characteristics of "stationary random noise." There is a growing body of literature (Allison, 1966; Schalow, 1968) discussing methods of estimating the parameters of a system in the presence of noise. This is a variant of the "black box" problem in which, given the box's inputs and outputs, one tries to deduce the nature of the mechanism inside.

The methods assume the functional form of the equations to be known (as will often be the case on the basis of general physical or biological laws) and that the equations can be treated as locally linear (linear for small perturbations about some standard condition). They aim at minimizing some function of the error between model and measured output, averaged over the interval of observation. In addition to furnishing optimum estimates of the parameters the methods enable confidence limits to be placed on these estimates.

Data for Validation

Clearly, one of the main limitations on the fidelity of any model will be the experimental data available for its construction and checking. Because new data may take considerable time to obtain it is desirable that any significant gaps in data be shown up as early as possible. The value of trying a preliminary overall model at an early stage has already been mentioned. The mere attempt to assemble such a model will reveal some gaps and by drawing attention to those parts to which the system is most sensitive, this early model can further help in revealing areas where there are likely to be data deficiencies.

Inadequacy of data is sometimes given as a reason for being unable to apply the modeling technique. This is seldom a sound reason as the mental models on which decisions will otherwise be based usually do not even take full account of all of the data already to hand. Generally it can be said that an appropriately constructed model will allow one to make the most of whatever data are available. As new data are acquired the model can be progressively improved. The predictions made with it at any time will then be the best estimates that can be made on the basis of all currently known facts.

It is desirable that all data acquired during the project be deposited in a "data bank" so as to be readily accessible to all members of the modeling teams. In some situations it would be desirable to set up a central panel to handle all requests for new data. The requests would specify not only what quantities were wanted and under what conditions, but also the required accuracy and frequency of measurement. The panel would vet these requests to ensure that all requirements were justified. This approach would be appropriate where it is proposed to set up a large experimental program in conjunction with the modeling program and it is important that the modelers and experimenters agree on firm data specifications. Where, on the other hand, it is intended to rely on existing data as far as possible and the sources of these data are many and varied, it may be better to let each specialist team ferret out its own data, so long as all data are catalogued and placed in the central bank. (See Section 7.3.3.)

5.5 Is Validation Necessary?

In the foregoing paragraphs, we have discussed the difficulties in attempting to validate models and concluded that, except in very special cases, complete validation is not possible, especially in the case of the large-scale policy models with which this book is concerned.

We agreed, however, that if and when validation is possible, it should be done, and we quoted one author concerned with how it should be attempted. But the question of whether validation is necessary remains an important one. The answer is difficult. If one argues that it is impossible to accomplish, then it is possible to question the usefulness of models. On the other hand, it would be illogical to suggest no computer models should be used, for without computer modeling and simulation, we are left with only a few other techniques to aid the decision maker, techniques that are as difficult to validate as computer models. If they too are denied the decision maker on the basis that they cannot be proved valid, he is left with his unaided intellect alone. Now how can that be validated?

6

Documentation

Documentation is one of the most neglected aspects of modeling and simulation, partly because it is largely noncreative and therefore uninteresting. Furthermore, because it should be everyone's responsibility, it frequently becomes the responsibility of no one. While documentation should commence at the very beginning of a project, it is often left until the project is otherwise complete. This in turn makes documentation more difficult because it requires searching old records. In addition, most workers find documentation distasteful because it is part of the cleanup operation.

In the broadest sense, documentation entails the furnishing of written (or otherwise recorded) information; therefore any information describing a model can be documentation. According to this definition, we have documented several models in this book, especially in Appendices I and II. Such documentation is certainly useful and has its place in the literature of modeling and simulation, but in no case have we given enough information to allow the reader to mechanize and run a model.

6.1 Definitions

In this book, we refer to furnishing the above type of information as *descriptive documentation*. We now define another kind of documentation that will allow technical evaluation of the documented model and, if circumstances warrant, the duplication and operation of that model. This we call *technical documentation*.

6.2 Requirements

Because almost anything recorded about a model can fit our definition of descriptive documentation, the literature is replete with examples. In contrast is the dearth of technical documentation. Yet without technical documentation there can be no evaluation of a model by others, no model transfer, and in all too many cases no model use by the developers if key personnel are lost to the project. For these reasons, if for no other, documentation—both descriptive and technical—should be a contractual requirement on the part of funding agencies and a rigorously enforced policy requirement in the case of in-house developments.

Furthermore, the developers should be required to start descriptive documentation with the inception of the project, and technical documentation as soon as work on the model begins. The documentation should then be updated with each change and at each milestone. This should be made a part of the regular reporting procedure.

6.2.1 The SEAS System

The following is excerpted from a set of applications (Ubico, 1973) designed for the SEAS system. If all models were as well documented, then some of the objections raised by the detractors of large-scale models would be obviated, and the feasibility of model transfer would be greatly enhanced. The manual describes the procedures and standards to be followed in the preparation, approval, dissemination, and control of design and programming documents for the SEAS system. These procedures and standards have been designed to strike a balance between the flexibility required by creative model building and the communication of information essential to orderly system development. Inherent in this approach is the need for close coordination between model designers and system programmers.

Documents produced for the SEAS system fall into one of three categories: system documents, study documents, and programming documents. Document types within each category are listed below:

Documentation Category	Document Type
System Documents	System Definition Document
	System Implementation Plan
Study Documents	Working Papers
	Design Papers
	Technical Memoranda
Programming Documents	Programming Task Description
	Program Design Specifications
	Program Specification
	Data Specification
	User Guide
	Test Documentation
	Run Book

The two System Documents set forth the design goals for the SEAS system, plus the performance milestones and contractor responsibilities for achieving these goals. These documents are periodically revised to reflect changing system requirements. All system development progress is measured against the objectives set forth in these documents.

The Study Documents represent the response of the SEAS module design contractors in developing methodologies for meeting system objectives. The work of each contractor is divided into tasks and subtasks, not all of which directly affect the SEAS computer system. All subtasks, regardless of purpose, must result in at least one Working Paper. If a study is to culminate in a new or modified system capability, the contractor will also prepare a Design Paper which sets forth the necessary development criteria. The Technical Memorandum represents the final product of a study task and, as such, must be of publishable quality.

Programming Documents are prepared by the system support contractor to document the incorporation of selected capabilities into the SEAS system. The Programming Task Description describes the programming effort required to develop a given capability. Once the capability is approved for development, the support contractor will prepare a detailed Program Design Specification. The remaining Programming Documents are then prepared to document the completed program coding and test work.

6.2.2 The Review Board

The primary body responsible for review and approval of technical documents on the SEAS project is the Design Review Board. This Board is comprised of three permanent members (or their designated representatives):

1. The government Project Officer, with responsibility for overall SEAS progress.
2. A design coordinator, with responsibility for the analytical quality of the SEAS system.
3. The project leader from the programming support contractor, with responsibility for SEAS system programming and implementation.

Other individuals can be asked to participate in Board meetings in which their work may be significantly affected by decisions then before the Board. The Board functions on a consensus basis and not as a voting body. Significant matters which cannot be resolved within the Board will be submitted to government management for review.

Major responsibilities of the Design Review Board include:

1. Preparation and maintenance of the two system documents: the System Definition Document and the System Plan.
2. Review and approval of documents at each phase in the design, development, and implemention of a new or modified system capability.
3. Setting of the agenda for each bi-weekly design review meeting.
4. Monitoring performance against the System Definition Document.
5. Monitoring of progress against the System Implementation Plan. (See Section 8.10 for a complete description of the SEAS documentation system).

6.3 Formats

While some standardizatiori is highly desirable, rigorous adherence to any single documentation format is precluded by the many different kinds of models and modeling equipment. Here, we publish some sample formats and a composite that can be used as a check list for documentation.

Regardless of the resulting documentation, however, there are two ultimate criteria that should be applied.

For Descriptive Documentation, the criterion for adequacy is an affirmative answer to the question: "On the basis of this documentation alone, would it be possible for anyone reasonably knowledgeable in the field to determine the suitability and availability of the model for a specific use?"

For Technical Documentation, the criterion for adequacy is an affirmative answer to the question: "On the basis of this documentation alone, would it be possible for anyone otherwise competent to duplicate and run this model?"

6.3.1 Sample I

The following is based on a suggested format in an article entitled, "Simulation: From Art to Science for Society" (McLeod, December 1973). As originally published, the lines under the letter T (standing for Technical) were not used. They have been added because of the varying purposes documentation is intended to serve and the authors' belief that the intended use should dictate the items covered. Items following the line under the T may be omitted from documentation meant to be descriptive only.

The documentation format should cover the following items describing the overall project, each model developed under the project, and each simulation for which each model is used.

Project Information

1. Project title
2. Responsible organization
3. Contact
4. Project objective
5. Project duration
6. Funding
   a. Source
   b. Amount
   c. Period

Model Development Information

1. Name of model
2. Name of modeler(s)
3. Purpose for which model was developed
   a. Specific
   b. General
4. Discipline(s) involved
   a. Primary
   b. Supporting
5. Data requirements
6. Method of development
7. Assumptions
8. Cost of development
9. Availability
   a. To developer
   b. To others
10. Compatibility
    a. Computer system used in development
    b. Other systems used
    c. Language(s)
11. Extent of use
    a. By developer
    b. By others

Description of a Model

1. Classification of model
   a. Focus
   b. Scope
   c. Sophistication
2. Block diagram of system modeled
3. Program listing and/or wiring diagram of model
4. Notation
5. Validation
6. Check run results
7. Reference information
8. Distinctive features
9. Antecedents of model
10. Current related models

Simulation(s)

1. Title
2. Purposes

   3. Assumptions
T 4. Experimental design
   5. Data requirements
T 6. Data used
   7. Run time
   8. Cost per run
   9. General description of results
   10. Listing or graphic display of results
T 11. Justification of assumptions
| 12. Analysis

Discussion

   1. Comments
   2. Conclusions

Literature

   1. Project reports
   2. References
   3. Bibliography

Obviously, it would be unreasonable to expect rigorous adherence to any such format. Some of the information requested may be considered "sensitive," while it might not be of sufficient pertinence to warrant inclusion in other cases. In some instances, the information may simply not be available; however, if simulationists will use the proposed format as a checklist to aid in the preparation of more complete and uniform documentation, it will certainly go a long way toward making simulation a more respectable technology.

6.3.2 Sample II

Dennis Meadows, who headed the team producing The Limits to Growth (Meadows, 1972), has furnished the authors with his own suggested documentation standard. It differs not only in format and wording from Sample I, but also in emphasis. However, it can be seen from the following that both approaches would elicit much the same information.

**Class II Documentation Standards
for Simulation Models**

1. ACCESS TO MODEL:

Name of model: _____

Name and current address of the senior technical
person responsible for the model's construction:_____

Who funded the model development?_____

In what language is the program written? _____

On what computer system is the model currently
implemented? _____

What is the maximum memory required to store and
execute the program? _____

What is the length of time required for one typical
run of the model? _____

Is there a detailed user's manual for the model?_____

2. PURPOSE OF THE MODEL:

For what individual or institution was the model
designed?_____

What were the basic variables included in the model?

Over what time period is the model supposed to provide useful
information on real world behavior?

Was the model intended to serve as the basis of:

an academic exercise designed to test the implications of a set of assumptions or to see if a specific
theory would explain historical behavior   _____

communication with others about the nature and
implications of an important set of interactions   _____

projecting the general behavioral tendencies of the
real system   _____

predicting the value of some system element(s) at
some future point in time   _____

3. MODEL SPECIFICATION AND
    THEORETICAL JUSTIFICATION:

Provide two diagrams illustrating the extreme behavior modes exhibited by the major model elements:

If they are not included in the body of the paper indicate where the
reader may find:

a model boundary diagram that indicates the important endogenous, exogenous and excluded var-
iables   _____

a causal influence diagram, a flow diagram, the
computer program and definitions of the program
elements   _____

Is the model composed of:

simultaneous equations _____

difference or differential equations _____
procedural instructions _____

Is the model deterministic _____ or stochastic _____

continuous   _____ or discrete   _____

4.   DATA ACQUISITION

What were the primary sources for the data and theories incorporated in the model?

Data _____

_____

Theory _____

_____

What percent of the coefficients of the model were obtained from:

measurements of physical systems   _____
inference from social survey data   _____
econometric analyses   _____
expert judgment
the analyst's intuition   _____

What was the general quality of the data? _____

5.   PARAMETER ESTIMATION

If they are not given in the publication, where may the reader
obtain detailed information on the data transformations, statistical
techniques, data acquisition procedures, and results of the tests of
fit and significance used in building and analyzing the model?__

_____

6.   MODEL PERFORMANCE AND TESTING

Over what period was the model's behavior compared with historical data?_____

_____

What other tests were employed to gauge the confidence deserved
by the model?_____

Where may the reader obtain a detailed discussion of the prediction errors and the dynamic properties of the model? _____

7. APPLICATIONS

What other reports are based upon the model? _____

Name any analysts outside the parent group that have implemented the model on another computer system. _____

List any reports or publications that may have resulted from an evaluation of the model by an outside source. _____

Has any decision maker responded to the recommendations derived from the model? _____

Will there be any further modifications or documentation of the model? _____
Where may information on these be obtained? _____

6.3.3   A Generalized Checklist

The following checklist is derived from the formats of Sections 6.3.1, 6.3.2, and elsewhere. If it is used as a guide for documentation and all pertinent items are covered in the order they are listed, then it will serve two purposes:

- It will ensure that no pertinent information has been omitted.
- It will result in a quasistandard format to make the evaluation and the comparison of the suitability of models for specified purposes easier.

Checklist for Descriptive Documentation

1. Project information
   1.1   Project title
   1.2   Responsible organization
   1.3   Name and address of best contact for further information
   1.4   Project objective
   1.5   Project duration
   1.6   Funding

      1.6.1 Source
      1.6.2 Amount
      1.6.3 Period
2. Model development information
  2.1 Name of model
  2.2 Name of organization for which model was designed
  2.3 Name of modeler(s)
  2.4 Purpose for which model was developed
      2.4.1 Specific
      2.4.2 General
  2.5 Discipline(s) involved
      2.5.1 Primary
      2.5.2 Supporting
  2.6 Basic variables included
  2.7 Real-time period for which model is intended to project
  2.8 Data requirements
  2.9 Method of development
  2.10 Assumptions
  2.11 Cost of development
  2.12 Availability
      2.12.1 To developer
      2.12.2 To others
  2.13 Compatibility
      2.13.1 Computer system used in development
      2.13.2 Maximum memory size required
      2.13.3 Other systems used
      2.13.4 Languages
      2.13.5 Time required for one typical run
      2.13.6 Availability of detailed user's manual
  2.14 Extent of use by organization for which model was designed
      2.14.1 By developer
      2.14.2 By others
  2.15 Transfer use
      2.15.1 Purpose
      2.15.2 Organization
      2.15.3 Name and address of contact for further information
3. Description of model
  3.1 Classification of model
      3.1.1 Continuous or discrete
      3.1.2 Deterministic or stochastic
      3.1.3 Number of state variables
      3.1.4 Number of computer instructions

3.2 Distinctive features
3.3 Antecedents of model
3.4 Current related models
3.5 Method of parameter estimation
3.6 Block diagram of system modeled
3.7 Diagrams of extreme behavior modes of major variables
3.8 Program listing or wiring diagram of model
3.9 Notation
3.10 Method of validation
3.11 Estimate of prediction errors
4. Simulation(s) run
  4.1 Title(s)
  4.2 Purpose(s)
  4.3 Results
5. Implementation of results
  5.1 Circumstances
  5.2 Contact for further information
6. Discussion
  6.1 Comments
  6.2 Conclusions
7. Literature
  7.1 Project reports
  7.2 References
  7.3 Bibliography

Checklist for Technical Documentation
(For complete Technical Documentation, the following items should be added to those listed for Descriptive Documentation.)

3.12 Theoretical foundations for model design
3.13 Sources and general quality of data
3.14 Sources of coefficients
3.15 Method of parameter estimation
3.16 Diagrams
    3.16.1 Boundary
    3.16.2 Causal
    3.16.3 Complete model
3.17 Plots of extreme behavior modes of major variables
3.18 Program listing (and/or analog wiring diagram)
3.19 Explanation of notation
3.20 Details of validation procedure
3.21 Sensitivity analysis
3.22 Estimate of prediction errors

4.4   Simulation assumptions
4.5   Experimental design of simulation
4.6   Data requirements
4.7   Actual data used and source
4.8   Maximum and minimum run times
4.9   Cost per run
4.10 Total computer cost
4.11 Sample tabulation or plot of results
4.12 Justification of all assumptions
4.13 Method of analyzing results

6.4   Further Information

Other documentation styles, formats, and comments will be found elsewhere in this book, especially in Sections 7.3.3 and 8.3, and in connection with the models described in Appendices I and II.

7

Use, Implementation, and Transfer

In Chapter 5, we emphasized that the primary question which should be asked when evaluating a model is not, "Is it valid?" but, "Is it useful?" Only when the question of usefulness can be answered in the affirmative does the question of validity become pertinent. Who cares whether a useless model is valid? To be sure, we contend that all models are useful for something, if only to enlighten the modeler. However, that in no way implies that all models are useful for the purpose for which they were intended. In this chapter we discuss some models that were useful for their intended purpose.

Implementation (as defined in Section 2.2) is another matter. In our view, it is possible for a model to be useful and used without implementation, for we have chosen to define implementation as putting into effect plans or policies based on simulation studies. Thus it is possible for a model to be developed and used in simulation studies designed to aid in the formulation of policy, but if the policymaker doesn't "buy it," the results of the simulation will not be implemented. Too many models are left unimplemented; this is another important subject discussed in this chapter.

Finally, if a model proves useful in any respect, either to the developer or the potential "customer," might it not be useful to others? Is transfer of a model for use by others desirable? Possible? Feasible? The transfer of models is also discussed in this chapter.

7.1 Useful Models

The authors have stated that all models are useful for something; but the subject of this book is policy models, and distressingly few models have been useful in shaping policy. Some exceptions may be found among those listed in Appendices I and II; but even then, it would be difficult to show the extent to which they contributed to the policymaking process. It is entirely possible that some policymakers have been influenced more than they care to admit. It is still degrading in the minds of many to acknowledge their thought processes can be improved by recourse to a machine.

However, it is certain that no matter to what extent a simulation study might influence a policymaker, unless the policies suggested by the simulation study are put into effect, the usefulness of policy models is suspect. This is true even though the study might have convinced the policymaker that a particular course of action would *not* be beneficial and thus influenced him to adopt another course of action that *was* implemented. Negative results can also influence policy.

7.2   Is Implementation Necessary?

If models can be useful even though the results of simulation studies making use of them are not put into effect, it can be said that implementation is not always necessary. However, if the objective of developing the model is not simply to study, but to *change* the system modeled, implementation *is* necessary.

7.2.1   *Difficulties*

One thing seems certain: simulation has not been used to its full potential to alleviate the problems of society. There are many reasons for this: the mystique of computers in general and simulation in particular, some disappointments due in large measure to overselling and premature starts, the mistaken notion that simulation can predict the future, and a lack of convincing methods of model validation.

The mystique is gradually being eroded by the more responsible representatives of the popular press as well as by well-balanced technical presentations. The other problems are treated elsewhere in this book. Here, we consider implementation as an activity required to make modeling and simulation truly effective in serving society.

7.2.2   *Approaches to Solutions*

Implementation as a Simulation System Component. A system relating simulation and implementation to real-world problems is conceptualized in Figure 7.1. That figure and the following paragraphs were taken from the newsletter *Simulation in the Service of Society* (McLeod, 1975). The figure is explained as follows:

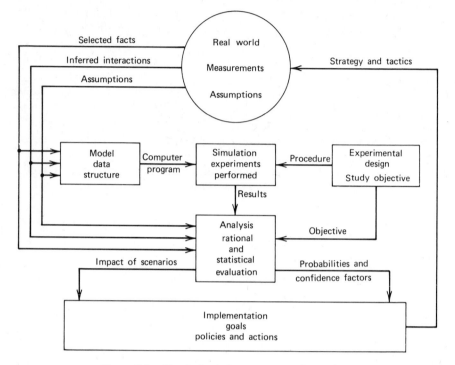

Figure 7-1. S^4—A simulation system serving society.

Pertinent facts and inferred relations from real-world measurements are selected as inputs for the development of a model. Assumptions are made where
necessary. The resulting computer model is used for the simulation studies.

However, for the studies to be meaningful, an experimental design must be
created, based on the objectives of the study and the need to produce meaningful
results suitable for analytical evaluation. Usually the procedure amounts to having the model act out a scenario based on actions proposed for the solution of the
problem under study. This yields a procedure for conducting the simulation
experiments.

The results of the simulation experiments are analyzed in the light of the original
assumptions and the experimental design, and the probable impact of alternative
courses of action is determined, preferably with a confidence factor attached.

In general the analyst should avoid making recommendations and limit himself
to presenting the simulation results with explanatory annotation as appropriate,
plus confidence figures if possible. Such activity may be considered to represent
one side of the coin. Now we turn the coin over.

The decision-makers operate on the implementation side of the coin. Theirs is
the responsibility to look at the simulation output and the analysts' explanations,
judge the confidence that can be placed in the results, modify that with other
information—such as past experience—that is exogenous to the simulation, and in

the light of their own or established goals, frame policies and/or institute actions. The strategies and tactics developed in support of policies are then applied in the real world, thus closing the loop.

Although we have made a distinction between simulation and implementation, if we expect simulation to contribute to the amelioration of world problems, the two can no more be separated successfully without damage to both than can the two sides of a coin.

A Revised Modeling Paradigm. The article expressing the foregoing thoughts elicited the following from a reader (Schultz, 1976).

A recent article argued, correctly I think, that the other face of simulation modeling is implementation. The main point of the discussion is that, to serve society, simulation [results] must be *used*, i.e., implemented. Thus, concern with building and testing models must be balanced with interest in how models *can* and *will* be used. Currently, however, implementation considerations are not an explicit part of simulation methodology. In this note it will be argued that S^4 (A Simulation System Serving Society, Figure 7-1) mandates a revised model-building paradigm. It is the interface between model building and implementation—the edge of the coin—that is crucial to success.

Simulation is one of the tools of operations research/management science (OR/MS). Despite the advances made in OR/MS *technology* over several decades, few OR/MS models, including simulation models, are used by organizations. Thus, the promise of OR/MS and of simulation *as a policy tool* is largely unrealized. Why is this so?

Within the past few years researchers have turned to this question with interesting results. The major insight is that, although OR/MS is a *technical* activity, implementation is a *behavioral* problem. Factors shown to be associated with successful implementation include the cognitive style of intended users, top management/administrative support (or lack of resistence), client-researcher relationships, goal congruence between model developers and intended users, quality and characteristics of the model, methods of model construction and presentation, personal characteristics of intended users, and a host of situational factors. These variables are now being asembled into models of the implementation process itself (Schultz, 1975).

When a simulation is intended for use as a policy tool, special considerations arise in designing the model (Schultz, 1974). These design factors arise precisely because of the purpose of the model: the simulation is supposed to influence policy; hence, it must be implemented before this influence can take place. What, then, can be done to enhance the probability of successful implementation?

Policy simulations are designed for policymakers, but created by model builders. The quality of the client-researcher relationship is thus important to central issues like (1) the correct identification of the problem, (2) congruence of goals (of the organization and the project) and, (3) *behavioral* understanding between the two parties. Model failure to match the problem has been called a Type III error and clearly depends upon how well the researcher and client *jointly* specify the problem space. The nature of the project should also be mutually understood, and furthermore, the use of the project should be clear to both researcher and client. Finally, the researcher must know the organization in the sense of understanding how policy is made and what changes can be made.

The simulation model builder is a change agent. If the model is adopted, then policy making will have been changed (and, with goal congruence and no Type III error, changed for the .better). Hence, the model builder should be as skilled in managing change as in constructing models. Managing change, however, requires it first be understood. This is the reason why current research is focused on the behavioral process of implementation.

A revised model building paradigm seems to be required if policy simulations are to be implemented to consequently influence policy. We have already stressed the importance of joint problem definition, goal congruence and the behavioral assessment of organizational needs, attitudes and action tendencies. The models themselves ought to be developed in stages so the client aids in the model-building process and isn't merely presented with the end result. By fitting the model's characteristics to those of the organizations or by knowing just how the organization must be changed to fit the model, implementation can be managed to enhance the chance of success.

The edge of the coin is the interface between model building and implementation; in practice, that interface is between model builder and policymaker. If simulation is to serve society, then the simulation builders have the responsibility to implement their models. To do this, we need to know a great deal more about human and organizational innovative behavior. Technical skill on the part of model builders is not enough.

Managing Implementation. An MIT Professor of Management of Technology offers the following excellent advice on implementation (Roberts, 1975):

My observations regarding model implementation are divided into four kinds of issue areas. The areas are: First, selection and identification of the problem to be investigated; second, the process for construction of the model; third, the characteristics of the recommendations that are made regarding the problem; and fourth, some general views on the overall setting.

PROJECT SELECTION

1. Purpose must be to solve a problem.
2. Problem must be important to "client."
3. Objectives must be credible.

Most corporate models, surprisingly, do not meet the first criterion—that is, most models are not built to solve a problem; they are built to model a system.

If you want to achieve implementation, that is have changes made as a result of your modeling work, the problem that you select must be important to the client. Furthermore, the client must in advance, or at least during the very early stages of the project, believe that the types of changes you are seeking to achieve are within the grasp of the organization.

MODELING PROCESS

1. Encourage maximum client involvement.
2. Expedite initial model development.
3. Model detail must be sufficient for persuasiveness.

4. Validity testing must be geared to management assurance.
5. Measures of effectiveness must be designed into the model, and consistent with real-world measures.

The greater the extent to which the job can be done inside the client organization, the better the likelihood that the job will result in implemented changes. The more that outsiders have to be relied upon, the more there are likely to be problems of communication and continuity.

An important point: the first model should be expedited so that you have a developed and operating model running on the computer quickly. The reasons are several—to reinforce client confidence, to communicate explicitly what kinds of work you are actually doing (in contrast to the work that people think you are doing), and to begin to define data-needs, so that you can begin resolving them.

And the model should have detail sufficient to be persuasive. You first meet the client's need for detail. After that, you meet the modeler's need for adequate problem representation. But the client is the boss. You must provide the level of detail that causes him to be persuaded that you have properly taken into account his issues, his questions, his level of concerns. Otherwise he will not believe the model you have built, he will not accept it, and he will not use it.

The problem of validation may be approached in several ways. However, no matter which way seems the most appropriate in a particular case, the validity testing of a model must be geared to the kind and the level that will give management assurance that the model is adequate for the task at hand.

Finally, I think it's important that when you begin trying to develop a complex model you decide upon the measures of effectiveness of results that you are seeking in the real world. Model the measures against which you will test the implementation, and within the simulation model itself give an opportunity to ask how that measure of effectiveness will change as a result of historical policies versus proposed policies or alternative strategies.

RECOMMENDATIONS FOR CHANGE

1. Account for ability to absorb change.
2. Consider possible impact on other systems.
3. Accompany recommendations by management re-education and/or by explicit decision rules.

Before making each contemplated recommendation one should consider whether the organization can absorb the recommended change.

Think of interdependencies. As you recommend a solution in one area, you are liable to be getting the organization into problems in another. Ask the cross-functional, cross-matrix, cross-organizational question: Will this recommendation impact other systems or other parts of the system?

Finally, recommended changes either have to be accompanied by a re-education program for management, or explicit decision rules. It will not be enough merely to say you are running the company wrong; you should run the company this way instead.

GENERAL CONSIDERATIONS

1. Implementation orientation from outset.
2. Continue work until implementation is achieved.
3. Project must be designed to produce—

implementable results;
desire to implement;
environment that enables implementation.

From the beginning of any project there should be consideration of the implementation issue that will arise. Consider the implementation issues with respect to problem finding, group composition, analysis method. At every point of the problem approach, you should be asking, "Are we doing this with an implementation perspective?" Then work should continue until implementation is achieved.

The people who had the commitment from the beginning for identification and analysis of the problem should not break up their working relationship when they submit a technical report containing recommendations. They should have as part of their responsibility the assisting of the organization in achievement of implementation.

Finally, in terms of overall perspective, the project process should be designed so that it's going to produce results that are implementable, that is the results must be practicable, and within the grasp of the organization. There must also be a desire to implement: you must have educated the people, persuaded them that the change is worthwhile, helped them to overcome their resistance barriers, motivated them to see the benefits. You must also have created an environment that enables the implementation to go forward. In many organizations, this may be a far broader task than all the modeling activities that were undertaken. This may engage you in significant human organizational development work; it may require that you have a *behavioral* scientist as part of your team (not just another *management* scientist); an applied psychologist who will help you anticipate and overcome those classes of issues within the organization.

7.2.3   Presentation of Results

An ancient Chinese proverb holds that one picture is worth more than ten thousand words. Certainly this seems to be true—qualitatively if not quantitatively—when it comes to presenting the results of using a computer model to make policy studies. The following excerpts support this view.

Department of Transportation Recommendations. The first recommendations are from a report (Schneider, 1973) of workshops sponsored by the Department of Transportation, which led to the recommendations (among others) that DOT seriously consider supporting "A General-Purpose Interaction Graphics System for Regional Planning Agencies."

Develop and implement an interactive graphics systems for general use planning agencies. The system should support the agencies' activites in the areas of: (1) browsing through existing data sets; (2) data editing and updating; (3) preparation of batch processing runs of large scale simulation models, and initial examination of their outputs; (4) network editing and analysis and (5) simple planning models. The proposed system should be inexpensive to purchase and operate. Development costs can be easily justified due to expected wide usage. The technology for the proposed system is available, and there are no problems in implementing it in the immediate future.

INTERACTIVE GRAPHIC CALIBRATION OF DISAGGREGATE BEHAVIORAL MODELS. An existing interactive graphics information storage and retrieval system oriented toward transportation data should be expanded to facilitate the use of these data to calibrate disaggregate behavioral demand models. This expansion would include such things as maximum likelihood logic estimation capabilities, residual displays, dynamic display of error measures as the estimation program progresses, and displays to compare the characteristics and results obtained with alternative model formulations.

The Situation Room Concept. The following excerpts from the Congressional Record of December 16, 1974 give some of the thoughts of another proponent of graphical presentation of simulation results (Lamson, 1974):

. . . we can and should do more through research to create a more holistic and accurate view of problems, causes, options and impacts, for example, through modeling and simulation of large complex systems . . .

A range of technologies exist to help improve the policy dialogue about the problems and options which confront us. These technologies include: maps and physical models; aerial photography and satellite imagery; gaming and simulation; computer modeling (involving the use of interactive computer graphics); social indicators and social graphics; citizen pooling and feedback systems; television-broadcast and cable.

To date, we have not brought together, assessed and employed such technologies in order to help policymakers and citizens grasp more easily the complex peace-time problems which they confront.

The key to putting such technologies together to aid the policy dialogue is the concept of the "situation room"—a physical location in which problems, trends, progress, options and the results of policy-related research can be displayed graphically in a form which decision-makers, including the public, can more readily see, comprehend and discuss.

Situation rooms can provide the neutral forums for policy dialogue and graphic communication of complex policy problems and options, at various levels—international, national, regional, state, city and community—and for various roles, involving policymakers and citizens, administrators, elected officials and legislators.

A situation room can provide a means whereby citizens and policymakers can more easily and intuitively see and understand the critical elements and interactions of large complex problems, obtain a sense of the degree of ignorance and uncertainty concerning the impacts of such problems and of the options to cope with them.

Moreover, by using graphic techniques, the situation room enables individuals who are in potential conflict (due to conflicts of personality, value, interest and power) to focus on the problem "out there" displayed through the use of various graphic techniques. Such a forum can provide a means whereby potential opponents over a policy issue can at least reach agreement about the nature of their disagreement.

By experimenting with and using situation rooms, we may be able not only to create a better synthesis, in thought, policy and institutions, but also to develop better perceptions and consensus on problems of dialogue, to develop shared values, increased thrust and agreement about desirable choices.

One possibility for synthesis and communication on the national level would be to create a policy-oriented exhibit building in Washington, D.C. possibly on the Mall as a new activity of the Smithsonian Institute.

The building could use the concept of the situation room and present policy-oriented exhibits and displays on the range of policy problems and alternatives which confront the United States.

A Demonstration Facility Concept. As an advocate of the concept, one of the authors of this book looked into the economic feasibility (the technology was available) of developing a specific kind of "situation room" in 1974. It was to have a large (visible from anywhere in the room) dynamic display driven by a computer model. The model was to be similar to World 2 (Forrester, 1971), but would differ in programming and mechanization in some important ways, all designed to improve the man/machine interaction and to make the presentation of the simulation results more intelligible, as well as dramatic. To this end, there would be calibrated dials labeled with the names of several of the more important exogenous variables and parameters that would be under the control of the experimenter. Furthermore, the computer would be programmed to run in "rep-op," a mode in which a complete simulation is run, and automatically repeated and displayed at a rate fast enough to make the presentation change in apparently real time with the movement of the dials. Thus, serious researchers and the curious public alike could immediately see the probable long-term impact of proposed policy changes or casual "dial twiddling."

Such a simulation could be invaluable both as a professional and a public relations tool. However, some caution would have to be exercised with respect to the public. Imagine an opinionated layman (or professional) who believes that the projected population increase is the only world problem. He moves the "Birth Rate" dial to match the setting of the "Death Rate" dial, immediately expecting to achieve "Zero Population Growth." His first shock is that world population continues to rise for some 70 years. The next disappointment is that the model indicates population control alone will not cure all the ills of society worldwide. The reaction to such an experience might be "Models are no damn good!" We have had enough of that attitude, so care will have to be taken to ensure that counterintuitive results are explained and hopefully understood.

The situation room sounded like a good idea. However, a cursory investigation indicated that such an installation would cost between two and three million dollars. That estimate was made before microprocessors were readily available. The economic feasibility should now be reexamined.

The worldwide controversy stimulated by the publication of *Limits to Growth* (Meadows, 1972) was the reason for thinking of mechanizing a similar model for the demonstration project. However, current computer technology would allow changing models by simply changing plug boards. There could be national models for Congress and interested citizens, state models, and even a model of New York City to demonstrate to the populace (and any politicians and union leaders who might be interested) what the trade-offs might be between public services, wages, and taxes.

As prices of hardware come down, every policymaker body, activist group, and concerned citizen could and should have access to such a facility.

7.3 Transfer

Large-scale models or policies are expensive in terms of talent, time, and money. Why, then, when a model has proven useful to one group or agency, should it not be transferred and adapted for similar use elsewhere? Obviously such models should be transferred, but they seldom are. Why not?

7.3.1 Problems

Few of those who study models and their formulation ever get around to studying the transfer aspect because it is less analytical and more institutional in nature. Our discussion here is limited to looking at just three facets of the problem: the NIH factor, the team factor, and the cost factor.

NIH (Not-Invented-Here). The factor glibly labeled NIH, or "not-invented-here," is one of the most self-defeating features of the way our scientific community is organized. All ideas, new or old, are continually required to compete for funding or recognition. Unfortunately, this often leads to a situation where no idea is considered valid or useful unless it has been originated by the particular group, person, or institution that has use for it.

Furthermore, little formal recognition is awarded those who transfer someone else's idea or process for local use. Such acts are usually deemed insufficiently worthy to be included in professional journals or to be the subjects of funding. In fact, in the non-social science disciplines there is a very clear distinction between the person who is expected to create new concepts (the scientist) and the person who implements these ideas (the engineer). In the social science or policy field, the person who carries out functions similar to the engineer is not yet afforded a legitimate place or recognition in the professional community.

There is no complex model built today that is honestly the product of a single person. Reports that describe the building of large-scale models (and proposals to build others) proudly point out the fact that it requires multidisciplinary teams to create these systems. Unfortunately, it has been less well recognized that it also requires multidisciplinary teams to utilize them. Again, we find that our institutional structure does not ordinarily reward a person for being a member of a team nor does it call for such teams to become standard parts of policy staffs.

Finally, although it is usually very difficult to get the substantial sums of money needed to design and build large-scale models, it is even more difficult to get funding to mechanize and use them in places other than where they originated. Those who would support research get the most benefit from being linked to a brand new idea. Seldom is there large internal payoff for supporting transferred projects.

The foregoing are general problems. In the following special case, other problems were found.

The River Basin Model Transfer. Soon after the Environmental Studies Division was formed, EPA received numerous requests for the gaming form of its RIVER BASIN MODEL, a large-scale, man-machine model. Since large portions of this model were incorporated in GEM (Sections AI-4, AII-5), it was decided that the transfer of the RBM could be accompanied by a research study that would give the agency some warning about the problems it might encounter in any subsequent attempt to transfer GEM. The model was therefore made available to a selected university research center in each of the 10 federal regions. In addition to the RBM manuals and computer programs, technical assistance was made available to the centers on request. The purpose of this limited experiment, as previously stated, was to see what kind of difficulties would be encountered in building and transferring a large and complex model. To provide the raw data for the study, each of the 10 centers was asked to complete an information sheet each month.

Although the RBM was successfully transferred to a number of places by this technique, there were difficulties. The following is a partial list.

1. Although the model was programmed almost totally in Fortran IV and for an IBM 360-40 and above, transferring was not straightforward.

2. Because the program had over 35,000 statements, considerably more analysis was required for adaptation than most centers had expected.

3.   The model is extremely complex and sophisticated. It required a great deal of dedication and study on the part of the user before he felt comfortable with it. This led to two ancillary problems:

a.   There was never enough documentation to satisfy a serious user.

b.   With a model of the size of RBM (with scores of subroutines and a large data base), there is always a new series of pathways possible that could lead to discovering a "bug." When the user who is not familiar with the model and cannot assess the severity of the bugs begins to doubt the veracity of the model output, he often will cease to put in the effort required to understand the model operation. The failure is, consequently, not attributed to him but to the model itself.

7.3.2   Requirements for Success

Experience and common sense agree that there are several requirements for successful transfer and reuse of models:

Need.

Institutional compatibility.

Suitable facilities.

Adequate documentation.

Technical support.

Need for a model having specific characteristics must exist, although that need might not be immediately recognized. If it is not, some "selling" on the part of the proponents of a transfer might be necessary. However, as in promoting the development and use of models in general, even when an available model seems suitable, overselling must be avoided.

In no case should wishful thinking allow a model to be represented as capable of delivering results for which it was not designed. Furthermore, even when a model is suitable for the purpose for which it is to be transferred, some problems will inevitably arise, and the customer should be prepared for them.

Institutional compatibility is difficult to define and, because of subjective components, impossible to measure. Of course, ways of coping with open hostility on the part of individuals or groups in either the sending or the receiving organizations should be devised, or the plans for transferring a model should be abandoned. If the transfer is forced against anyone's will, the project is courting either overt or covert sabotage.

How about latent psychological factors—people who fear (consciously or subconsciously) that the transfer threatens their image or security? Or institutional factors related to the organizational structures and their relative place in their respective hierarchies? In other words, how about the politics of the situation?

Because of the nature of the foregoing problems, we can only recommend that their existence or probable existence be recognized, and a general approach to alleviate them be instituted. This should start with establishing good lines of two-way communication. In the direction from developer to potential user, this can serve to educate the latter in the nature and advantages of the subject model. In the other direction, it can warn the developer of areas of possible friction which might have to be treated on an ad hoc basis.

Technical competence on the part of the potential user must be ensured. It is possible to drive an automobile without knowing how an internal combustion engine works, and it is possible to conduct simulation studies without knowing how a computer works; but driver tests are required that are designed to show that a person knows everything necessary to operate an automobile without getting into trouble. Much more technical knowledge is needed to prevent the user from getting into trouble while operating a complex model. Therefore, means should be devised to ensure the competence of potential operators. This should be a joint responsibility of both parties to any proposed transfer: the developer, lest failure of the transferred model to meet expectations accrue to his discredit; and the new user, lest he obtain unsatisfactory, or even misleading, results from his use of the model.

Suitable facilities are an obvious requirement, but these are sometimes overlooked because of the vagueness of the term "suitable." Equivalent facilities might not be suitable if corresponding but slightly differing components require substantial computer program modification.

This matter should be checked carefully before plans for transferring any model are consummated.

Adequate documentation is a requirement that has been discussed previously, especially in Chapter 6. No more is said here, except that it should not be overlooked when first considering transferring any model.

Technical support to the would-be user by the developers of the model is required in roughly inverse proportion to the adequacy of documentation. Theoretically, if documentation were perfect, no technical support would be required. But perfect documentation is too much to expect, and therefore technical support by the developer should be included in any plans for transfer.

Other insights concerning institutional factors were developed in a survey covered in Section 8.3.4. This same survey indicated that many respondents favored the establishment of a clearing house for models to make them centrally available to researchers. A discussion of this concept follows.

7.3.3 The Clearinghouse Concept

The idea of a "clearinghouse" for modeling information is such a natural one that it has been suggested by many simulationists and others (see, for instance, Section 8.5.5). However, when it comes to details, opinions differ widely as to what services such a facility should furnish, how it should be organized, and who should pay for it.

For instance, services could range from simply cataloging model names and sources for further information, to completely checking out, documenting, and certifying models. Methods could vary from card files to computer storage and retrieval, while the cost might be borne by the users or granting agencies. These points are considered in the following paragraphs.

How Much and By Whom? The primary questions when considering the establishment of some sort of "clearinghouse" are:

What should be the criteria for the inclusion of a model?

How much information should be stored and disseminated?

To what extent should the format be standardized?

Who would be responsible for its adequacy and accuracy?

Who would pay for the service?

De Facto answers to some of these questions have been supplied by several services; they range from a simple listing of model names and contacts where further information can be obtained, to fairly complete model descriptions. To date, however, we know of no information storage and retrieval service that furnishes documentatation complete enough for a client to mechanize and run a model. Nor does any such service assume responsibility for the validity or usefulness of the models they list. Some, however, give valuable information concerning what is available.

Some Model Information Sources. Although they do not qualify as model clearinghouses in the sense that we have discussed, there exist some sources of information that can be helpful to those interested in models for possible transfer, or who just want to know what is going on. The following are illustrative of the kinds of information available; an exhaustive listing would be beyond the scope of this book.

Probably the source most pertinent to the subject of this book is *Federally Supported Mathematical Models: Survey and Analysis* (Fromm, 1975). This is a 293-page report which, after 39 pages of introductory material, lists 289 models by author, by developing institution, by sponsoring agency, and by subject area.

The author listing assigns a number (for cross-referencing), gives the author's name, title of the model, the developing organization, and the sponsoring agency. This is followed by a one-paragraph description of the model and—usually—references. The following is typical.

209.   Environmetrics, "River Basin Model."
Environmental Studies Division, U.S. Environmental
Protection Agency, Washington, D.C., U.S. Environ-
mental Protection Agency 018.

The River Basin Model is a man-machine simulation model that represents the working of a water system within the context of a full range of spatial, economic, social and government activity. The model may be used to represent any actual or hypothetical river basin area. A wide range of decisions and their consequences may be illustrated by the model. For example, in the economic sector the impacts of response to water pollution regulations, fines, comprehensive planning, and quality of the local water system may be shown. The impacts of many government decisions may be shown; comprehensive water management programs, changing utility district boundaries, intergovernmental cooperation and many more.

References "An Environmental Laboratory for the Social Sciences" Peter W. House and Philip D. Patterson, (eds). U.S. Environmental Protection Agency, Washington, D.C. 1972.
Laska, Richard M., "Player's Guide: River Basin Model." U.S. Environmental Protection Agency, Office of Research and Monitoring, Environmental Studies Division, Washington, D.C., 1973, 290 p

Just as the foregoing listing is limited to federally supported models, most other lists are just as specialized. For instance, the International Institute of Applied Systems Analysis has published two reports (Charpentier, 1974, 1975) which together list and briefly describe 145 models in the energy field alone. The following is typical.

Sample IIASA Model Description
E.E.C.

The Model	H. Neu, Ispra Establishment, Italy, 1975[49]. Energy Simulation Model.
Subject and Goal	A simulation model to study the impact of different supply strategies (nuclear, exploitation of home resources) and to develop energy demand and supply scenarios for the year 2000

and beyond. A special goal is the study of the impact of new technologies on the dependence of the E.C. on primary sources imports.

System Described		The system is divided into 4 interconnected subsystems: Demand, Supply, Conversion and Economy. Demand is subdivided into electricity and heat (fuel) for 4 economic sectors (industry, household and commerce, transportation, and energy). The Demand subsystem is connected to the Economy subsystem through the GNP growth rate by functional relationships. From the total electricity demand the required primary energy (fossil, nuclear, hydroelectric) is calculated in the Conversion subsystem and fed into the Supply subsystem, which is structured into production, imports and exports of different primary sources (coal, crude oil, natural gas, primary electricity, primary heat). The costs of imported primary sources influence the GNP growth rate (feedback loop).
Area	Time	1960–2000.
	Space	Nine nations of the European Communities; can be applied to any industrialized nation or world region.
Modelling Techniques		The computer language is DYNAMO III. Time series are generated by a loop structure and time varying growth rates. Functional relationships are given in the form of tables (systems dynamics approach). Output data are printed out and plotted by the DYNAMO compiler.
Input Data		For the time period 1960 to 1974: —Statistical data for 1960, —Average growth rates of time series. For the time period after 1974: —Policies for the exploitation of primary sources, —Nuclear installed capacity, —Estimated growth rates of various parameters, —Table functions for the sectorial demand, —Table function for the impact of primary sources import costs on the GNP growth rate (hypothetical), —Oil and gas reserves, —Inflation rate, oil price and other parameters.
Output Data		Plotted curves 1960 to 2000 —GNP at fixed prices, GNP growth rates, —Total inland consumption of primary sources, —Production of primary sources (nuclear, hydro-, natural gas, crude oil, lignite, hard coal),

	—Imports of primary sources (oil, natural gas, coal), —Sectorial consumption of primary sources, —Sectorial energy consumption per capita, —Sectorial share of primary sources consumption, —Share of different primary sources in total inland consumption. Time series of 70 parameters are printed out.
Observations	An extended model should include other conversion processes besides electricity production. The Economy subsystem should be more detailed, and more sophisticated linkage should be elaborated with the Demand subsystem. The model results suffer from the poor knowledge of functional relationships.

Summary supplied by the author of the model.

Another specialized listing is limited to growth models (Library of Congress, 1975). Twenty of these are listed and described in a format similar to the sample given in Section AI-1.3.

In addition to such listings, information concerning models can be obtained through more generalized information storage and retrieval services such as SSIE (Smithsonian Science Information Exchange). This is "A National Collection of Current Research Information; A Comprehensive Single Source for Ongoing Research Information in All Sciences." For a fee that varies with the amount of material found, this organization will make a computer search of selected subject areas. The sample shown is typical of some 300 NRPs (Notice of Research Project) that were furnished in response to a request to search for "projects involving computer modeling and simulation in the social sciences." About 60% were actually pertinent to the areas of interest, the others apparently were picked up by misleading key words.

ERIC/CHESS (Educational Resources Information Center/ Clearinghouse for Social Studies Social Science Education) is also a storage and retrieval service that can furnish information on models and simulation, but only if they relate to education.

There are many other services in both the public (e.g., NASA) and private (e.g., Lockheed) sectors which, while designed to serve much broader areas, list considerable information on policy models.

7.4 Challenges to Modelers

There are several schools of thought concerning what types of models (not only in form but in content) would be of most use to the policymaker.

FORM APPROVED
BOB NO. 108 R0002
EXPIRES 11/76

SMITHSONIAN SCIENCE INFORMATION EXCHANGE
Room 300 • 1730 M Street, N.W. • Washington, D.C. • 20036
Telephone (202) 381-4211 • Telex 89495

SSIE NUMBER

GY-64729-1

NOTICE OF RESEARCH PROJECT

SUPPORTING ORGANIZATION:
OKLAHOMA STATE GOVERNMENT

SUPPORTING ORGANIZATION NUMBER(S):
0064729

OKL01564

PROJECT TITLE:
ECONOMIC AND ENVIRONMENTAL IMPACTS RECREATION DEVELOPMENT AND MANAGEMENT STRATEGIES

INVESTIGATOR(S):
DD BADGER

DEPARTMENT/SPECIALTY:
AGRICULTURAL ECON

PERFORMING ORGANIZATION:
OKLA. ST. UNIV.
  AGRIC. EXPERIMENT STATION
  107 WHITEHURST HALL
  STILLWATER, OKLAHOMA 74075

PERIOD FOR THIS NRP:
7/75 TO 6/76
FY76   FUNDS UNKNOWN

PROJECT SUMMARY:
OBJECTIVE: Estimate economic effects of alternative water-based recreational development and management strategies. Analyze factors causing environmental impacts on both recreational users and on the physical sites. Develop a simulation model which will measure the environmental externalities and economic impacts associated with the water-based recreational uses. Determine the level of physical development, and the level management that will optimize the trade-offs between environmental externalities and economic values.

APPROACH: Regression and input-output models for several regional man-made lakes will be used to measure economic effects. Qualitative models will be constructed to measure seasonal and yearly variations in environmentally related variables. These variables will be stratified as to physical site, and location of recreational area (rural or urban). Effects of fluctuating water levels on use, quality of the recreational experience, and resulting economic impact will be determined. Current and proposed management strategies for the water-based recreational facilities, as well as effects of over use and under use, and complementary and competitive relationships among old and new reservoirs. Develop a simulation model to demonstrate quantity of use-quality of experience erlationships for these alternative recreational development and management strategies.

PROGRESS: Lake Tenkiller, a medium size lake (12,500 surface acres) built by the U.S. Army Corps of Engineers in 1952, was selected for study. Lake Tenkiller is located in a rural area of eastern Oklahoma. It is intensively used by recreationists, recording over 4 million visitor days in 1973. A sample of both recreationists and home owners around the Lake was selected. Personal interviews with 320-on-site (in state park or at Corpes of Engineers public use areas) recreation groups and 127 home owners (73 permanent residents and 54 seasonal residents) were completed in the summer of 1973. Analysis of much of the data is still incomplete. The mean annual household income of permanent property owners around the lake was $12,197; for seasonal property owners, $17,550. This compares with the 1970 average of $6,225 for residents of the two counties where the lake is located, and $9,110 for Oklahoma residents in 1970.

As with all problems, one will find that at various levels of abstraction various alternatives are relevant. For instance, if a specific public issue reaches significant proportions it will rise to the policy level, which tends to deal in fairly aggregate terms. Because most issues are fairly specific, the policymaker finds himself dealing with an issue in greater detail than generally handled at this level; it may therefore require more precise inputs and rigorous handling. Perversely, the detail and data requirements of such models, although potentially of great use to the policymaker, generally preclude their application. Furthermore, problems of this sort often encompass a time constant that coincides only by accident with the time constant of the scientific community manipulating the models.

More to the point, there seems to be a class of problems that the policymaker deals with all the time, and which the modeling community only recently has begun to address. The policymaker, like the biblical Solomon, continually must adjudicate between areas with competing needs for scarce resources. He will tend to prefer those policies that appear to be most effective in pursuing his goals and in satisfying his constituency and, at the same time, minimize the negative effect from those parts of the system that he has been forced to deemphasize. Such models are the type that trade off various policy choices among comprehensive alternatives. In fact, such tradeoffs must be made to relate all the parts of the policymaker's area of interest to each other. They must also be related through time so that a short-run decision maximizing an immediate gain does not turn out to be suboptimal in the long run. Consequently, what appears to be called for is a model which (1) is at a gross or aggregated level of detail, (2) allows manipulation of a large number of alternative choices, (3) is sensitive to the time dimension, (4) is relatively easy and quick to load and run, and (5) gives an output easy to interpret in policy terms.

If it is true that the policymaker really could make use of such models, why is it that they generally have not been built or applied? A perusal of the literature suggests three general answers to this question: (1) theories needed to build such models, particularly those of the social/political institutions, are barely hypotheses; (2) the specific functions constructed that purport to represent the system under consideration are open to question; and (3) the required data is either unavailable, questionable, or in the wrong form.

One of the largest single issues subsumed in the above is that a rigorous method of validating policy models is unknown. Since such models may claim completeness or a comprehensive base, apparently the only test that can be made is to see whether they will replicate a historical time period. However, if it is a comprehensive model, it will only do this on a probabilistic basis. Consequently, the lack of precision generally found in many models leaves the analyst with no rigorous method of validation. Since large-scale forecasting models often can be used to generate a series of possible alternative futures, the range of outputs must be evaluated on a "most likely" basis rather than on a deterministic one.

Since we continue to apply models despite the fact that perfect validation of such models is impossible, given all the time and details represented, this raises a question for modelers: Should we avoid developing policy models? As discussed in *Urban Dynamics* (Forrester, 1969), complex systems (e.g., urban areas, national governments, the environment) are subject to such interactive behavior that unexpected and counterintuitive results may well be the rule rather than the exception. With this phenomenon in mind, how can we rationalize the development of complex models? It is clear more attempts *must* be made to model systems. Lack of validation cannot by itself be allowed to obviate the building and use of policy models. On the other hand, this statement should not be mistaken for license. Some test of reasonableness will have to be made and the standards of scientific integrity kept high. In short, the plea is made for further experimentation and limited use as an alternative to the presently fashionable rejection. The significant principle should be explicit and objective specification of goals for the system.

The question of unavailable data is interesting. Probably little frustrates the policymaker who supports a large organization more than to be told that there is not enough data available to answer his questions. This reply, in fairness to both sides, is probably both right and wrong. From the perspective of the researcher or analyst, the policymaker has a habit of changing his mind concerning information he wants. He thus changes his long-range information needs. The time frame is often such that just as the researchers begin to gear up and handle questions of one type, the policymaker, having made his mind up in that area, is anxious to move on to other questions. This means that the scientifically trained analyst is eternally frustrated as he attempts to get the ever-finer detailed information. This is particularly true since, again, his judges are his peers and not necessarily the elected and therefore changeable policymaker.

Nevertheless, it is counterproductive to tell a policymaker that in two years a finished model can give him an answer when he needs an answer today (Brewer, 1973). From the policymaker's perspective, responsibility is to his goals and to those of his constituency. The issues and questions that need answers are not necessarily those that are amenable to the scientific method. Issues and needs change more rapidly than systems for data collection and use. Pressures demand that answers be given and policy choices made, whether or not enough data are available.

When modelers from various disciplines assemble, their interaction problems are similar to those of getting any multidisciplinary team to work together. The journals they read, the training they have, the vocabulary (not only that peculiar to their discipline, but also that of the mathematics and computer languages) are all different. Most ad hoc groups gathered together to support the policymakers spend an inordinate amount of time in just fighting communication problems among themselves, not to mention the substantial difficulties they encounter interfacing with the policy people.

There is a need for a group of policy-oriented scientists to support the policymaker. These people would have responsibility for making available, to the policymaker, on demand, information that would help him make his policy decisions. The information would be the best available at a particular time, and the specific requirements of the policy may or may not engender research projects by the general R&D staff. Models could and should be a basic tool of such a support group. Of course, it is recognized that since the development of data and structures for such models is still in its infancy, advice to the policymaker as a result of using general purpose models will have to be probabilistic in nature. Furthermore, such advice should give the policymaker some confidence level indicating how good or reliable the estimates are. Such timely advice could be of great value for the solution of policy-level problems.

As an example of such analytical support of the policy-level decision maker, let us again focus on the environment. Conceptually, a policymaker in any area could be supported in essentially the same fashion.

It has been assumed throughout this work that there must be comprehensive and long-run planning if policy intended to both clean up and preserve environment is to be promulgated. In practice, however, the day-to-day implementation of policy often does not accommodate such concerns. This feature is obviously not a function of capriciousness of the advisors, but may be a function of the fact that these people are constrained by training and by their attempts to satisfy their professional community. For instance, perusal of college catalogues shows that of those who majored in the areas of law, social science, business, public administration, and liberal arts more than a decade ago, few had any training in analytical methods. This means that a large portion of our policy leaders and their advisors are conversant with modern decision-making tools only to the extent that they have educated themselves. The subsequent fear of the new and unknown is a serious impediment to change.

There does not appear to be any group that would be dedicated to supporting the policymaker in environmental issues as a full-time vocation. To further illustrate the void, visualize the following typology:

Basic Research	Transfer Agent	Transfer Process	Output
Physical and natural sciences	Engineer	Market place	Product
Social sciences	—	Political arena	Policy

The policymaker in society really needs technical support. Unfortunately, many who would otherwise fulfill this function find it too risky, in a professional sense, to become tainted with "merely" implementing somebody else's research. Those who made the transfer between basic social research and the political arena have sometimes been labeled "popularizer," especially by the basic scientist who does not see the necessity for translating his jargon to a more readable and useful form.

A more readily identifiable group has attempted to fill the gap. This group consists of the planners. Their profession is seen as complementary to that of the policymakers because they have tended to define areas of interest in line with political and administrative jurisdictions. Unfortunately for the policymakers, these people usually do not possess the skills necessary to handle the analytical chores required by comprehensive, long-range policymaking. This requirement is being rapidly filled by still another contingency, the operations researcher or management scientist.

By considering the need for a policy scientist (or an environmental analyst) one suggests that only when such a profession is developed will the policymaker have the incentive and the ability to take the future into consideration more than he currently does. The environmental analyst will have a long-range viewpoint because of his training, and his logic will be reinforced by his peers. The policymaker should then have the confidence (rightly or otherwise) to meld long-range factors into his policies. His advisors will attest to the soundness of the practice, and communicate it well to him. It is not, in short, logical to assume the policymaker will change his pattern without such encouragement. Therefore, the change will have to come from his advisor, who concomitantly will have to receive support and encouragement either from other social scientists or from their own peer groups. Therein lies the challenge to modelers.

This treatise would not be complete if we omitted a discussion of the ways in which policymakers can make better use of analytical support in the policy process. The policymaker has a responsibility to ensure that public policymaking is as rational as possible and takes into account the full ramifications of short- and long-run policy decisions.

What this means in terms of the development and use of models is that policymakers should insist on being involved in the process. Most effective model builders would be elated to have policy-level scrutiny and input throughout the design process; such input would enhance greatly the utility of the models.

Furthermore, policymakers should take the time to stay abreast of the field. Seminars, literature, and staff briefings are important methods to maintaining a continuing analytical capability. An intimate knowledge of the responsibilities of the job coupled with a general understanding of analytical tools can produce a credible and rational framework for not only making policy decisions but also guiding research studies and other developmental efforts before projects or issues become crises or failures. It is recognized that time is critical to a policymaker; however, the value of effective and relevant seminars has proved to be significant.

Finally, policymakers should be innovative and willing to experiment with new tools. Just as modelers have a responsibility to develop tools for policymakers, management should be receptive to new approaches. This is an extension of the interviewing dialog that goes directly to the use of new tools, their criticism, and feedback for their improvement. Improved public policy can only evolve from a better understanding of the relation of policy needs to their impacts and implications.

7.5 Conclusions

We have claimed that all modeling, even the attempt to model, is useful in some respects. It forces us to order our thoughts and consider the overall problem; but distressingly few models have been used to guide policymaking. We suggest that some of the models described in Appendices I and II may be successful candidates for that honor, depending, of course, on our criteria of usefulness.

We have stated that implementation is necessary if models are to influence policy and have discussed the attendant problems and possible solutions. The opinions for improving model use, the implementation of simulation results, and the transfer of models can be summed up as follows.

- Try to involve the policymaker with the problem to be solved in the model developing process from its inception, and work as closely as possible throughout the model development, the simulation experiments, and the implementation of results. Ask and try to understand the policymaker's view of his problem, and be sure the model reflects it.

- Consider keeping a simple version of the model for reference and demonstration, while using a similar model as a point of departure for making refinements and developing a more sophisticated, and necessarily a less transparent, model.
- Try to build enough of the decisionmaker's information and ideas into the model to make him feel it is "his model". There is no better way of increasing the probability that the model will be used and the resulting policies implemented.
- Pay attention to the presentation of results. Regular and clear progress reports during development will help all concerned to know what to expect. Demonstrations, preferably "hands-on", but at least in close cooperation with the "customer", should be arranged at appropriate stages of the development. These should be arranged not so much as sales pitches, but as means of eliciting feedback and guidance.
- Graphic displays of simulation output can be used to great advantage for improving communication, understanding, and mutual respect.
- Document the model in a way that will assure that it can be transferred, thoroughly understood, and used by others.

Many situations make the idea of transferring an already-developed model to a new task seem attractive. However, in the past the transfer of models has entailed considerable rebuilding on the part of potential users. Although simple in concept, this has seldom been done well anywhere with any model. The transfer of the same model to several places has almost never been accomplished, and to our knowledge, transfer has resulted in dismal failure in terms of model utility. The changes required to handle these problems appear to be largely institutional, but if the pressure for such models continues, such changes will probably come about with time.

At this point, it is clear that the evidence leads to a verdict of "possible" for the transfer of large-scale policy models. It is equally clear, however, that the verdict can be considered possible only if advances are made in three critical areas:

1.   The responsibility for adequate and available documentation must be assumed by model builders.

2.   The area of model validation must be further researched and refined so that the extent to which models can be validated will be increased.

3.   Institutional changes must accompany progress in the areas of documentation and validation if transfer is to become feasible.

Thus, the challenges to modelers are substantial. If the modelers really want policymakers to use their tools for improving public policy, then it appears that the standards must be modified, as should the ways of going about developing models and communicating and sharing them with policymakers. The process should be opened to more involvement on the part of policymakers (and to the public, too, for that matter).

8

Cogent Comments

In this chapter we bring the reader varied (not necessarily contrasting) points of view concerning what is right and what is wrong with computer modeling and simulation. The writers quoted are, in the opinion of the authors, astute observers, even though they do not always agree with us, or with each other. This is not surprising as they are discussing a relatively new and certainly a developing field. None of us has plowed all of it. Perhaps, however, if we can piece together the observations of several authors, we can make headway toward a synthesis. At present, the field reminds one of the oft-used example of "The Blind Men and the Elephant" (Saxe, 1969).

It was six blind men of Indostan
To learning much inclined,
Who went to see the Elephant
(Though all of them were blind),
That each by observation
Might satisfy his mind.

Admittedly most of the material that follows in this chapter was selected to support *or* cast a different light on the material in the preceding chapters. We hope that it will prove more enlightening than confusing.

8.1 Alonso on Predicting Best With Imperfect Data (Alonso, 1968)

Long chains of argument are the delight of theorists and the source of their mistrust by practical men. There is some merit in this mistrust. Imagine that we argue that if A then B, if B then C, and so forth. If we are 80 percent certain of each step in the chain, from the joint probability of the steps it follows that we are less than 50 percent certain of where we stand after four steps. Thus the brilliant deductive chains of Sherlock Holmes or the young Ellery Queen, while dazzling, leave us with the feeling that they will not secure a conviction. In this paper I will raise the issue of the effect of errors and their propagation in models for prediction, and suggest some strategies for the selection and construction of models which are intended for applied work. The gist of my argument is that the use of sophisticated models is not always best in applied work, and that the design of the model is not always best in applied work, and that the design of the model must take into account the accuracy of the data on which it will be run. There exists the possibility, which should be explored, that some of our intellectually most satisfying models should be pursued as fundamental scientific research, but that simpler and more robust models should be used in practice.

8.1.1 Types of Errors

Let us distinguish two types of error: error of measurement and error of specification. Error of specification arises from a misunderstanding or purposeful simplification in the model of the phenomenon we are trying to represent. A simple instance is the representation of a nonlinear relation by a linear expression; another is the omission from the model of variables which have only a small effect, or the aggregation of variables. Measurement errors are those that arise from inaccuracy in assessing a magnitude. If I say that a man is six feet tall, or a nation has a population of 200 million, I really mean that he is six feet give or take an inch, or that the population is 200 million give or take 10 million. Thus, in scientific work it is customary to indicate measurement, M, as having an error, e, attached, and we may write the height of a man, the population of a nation, or the density of a population as M ± e. It is customary to use either the standard deviation or the probable error as the measure of error. The probable error is a distance from the mean such that one-half of the probability distribution lies within the mean plus or minus the probable error; in other words, there is a fifty-fifty chance that the true magnitude lies within M ± e. The probable error is approximately 0.675, the standard deviation. I will not deal in this discussion with the question of an asymmetric error distribution.

8.1.2 How Error Cumulates

A quantitative model puts together various numbers obtained by measurement, and combines them through algebraic operations. Normally we consider only the measurements and forget the error terms, and give the result of our calculations as a number without indicating its error. Too often we seem to hope that the errors in the inputs somehow cancel out as they go through the model, but in fact they do not. There exists a well-known formula for estimating the error in the output which results from the propagation of errors in the inputs. If we have

$$z = f(x_1, \ldots x_n),$$

$$e_z^2 = \sum_i f_{x_i}^2 \, e_{x_i}^2 + \sum_i \sum_j f_{r_i} f_{r_j} \, e_{x_i} \, e_{x_j} \, r_{ij}$$

where e_z is the error of z; f_{x_i} is the partial derivation of f with respect to x_i; e_{x_i} is the measurement error in x_i; and r_{ij} is the correlation between x_i and x_j.

This formula is exact when the function is linear, but an approximation when it is not. However, recent work has shown it to be a much better approximation than had been previously thought. Thus, by applying it to a model, we may estimate the probable error in the result that arises from errors of measurement in the input variables.

Examination of the formula gives several simple rules of thumb for the construction of models or the selection of models, and these may be useful when, as is often the case, the investigator has several choices in the formulation of the model.

The first rule is to avoid intercorrelated variables whenever possible. The second term on the right-hand side shows that the error in the dependent variable can increase very rapidly from this source.

Let us now examine the most basic algebraic operations to derive some other general rules. For simplicity, let us have $z = f(x,y)$, where $x = 10 \pm 1$ and $y = 8 \pm 1$. We will assume that x and y are mutually independent.

Addition:

$$z = x + y$$
$$18 = 10 + 8$$
$$e_z^2 = e_x^2 + e_y^2 = 1 + 1 = 2$$
$$e_z = 1.4$$

We see therefore that, in the case of addition, the absolute magnitude of the error in the dependent variable is greater than in the independent variables. On the other hand, the percentage error is smaller (8 percent) than in the independent variables (10 and 12.5 percent). It may be said, then, that the operation of addition is relatively benign with respect to the cumulation of error. With one exception,* it is the only operation which reduces relative error. It must be noted, however, that the size of the absolute error increases.

Subtraction:

$$z = x - y$$
$$2 = 10 - 8$$
$$e_z^2 = e_x^2 + e_y^2 \quad 1 + 1 = 2$$
$$e_z = 1.4$$

The deceptively simple operation of subtraction is explosive with respect to relative error, especially when the difference is small relative to the independent variables. In this case the relative error is 70 percent.

Multiplication and Division:

$$z = xy$$
$$80 = 10(8)$$
$$e_z^2 = y^2 e_x^2 + x^2 e_y^2 = 64(1) + 100(1) = 164$$
$$e_z = 13.3$$

It can be seen that multiplication not only raises the absolute error, but also the relative error (in this case to 17 percent). Division behaves exactly like multiplication.

Raising to a Power:

$$z = x^2$$
$$100 = 10^2$$
$$e_z^2 = (2x)^2 \, c_x^2 = 400(1) = 400$$
$$e_z = 20$$

*The exception is when an independent variable is raised to a power with an absolute value smaller than one, in which case both the absolute and the relative error are reduced.

Raising to a power is another explosive operation. In this case the relative error has climbed to 20 percent. It may be thought of as multiplication of perfectly correlated variables, and thus, from the second term in the basic equation, we may expect the error to be substantially higher. However, if the variable is raised to a power between 1 and −1, both the absolute and the relative error decrease.

8.2   Drake on Failure of Transportation Models (Drake, 1973)

Why do many computer-based transportation models fail? The failures are not primarily technical in the sense that the model simply will not run on a computer. What are the failures, then? Failures of transportation knowledge? Failures to build a *good* enough model? Failures to understand the problem? Failures to communicate results adequately? Failures to deliver in a timely fashion? In short, if the failures are failures of administration of the projects, what sorts of administrative practices lead to models which are considered useful by their recipients and what practices are associated with models which are considered less useful?

8.2.1   Eleven Hypotheses

A number of hypotheses are examined relative to the various aspects of the conduct of modeling projects. Included among these are that modeling usefulness will be enhanced by:

1.   Greater decision maker-modeler contact
2.   Greater decision maker-modeler communication
3.   Greater decision maker-modeler desire for success
4.   Smaller size of model
5.   Greater modeling of social and political aspects in non-technical problem areas as opposed to simply making assumptions
6.   Less bureaucratic environment in the client organization
7.   Less complexity of modeling techniques
8.   Greater formality of planning and conduct of the project
9.   Greater similarity of cultural and employment backgrounds of the principals involved
10.   A successful early start on the project
11.   The models being undertaken in a European environment rather than in the United States

A general framework for transportation analysis is presented which places modeling in the larger context of the analytic process, and makes clear many of the ways in which misunderstanding of the system nature of this process leads to failure. For example, paying too little attention to the goals and institutional environment within which the problem must be solved, improperly framing alternatives for study, viewing the process as a linear one without feedback, unsatisfactorily transforming the measure of various parameters into comparable terms and inadequately examining results in terms of initial criteria.

Most transportation modeling funds come from national governments. Most modelers come from technical fields rather than transportation. Because of the way projects are contracted for, the portability of skills, and the ease of entry into the business, the modeling industry is very fragmented, leading to a great deal of lost time on projects as the uninitiated are educated in the subject matter.

8.2.2.   *Twenty Interviews and Questionnaires*

Principals in over twenty diverse transportation modeling projects were interviewed at length. The projects spanned nearly all transportation modes, sizes of models, types of clients and modelers, durations, purposes, types of problem, techniques, and geographic locations.

In addition to being interviewed, the decision-maker and modelers were asked to complete a detailed questionnaire concerning a variety of aspects of project conduct. It proved that strong statistical inferences could be drawn from these data.

Conclusions drawn from the research fall into a number of areas, including the nature of the problem addressed, the nature of the model itself, the nature of the organizations involved and how they organize the project, the conduct of the project and the geographic location.

For a model to be perceived as useful by decision makers, problems modeled should:

1.   Have a high technical component and few social, political or economic aspects.

2.   Be well thought out within a framework of institutional goals needed to translate the problem into meaningful criteria.

3.   Be extraordinarily well defined with clearly set boundaries if the problems inherently contain significant social, political or economic factors.

Models will be perceived as more useful by decision makers if:

1.   They are small.

2.   They are modular.

3.   They are well documented.

4.   They use very common programming languages.

5.   They deal with specific rather than generalized problems. Generalized models are rarely suitable or efficient for specific use.

6.   They avoid complex techniques, except in the case of the most technical problems having little social or political content.

7.   They provide for substantial user ability to see intermediate results, to modify the data prior to the next step, and generally intervene in the overall process of model use.

To organize a modeling project in such a way as to best enhance the likelihood of useful results, one should:

1.   Base employment of a modeler not on his resumé, but rather on his past record with the client or with clients whose recommendations are to be trusted.

2.   Put the modelers in a position of contact with, and responsibility to, line personnel rather than staff.

3.   Recognize the diffuseness of the decision making process in large bureaucratic organizations.

4.   Employ modelers with background as similar as possible to those of the decision makers.

5. Employ modelers in as close a relationship as possible to the decision makers, i.e., employed by and reporting directly to them, rather than in a consulting relationship from a distant location.

6. Ensure that if the decision maker is likely to be unavailable to the modelers, that frequent contact is available with a subordinate.

7. Employ joint client/modeler teams but not as a substitute for true decision maker participation.

8. In general employ modelers for their transportation experience first and modeling skill second.

9. Recognize that the less bureaucratic (i.e., large, structured, and burdened with necessary adherence to established procedures) the character of the client organization, the better the results are likely to be.

In the conduct of transportation modeling projects, one should:

1. Clearly articulate the roles to be played by both client and modeling groups making certain that the distinction between decision maker and analyst is clearly understood and accepted. This appears to be the single greatest determinant of project success.

2. If the client group is large and diverse, go to extraordinary lengths to get out "onto the table" (and into written memoranda) the goals, objectives, values, and criteria of the various participants, and to constantly reevaluate these.

3. Confront problems rather than attempt to smooth them over or accept the will of the most powerful participant.

4. Halt the project if, as the result of step 2 above, major differences are discovered which will take a significant time to resolve or appear irreconcilable.

5. Halt the project if, early in the work, the decision maker is very pessimistic concerning the likelihood of useful results.

6. Employ an experienced, respected coordinator to assist the client and modelers in working together and resolving problems.

7. If a qualified full-time coordinator is not possible, employ a number of outside (usually academic) experts to critique progress and results.

8. Conduct a substantial, formal, feasibility study. This is often the best means of ensuring adequate definition of the problem.

9. Phase them in parts, each one small enough to define.

10. Do them on a fixed price rather than a cost plus fixed fee or other open-ended basis if technical in character, and in the opposite way if nontechnical.

The geographic location of projects appears significant in two senses:

1. European projects appear more successful than those in the United States. This is primarily due to greater role recognition (see above) and greater correspondence of backgrounds (also see above).

2. Success is enhanced by very close physical proximity of modelers and decision maker.

Finally it may be said that nothing discovered in the course of this research suggests that the conclusions should be confined to transportation projects alone. Quite to the contrary: the author's belief is that they would prove equally applicable to all fields except to some degree, modeling of computer problems for computer scientists, and modeling purely scientific problems for pure scientists.

Sections 8.3, 8.4, and 8.5 that follow are taken from a single report but are separated into three main subject headings. All reflect the results of a survey to which 230 project directors (those responsible for assuring that the work is properly done) and 80 federal agency project monitors (those responsible for funding and overseeing the projects) responded. Because the complete report runs to 193 pages, we can only give relatively short excerpts here.

8.3 Fromm on Documentation (Fromm, 1975)

Modelers and model users have often suggested the establishment of policy or standards governing model documentation. One writer (McLeod, 1973) makes the case strongly:

It is time simulationists grew up and stopped acting like youngsters playing with toys. Simulation can and should be more of a science. A big step in that direction would be the development and use of a standard format that would assure adequate and uniform documentation.

Movements toward documentation standards have occurred in individual Federal agencies supporting models, and on a cross-agency basis. The General Accounting Office (GAO) recommends that standards be developed by GAO, Office of Management and Budget (OMB) and General Services Administration (GSA), and applied to all Federally funded models. The report cites a set of standards under development in the Department of Transportation.

There is certainly logic in the focus on documentation. Without an explanation of the premises and assumptions of the model, one can not adequately interpret or act upon the model's results. Without knowing something of the purpose, logic and capability of the model, one cannot decide whether it applies to a particular problem. Without detailed instructions and records, one cannot set up and operate the model independently of its developer. And substantial criticism has been aimed at models and modelers on all three points. Brewer, for example, found documentation "largely of uneven quality, not available, or non-existent." (Shubik, 1972)

To some degree, the perceptions of the Project Directors and the Agency Monitors dispute these criticisms: the minority consider the model documentation weak. Yet, less than a quarter of the Agency Monitors feel that the models could be picked up and used, simply with the available documentation. Thus, there does seem to be a problem, and it is particularly acute with programming materials— i.e., the materials needed to set up and operate the model. Most documentation appears to be in the form of reports and articles, seldom with user manuals or program decks (although private research institutions working under contract produce these somewhat more frequently). Finally, the documentation that does exist appears not to be generally available through centralized sources, but usually must be obtained through direct contact with the developer.

8.3.1 Quality of Documentation

Few Project Directors and Agency Monitors reported major problems in the documentation of their models. Their assessment is shown in Table 8.3-1. While neither Project Director nor Agency Monitor responses showed more than 27% of the model documentation in the weak-uneven-unavailable categories, the two respondent groups disagree on how good the remaining documentation is. Project Directors are far more positive about the excellence of the work, particularly in the case of structural documentation, where they find problems in only 10% of the models.

The divergent views represented in the above table suggest a substantial gap between the model developer and the potential user, a gap which would almost certainly limit the utility of the model. An additional limitation is posed by the consensus that program documentation—i.e., the materials which would be needed to run the model—is of lower quality than the structural documentation. In this situation a potential user might understand the model, but if he wanted it applied to his problem he would have to rely on the designer to do so.

The overall ratings deserve a cautious reading. Of the two respondent groups, the Agency Monitors are almost certainly the less biased in assessing documentation. But many people in the field would question whether the general standard of documentation is even as good as the agency respondents say. The definition used for the "excellent" category was: "The documentation can be understood and the model used with a minimum of long-distance telephone calls." Reviewing the documentation available for many of the models included in the survey makes us doubt that as many as 20–26% of the models funded by Federal agencies would meet such a standard in practice.

8.3.2 Publications

The materials published in connection with particular models give some idea of the form which documentation takes. The most common publications are reports

Table 8.3-1. *Quality of Documentation*

	Structure*		Program†	
Quality Assessment	Project Director	Agency Monitor	Project Director	Agency Monitor
Excellent	53%	26%	39%	20%
Average	39	51	32	48
Weak	2	16	12	21
Uneven	1	0	3	1
Unavailable	6	5	12	5
Number of Models	156	53	149	53

*Structure is defined as the underlying theory, equations, etc., of the model.
†Program is defined as the technical instructions and computer program required to construct and operate the model.

and articles. Of those citing any published documents, 67% indicated reports had been produced and 64% mentioned articles. Most of the projects which had produced any reports noted only one, although seven projects indicated that 10 or more reports had been written. Multiple articles were much more common in more than half of the projects where articles were published. The number was at least three, and nine projects reported 10 or more articles.

Books, user manuals, and program decks were much less frequently published. Only 17% of those reporting any publication mentioned a book. The rates for user manuals and program decks were 21% and 13%, respectively. Very few projects reported more than one instance of any of these documentation categories.

The publication pattern confirms the indication of the quality assessments, that structural aspects of models are considerably better documented than the programs. A report or article will normally present model findings and a general discussion of methodology. But to use the model requires the programming details, which are found in the user manuals and program decks—which means, according to the preceding figures, that they are seldom found.

8.3.3 Availability

Model documentation does not seem to be available through any single source, or small number of sources. Only 26% of the Project Directors indicated that their documentation materials would be available through the National Technical Information Service (NTIS—which is supposed to maintain copies of all reports filed with Federal agencies), and smaller proportions named other central sources. Model developers in many cases may not know that their reports have been filed with NTIS, so this figure many understate the reality. (In fact, more than a quarter of the models included in the survey were identified through NTIS.) On the other hand, the report on file at NTIS is frequently less than the complete documentation needed to construct and operate the model.

The source through which documentation was most often said to be available was the author. About 72% of the Project Directors said that materials would be available through the author, and 53% indicated the institution at which the model was developed as a source. Commercial publishers or distributors were mentioned in only 11% of the cases.

Although documentation sources appear scattered, there is little problem of legal access. Almost all Project Directors indicated that their documentation materials were in the public domain. Only about 10% said the materials had a proprietary status, and only a handful mentioned a restricted or classified status.

The pattern of documentation sources varies somewhat by subject area of the model, as illustrated in Table 8.3-2. Apparently, this reflects both differences in sponsoring agency practice (e.g., the Department of Labor appears to be particularly conscientious about filing reports with NTIS and/or letting the authors know that this is happening) and differences in publication patterns of different academic communities (e.g., the comparatively high proportion of commercial publications in the economic area).

8.3.4 Institutional Factors

Documentation seems to vary according to the practices of the developing institution and the demands of the sponsoring agency. This variation is seen principally

Table 8.3-2. *Sources of Documentation (% of Models Available from Specific Sources)*

		Source				
Subject	Author	Developing Institution	Commercial Publisher/ Distributor	Library of Congress	National Technical Information Service	Defense Documen- tation Center
Business and finance	55	70	5	5	10	0
Economic theory and policy	75	50	22	6	16	0
Agricultural economics and sciences	88	44	9	0	3	0
Natural sciences and resources	85	52	3	9	42	3
Labor, manpower and population	59	41	23	9	46	0
Public administration and services	64	62	8	2	34	0
Total	72	53	11	5	26	1

in the types of documents produced, and to lesser extent in the assessment of documentation quality.

Project Directors at universities tend to publish more articles and books on their models, while those at research institutions more often produce reports and user-oriented program materials. Nearly 80% of the university projects reporting any publications cited at least one article, and 55% indicated that more than one article had been published. This compares with 54% of the projects at private institutions publishing any articles at all, and 48% of the government projects. In contrast, 84% of the privately developed projects submitted at least one report, as compared with 74% of the government and 58% of the university projects.

Although user manuals and program decks were infrequently produced, the variation by developing institution is particularly interesting. Projects developed at research institutions reported users manuals to be available in 36% of the cases, compared to 18% of the government projects. The research institutions work much more often under contract, with comparatively high levels of specification from the funding agency, and it is reasonable to believe that this greater production of user-oriented documentation is one result.

Reported quality of documentation does not vary much by type of developing institution, but there is some confirmation of the pattern of user-oriented products. Structural documentation, as assessed by the Project Directors, is rated about equal at universities and research institutions, and under grants and contracts. Program documentation, however, is considered worse for grant-funded than contract-funded models: 35% of the grant-funded projects were in the weak-uneven-unavailable category, compared to 21% of models supported by contracts. This suggests that articles (produced under grants) and reports (produced under contracts) are equally good means of documentation models' structures. But good documentation of programs requires user manuals and program decks, and these are more commonly produced under contract.

8.4 Fromm on Model Use (Fromm, 1975)

Not all models are intended to be used for policy decisions. When Agency Monitors were asked to name the principal reason they funded particular models, only half mentioned specific problem-solving; the remainder cited reasons evenly divided between desires for increased knowledge in the subject area and advances in the methodology.

Nonetheless, the focus here is on model use in policy decisions. There is good evidence that such a focus is appropriate for examining the sample models: nearly three-quarters of them had some stated purpose directly related to policy decisions; and in response to an open-ended question about what would constitute "success," the vast majority of the Project Directors cited use of the model's results in decision making.

The survey data suggested that limited utilization of models is a major problem. The extent of use is hard to measure, and different questions yield different apparent utilization rates. But the most generous estimate would be that more than a third of those models intending policy use fail to achieve it, while a conservative estimate could put the failure rate as high as two-thirds.

There are several points of evidence that institutional and procedural factors have a great deal to do with use. Comparing intended to actual users, we find the highest achievement rates where the intended user was the developer. The next highest rates existed where the relationship with the developer is relatively close (funding agency) or where the utilization requirements are non-specific (other universities). Least utilization occurred where both distance and specific requirements are great (other governmental agencies).

Similarly, we find high rates of reported use among models developed inside federal agencies. Models which originated with the user, were developed under contract, were developed by for-profit private institutions, and were accompanied by a high degree of agency specification of model characteristics were more frequently used. Each element of this pattern suggests a means of overcoming the distance between developer and user or meeting the specific nature of the user's requirements. This distance would not seem much reduced by current procedures for using models: reports are most common, followed distantly by direct analysis by the user and personal briefings.

The survey shows no significant difference between model cost or complexity (number of equations) and the rate of policy use. This casts doubt on a thesis that small models, oriented to a single type of decision, are more useful. In fact, the pattern within the sample was for the lowest cost models to be used somewhat less.

The pattern within the sample was also for better documented models to be used more, but while the pattern was consistent, the individual relationships were not statistically significant. Characteristics of model design, such as cross-sectional vs. time series data, or stochastic vs. deterministic structure, were not significantly related to use.

8.4.1 Model Users

In general, one would expect a model to be used by those whose resources contribute to developing it—that is, the funding agency and the developing institution. The models surveyed conform to this expectation. Most Project Directors (61%) reported that the developing institution was the intended user of the model; nearly half (47%) named the federal funding agency. The intention for the developer to use the model is reasonably consistent, regardless of which federal agency was providing support. Expectations of agency use, however, showed a few substantial deviations from the norm: only about a quarter of the projects funded by NSF and DOI named the funding agency as an intended user, while DOT (78%), HEW (73%), and EPA (69%) were at the other extreme.

When models are intended for use by a federal agency, a research unit within the agency is the most frequently expected user. More than 60% of the Project Directors who said the model was intended for use by the federal funder named a research unit as the specific user. Policy level units were named in 25% of the cases, and program units in 11%. Agency Monitors expected much more use at the program level (35%) and less by research units (42%). This probably reflects a better understanding of where the model would have to be used in order to have operational impact.

Although developers and funders were most often mentioned as intended users, they represent only part of the story. Substantial numbers of Project Directors expected their models to be used by some federal agency other than the funder (29%); a state (26%) or local governmental agency (24%), or a university (24%) or private organization (26%). The pattern of such "beneficiary" users reflects some of the divergent intentions of federal funders. Models funded by HEW, for example, were targeted for state and local governmental agencies more often than the norm. Department of Interior models expected high use by other federal agencies and state agencies. Models with NSF funding were often intended for use by universities.

Intended users did not always turn out to be actual users as shown in Table 8.4-1. With one exception—that of the institution which actually developed the model—the rate of actual use fell far short of intentions. Four classes of users can be distinguished: the developing institution where the rate of actual use approximately equals the intention, the federal funding agency with an accomplishment level of 59%, non-governmental beneficiaries at 62–77%, and governmental beneficiaries at 40–47%.

This pattern suggests that a model's chance of being useful declines as a function of *distance* from the developer and lack of *specificity* of user requirements. The developing institution is inevitably close to the development process, and is likely in addition to find a way to adapt its requirements to the model's features (this is particularly true in the academic or general research setting where most new knowledge in a field of interest can be used). The funding agency is next closest to the development process but has more specific problem-solving requirements. The non-government beneficiaries are farther removed from model development than the funding agency, but their non-specific requirements allow accomplishment ratios similar to that of the funding agency. Finally, the governmental beneficiaries suffer from both distance and specific problem-solving requirements.

8.4.2 Modes of Use

If distance between the developer and the user of the model is a major factor in determining use, the utilization procedures (i.e., the means by which that distance

Table 8.4-1. *Model Users—Intended and Actual*

Potential User	Neither Intended Nor Actual User	Intended But Not Actual	Actual But Not Intended	Intended and Actual	All Actual ÷ All Intended
Developing institution	30	10	9	51	98
Federal funder	53	20	1	26	59
Other federal	65	20	4	10	47
State agency	71	17	3	9	46
Local government	74	17	2	8	40
University	70	12	6	12	77
Private organization	67	16	6	12	62

$n = 182$ (excludes models not yet operational).
Cell figures in columns 1–4 represent % response distribution, and add to 100% (barring rounding error) horizontally. Column 5 is columns 3 + 4 divided by columns 2 + 4.

Table 8.4-2. Modes of Communicating Results

Mode	Project Director	Agency Monitor
Direct run of the model and analysis of results by user agency	61%	34%
Model designer runs model, presents results in briefing to policy makers	24%	19%
Model designer runs model, presents results in policy memorandum or reports	48%	53%
Other	10%	13%

is overcome) might be expected to be equally important. Both Project Directors and Agency Monitors were asked to identify the procedures by which their models were used in decision making, with the results shown in Table 8.4-2.

The discrepancy in the reported rates of direct analysis by the user suggests a distinction between policy-related use and more general use for problem analysis, research or educational purposes. Agency Monitors were restricted by the question to considering uses by the *agency*, while Project Directors could interpret "use in decision making" more broadly.

Assuming that the Agency Monitor response on direct use is the closer approximation of the policy situation, we note that analysis by the model developer, with subsequent communication of results, occurs more than twice as often as direct analysis by the user. Further, when the developer conducts the analysis, he presents results in written form twice as often as through personal presentation. In short, the distance between the model and the user seems to be maintained rather than diminished in utilization.

Mode of use varied to some extent by supporting agency. The Department of Agriculture and the independent financial agencies showed a high incidence of direct analysis by the user; the Department of Commerce had higher than average rates of briefings and reports; and DOL and HUD both had high use of the report mode. There was also some variation by subject matter, but this appeared largely to reflect agency practice (e.g., models in the area of agricultural science and economics reported high direct analysis by users).

No other factors appeared closely related to modes of use. For-profit developing institutions presented results in briefings at more than twice the average rate, but otherwise the varying institutional types behaved similarly. Although differences by supporting agency were noted, utilization mode was remarkably similar for differing categories of user. Model size, as indicated either by development cost or the number of equations, did not influence the way the models were used.

8.4.3 Rates of Use

It is extremely difficult to measure model use satisfactorily. The major part of the problem is definitional: what is use? If a model designer improves his understanding of a process by attempting to model it, has the model been used? If he publishes a paper based on model results, is that use? If the designer responds to ten different requests to apply his model to a policy problem, and in one of the ten cases the results enter the policymaking process, how many times has the model been used?

The survey included several different questions related to use, attempting on the one hand to surmount the definitional problem, and on the other to deal with the lesser problem of respondent reliability. The latter derives from the reasonable assumption that few model designers or funders would like to have their model classified as "useless." Questions designed to counter this bias requested detail on how the mode was used but suffered from a general tendency for detailed questions to have higher non-response rates.

Depending on which question is examined, and how it is interpreted, a range from nearly all to less than a third of the models surveyed have been "used." Despite this variation the overall impression is that the models are not used as much as intended, especially for policy purposes.

Most of the models surveyed had policy-related intentions, but these intentions were the least frequently implemented of all identified model purposes. Table 8.4-3 shows the percentage of Project Directors indicating that their models had been used for each purpose and shows the number reporting actual use as a percentage of those reporting intended use, an "accomplishment ratio."

In all cases including both policy and non-policy purposes, the majority of the models were used for the purposes intended. However, the accomplishment rate was 67% or under for developing, selecting, or evaluating policies or programs. The purposes which would impose only fairly general requirements on the modeling effort—problem analysis, methodological development, and training or education—all reported well over 90% accomplishment. This supports the hypothesis advanced earlier, that policy requirements tend to be more demanding, harder to meet, and less often met than the requirements for non-policy use.

The question on intended and actual use, like that on intended and actual users, is open to a wide interpretation of "use" and might be expected to over-state the real rate of model use. A more restrictive question asked respondents to state the number of times the model had been used in each year from 1968-1973, defining use as "an application to a specific problem." Table 8.4-4 shows the results.

Table 8.4-3.   *Rates of Use by Purpose*

Purpose	Actual Use	Actual Intended Use
Selection among policies or programs	33%	67%
Developing policy or program concept	20	63
Evaluation of policy or program effectiveness	29	61
Program management	5	63
Forecasting	35	75
Problem analysis	50	93
Training/education	15	103
Research methodology	33	94

$n = 194$ (excludes models not yet operational).

Table 8.4-4. *Number of Model Uses*

Year	Any Use	% Reporting One Use	Two Uses	10 or More	Median of Those Reporting Any Use
1973	38%	10%	7%	9%	3 Uses
1972	31	9	4	10	3 Uses
1971	27	8	3	7	3 Uses
1970	15	3	2	4	3 Uses
1969	10	3	1	3	3 Uses
1968	8	1	2	3	4 Uses

n = 194 (excludes models not yet operational).

Slightly under 40% of the Project Directors reported at least one use of their model in 1973. The decreasing proportion of positive responses in prior years mainly reflects the smaller proportion of models in operational status. The number of uses of active models has been reasonably consistent throughout that period. The median was about three uses, with about 1/4 to 1/3 of the models being used only once and an equal proportion used 10 or more times. A few models have reported more than 100 uses in a year.

In the most demanding of the utilization questions, about 30% of the Project Directors indicated that their models had been "used." This question required the respondent to describe a *decision* in which the model was involved, to state the number of times the model had been used for that type of decision, and to evaluate the model's influence on the final decision. The complexity of the question undoubtedly caused some respondents whose models actually had been used in decision making not to respond. Unfortunately, the design of the questionnaire did not allow a distinction between non-respondents to the question and models which had not been used. Some who did respond did not clearly relate the model operation to a decision; a macro-economic forecasting model, for example, was simply said to have produced forecasts, but with no indication of how or whether the forecasts were used in decisions. These countervailing problems cannot be measured accurately, but if they do offset each other, the figures mean that less than one-third of the models were used in decision making.

Where Project Directors did describe decisions in which their models had been used, most felt that the model had a substantial influence on the decision. In 48% of the examples, the model was described as "one of a number of equally important decision inputs," and 32% held the model as the "most important input to the decision." Only a few instances were cited in which the model was either a minor element (8%) or simply an ex post justification (12%) of the decision. This pattern almost certainly overstates the case because of selective non-response; the respondents were probably less inclined to take the trouble of writing about decision in which the model was less important.

8.4.4 Benefits of Use

Additional perspective on the rate and importance of model use is provided by the Project Director's view of their models' benefits. Actual assistance in policymaking is next to the bottom of the benefit list. The most commonly seen benefit is the education which the model builders receive, but the education benefit is not considered as important as providing a tool for policy analysts. In short, policy considerations are very important to model builders, but real policy impact is achieved infrequently. The easier targets, which could be summarized under the heading of advancement of knowledge, are more often hit, and it is the researcher's own knowledge which is most consistently advanced, as shown in Table 8.4-5.

8.4.5 Correlates of Use

A low rate of use of models for policy decisions purposes appears to be the key problem demonstrated by this survey. But some models have been used. The present analysis contrasts those models to the less successful examples in search of means to improve future utilization.

Most of the analysis reported in this section is based on two variables constructed out of the "intended and actual use" question. In one variable, models reporting "actual" use for "selection among policies/programs," "development of policy/program concepts," or "evaluation of policies/programs" were classified as "used for policy." All other models responding to the question were put in the "not used" category. The second variable uses the same classification for "used for policy," but the "not used" category includes only models which reported "intended" use for one of the three policy purposes. These two variables are referred to as "Policy Use" and "Policy Accomplishment," respectively. Their overall distribution is as follows:

	Policy Use	Policy Accomplishment
Used for policy	49%	66%
Not used	51%	34%
n (excluding models not operational)	194	142

The variables as defined are somewhat "generous" but reasonably consistent indicators of model use in policy decisions. The questions from which they come do not require the respondent to provide details about use, but have a higher

Table 8.4-5. *Model Benefits*

Benefit	% Assigning Any Benefit	Average % Benefit Assigned
Educated the model builders	78	20
Pointed a way for future research	76	16
Provided a tool for policy analysts	74	23
Helped clarify the system modeled	67	17
Helped in making policy choices	58	15
Created a need for more/better data	52	7

n = 168.

response rate than the variables which demand such extra effort. Both variables are strongly related to other use indicators such as number of uses per year, number of decision examples cited, and benefit attributed to policy contribution. Policy use and policy accomplishment, because they are definitionally related, are for the most part similarly related to other variables. Except where otherwise noted, therefore, only the policy accomplishment figures are cited. The policy accomplishment variables have a somewhat more intuitive meaning and can be read as a "short-fall" indicator.

8.4.6   *Institutional Factors*

Use rates showed marked variations according to the type of institution developing the model and the federal agency providing the money. Models developed inside federal agencies or by for-profit research organizations were much more often used for policy purposes. The policy accomplishment rates were 83% for government, 69% in for-profit institutions. Use rates by sponsoring agency generally reflect this pattern: models supported by agencies which emphasized internal development, such as the Department of Commerce and the independent financial agencies, reported high utilization, while most low utilization rates were found where universities or non-profit institutions were the principal developers. The main surprise in the pattern was the Department of Transportation, where 12 of the 13 models intending policy use reported that it happened.

The high utilization of models developed within government agencies supports the earlier hypothesis that distance between developer and policymaker is one of the primary obstacles to use. But it is impractical for all models to be developed inside the user agency. The high rate of use of models from for-profit developers suggests an alternative path around the obstacle. The for-profit institutions more commonly work on a contract basis with greater specification by the supporting agency of the output desired. Perhaps, then, the "distance" problem can be overcome by user specifications and contracts which require the developer to produce a useful and usable model when policy use is the intended goal.

This hypothesis seems to be supported by the following relationships:

- When the model idea is originated by the intended user or funder, the policy accomplishment rate is 69%. This compares with 64% for models originated by the developer.
- When the idea originates in a federal funding agency, it seems to be important *where* in the agency it comes from. Models originating at the policy level had an 86% use rate; the program level rate was 75%, and only 50% of the model ideas originated by research units were used.
- Model development funded by competitive contract had a use rate of 70%. Sole source contracts and grants were slightly lower at about 63%.
- Where the funding agency was considered highly specific or moderately specific about the desired output, the policy accomplishment rate was 66%. Where the agency was not specific, the rate was 58%.

Although most of these relationships are not statistically significant, the consistency of their direction lends some support to the hypothesis that when the policymaker knows what he needs, communicates that to the developer, and holds the developer responsible for performing according to specifications, the resulting model has a high probability of being used.

8.4.7   Cost Factors

Among the sample models, there was some tendency for models with greater resource inputs to be used more for policy purposes. The principal findings were:

- Models with four or more man-years of professional effort in development had a policy accomplishment rate of 77% compared with 63% rate for those with lesser development effort.
- Models costing less than $25,000 to develop were used 71% of the time compared with 54% for more expensive models. When the sample is restricted by eliminating models developed at universities under grant support, the pattern remains: 63% of those costing less than $25,000 are used, compared to 76% of those costing more.
- An accomplishment rate of 71% where data costs were less than $10,000 was contrasted with 61% where data was more expensive.
- Where annual costs (subsequent to the model becoming operational) were less than $25,000, policy accomplishment was 68% compared to 79% where annual costs were higher.

However, because none of the relationships examined meets a .05 level of statistical significance it is impossible to reject the null hypothesis that model development cost is unrelated to utilization. The consistent direction of the pattern, however, lends some support to the concept that more policy use requires more resources.

The survey does suggest one way in which high cost may be a barrier to use: transferring from one location to another. Only about 11% of the Project Directors estimated a cost of $5,000 or more. However, the policy accomplishment rate for this group was 58%, as compared with 70% for the rest of those responding. Since a model transfer from developer to user would be one logical means of overcoming the distance problem, it may well be that sizable transfer costs pose a special obstacle to policy utilization.

8.4.8   Documentation

The general concern about model documentation rests on an assumption that poor documentation is an obstacle to use. The survey results support this assumption.

Where models were reported to have poor documentation, policy accomplishment rates were quite low as illustrated by Table 8.4-6. Similar results are obtained by examining project output in terms of publications:

- Models with no associated published articles have a 63% use rate. The rate climbs to 67% with one to three articles, and 78% with more than three.
- Where user manuals were published, the policy accomplishment rate was 82% as compared to 64% when manuals were unavailable.
- Where no reports were written the rate was 61%, the rate was 72% with one or more reports.

There is, of course, substantial intercorrelation among the various forms and indicators of documentation. Even so, the observed pattern suggests no particular difference in the effectiveness of various forms of documentation but rather a tendency for any reasonable documentation to enable more policy use of models.

Table 8.4-6. *Effect of Documentation on Policy Accomplishment*

Documentation	Excellent	Average	Weak, Uneven, or Not Available	n
Structure (i.e., underlying concepts)	69%	71%	29%	124
Program (i.e., mechanics of use)	77%	66%	57%	119

8.5 Fromm on Modeling Policy (Fromm, 1975)

If any Federal policies on modeling are established, it is the model developers and their sponsors in the Federal agencies who will be most severely affected. It is useful then, to examine their views about model utility and potential modeling policies—without committing ourselves to policy formulation by popularity poll.

The survey data on model strengths and limitations suggest that modeling is a case where technology has outstripped application capacity. The strong points seem to be the methodology—the capacity to deal with complex systems, particularly in a comparative and/or predictive sense—and some of the side effects of the methodology, such as the forced expression of hitherto vague goals and assumptions. Constraints are set by the limitations of data and measurement, and by characteristics of the developers and users (the developer's inattention to user needs, the user's inability to use the model appropriately.

Four policy possibilities were presented: a clearing house for models, a Federal effort to develop standardized model components, the use of professional review panels, and the establishment of Federal standards for validating and evaluating models. The first two were seen principally as aids to modelers, and were favored. The second two, though recognized as helping to overcome problems such as documentation deficiencies and non-credibility of model, were disliked on the grounds of too much Federal control and bureaucratic process. Project Directors made some creative additions to the policy list, aimed at reducing developer-user distance and increasing user capability.

8.5.1 Model Strengths

Agency Project Monitors were asked to identify the most useful functions which they felt models could serve. Their responses suggest that the major strength of models is the capacity to deal with complex analytic situations.

The largest number of respondents focused on characteristics of modeling which made it particularly useful in their situation. Most admired was the model's systematic approach—i.e., its capacity to take into account numerous related elements of a problem. Related characteristics were also mentioned: the ability to handle large numbers of variables, and to identify the key variable(s) or element(s) in a system; the ability to handle huge quantities of data; and the ability to derive quantitative values (or approximations) where other techniques might provide qualitative or noncommensurable outputs.

Certain types of problems or decisions were identified as particularly susceptible to the application of modeling. Using a model to compare alternative policies or programs was most frequently mentioned. Where alternative policies are considered for application to a given situation, the model is able to predict comparative outcomes (e.g., impacts on a program's target population; size of the target population and coverage of the program; benefit-cost or cost-effectiveness ratios) more accurately or comprehensively than simpler analytic techniques, and less expensively than experimentation.

Some of the models' utility was seen in terms of the impact on the model builders or users. A model condenses and applies substantive knowledge about a problem, and thus may allow a user unfamiliar with the field to make an intelligent decision. One Project Director said his model could be considered a success "if an inexperienced person using the model can come to the same decision that a very experienced person would reach without it." More commonly, respondents argued that the modeling effort itself, almost irrespective of the final product, was instructive: it educates the model builder in the detail of the problem, it forces the user to make his assumption explicit, and to translate his goals into measurable objectives and it establishes a common language and understanding of the problems.

8.5.2 Model Limitations

In a companion question to the one just discussed, Agency Monitors described the limitations of modeling in their experience. Very few cited limitations connected with modeling techniques or methodology. The major emphasis was on the problems of applying models to decision making.

The greatest number of responses noted factors left out of the model but necessary in the decision process. Some were apparently left out by design (e.g., regional disaggregation of the results); omissions which could result either from poor understanding of the decision need, or from funding or data constraints. In other instances the limitations were phrased in terms of factors which could not be quantified or predicted. The failure of a model to take into account the political factors which might be a key to a decision was cited more than once. A few respondents noted an absence of documentation, which they said prevented the model from having enough credibility to be used.

The second major group of responses focused on human and institutional factors in the creation and use of models. Model builders were criticized for "wanting to go their own way," and taking an "academic approach" which led the models away from usefulness in decisions. But more attention was given to problems at the user end of the process. Many decision makers, it was argued, do not have sufficient understanding of individual models or modeling in general to use them appropriately. This may lead either to a failure to use the model at all, or to a "false sense of security" in which model results are not questioned.

An additional perspective on model limitations is provided by a survey question asking both Project Directors and Agency Monitors to identify constraints on their models. The results are shown in Table 8.5-1. Data constraints are seen as the most critical problem, with ease of use in second place, while the methodological and technological areas pose the smallest constraint. In other words, the tech-

Table 8.5-1. *Model Constraints*

Constraint	Project Director		Agency Monitor	
	Score	Rank	Score	Rank
Transferability of the model	1.10	6	1.16	6
Ease of use by non-technicians	1.72	2	1.86	2
Ease of interpreting output for non-technicians	1.47	5	1.56	4
Conclusiveness of policy indication	1.57	4	1.38	5
Theoretical or substantive knowledge	1.64	3	1.60	3
Data availability	1.93	1	2.18	1
Statistical techniques	0.99	8	1.02	7
Hardware/software techniques	0.75	10	0.93	9
Solution/simulation techniques	0.79	9	0.82	10
Dissemination/communication paths	1.02	7	0.95	8
Inappropriate level of detail[2]	—	—	1.00	(7)
Reliability and accuracy of results[2]	—	—	1.32	(5)
Number of models	192		55	

Score represents mean response where 0 = no constraint; 3 = severe constraint.
[1]Excludes models developed within federal agencies.
[2]Not asked in Project Director Survey.

niques of modeling are viewed as substantially in advance of either the quality of the inputs or the capability to use the outputs. Project Director and Agency Monitor preceptions are almost identical on these points.

8.5.3 *Models Compared to Alternatives*

As shown by Table 8.5-2, both Project Directors and their Agency Monitors seem fundamentally happy with modeling as a technique—perhaps not surprising, since they are doing it and funding it, respectively.

About 20% feel that the purposes served by their models could not be achieved by any other means, but most recognize an option. Quantitative analysis is the most frequently mentioned substitute, accounting for about 40% of those who will admit to an alternative. Although comments were not generally provided in response to this question, it seems likely that the respondents are thinking of reaching the desired result either by disaggregating the model—doing in pieces what the model does all at once—or by simplifying the problem and leaving out some elements of the analysis. Case studies, or historical information was the next most frequently mentioned alternative to models, followed closed by experience. No other single alternative was mentioned by more than a handful of respondents.

The advantage of the models, as compared to any alternative technique, is seen principally in the results. The only points on which the model is conceded to be at a disadvantage are its requirements for skills and facilities. Perhaps significantly,

Table 8.5-2. *Model Advantages*

Characteristic	Project Director[1]		Agency Monitor	
	Score	Rank	Score	Rank
Satisfaction to user	1.34	1	1.27	2
Reproducibility	1.35	2	1.10	1
Speed	1.40	3	1.45	3
Cost	1.62	4	1.65	4
Skill requirements	1.99	5	2.20	6
Facilities requirements	2.10	6	2.02	5
Number of models	167		49	

"Score" represents mean response value, where a 1 indicates that the model was considered better, a 2 means the model and its alternative were the same, and a 3 means that the alternative technique had the advantage.
[1]Excludes models developed within federal agencies.

the Agency Monitors are slightly more sensitive to the skill problem than the model directors—suggesting they had encountered a need for learning in order to use the models.

Most surprising is the opinion about cost. Models have a reputation for being costly, and the survey has shown this image to have considerable validity. Yet more than 60% of the respondents felt the model would cost less than the alternatives (although this item did have the highest variability—standard deviation—among the Agency Monitor respondents). This may reflect a sophisticated perspective about the cost of the alternatives. Carrying out the analysis in separate pieces, for example, may cost more than putting it together in a model. There are not data in the survey to test this hypothesis, but the question is worthy of future research.

8.5.4 Policy Options

The survey asked for reactions to four possible policies which the Federal Government might undertake. Both Project Directors and Agency Monitors reacted warmly to offering some assistance to the model developer, and negatively to the ideas implying increased Federal control, as seen in Table 8.5-3. Over half of the respondents were positive about the clearinghouse and standardized routines, and negative about the review boards and validation standards. There were no substantial differences among responses from universities, for-profit and non-profit research organizations, and public agencies.

8.5.5 Clearinghouse

The popularity of the clearinghouse was based on two principal arguments. First, it would prevent duplicative efforts—"avoid reinventing the wheel," as several respondents put it. Second, it would reduce the time and effort spent by researchers in attempting to identify related efforts and useful ideas. Some respondents

Table 8.5-3. *Policy Options*

Policy	Project Director	Agency Monitor
A clearinghouse for models to make them centrally available to researchers	1.73	1.63
A centralized effort to develop standardized routines and procedures	2.08	2.25
Review boards for validation or evaluation of federally sponsored models	2.69	2.53
Federal standards and procedures for validating and evaluating models	3.01	2.69

Figures cited are mean response, where coding was: 1 = very positive; 2 = somewhat positive; 3 = somewhat negative; 4 = very negative. Thus, a lower number is a more positive response, and 2.50 is the dividing line between positive and negative.
Excludes models developed within federal agencies.

felt that the clearinghouse might stimulate communications among researchers, although the opposite argument was also presented: that the clearinghouse would replace existing, presumably more meaningful personal contacts. A few respondents saw important benefits for the policymaker. They indicated that it would make him more aware of alternative approaches to the problem, offer greater opportunity to compare the results of different models, and facilitate information exchange among agencies.

While the clearinghouse idea was well received, several problems of implementation were noted. The job of establishing and administering a clearinghouse would be huge and costly, given the number and diversity of models. The model documentation made available through the clearinghouse would have to be reasonably high quality in order to be useful: the question was raised of who would pay the cost of improving the documentation beyond that which the model developer would ordinarily produce. Perhaps the greatest identified danger of the clearinghouse is that models of poor or unproven quality would be disseminated to individuals incapable of identifying flaws, leading to inappropriate or damaging decisions.

These arguments suggest that a clearinghouse for models, in order to be maximally effective, should be more than a simple library. It would have to impose standards on the materials submitted, and be able to provide technical help in evaluating model structure and utility. The cost of such an institution might make it impractical in the short run, but the high level of support from modelers and agency personnel argues for serious consideration of the idea.

8.5.6 Standard Routines

Most respondents favored the idea of developing more standardized routines and procedures for modeling. They saw this as a means of cutting costs and development time, and possibly as a means of increasing standardization and compatibility across models. Such products would be especially useful to people just entering the field of modeling and to modelers at institutions without large computer centers and in-house libraries of routines.

Principal points in the arguments against such development were:

- It is unnecessary, because such routines are already being produced. Several agency respondents saw a danger of government competition with private enterprise.
- Numerous implementation difficulties were cited. The diversity of models means that general routines need much modification to apply them. The variety of computer equipment would require multiple versions of routines, or would tend to favor one manufacturer. Changes in the state-of-the-art, both of modeling and of machinery, would require continuous updating.
- Packaged routines would tend to limit the flexibility of models, and might inhibit the creativity of model developers.

The responses demonstrated not only a considerable range of opinion about what should be done, but also different perceptions of how much has been done, and how good it is. This lends support to the argument of one respondent, who suggested that the best first step might be to catalogue, test and disseminate information about existing routines and development efforts, rather than to undertake further development.

8.5.7   *Review Panels*

Opinion about the review panels was mixed, with strong comments on both sides. The most commonly perceived benefit was the identification and avoidance of poor quality models. Given high professional quality among the panel members, it was argued, a review could be sensitive to the unique situation of a particular model. The review could provide a learning experience for the modelers, assurance to the model sponsors that the product was worthwhile, and a measure of credibility and stature to the model.

Opponents of the review concept presented two main points. First, administering a review panel policy would be a slow, cumbersome and costly generator of bureaucracy and red tape. Second, it would be impossible in practice to obtain enough highly qualified, objective reviewers: instead, the process would "simply create more prima donnas," whose biases would lead to non-objective reviews and inhibition of innovation.

One respondent, recognizing both the benefits of a review process and the inherent problems, suggested selective reviews. Review panels would be established for big or important models, where the cost of errors or the need for credibility would be particularly great.

8.5.8   *Validation and Evaluation*

Although respondents expressed more dislike of the concept of Federal standards for model validation and evaluation, most arguments pro and con were essentially the same as for review panels.

Validation standards were seen, on the positive side, as a means of avoiding or discarding bad models, and enhancing the credibility of good ones. The main advantage over the review panel would be the greater uniformity of criteria, and thus perhaps more even and comparable results.

But validation standards also brought forth the strongest arguments against "government intervention in scientific matters." The need for uniformity in such standards would make them either too vague to be effective, or inapplicable across all models. Further, they might inhibit good developments that would conflict with the standards, and possibly curtail support for exploratory efforts. Finally, it was argued that a model should only be as good as its use requires, and that only the user can determine appropriate standards.

8.5.9   Other Policies

Although the survey requested comments only on the four potential policies listed above, a few respondents were moved to place write-in nominations. Four of these are particularly salient in the light of the study's findings on utilization problems:

- Model review and evaluation should not be limited to *ex post* critiques. Rather, the initial idea should be reviewed for relevance (if it works, will the model be providing a needed product at the appropriate time?) and feasibility (will it work?) prior to funding.
- Data is a critical constraint. Federal policy should attempt to increase the data resources available to modelers, working towards a goal of generally available, systematic bodies of integrated social and economic data.
- Review and monitoring procedures should increase the contact between modelers and users. Including conferences as a part of modeling efforts and establishing advisory boards of potential users might accomplish two-way education and make the resulting models more useful.
- In addition to attempting to control the model development and dissemination process, effort should be directed to potential users. Training agency and Congressional personnel in model use and interpretation might improve both the quantity and quality of model utilization more than refining the models themselves.

8.6   Hamilton on Management of a Multidisciplinary Research Project (Hamilton, 1969)

The following discussion concerns problems and ideas relative to the management of multidisciplinary research projects. Although many of the problems discussed are presented within the context of the Susquehanna River Basin Study the authors have encountered similar problems in relation to other studies. Some of the management techniques employed in the Susquehanna study in an attempt to avoid these problems are a result of this prior experience.

The discussion focuses upon project management. This particular focus is needed because the research management literature is surprisingly sparse in

relation to how relatively small, multidisciplinary efforts should be managed.*
The literature is probably thin in this area because the interests of those who
usually coordinate small projects normally lie in specific subject areas rather than
in project management. That is, most small projects are coordinated by individuals whose interests are largely associated with doing parts of the research and who
have much less interest in managing the work of others.

Too often there seems to be an implicit assumption that assembling a group of
individually competent personnel will automatically lead to an efficient and competent research team. However, the truth of the matter is that many highly
competent individuals cannot be integrated into effective research teams; many
more have neither the interest nor the ability to coordinate the work of others.
This is especially true once the constraints of time and budgets are superimposed
above and beyond those involving the research problem, per se.

It is becoming clear that the nature of modern problems dictates the need for an
increasing amount of multidisciplinary research. We must learn to manage such
research. The comments offered present a few guidelines and point out some
pitfalls in relation to multidisciplinary research, or for that matter, any multiperson study, particularly those in the modeling field.

8.6.1 The Nature of the Problem

Research programs may involve a number of individuals for a variety of reasons.
First, there is often a desire to condense the time period encompassed by the
study, and this can be accomplished by bringing more manpower to bear over a
shorter time span. Of course, the study may require inputs from a variety of
disciplines. It is often the case that individuals with different points of view within
the same discipline may make valuable contributions. Perhaps more often, a
combination of these and other reasons generates the need for a team effort.

Because efficient use of personnel on a research project dictates that all those
assigned to the project not work on the same tasks, subdivision of effort is
required. It is this subdivision of effort that brings about the need for coordination
and management.

The research manager or project coordinator encounters a number of problems
in directing a research team. These often involve the personal characteristics of
the individual team members as much as any other one factor. For instance, some
individuals will wish to be kept completely abreast of developments on all phases
of the program at all times, often to the point that work on their subtask suffers.
Others will attempt to proceed with their work without regard to the overall
program, viewing their subtask as an end in itself. Both these extremes must be
curbed. In the former case too much time is wasted through curiosity about the
over-all. In the latter case work on subtasks, once completed, may not fit the
over-all study objectives.

---

* There can be no hard and fast definition of what constitutes a "small" study. Small studies
in the aerospace industry are often viewed as enormous studies when performed at the same
level of effort in the social sciences. A small study, as referred to here, is one that does not
reach the proportions where formal management techniques are obviously required in the
eyes of most researchers. Efforts requiring inputs from three to fifteen people often fall in
this class.

In relation to the Susquehanna study, both formal and informal exchanges were encouraged among the project staff developing various portions of the model. Such meetings were very necessary because at times this project team was composed of as many as fifteen professionals—professional Battelle staff members from a variety of disciplines, consultants, and research aids. Some of these individuals were geographically separated from the Battelle facilities in Columbus, Ohio. To ensure that at least a minimum of such interaction took place, formal project meetings were held in which progress and problems on each of the program's major tasks were discussed. The frequency of the meetings was varied in relation to the then current pace of the project and the amount of informal exchange known to be taking place. In addition, the project manager encouraged meetings between selected individuals to discuss how the sectors they were developing were to eventually mesh.

It is much more difficult to control "idle curiosity" than lack of communication because the former is so difficult to define. However, idle curiosity often takes the form of too much interest by one team member in the incidental details of the work being done by others. Such curiosity is often regarded as meddling by team members. During the Susquehanna program such idle curiosity did not appear to be a major problem.

Modeling programs have desirable attributes from a communications point of view. This is because the model can be used as a communications tool by the research team. Because models are explicit, everyone on the team can use the model to define how this subtask meshes with the over-all program. Thus, the risk of a mismatch between the output of a subtask and input needed by the overall program (model) is lessened in relation to the risks that exist in more qualitative research undertakings.

On the other hand, a model can be a terrible taskmaster. Models demand precision, and each little odd and end must be accounted for before a sector is inserted into the overall model. For example, all linkages to the main model from the sector must be specified. The model is not "sympathetic" when the researcher finds time to study only three of four mechanisms generally agreed to be important or if the main model demands an input not provided. In such cases, the modeler may be forced to omit the link, admitting it could be important, or he must quantify his best judgment on the nature of the link without the benefit of extensive research. In any case, what he has done will be evident. Thus, the modeler is not allowed the luxury often enjoyed by those involved in more descriptive and nonquantitative studies in which it is usually possible to make a few last-minute comments about how a variable might affect other variables but leave rather unclear just how the variable was actually blended into the overall analysis.

Modeling studies demand more rigorous scheduling than more qualitative efforts. The development of one model sector often requires definitive information concerning the nature of the input requirements and outputs of other sectors. Therefore, problems encountered attempting to define and complete one sector can delay the research on other sectors. Of course, qualitative research can be delayed by incomplete tasks also, but the problem seems more serious in modeling studies. Perhaps the reason for this is that in qualitative studies so often only the general nature of the output from one task is needed in order to begin the next, while quantitative programs often require very specific task results, e.g., equations, before succeeding steps can get under way.

8.6.2 Scheduling

In order to keep the Susquehanna project on schedule, several kinds of rather elaborate flowcharts of the project were constructed. The charting technique employed in the earlier phases of the study embodied many of the concepts of critical path programming, although the problem was never programmed for computer analysis. These charts defined the sequence in which tasks had to be completed and identified those tasks which seemed to be the most critical from the point of view of their potential for delaying the overall program.*

. . .

While simple charts of the type shown are useful, they will often fall far short of the mark in terms of yielding an understanding of the complexity of the problem being faced. In particular, such simple tools do not shed much light on the range of uncertainty surrounding the completion of a given sequence of events on a given date. Further, more complex charts that specify the assignment of manpower to the identified tasks must be used in order to ensure that intolerable peaks and valleys of effort among individual team members are avoided.

Many in the research field argue that the whole problem of the scheduling, planning, and control of research projects is not one amenable to detailed direction. These people point out that even if estimates of required effort can be made, these estimates must be continually revised. Our belief is that the effort required to plan and control is worth while even if constant revisions in planning are necessary. The alternative is to allow research programs to drift and to face problems as they arise instead of anticipating these problems and attempting to take corrective action at an early date. However, the skeptics about the usefulness of positive and aggressive overall study management are correct to a degree in that it is certainly doubtful that all problems will be anticipated. For this reason, adequate reserves of resources, including time, must be incorporated into any program plan and budget.

8.6.3 Producing a Balanced Model

In a modeling study, the major responsibility of the program manager is to produce what may be termed a "balanced model." A balanced model may be defined as one in which the level of research effort devoted to developing each of the model's sectors and subsectors is commensurate with its importance to the overall problem being investigated. The level of effort devoted to a model sector is not always correlated with the size of that sector that finally evolves when size is measured in terms of number of equations. Often, a rather large sector is fairly easy to assemble; just as often, much research is required merely to define the functional form of one important equation.

As a research unfolds, it is necessary to review continually the goals of the overall study and to assess the question of balance in light of the program's prior findings. Further, it is necessary to remember that the goals of the work may be modified with time. In light of prior findings and redefinition of research goals, the

---

* A relatively complex but useful technique used during the early part of the study was recommended by J. J. Moder in *Engineering News-Record*, March 14, 1963, p. 31.

view of what constituted a balanced model changed a number of times during the evolution of the Susquehanna study.

The creation of a balanced model requires that the program manager have flexibility in assigning talent to various subtasks. Such flexibility can be lost at the initiation of a project when the initial research team is selected unless the manager realizes the program management implications of this team selection process. A good team is seldom selected by a completely authoritative procedure. In some research settings it may be necessary to spend much time convincing people that they should join the team. In any setting, some degree of ''selling'' the team on the study is usually necessary. This process normally involves a very critical element, namely, a commitment to the individuals concerned in terms of some range of effort for a given period of time.

As the study evolves, the need for the capabilities of a given individual may change radically from that originally anticipated. For instance, a problem element originally conceived as important may be found to be noncritical. Thus, the demand for the inputs of the individual(s) originally assigned to this problem may be lessened or eliminated. Depending upon the institutional environment, the flexibility of the individual, and the nature of the original commitment, attempting to alter the nature of a commitment may present various kinds and degrees of problems. Certainly, no individuals or organizations are infinitely flexible in terms of assignments. Therefore reorientation of effort is usually accompanied by some kind of difficulty. The problem is minimized when the individual concerned has a variety of alternative tasks that he can undertake, either related to the same overall program or to other programs. However, change of alternative assignments readily available for the individual also forms the basis of his financial support and the basic elements of a dissertation or thesis. When a study is staffed by a number of such individuals, program management may not include the option of reallocation of effort except within very narrow boundaries. In instances where program direction and flexibility are restrained by commitments such as those cited, the research sponsor should recognize that the financial commitment made is often in terms of training men rather than the solution of a problem.

Perhaps a good way to minimize the team selection problems is to begin multidisciplinary and other multiperson programs with a small staff of flexible individuals and to proceed initially at a low rate of effort. Once preliminary results point toward the critical elements in the overall problem, specialists can be brought to bear on these elements and firmer commitments established. Still, the problem of assignment flexibility always exists, and any time the allocation of effort to study becomes completely ''frozen'' the research is apt to suffer.

In regard to the Susquehanna study, a feasibility or planning study was conducted first. This study resulted in several revisions in thought concerning the nature of the problem. Prior to and in the early phases of this ''initial cut,'' a 2-sector model was generally conceived; one with an economic sector and a water sector. However, initial study revealed that (1) water of useful quality seemed in general abundance in the region, and (2) regional economic studies often neglected the role of the region's population in the development of an area. In light of these findings, it was decided to build a model (1) containing an explicit and detailed population sector and (2) suitable for testing the criticality of water in the development of the region. Subsequent study was then planned to refine and expand problem areas where water appeared important. This decision led to much less emphasis on water than was anticipated originally. As can be seen, an original commitment to construct a detailed hydrological model would have to be revised because the research problem was the major criterion for defining the research program. Personnel commitments would have had to be adjusted correspondingly.

Throughout the Susquehanna program, the nature of the research inputs to the study shifted. To a degree, some of these shifts were foreseen. In assembling the first workable model, much data assembly effort was involved. However, after the assembly of the first model, data collection was de-emphasized for two reasons. First, much more attention was devoted to analysis, and second, the data assembly was routinized by exploiting the experience gained in the assembly for the first model. This change in emphasis resulted in a change in the complexion of the research group, with nonprofessional and clerical assistants taking a large role in data assembly because much less judgment was required in the subsequent phases of this activity. This particular change in the nature of the research and of staff needs was foreseen.

Sensitivity experiments with the original model gave substantial guidance to the remainder of the research program. Critical elements in the system were defined through model simulation, and work to investigate these elements was organized and planned. At this point in the program, it became possible to organize the studies of these critical problem areas on a semi-independent basis as the model itself provided guidance to the researcher as to where his task fitted in the scheme of things. The management problem then became one of keeping the model in balance by ensuring that the individual problems being investigated did not receive attention out of proportion to one another and to the goals of the program.

To accomplish this coordination and guidance, constant effort was maintained to keep the staff members aware of the over-all problem so that they themselves could aid in deciding how far to carry their work. But the nature of a good researcher is to immerse himself in his assignment. Thus, a reluctance to "let go of the problems" is only natural. However, when the researcher takes on the attributes of what might be termed a "research alcoholic," always wanting to use "one more" hour of computer time, to investigate "one more" variable, to spend "one more" day on a problem, he has often gone too far and must be redirected.

Nevertheless, discontinuance of the research effort in a particular problem area against the advice of the team member directly involved is not an easy decision for a program manager to make. Disregarding problems of team morale as a consideration (which is usually impossible), contentions that a little more effort will bear large returns may be correct. Of course, it may also drain resources from more important problems and lead to no concrete results.

8.6.4 Acceptance of Results

The preceding paragraphs have largely stressed the role the problem should play in the guidance of a research program. Of course, there are other pressures that shape the scope and direction of research, and these must be recognized and dealt with. One of the most interesting of these involves the acceptance of the research by the lay and professional worlds. It is often necessary to do things as part of a research program basically for the purpose of making the work convincing to others. In terms of modeling research, one must face the fact that many people will judge a model by the sophistication of the model sector relating to the subject matter with which they are most familiar. Taking the Susquehanna model as a case in point, a demographer will usually study the demographic sector of the model first. If he finds it "uninteresting," perhaps only in the respect that he feels it does not make a contribution to his field, he is apt to judge the whole model on this basis. Therefore those interested in gaining a measure of acceptance for a model often feel pressure to develop certain sectors far enough to please experts in the subjects treated by those sectors regardless of whether such sophistication is needed from the point of view of the main research problem.

Depending upon the importance of widespread model acceptance, the research manager will or will not yield to this latter pressure as a practical expedient. However, the program manager should avoid the trap of carrying the work too far from the point of view of the overall problem faced, and yet not far enough to satisfy the "expert" whose acceptance is sought. This middle area of no man's land is often quite broad, and the jump from the problem-oriented level of development to that which the expert regards as "interesting" is often a big one.

8.6.5 *Aids to Research Management*

Unlike his modern counterparts in the production and sale functions, the research manager is not blessed with an abundance of management tools. Perhaps the only such aid commonly found is an accounting system whereby research costs are reported. If such a system is not available to the program director, he will be wise to devise one of his own, even if it is designed and maintained on only an informal basis. Even within organizations providing cost accounting services, the project director may find it desirable to augment this system with some bookkeeping of his own in order to fill in for obvious deficiencies in report timing and the formats provided by the system.

Although a properly designed accounting system is obviously useful in terms of project management, it is a fact that many research organizations and research laboratories make little use of such systems. For instance, many laboratories have only a general R&D budget and do not attempt budgeting and costing at the individual project level. While many argue that research cannot and should not be controlled with precision, perhaps a more likely reason for this low level of application of accounting systems to project management is that so many research personnel strongly resist the discipline imposed by an accounting system.

Despite the apparent lack of intensive application of accounting systems, a good accounting system is often about the only formal aid to project management that is ever given to the project director. Project managers must normally devise their own systems for judging the research progress that is being made in relation to costs. Of course, flowcharts such as those mentioned earlier may be used to plan the project and to monitor progress, but such aids are not services normally provided to the manager. Instead, he must usually devise his own procedures. In some organizations, critical path programming services may be available, but these are often too expensive to use on small projects.

It would appear that considerable research is warranted for useful management services that can be provided to the coordinators of small research efforts in order to raise research efficiency.

8.6.6 *Summary*

This discussion has stressed the fact that management is an important ingredient in multidisciplinary studies. It has also stressed that the management role in such studies is often virtually ignored because small project coordinators often have little interest in project management per se, emphasizing instead their research specialties.

In small studies, the personal traits of the various research team members are often important. Some must be urged to communicate with other project staff, others must be constrained from over-communicating.

In modeling studies, the major goal of the research should be to study the problem at hand by construction of a balanced model. To do so, the project manager must have the management flexibility to reassign people among tasks and to alter the make-up of the research team. Without such flexibility, the research effort will suffer.

A good accounting system is about the only management aid a manager of a small project can expect to have. He will often need to devise other aids on an ad hoc basis. Because so much research is carried out by small groups, more attention should be devoted to the management of such studies and to providing the directors of this research with better tools for achieving higher research efficiency.

8.7 House on Building a Man—Machine Model: Administrative Aspects (House, 1972)

This selection is a discussion of the experiences in the building of a gaming simulation that was computer based. Although it covers a completely different type of "modeling," the experiences are very similar to the Susquehanna ones. It is taken from an article entitled "Building Games: Retrospection" and is narrated by the author in the first person.

Now that the project which created the CITY models is completed, it would certainly be possible to delineate a neat set of design stages similar to those posited by others. However, our approach to the problems of building a model was not completely systematic, and so it appears useful to relate this experience in such a fashion that a portion of it might be of some use to others.

8.7.1 City I

As will be indicated throughout this article, the surrounding circumstances had a great deal to do with the building of the model itself. In the first place, all the original designers of CITY I got involved in building models quite accidentally. None of us was trained in model-building, nor had we any previous experience with it. Second, the money for the project was supplied by an Office of Education grant, almost completely free of research strings and given by an office which had no knowledge of man-machine simulation. Third, the purpose of the study was to wed role-playing and systemic gaming. For a couple of years, the role-playing game of Richard Duke called METROPOLIS and the systemic game of Allen Feldt called CLUG were each thought to hold strengths that the other lacked. Our goal was to take the best of each of these and combine them. Fourth, the model was to be computerized. Fifth, the model was to be completed in six months.

During the six-month period, a staff was to be hired and moved to new quarters, a computer was to be procured, the staff had to learn a new field and, of course, build a model.

The staff sort of "got together" in a haphazard way. A high level of controlled havoc (loosely translated as esprit de corps) prevailed throughout the beginning as the group of us literally did everything required to set up a small business.

To familiarize ourselves with gaming, we built a manual game model called REGION. Later, we decided to put this model on the computer, before designing CITY I, to test the concepts we were beginning to develop. This effort never really resulted in an operational model.

CITY I was begun and REGION aborted because we were running out of time. As REGION was an adaptation of Feldt's CLUG, CITY I grew from REGION. Once the model was roughly defined, each of the programmers was assigned a section of the model to program. Because no overall systems work was done on the program to begin with, the resulting program was a systems analyst's nightmare.

While the model was being programmed, the rest of the staff gathered data for the model, designed the starting metropolitan configuration, and wrote a manual of play for the yet to be completed model. As the end of the contract period drew near, we scheduled a play despite the fact that the model was not yet fully coded. No one slept for a week in the attempt to build the model. It did not run.

We continued to schedule monthly plays and succeeded in nursing through one section after another of the code—arguing among ourselves all the way about content and method. The author developed an amazing ability to describe a nonexistent model; the staff was rapidly ageing, and then, suddenly the model ran.

This was a time of great celebration. No longer did we wait with bated breath to see if we had a first-round output (we always waited until the last minute to make one more change). This period of bliss lasted one month.

We decided that there were a number of small changes to make and that the program had to be completely redone. The programmers blithely began this task by junking the old model and starting the whole cycle over again. In the end, we had a truly operating model for no more than four or five months.

As a footnote, we later redid the whole model for still a third time to correct the further errors.

8.7.2 Cities II and III

The organization and physical construction of the CITY II and III models was done in the same uncoordinated, frenetic manner as CITY I and was as successful. The design was somewhat more organized, as we learned from CITY I what we wanted to add to this model, how we wanted to add to it, and how we wanted to expand the computer program from its earlier version. Further, there were several programmers who had suffered through the earlier model with us and so could transfer their knowledge to the new one. However, because of the decision to abandon the basic design used to program CITY I in favor of one which was more comprehensive, we again found ourselves with too little funds, manpower, or time to complete the model.

Again, a play of the game was scheduled well before many modules had been programmed. Consequently, the model was never tested before the run. Because of time constraints, the model was loaded into the computer with a wish that it would run on the first try. It did not. Nor did it run without major bugs for several months, as the design staff split its time between designing the emerging model (CITY III) and patching the existing one (CITY II). The resulting model had never been fully documented, and likely no one could accurately describe how all the parts were built.

8.7.3   City IV

At the final stage, on the basis of our growing experience, we attempted to design City IV with rigorous constraints so that problems we had in the past would not spring up again to confound our methodology; the effort was highly successful.

In general, the design was still by consensus, with meetings to discuss different aspects of the model and to arrive at specifications for the programmers. These subroutines had been previously set up so that their interrelationships were at least functionally defined.

We adopted the use of a time-phased plan for each of the modules, as it was to be designed and sent to the programmers for mechanization. The finished module was to return to a section of the design shop, where it was to be tested to make sure it did what it was supposed to do. The modules were then to be tied together a few at a time to test the results. Finally, all modules were to be tied together to provide an operating program.

After a full cycle, our research methodology finally appeared to resemble the more conventional scientific method. If we had been lucky, this might have been the way the model was completed. In fact, the actual schedule never came to pass. External pressures dented and finally punctured the scholastic isolation of the design team. The model runs had to be scheduled before there was any certainty of model cohesiveness. While still trying to patch this version of the model on a UNIVAC 1108 computer, we had to completely rewrite the model program again to convert it to an IBM 360/65 computer. The situation was further confounded in that we were simultaneously doing another contract to design an even more complex and sophisticated model.

After the completion of the CITY IV model, we decided for a variety of reasons not to accept other contracts and to go our separate ways to carry on other projects. With the research project over, it seems useful to make a few suggestions which accrued from our experiences.

8.7.4   Suggestions

Staff. Separate the design staff from the programming staff during the formative stages of the model. Only allow interaction when actual programming begins and make sure that it is the design staff who specify the model, not the programmers.

From the early days of our modeling effort, and pretty much to the end, I had made a concerted effort to keep programmers away from the actual design of the models. The programming of these models, albeit a very difficult task, was taken to be a technical problem and a definite second stage. It seemed to us that a large number of the social science models were being designed by engineers or mathematicians trained in the hard sciences. Although these people were usually very qualified to handle the problems from a technical point of view, they lacked sufficient knowledge of the social sciences. In the case of our models, the workings of the social system (as best we could understand them) were described to the programmer or analyst, and it was his job to fashion algorithms to accomplish the task.

Theory. Design a social simulation in the same way you would construct a set of detailed blueprints—one set of descriptions after another. Let the final model be the description of the over-all theory.

It would have been wonderful if we could have discovered a general social theory, or even a set of theories, which described the social system and simply programmed them. We have all heard the expression that political science does not describe what a politician does, nor does business administration describe what a businessman does. Because our models were designed to be highly dynamic and to interact with humans, they were not constructed around any specific theoretical framework. Rather, they were laboriously shaped in a descriptive fashion, one function after another, to yield a total model which described how various sectors functioned and how those sectors interreacted with one another. This design technique, we believe, yielded models which could be used to test numerous theories and, in a general sense, contained most specific theories in one form or another.

8.8   McLeod on A Specific Methodology for Building Models (McLeod, 1974)

In the 1960s Professor Jay W. Forrester of Massachusetts Institute of Technology pulled together some existing techniques of feedback control, mixed in some of Norbert Wiener's principles of cybernetics, added inventions of his own, and developed a methodology that is now known as system dynamics.

System dynamics makes it relatively easy for an engineer, or others with a suitable technical background, to develop and use computer models. In fact, when used in connection with the DYNAMO simulation language—a convenience for those who have a DYNAMO compiler but, fortunately, not a necessity—system dynamics makes simulation so easy that it has enjoyed worldwide acceptance. (This is both good and bad for simulation; on the one hand, it promotes the use of the technology; on the other, it encourages simulation by some who understand little of what they are doing and who thus can give simulation a bad name.)

Dennis and Donella Meadows left MIT, where they were awarded their doctoral degrees and where they became system dynamics enthusiasts, and established a system dynamics laboratory at Dartmouth College.

The following description of the system dynamics methodology was taken from a "How to Simulate" report on the Third Annual Advanced Study Institute on Social System Dynamics, held in Dartmouth in 1974.

Basic Methodology

A model is a set of simplified assumptions about a complex system. The essence of modeling is *simplification*. One tries to reduce previously incomprehensible phenomena to general abstractions that are understandable and that still have explanatory or predictive value.

The model is built up in steps of increasing complexity until it is capable of replicating the observed real-world behavior of the system.

However, modeling is an iterative, trial-and-error process. A modeler does not usually proceed smoothly from start to finish, but he does generally follow a set of logical steps, repeating them until the model satisfies him.

8.8.1   Basic Steps in Formulating A System Dynamics Model

1. Verbal description of the system
2. Precise definition of the problem
    a. Reference mode
    b. Definition of boundaries   CONCEPTUALIZATION
    c. Time horizon
3. Construction of causal loop diagram
4. Formulation of a flow diagram
5. Writing the equations   REPRESENTATION
6. Mechanization of the model
7. Analysis of the model
    a. Comparison with reference mode
    b. Sensitivity testing   ANALYSIS
    c. Policy testing
8. Evaluation, communication, implementation of recommendations.

Some brief comments on the foregoing steps are in order.

8.8.2   Verbal Description of the System

This is a verbal summary of the information available about the system as the study begins. This first, rough system description serves as a starting point, a collection of perceptions about what may be important to include in the model.

Although the Institute covered models of several kinds of real-world systems—or simulands—for simplicity we will use only one of them to illustrate the fundamental concepts which we believe apply to modeling in general. The verbal description of this system follows:

Prior to 1907, the deer herd on the Kaibab Plateau, which consists of some 727,000 acres and is on the north side of the Grand Canyon in Arizona, numbered about 4000. In 1907, a bounty was placed on cougars, wolves, and coyotes—all natural predators of deer. Within 15 to 20 years, there was a substantial extirpation of these predators (over 8,000) and a consequent and immediate irruption of the deer population. By 1918, the deer population had increased more than tenfold; evident overbrowsing of the area brought the first of a series of warnings by competent investigators, none of which produced a much needed quick change in either the bounty policy or that dealing with deer removal. In the absence of predation by its natural predators (cougars, wolves, coyotes) or by man as a hunter, the herd reached 100,000 in 1924; in the absence of sufficient food, 60 percent of the herd died off in two successive winters. By then, the girdling of so much of the vegetation through browsing precluded recovery of the food reserve to such an extent that subsequent die-off and reduced natality yielded a population about half that which could theoretically have been previously maintained. Perhaps the most pertinent statement relative to the matter of the inter-regulatory effect of predator and prey is the following by Aldo Leopold, one of the most significant of recent figures on the conservation scene:

We have found no record of a deer irruption in North America antedating the removal of deer predators. Those parts of the continent which still retain the native predators have reported no irruptions. This circumstantial evidence supports the surmise that removal of predators predisposes a deer herd to irruptive behavior.*

8.8.3 Precise Definition of the Problem

This requires a clear statement of the exact problem that the model will address. This step is extremely important, because all the modeling decisions to follow will refer back to the problem definition.

In the case of our deer population example, the problem definition begins with two questions:

What caused the irruption of deer on the Kaibab plateau? Can we design a policy to maintain a stable deer population on the plateau in the absence of predators?

Reference Mode.   The reference mode is a sketch of the variation of several important system elements through time. It may be a picture of the dynamic problem that is already occurring, or a set of possible future behaviors that one might want to encourage or avoid. The deer population reference mode is somewhat as shown in Figure 8.1.

Definition of Boundaries.   The boundaries that separate the elements of the system must then be defined. Those elements which produce the dynamic characteristics displayed in the reference mode are the endogenous elements. Outside the boundaries enclosing them there may be factors which affect the reference mode but are not affected by it, and others which are affected by it but do not in turn affect the dynamics of the system of interest. These are the exogenous factors.

Note that factors which affect the reference mode and are also affected by it constitute part of a feedback loop and are thus endogenous to the dynamic system.

The mnemonics used are as follows:

DP = DEER POPULATION

DPI = DEER POPULATION INITIALLY

DNI = DEER NET INCREASE

NIR = NET INCREASE RATE

* In E. J. Kormondy, *Concepts of Ecology*, Wisconsin Conservation Bulletin No. 321, 1943.

DPR = DEER PREDATION RATE

DKPP = DEER KILL PER PREDATOR

DKPPT = DKPP TABLE

DD = DEER DENSITY

A = AREA

PP = PREDATOR POPULATION

PPT = PP TABLE

Boundaries of our example system might thus appear as shown in Figure 8-2.

Time Horizon.   The time horizon is the length of time over which the system's behavior develops—it is implicit in the reference mode. The time horizon provides a rough guideline for choosing what dynamic processes to include in the model. For example, one would not represent the dynamics of a 200-year process in a 2-month model, nor a 2-month process in a 200-year model.

8.8.4   Construction of a Causal Loop Diagram

This is a non-quantitative, preliminary sketch of the system structure. It indicates the major elements of the system, and it illustrates the important interactions among these elements by means of causal arrows, as shown in Figure 8-2.

8.8.5   Formulation of the Flow Diagram

This is a more precise picture of the system structure, distinguishing between levels and rates, and between information flows and materials. Figure 8-3 shows flow diagram using System Dynamics symbols, but readers might prefer to use symbols with which they are more familiar.

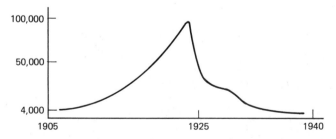
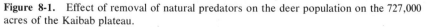

Figure 8-1.   Effect of removal of natural predators on the deer population on the 727,000 acres of the Kaibab plateau.

Elements and factors having no significant
influence on the reference mode

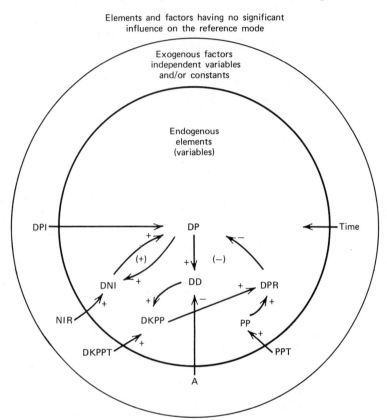

Figure 8-2. System boundary and the concept of closed systems interaction of *endogenous* factors explains reference mode.

8.8.6 Writing the Equations

These constitute the final, quantitative statement of the model assumptions, including the mathematical equations and numerical parameters that define all inter-relationships.

These equations can be written in any of several languages that are suitable for computer modeling. However, the program below is given in DYNAMO because that was the language of the Institute.

BANK FILE NAME: DM1

```
0010  *          DEER MODEL ONE
0020  NOTE
0030  NOTE CONSTANT NET INCREASE
0040  NOTE
```

```
0050   L  DP.K=DP.J+(DT) (DNI.JL−DPR.JK)
0060   N  DP=DPI
0070   C  DPI=4000
0080   R  DNI.KL=DP.K*NIR
0090   C  NIR=.2
0100   R  DPR,KL=PP.K*DKPP.K
0110   A  DKPP.K=TABLE(DKPPT,DD.K,0,.025,.005)
0120   T  DKPPT=0/3/13/32/51/56
0130   A  DD.K=DP.K/AREA
0140   C  AREA=800,000
0150   A  PP.K=TABLE(PPT,TIME.K,1880,1960,20)
0160   T  PPT=300/300/300/300/300
0170   NOTE
0180   NOTE CONTROL VARIABLES
0190   NOTE
0200   N  TIME=1880
0210   C  LENGTH=1970
0220   C  PLTPER=3
0230   C  DT=.1
0240   PLOT DP=D(0,20,000)/PP=P(0,400)/DKPP=K(,0,56)
```

8.8.7 Mechanization of the Model

In our example case, this required only typing the above lines into the computer via any of the numerous computer terminals distributed around the Dartmouth campus. (There were 12 in the basement of our dormitory! All were available to Institute participants 24 hours a day, seven days a week, except for a 12-hour maintenance period beginning at 2000 hours each Wednesday.)

Usually, however, there is much more to implementing a program on a computer than that. "Debugging" the program might be a considerable chore, depending on the complexity of the program and the competence of the user. This step,

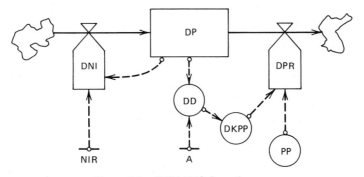

Figure 8-3. DYNAMO flow diagram.

which we refer to as Verification, involves making sure that the program runs as intended. It should not be confused with Validation, which is concerned with assuring that the computer model displays all those characteristics of the real-world system—the simuland—that are pertinent to the study to be undertaken, with the degree of fidelity required for that study.

8.8.8 Analysis of the Model

This involves computer simulation of the model equations to determine the resultant behavior mode. The analysis typically includes three stages:

a.   Comparison of the model's behavior mode with the reference mode; then additions, corrections, and revisions of the model until the comparison is satisfactory.

8.8.9 Evaluation, Communication, and Implementation

System dynamics models are interpreted and evaluated with regard to their ability to reproduce the *behavior modes* of a system. Behavior modes are the general dynamic tendencies of the system (growth, decline, stagnation, oscillation, stability, instability) rather than the precise values of state variables at any given time.

The importance of communication cannot be overemphasized, but we will not lecture on the subject here. It is enough to remind our readers that good communication is necessary both internally—among those developing the model and designing the simulation experiments—and externally, with the "customers." The latter would include both the funding agency and the potential user of the results of the simulation study, who may or may not be the same. Further, good communications as a means of fostering good public relations should not be overlooked. In this respect it should be remembered that the model itself is an excellent communication tool; it is something concrete to which people can refer to be sure they are discussing the same thing, and it is unambiguous. And Dennis Meadows reminded us, decision makers respond to what they *think* they understand!

"Implementation" as used here refers to making use of the results of a simulation study to influence some real-world system. While this might not be considered a part of the art or science of simulation per se, it is usually (though not in all cases) the reason that a simulation project is undertaken in the first place. And certainly it is the only way simulation can directly alleviate any of the problems of our society—which was the goal of the Institute, and is the *raison d'être* of this Newsletter. So important, in fact, do we consider the problem of "selling" simulation results that we plan to treat the subject separately in a future issue of S^3. We will, therefore, say little more about it in this issue although there was an excellent presentation on the subject during the Institute.

8.8.10 Supplemental Thoughts . . .

System Dynamics is a way of thinking that emphasizes that " . . . de neckbone is fastened to de headbone . . . " etc. ad infinitum or, as Barry Commoner has written, "Everything is connected to everything else." "Everything must go somewhere."

Nevertheless, the behavior mode of a model is not sensitive to parameter changes in the equations. These changes affect the timing and severity of response, but do not alter the basic dynamic pattern. In contrast to this, *structural* changes that effectively alter the polarity of feedback loops or that add or remove them altogether may have a major effect on the system's behavior.

The *feedback loop* is the basic unit of system dynamics models. A feedback loop is a closed chain of causal relationships. The most basic representation of any feedback loop consists of just two elements:

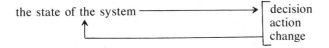

A negative feedback loop tends to be self-correcting or goal-seeking. A change in one element is propagated around the loop to result in a *counteracting* change in the same element.

A positive feedback loop is self-reinforcing or explosive. A change in one element is propagated around the loop to *augment* the original change.

Causal loop diagrams can therefore aid in the communication of ideas and the conceptualization of a problem even if the remaining steps of modeling are not completed.

Levels (state variables) to be included in a model are determined by the questions you are asking. Levels are the measurable quantities left when the system is brought to a stop. The number of levels determines the "order" of a system. Levels introduce delays into flows by acting as reservoirs. The inputs to levels are material flow rates.

Rates control the flows between levels. Rate equations are statements of *policy*, or general decision rules. Once the principal levels and rates have been chosen, the formulation of the rate equations determines the system behavior.

One method of causal loop diagramming consists of identifying levels and the rates affecting those levels, and then determining the feedback mechanisms affecting the rates

A tradeoff between *amount of detail* and practicality exists. A highly aggregated, less accurate model may be as useful as a detailed, accurate model because the former can be understood in an intuitive way while the latter cannot.

Determining the causal structure interrelating the system variables makes it possible in many cases to understand system behavior even without use of a computer.

There are basically two types of policy tests that may be made using a system dynamics model: (1) tests involving structural changes (i.e., different equations); and (2) tests involving parameter changes (i.e., different constants or table functions).

In general, reasonable structural changes result in more dramatic effects on system behavior than do reasonable parameter changes (reasonable is taken to mean a change that could conceivably occur in the real world).

Testing policies using random noise inputs may yield different results than when using standard inputs (i.e., a step function, sine wave, etc.).

Delays characterize the real world. We base our decisions on our perceptions of the real world, not on the actual state of the real world. It takes time to form and alter our ideas of what the real world is. When we do take action, time must pass before the effects of our decisions can be observed. Systems have momentum; time, as well as energy, is required to change their direction or velocity.

Perception (information) delays result from the need to observe and store information from the system in order to assess this information and to make decisions. Material delays result from the existence of system elements which store material flowing in the system.

Delays transform information and material flows in characteristic ways. The *order* of a delay (the number of internal levels) determines the shape of the response to an input and the *adjustment time* determines how fast the response takes place. First-order delays give an immediate partial response and adjustment is essentially complete in about three adjustment times. Third-order delays do not show a response immediately but adjust more rapidly later so that adjustment is essentially complete after three adjustment times.

Delays may stabilize a system's response. If the delay slows or attenuates the actions of a system so that a controller can respond to changes in sufficient time, the delay stabilizes the system. If the delay increases the time for perception of an effect in a rapidly changing system, the controller will not be able to respond to changes rapidly enough and the delay destabilizes the system.

It is necessary to define a unit of measurement for all the variables in a model. This is easy for concrete variables like people, and birth and death rates. For abstract variables such as attractiveness, an "attractiveness unit" has to be defined, which is meaningful only if it is made operational by being linked to observable qualities.

Depending on the purpose of the model, it may be advantageous to initialize (start) to in an historically interesting state or in approximate equilibrium (i.e., in a state where changes are few and slow).

In order to increase one's belief in the conclusions obtained with the aid of a model, one should check whether it is in fact valid for all differing but reasonable assumptions about how the simuland operates. Such sensitivity testing should definitely be done for the uncertain relations in the model.

Simple dynamic structures (first and second-order systems) have a small set of behavior modes. An understanding of these modes is useful for understanding the behavior of more complex systems of which these simple structures are parts.

A useful concept for understanding the behavior of a complex system is the notion of dominant loops. A dominant loop is the feedback loop with the strongest influence on a given level at any time.

The simplest feedback structures are those containing a single level (i.e., first-order system). In a first-order feedback loop the rate of change of the level depends directly (without delay) on the level itself. If the flow into the level increases as the level increases, then the feedback loop is positive. If the flow into the level decreases as the level increases, then the feedback loop is negative.

A linear first-order negative feedback loop creates exponential decay or goal-seeking behavior, also commonly observed in the real world.

Sigmoidal growth, in which the level grows over a period of time and then continues asymptotically toward a limit, can be created by a level which is part of the two first-order feedback loops—one positive and one negative. The behavior of this system results from the dominance first of the positive, and then of the negative loop.

A second-order system has two levels imbedded in up to three feedback loops, i.e., one major and up to two minor loops.

A major loop connects the two levels to each other.

A minor loop connects a level to itself like a first-order system.

Linear second-order systems have rates which depend linearly on the two levels. These systems may show growth, decay, overshoot and decline, decaying oscillations, steady (constant amplitude) oscillations and growing oscillations.

Non-linear second-order systems have rates which depend non-linearly on the two levels. These systems may show all of the above behavior modes as well as more general periodic behavior which is not sinusoidal oscillation.

The modeling of a system may be thought of as a two-stage process: conceptualization and representation. In practice the procedure is always iterative—the individual steps are re-done several times.

The diagram below shows this procedure as it was actually followed in a study of solid waste.

1. Define general problem

2. Decide on specific question

3. Identify dynamic behavior

4. Determine system boundary

5. Choose system descriptors

6. Draw causal diagram

7. Construct flow diagram

8. Choose parameterization

9. Write equations

10. Make runs

11. Perform policy experimentation

12. Carry out implementation

6/1/70 7/1/70   10/1/70 1/1/71 1972

8.8.11 . . . And Cautions

In contrast to the wealth of constructive information, we are indebted to Douglas Lee, famous (or infamous, depending on your point of view) as a result of his *American Institute of Planners Journal* article for his astute observations concerning "characteristics of most large scale simulation modeling studies that make them of little use to policymakers."

Essential Points (See Section 8.11 for details). Most models fail to have any impact on policy because the model builders attempt:

To include too many details and phenomena in their models (hypercomprehensiveness).

To represent detailed behaviors with data that is not fine enough (grossness).

To construct models that require so much data that the analytical effort cannot be supported by the sponsoring agency (hungriness).

To use models that do not in fact portray the real world behavior of interest to policymakers (wrong-headedness).

To use models in which there may be mechanical errors associated with the computer or the structure of the programming language (mechanicalness).

A program too large to be supported by the client (expensiveness).

In the same vein we can quote Jørgen Randers' talk at the Institute in which he gave a list of:

"UNDESIRABLE TENDENCIES IDENTIFIED IN THE ACTUAL MODELING PROCESS"

To ramble due to lack of an explicit goal.

To make excessively complex models to avoid inadvertent omission of important elements.

To exclude too much detail subsequent to failures with overly complex models.

To contract the scope of the model to make feasible a complete, respectable analysis.

To stick to earlier formulations to justify the effort put into their development.

To overemphasize causal diagramming, since causal diagrams constitute a tangible result without the finality of a completed model.

To go stale in unending formulation problems actually resulting from lack of understanding of the simuland.

With the foregoing caveats in mind, let us return to some additional points gleaned from the Institute lectures and commentary, which we will collect loosely under the heading:

8.8.12   How to Cope . . .

. . . *With "Soft" Variables.* All who have followed the controversy precipitated by the publication of *The Limits to Growth* will recall the questions raised with respect to representing unquantified difficult-to-measure, soft variables. Concerning this we quote from notes on a lecture by Donella Meadows.

The behavior of social systems is often determined by relationships that have never been quantified or can only be roughly measured. These relationships are typically dependent on psychological variables, such as preferences, values, expectations, dissatisfactions, or aspirations. They usually involve the representation of human decisions. The main sources of information about these soft variables are personal experience and subjective impressions.

Ignoring soft variables because of an inability to measure them may lead to a model that is unable to reproduce observed behavior. Inclusion of even a rough guess about the impact of these variables usually provides a better model than can be obtained by ignoring them; the structure will be correct although the parameters may be inaccurate.

There are two steps to including soft variables in a model:

Conceptualization, or the choice of an appropriate concept or structure to represent the dynamic phenomenon; and

Parameterization, or the choice of a range of reasonable numbers to quantify the variables. Here are some guidelines that may help.

a.   Ignore the kinds of measures found in standard data banks and think hard about what's really happening in the system. Put yourself in the place of the decision-maker you're modeling. Even better, go talk to him and watch him in action.

b.   Be aware of information inputs to the decision, of their time lags and biases. Look for unspoken goals, constraints, pressures.

c.   If it seems that the inputs to a decision are numerous, list them. Try to eliminate minor or dubious variables from the list. Aggregate others into categories with similar dynamic properties.

d.   Define your aggregate variables as clearly and carefully as possible. If necessary, invent a scale by which to measure them, with easily perceived end-points or a familiar standard reference point.

e.   Draw a "most likely" guess of each relationship, paying special attention to extreme points and end-points. Draw upper and lower limits around this line to illustrate what you believe to be a reasonable range of values for the relationship.

f.   Test the "most likely" and the upper and lower limits in the model to determine the system's sensitivity to inaccuracies in your parameter estimates. If the system does seem to be sensitive to a "soft" variable, further definition, experimentation, or study may be indicated.

g.   Remember in interpreting your model outputs that the computer assigns very precise values to variables and concepts that may be in fact be imprecise and "fuzzy." It is up to you to read the proper degree of (im)precision into the final conclusions.

h.   BE BRAVE. Although scientists have been trained to avoid variables that are difficult to measure, especially those involving human behavior, in fact a great deal of imprecise, subjective knowledge about such variables exists. Almost no social system model is complete without them. Searching out and representing "soft" variables explicitly will lead to better models and may inspire new research and better understanding of social systems.

. . . *With Aggregation.* Another "Achilles heel" of *The Limits to Growth* was the extent of aggregation. Again we quote from Dana's lecture.

Aggregation is the practice of grouping quantities with common properties together and discussing them as a generic whole. A model with general, broad groupings and little detail is said to be highly *aggregated;* a model with much detail and little generalization is said to be *disaggregated.*

One can often make statements about aggregated quantities that cannot be made with certainty about individual quantities (death rates, but not death of a particular individual; gas temperature, but not energy content of a particular gas molecule).

No system can be understood completely by viewing it at only one level of aggregation.

The proper degree of aggregation for any particular model depends on the model's purpose. A model may be built for all of the following purposes, and each one has some bearing on the aggregation decision:

a.   Simulating a behavior mode (dynamic understanding)
b.   Exploring policy alternatives (analysis)

   c. Integrating existing literature and data (communication)

   d. Convincing a client (implementation)

Within the rough level of aggregation implied by the question being asked, there is a difficult choice between too little aggregation (which leads to unnecessary detail, waste of modeler's and computer's time, and confusion), and too much aggregation (leading to loss of important distinctions and behavior modes). The following hints are useful to keep in mind.

   a. Usually larger space boundaries and longer time horizons imply more aggregation.

   b. Always start at the highest possible degree of aggregation. The model can be made more elaborate later, if necessary.

   c. Model elements can be aggregated if they are dynamically similar—that is, if they are controlled by similar rates, if their outputs are used for similar purposes elsewhere in the system, and if their "mix" is relatively constant.

   d. Nonlinear table functions should be chosen with the "mix" of aggregated quantities in mind.

   e. The level of aggregation should be consistent throughout the model.*

   f. BE FLEXIBLE. Do not accept without question an accepted level of aggregation within a given discipline or profession. Experiment with different levels until you find the best (and simplest) for your purpose.

Model Validity Versus the Utility of a Model. Model validity is not an absolute concept; whether a model is valid or not depends on the purpose for which it was constructed. Model utility—the extent to which it helps its user—is a more sensible criterion for evaluating a model.

A model cannot be useful to the client unless he believes in the model—i.e., unless he sees a certain degree of correlation between model assumptions and overall behavior and the real world. A model becomes more believable and interesting for practical use when the model assumptions are made more realistic. The assumptions and the overall system behavior have been made sufficiently realistic when the user believes that the model can tell him something useful.

Models can be separated into four relatively distinct classes according to the degree of formal correspondence between model assumptions and reality:

CLASS 1—COMMON SENSE MODELS. Model assumptions are based on the modeler's intuition and general knowledge about the system.

CLASS 2—EXPERT OPINION MODELS. Model assumptions (hopefully) represent the consensus of the existing knowledge—as found in the literature and among experts.

CLASS 3—PARTIALLY ESTIMATED MODELS. Model assumptions satisfy the requirements for Class 2 models. In addition, formal techniques are used to demonstrate the capability of the individual assumptions to reproduce real world data.

CLASS 4—FULLY ESTIMATED MODELS. Besides satisfying the Class 3 requirements, the *full* system can be shown to reproduce reality through formal tech-

*No! Often a particular subsystem of a complex system must be disaggregated to allow it to be studied in detail while the rest of the system can be highly aggregated, as it is only required to close the feedback loops around the subsystem of interest. This is the broad and shallow versus narrow and deep compromise.   JM

niques (like simultaneous equations estimation, by regression or Box-Jenkins' technique).

In general one's confidence in a model increases as its class number increases, but that does not mean that a Class 4 model is "better" for all purposes. First of all there are large time and other costs connected with moving a model to a higher class. Secondly, the user may have confidence enough in a lower class model to rely on its results.

This classification of models corresponds closely to a classification of information which ranks information in a spectrum consisting of intuitive perception, expert opinion, tentative measurement and high-quality measurements.

Data should not be used to *obtain* the assumptions, but to check to assure that seemingly reasonable assumptions constitute a realistic representation of reality.

8.8.13 Criteria of Model Utility

Depending on the goal served, a model may be evaluated by how satisfactorily it meets 16 criteria:

1. What is the cost in money, man-hours, or computer time to develop, validate, redesign, the model or modify it to represent another system?

2. Is the model subject to general analytical solutions so that system elements can be evaluated for any point in time and so that boundary conditions can be established for its different behavior modes?

3. Can the form of the model accommodate nonlinearities, delays, and arbitrarily large numbers of variables?

4. Is the form of the assumptions one that permits critical analysis by those with the most information about the real system, or with responsibility for responding to the results of the model analysis?

5. Can the model be traced to its logical implications without error?

6. Can the model be used to determine the behavior of system elements over time?

7. Does the form of the model lend itself to regression analysis?

8. Does the form of the model accommodate information from any level ranging from intuition to controlled physical measurements?

9. Does the model reproduce the behavior it was built to understand or alter?

10. Does the model permit one to represent the effects in it of specific policy measurements?

11. Does the model permit modifications to be incorporated and analyzed quickly?

12. Is the model isomorphic with mental impressions of causal relationships?

13. Does the model predict past time series data when initialized for some earlier time period?

14. Are the spectral characteristics of the model elements over time similar to those observed in the real world?

15. Does the model permit automated sensitivity analysis or automated search for optimal points in the parameter space?

16. Does the model contain sufficient information on real world parameters to permit relevant policy makers to assess preferences among alternative outcomes?

The relevance of each question certainly depends upon the goals and resources of the model user. Nevertheless, the 16 dimensions appear to include most of the considerations that might be involved in the choice among alternative models of the same system. The criteria are incommensurate and thus do not lend themselves to identification of the optimal model. Moreover, each model's performance along each of the 16 dimensions is not a purely objective fact; some intuitive judgment would be involved in the ratings. However, through use of a 16 by N matrix, it would be possible to provide a concise, subjective comparison of N models along the 16 indicated dimensions. An example of the matrix developed by one analyst to compare three models is given below. The result is a far better guide to the preferred model than is simple reliance on a single index such as the model's ability to reproduce past time series data.

Matrix Comparing Three Commodity Models Along 16 Dimensions

Criterion Model	1	2	3	4	5	6	7	8	9	10	11	12	13	14	15	16
Cobweb	3	3	0	2	2	1	2	1	1	0	3	2	0	2	3	0
Econometric	1	2	1	1	3	2	3	2	3	2	2	1	3	3	2	2
System dynamics	2	1	3	3	3	3	1	3	2	3	3	3	2	3	1	2

Rating: 0 — inadequate   2 — medium
         1 — very poor   3 — very satisfactory

8.9   Hummon on A Methodology for Model Evaluation (Hummon, 1973)

This section addresses a rather limited topic in the broad spectrum of issues that relate to simulation and gaming: How can an evaluation be made of that part of a simulation model or game which is incorporated into an algorithm (i.e., programmed on a computer)? Thus the discussion may have little applicability in those situations where game players construct their game during the game play, but have high applicability in those situations where the computer performs the entire simulation. We will address primarily the latter case recognizing that the degree of applicability varies with the specific situation.

The approach suggested here bears a strong similarity to evaluating empirical social science research; the evaluation of much research is based on an examination of the methodology used in conducting the research. Of course, it is recognized that an evaluation based on an examination of the research methodology is more apt to find difficulties and inadequacies rather than invention and imagination, and thus must be viewed as a beginning, albeit an important one.

To suggest the evaluation of simulation models by an examination of the methodology used to construct the model presumes that such a methodology exists. Such a presumption may not be totally justified. The relative newness of the field of simulation, the diversity of substantive applications and the multiplicity of simulation techniques make the specification of a simulation methodology both tenuous and difficult. Nevertheless, that is the direction this discussion takes in the hope such a specification provides insight into the issues of evaluating simulation models.

8.9.1   Components of the Methodology

A methodology is a system of rules which guide scientific inquiry. A breakdown of the components of the methodology depends on the substantive nature of the inquiry, its use or purpose, and the predilections of the investigator. It is possible to identify three, and possibly four, components of a methodology for constructing simulation models. They are:

1.   A substantive or theoretical component which specifies how a model's variables and relations are selected;
2.   An epistemological component, which provides a set of criteria that can be used to determine whether the results generated by a model are acceptable or unacceptable;
3.   A technique or set of techniques which are used to build and run the model; and
4.   A component composed of criteria which are used to evaluate whether a model is suitable for some specific purpose, e.g., simulation models designed to aid decision-makers ought to include realistic decision variables.

In the interest of maintaining a certain level of generality, we will focus on substantive and epistemological components of a simulation methodology. The specialized technical problems of programming, as opposed to designing, a simulation model are fascinating—at least to some people—but a discussion of the merits of different languages and computer techniques is best reserved for another forum. Similarly, the component that reflects the specialized purpose of a model is difficult to discuss as a generalized set of issues. The purpose of this discussion is to address evaluation problems which are common to most simulation models, namely, "How can the substantive content and performance of a simulation model be assessed?"

Before defining and elaborating the nature of the two more general components, it is useful to set forth the context in which they were developed. This writer's experience with gaming and simulation has focused primarily on the study of urban simulation models. Thus to some degree, the discussion that follows reflects the problems and issues of simulating contemporary American cities. The urban-based examples which are used to illustrate the components of the simulation methodology reflect the following biases: a concern for dealing with complexity, a concern for being substantively comprehensive at the risk of being theoretically simplistic, and finally, a concern for generating results that are useful to decision-makers and policy formulators. These biases result in simulation models which are inelegant when viewed through academic disciplinary blinders. Therefore, a strict translation of criteria generated within a discipline may well overpower a simulation model if they are used for evaluation. The view taken here is that criteria should be derived from, and therefore reflect, the nature of the model being evaluated. With this background in mind, we now turn to an elaboration of the two general components of a simulation methodology.

8.9.2 The Substantive Component

The substantive component is not normally *explicitly* included in discussions of social research methodologies. However, it would seem obvious that any methodology operates in a substantive context. At a minimum, this component consists of a vocabulary and a system of definitions. As this component increases in importance, it converges to a substantively based theory of the subject of study. Of course, this component is not the theory; it does, however, reflect the structures, perspectives, and orientation of the theory. In short, the substantive component of the methodology should describe the correspondence between structure and process in the simulation model. The problem of evaluating the substantive aspects of a simulation model then involves a critical assessment of the correspondence between the model and the real world.

This task can be broken down into a series of steps which, in sequence, become both more critical and more difficult to perform. First, we can assess the appropriateness of the variables included in the model. This involves assessing both the definition of the variables and, taken as a set, their substantive scope. In evaluating the variables, one overriding consideration must be taken into account; the number of variables that can be practically included in a simulation model is normally a small fraction of the number of variables thought necessary to describe the real world. Where a sociologist may use fifteen or twenty attributes to describe the social class of an individual, most urban simulation models use but one or two variables to represent social class. Where an economist may describe an urban economy in terms of fifty sectors, many urban models involve only the gross description of primary, secondary, and tertiary sectors. Thus, the question "What variables?" must be dealt with within a highly constrained framework.

The scope of the set of variables included in a simulation model can be examined in two interrelated ways. First, does the set of variables represent all or most of the major structural attributes of the phenomenon being modeled? For example, if one were evaluating the set of variables included in an urban simulation model which was supposed to be comprehensive with respect to the major structural attributes of American cities, one might check whether the model variables reflected: (1) the spatial/physical system of the city, (2) the demographic characteristics of the population, (3) the social characteristics of the population, (4) the economic structure of the city, (5) the political structure of a city, and (6) the technology system of the city. An urban simulation model which included variables for all these major urban structural attributes can be said to have satisfied some sort of completeness criterion.

Closely related to the completeness of the set of variables is the issue of the efficiency of the variables. By efficiency we mean the degree to which variation or change can be captured by the variables included in the model. For example, consider the situation where we have only two variables to describe an urban population. What should they be? Using the household as the basic population unit, two possible candidates are income class and educational level. However, given one of these variables, say income, the other is to some extent redundant, and redundancy reflects inefficiency in variables selection. A more efficient pair of variables might be education and some age-dependent variable such as stage in family life cycle. The problem of efficiency can be made more complicated when other factors are considered. While a household's educational level and stage in family cycle may be a good combination for modeling urban migration patterns, modeling the urban employment process may be facilitated by the inclusion of wage rates or income levels.

In summary, it if difficult to specify exact evaluation criteria for the scope and efficiency of a set of variables. To some extent judgment must play a role.

The foregoing discussion also applies to the set of relations in a model. Instead of evaluating the correspondence between the set of variables and the structure of the real world phenomena, we examine the correspondence between relations in the model and the major processes inherent in the real world.

It should be clear that if variables are chosen according to the criteria of their scope and potential efficiency, this potential is only realized when the degree of variation we observe in the real world is captured by the functional relationships in the model. Moreover, the same problem is faced in selecting relationships that is faced in selecting variables; a severe limitation exists on the number that can be included. Thus care must be taken to select relationships that represent at least the major first-order sources of variation, often at the expense of secondary variation. For example, in modeling an urban system, the migration process which brings about basic changes in land use and the employment probably take priority over modeling urban education institutions or health care delivery systems unless, of course, the latter cases are the primary focuses of study.

Given that a simulation model includes relationships that capture the basic system phenomena, the next question is, "Are the functional forms of these relationships reasonable given theoretical and empirical knowledge of the phenomena?" To answer, professional judgment must be brought to bear recognizing the severe limitations under which most models must be constructed. This becomes a critical problem where theoretical results generated within disciplinary fields suggest relationships are multivariate, non-linear, etc. First, the criterion of parsimony is useful; that is, maximizing the explained variation with the minimum number of variables. Secondly, we can assess the quality of the homomorphic transformation. Such a transformation compounds elements and relations, but preserves the basic structural characteristics. A homomorphism is not a false representation; it is only a partial representation. A homomorphism of the same degree is an isomorphism. Thus the question becomes, "Are the relations in the model sensible aggregations of the more complex theoretical relations?"

One final evaluation criterion can be included in the substantively based component of our methodology. The reason simulation is used in the study of social phenomenon is its potential capability of incorporating complexity. As already indicated, this complexity does not result from the nature of the individual relationships of variables, but instead results from linking relationships and variables into networks. An evaluation of the network or connectedness of the simulation model is a most difficult task because the evaluator cannot resort to disciplinary based empirical and theoretical studies as a basis of comparison. And yet, we can normally find connections that make intuitive or experiential sense though hard data may be lacking. For example, over a period of time it has been observed that certain kinds of urban development such as the building of an expressway influence migration patterns in a city, and in turn, the relocatees increase demand for transportation facilities which stimulates further development of the highway system. This particular kind of development suggests a positive feedback loop exists between the migration process and the transportation system in an urban area. A simulation model that does not represent this feedback loop omits one of the major mechanisms that has facilitated change in American cities.

To summarize the substantive component of our methodology, we have noted three levels of evaluation. The first concerns the scope and efficiency of the variables included in the model. The scope condition focuses on the completeness of the model's representation of the structure of the real world phenomenon. The efficiency criterion focuses on the substantive redundancy or independence of the variables. An evaluation of the relationships in the model can be based on their ability to capture the range of variation observed to the kinds of change observed. Finally, evaluation of the linkage system or connectedness of a simulation model can be approached by asking what are the major feedback loops, both positive and negative, that drive and control the system. As already mentioned, as evaluation proceeds from variables to relations to linkages, the criteria become less clear. At the same time, however, the evaluation becomes more concerned with the creativity and ingenuity exhibited in the model. Thus, problems encountered at the more mechanical level may be compensated for by creative solutions where standard procedures and hard data on the real world are missing.

8.9.3   The Epistemological Component

The epistemological component of traditional social science methodologies is based on the conditional statement of the form: If X, then Y. Statistical inference is often used to determine whether result Y is obtained under the conditions of X. The validity of such an evaluation criterion rests on a basic assumption, namely, *ceteris paribus*, i.e., that other factors are equal. In many types of social research, this assumption can be approximated through the technique of randomization.

The problem of using this traditional approach in evaluating simulation models is twofold. First, the number of possible conditions to be specified in a simulation model of even moderate complexity may be so large as to be infeasible. Second, from a systems perspective, it is not clear that an "If X, then Y" approach is desirable. The fact is that the probability of obtaining *ceteris paribus* conditions in the real world is infinitesimal. While simulation models are abstractions of the real world, they are generally of a different kind than the abstractions generated by traditional social science. Simulation models are not constructed to study a purified version; they are constructed to study precisely the opposite—the complexity inherent in the real world.*

We are not arguing that the epistemological criteria used to evaluate simulation models are illogical. However, we are observing that traditional uses of logic are either extremely cumbersome or miss the point of the evaluation. These problems pose a serious dilemma to one interested in establishing a set of criteria that can be used to determine whether the results generated by a model are acceptable or unacceptable. The following suggestions for circumventing this dilemma are tentative. They are based in part on trial and error experience in evaluating simulation models and in part on the growing body of literature on the philosophy of systems. In the latter instance, the writings of Churchman have strongly influenced these tentative suggestions.

At the risk of oversimplification, we contrast the systems approach with its more traditional counterpart. The traditional approach asks the question, "What are the relative effects of a set of independent variables on a dependent variable?" It is suggested that the systems approach turns the question on its head, namely:

---

* It is realized that statisticians often resort to "computer simulations" to generate statistical distributions for which they cannot derive analytic solutions. However, this use of simulation in support of traditional evaluation procedures is beyond the scope of this paper.

"Given a change in a system component, what are the relative propagated effects on other components in the system?" But, having posed the question with respect to a change in one component with the resulting propagated effects on others, the question must be repeated. In short, this approach to evaluating a simulation model amounts to assessing the behavior of the constructed system. This raises the question: "Are there certain classes of system behavior which can be used to characterize, and therefore, evaluate simulation models?"

One possible set of criteria comes to mind that is based on the properties of complex systems. As mentioned previously, systems can be described in terms of their connectedness, and this property can often be translated into a language of positive and negative feedback. The nature of feedback tells us something about the behavior of the system. We can attempt to assess whether a system is tending toward an equilibrium state and whether this state is similar or quite distinct from the state we are using as a basis of comparison, often the initial state of the system. We can also attempt to assess whether an equilibrium state is stable or unstable. Of course, when positive feedback is present in a system, behavior characteristics of a system tending toward equilibrium may not exist.

The application of these criteria to the evaluation of the simulation model depends heavily on one's substantive knowledge of the phenomenon, sometimes on knowledge not incorporated into the simulation model. For example, when Lowry assessed the validity of his simulation model of the Pittsburgh Metropolitan Region, he discovered that he underestimated population densities in the western sector of the region and overestimated population densities in an eastern sector of the region. He attributed this error to a failure in system specification; the model did not reflect increased access in the western sector due to the construction of a major expressway. In other words, the model failed to incorporate a positive feedback loop which affected the development of the region.

Another example can be provided. One of the best known urban simulation models is Forrester's Urban Dynamics Model. The behavior of this model is interesting because the equilibrium state reached at the end of the simulation run is quite independent of the initial state. Moreover, this equilibrium state is extremely stable. Urbanologists might raise serious questions about the existence of a stable equilibrium for any realistic urban model, and the independence of this state from initial conditions.

The use of the phrase "tending toward equilibrium" has implicitly introduced time into our discussion. We can make further use of a temporal framework. If the behavior of the model reaches equilibrium, or more likely, a set of equilibria, we can ask whether the sequence of this set of events is reasonable. By implication, those variables or subsystems which stabilize first are subject to more negative feedback than those which stabilize at later times. Do the relative amounts of negative feedback implied by the time sequence match with experience and theory?

Given that it is possible to generate actual time trajectories of the system being modeled, even more complex questions can be posed. Can the graphic patterns for variables such as growth, decay, or oscillation be explained? Can they be explained in combination as we might expect for the supply and demand of markets? Anomalous patterns may be surprise findings, but they should be suspect until those structural properties of the system that generate them are scrutinized.

In summary, the behavior of a system sometimes allows the evaluation to localize problems in modules that are not apparent when the model is constructed. This approach is particularly useful for assessing the network properties of a model.

I would like to conclude by noting that a system-based epistemology is probably impossible to construct if one applies systems philosophy and logic in a rigorous manner. The reason is that the process of constructing abstract systems is one of synthesis; a component is defined by its relations with other components, a system is part of a larger system, etc. We can never know enough. But rather than be pessimistic we can follow Churchman's advice and try to understand enough to get on with the problem, even though the enough gets to be very large indeed.

8.10   EPA on Model Documentation Standards

The following set of standards was prepared by the SEAS team at EPA and Ralph Ubico of CDC. It is likely the most complete set of standards ever designed but, in large part, helps explain the success of getting the system built.

8.10.1 Document Review Cycle (Ubico, 1973)

The Module design contractor will prepare a Design Paper to cover the requirements for any capability approved for development of the SEAS computer system. This paper will be reviewed by the programming support contractor, and a sequence of document reviews required to support this flow is described below.

Review Phase	Documents Reviewed
Preliminary Design	Working Paper
Development	Design Paper
	Programming Task Description
Implementation	Program Design Specification
	Technical Memorandum

Preliminary Design Phase. Each Working Paper will be reviewed by the appropriate government Task Monitor and approved for circulation before presentation at a bi-weekly design review meeting. Following this presentation, the SEAS Design Review Board will meet to evaluate the paper in light of the comments it has received.

Agreement will be reached at the Board meeting as to the disposition of the paper. Four subsequent sets of action are possible:

1.   Work on the subtask may terminate with the Working Paper.
2.   If the paper calls for an acceptable action or change to the SEAS computer system, the contractor will be asked to prepare a Design Paper describing these requirements.
3.   If the paper does not affect the SEAS computer system, but is sufficiently significant to warrant further dissemination, the designer's work may lead directly to a formal Technical Memorandum.

4. The designer may prepare both a Design Paper and a Technical Memorandum.

Development Phase.   Module design contractor will prepare a Design Paper to cover the requirements for any capability approved for development of the SEAS computer system. This Paper will be reviewed by the programming support contractor, and a mutually acceptable product will be worked out. The support contractor will then prepare a Programming Task Description describing the programming effort required to implement the capability. The Design Paper and Task Description will then be submitted to the SEAS Design Review Board for review and approval. Following Board action, the support contractor will prepare a detailed Program Design Specification and will begin his programming effort.

Implementation Phase.   Each Technical Memorandum will be reviewed by both the ESD Task Monitor and Project Officer prior to circulation and presentation at a bi-weekly design meeting. After this meeting, the Design Review Board will meet to discuss the comments generated by the Technical Memorandum. The Board will agree on changes to be incorporated into the Technical Memorandum. It will also compare the design criteria described in the Technical Memorandum with the programming requirements detailed in the latest version of the applicable Program Design Specification. The module design contractor may then proceed to publish his Technical Memorandum. At the same time, the support contractor will complete the required programming task and document this work through Program Specifications, Data Specifications, and Users Guides.

8.10.2   Document Identification

All technical documents produced for the SEAS system will have a covering title sheet containing the following elements:

1. Document Type (i.e., Working Paper, Design Paper, etc.).
2. Number of task or subtask under which the document was prepared.
3. Title of document.
4. Document author(s).
5. Contractor identification.
6. Date of document release.

Any document subject to change or to continuing maintenance should also carry its release status in the upper right hand corner. The following designations are recommended for this purpose:

DRAFT COPY
ORIGINAL ISSUE
REVISION 1
REVISION 2
etc.

8.10.3   System Definition Document

The system Definition Document sets forth the overall objectives of the SEAS system and describes the major functions to be performed. The format of the

System Definition Document is unrestricted. In general, it will begin with a statement of purpose, followed by the assumptions and design philosophy on which the system is based. Subsequent sections will identify the models which comprise the system, the functions which these models perform, and the interrelationship requirements which the system must meet. Finally, it should include a definition of contractor responsibilities, cross references to related documents, and a glossary of unique terms. The language used in the System Definition Document is generally that of an Agency administrator, rather than that of the model designer or the data processor.

8.10.4   System Implementation Plan

The System Implementation Plan specifies the milestones to be met in the design, development, and implementation of SEAS capabilities. It will identify each subtask expected to result in a new capability or in a modification to an existing capability. Scheduled dates for document submittals and programming completion will be presented for each subtask. Plans for component testing, system implementation, and system testing will also be presented. A tabular format, similar to the one shown below, will be used for schedule display:

Task No.	Task Description	Contractor	Study Plans			Programming Plans		
			Due Dates			Design Spec.	Prog. Compl.	Prog. Doc.
			WP	DP	TM			
P5.3	Land-Use Stock Model	IRT	11/2	11/20	12/7	11/27	12/17	1/15
P7.5	Metals Stock Model	IRT	10/5	10/24	11/12	10/31	11/20	12/10

A maximum of three weeks will be allowed between the presentation of a Working Paper and the submittal of its resultant Design Paper to the Design Review Board. The corresponding Program Design Specification is to be prepared within a week after authorization to proceed with programming is received from the Board.

8.10.5   Study Document Standards

Working Papers (WP). A Working Paper will be scheduled for submittal early in each subtask and at appropriate times thereafter. The content of each paper will be oriented toward identifying important technical issues and suggesting directions in which research should proceed. The format will be generally informal.

Working Papers should be generated rapidly and require only minimal review by the Task Monitor prior to distribution. They should be designed to elicit comment from within the SEAS project and, therefore, the project team. No Working Paper may be circulated outside the SEAS project without the prior approval of project management.

Design Papers (DP). Design Papers are prepared by SEAS module design contractors to describe the requirements for new or modified capabilities to be developed for the SEAS system. No rigid formats will be specified for these papers. They should be brief and concise, containing only that essential information needed by the Design Review Board for evaluation and by the programming support contractor for preparation of a Program Design Specification.

Guidelines to be followed in the preparation of Design Papers are presented below. An example paper on space heating is presented in Appendix J as a further aid.

1. PROBLEM STATEMENT. Give a general description of the problem and the proposed technical approach.

2. GENERAL DESCRIPTION. Define the purpose of the proposed capability. Summarize the basic concepts and methodology to be employed. Describe the relationship between the proposed capability and other capabilities within the SEAS system; if helpful, present a generalized flowchart depicting this relationship. Provide a bibliography as appropriate to a further understanding of the methodology.

3. SPECIAL PROCESSING REQUIREMENTS. Present exact specifications for all calculations and other special algorithms and functions to be performed. Where appropriate, support this discussion with generalized flowchart indicating the sequence of desired operations. Discuss any special assumptions, restrictions, and considerations which have influenced the design. Specify any desired data update, error handling, and processing accuracy requirements.

4. DATA SOURCES. Identify sources of data required by the model. If the data is not included in the paper, reference its physical location and indicate in what forms it is available (magnetic tape, published tables, etc.). If the data is available in machine readable form, give as much information as known about the file organization, type (decimal, binary, hexadecimal, etc.), size and field definition. If appropriate, include a brief statement as to work expected of the programmer in further defining input requirements.

5. OUTPUT OBJECTIVES. Describe the form and content of the output to be produced by the model. Discuss its potential benefits to SEAS information users.

6. CONCLUSIONS. Include a justification for adding the proposed capability to the SEAS system. Identify known limitations and problems and give recommendations for further developments.

8.10.6   Technical Memoranda

The Technical Memoranda are prepared by a contractor at the conclusion of a subtask or task to document his solution to a particular research or design problem. The technical approach is described, alternatives are discussed, and references are presented. At least one Technical Memorandum will be required for each task. It will be developed to standards normally prescribed for a high quality professional journal.

All Technical Memoranda require the approval of both the Task Monitor and the SEAS Project Officer before being circulated. Review and critique will then be sought from selected experts in the research community, as well as in EPA and other Federal agencies. Since each document will cover a different set of problems, a specific review process will be determined for each Technical Memorandum.

A Technical Memorandum may be made available for public distribution, depending on the quality of the final version and the sensitivity of the problem area. The objective in most cases is to arrive at a consensus document that, upon approval by government management, can be released as a formal technical report.

8.10.7 Programming Document Standards

Programming Task Descriptions (PTD). The Programming Task Description represents a transitional document between the model builder's Design Paper and the programmer's Program Design Specification. Its chief purpose is to estimate the programming and test effort required to implement the capabilities described in a Design Paper. In practice, the Programming Task Description documents the work of the programming support project leader in analyzing the requirements set forth in each Design Paper. The Programming Task Description will be generally narrative in form, but will contain the following kinds of information:

1. A restatement of functions so as to facilitate their division into programmable components.

2. A general discussion of implementation requirements from the programmer's viewpoint.

3. An estimate of the time and cost required to implement the proposed capability.

4. A discussion of the impact of the proposed work on the total system.

5. A determination of the availability status of all intermediate and permanent files required for processing.

Program Design Specifications (PDS). The programming support contractor will be responsible for the preparation of design level flowcharts and specifications. This documentation will form the primary means of communicating design criteria to the programmer.

Design level documentation will begin with the development of macro flowcharts. These flowcharts will start with an overview of the total SEAS prototype system and will ultimately cover all SEAS application program and file management components. The logic displayed will be sufficient to reflect all significant design requirements. The macro chart for each program will depict all input/output functions to be performed in passing data to and from permanent and intermediate data files. It will also identify all major processing steps to be performed by the program and its subroutines. Flowcharting symbols of the American National Standard X35-1970 will be used for all SEAS flowcharts.

A Program Design Specification will be prepared to accompany the macro flowchart for each program to be coded. Normally, this specification will be developed from the Design Paper prepared by the module design contractor. The general form of the Program Design Specification is presented below:

1. PURPOSE. Give a brief description of what the program accomplishes and how it relates to the total SEAS system.

2. PROGRAM ENVIRONMENT. Describe any restrictions or assumptions which affect the environment in which the program will operate.

3. PROCESSING LOGIC. General Logic: Supplement the macro flowchart with a narrative description of the required processing logic. Special Processing: Give the exact specifications for all equations, special algorithms, and functions to be performed.

4. INPUT DESCRIPTION. Give the exact format specifications for all input to be used by the program, supported by data record layout charts. Include information on file organization, blocking, data type and volume, and field definitions.

5. OUTPUT REQUIREMENTS. Give the exact format specifications for all output to be produced by the program, supported by printer layout forms where appropriate. Include information of data storage medium, type and volume.

6. ERROR MESSAGES. Give the exact specifications for all edit checks and the corrections to be performed or error messages to be printed.

7. CROSS REFERENCES. Give the identification number of all programs and files with which this program interacts.

8. APPENDICES. Include the macro flowcharts, record layouts, and, if the program is to be a modification of an existing program, the source listing of the existing program.

Program Specifications (PS). A detailed Program Specification will be prepared by the programming support contractor for each program coded. Preliminary versions of these specifications will be placed in a common notebook as each program is successfully compiled and subjected to component testing. This notebook will become the SEAS Programmers Manual after successful completion of system testing. The form of the Program Specification will be as follows:

1. PURPOSE. State the basic objectives which the program accomplishes.

2. GENERAL DESCRIPTION. Give a general description of the major functions performed by the program. Describe the relationship between the main program and each of its subroutines. Support this discussion with macro flowchart of the overall program.

3. ROUTINE NAME. Give the following information for the main program routine and each of its subroutines: Purpose; Processing Logic (supported by micro flowcharts); Entry Exit Points; Data Communicated (a definition of all arguments passed or obtained from Common); Description of Tables (name, size, purpose).

4. TREE STRUCTURE. If the program includes overlays, include a tree structure showing which routines reside in each branch.

5. SPECIAL ASSUMPTIONS AND CONSTRAINTS. Indicate core requirements and run time estimates. Present any additional information which might prove helpful to a maintenance programmer.

6. CROSS REFERENCES. Give the identification number of all programs and files with which this program interacts.

7. APPENDICES. Include flowcharts, record layouts, and source listings.

Following completion of system testing, all program specifications will be updated to reflect actual prototype system conditions. An overview of the SEAS prototype system will then be added to the front of the notebook, which will then be issued as the SEAS Programmer Manual.

Data Specification (DS). Data Specifications will be prepared by the programming support contractor to document all data records used by the SEAS prototype system. These specifications will be included as a separate section of the Programmers Manual. The general form of each Data Specification is presented below:

1. GENERAL USAGE. Indicate what purpose the file serves in the SEAS system.

2. DATA SOURCE. Identify the program which creates the file. Give appropriate background on original sources.

3. RECORD DESCRIPTION. Give the content, form, type, and length of all fields in the header and data area of each record. Support this discussion with a record layout.

4. FILE ORGANIZATION. Discuss the physical and logical organization of records in the file. Identify all prime and secondary keys used to access records.

5. PHYSICAL CHARACTERISTICS. Give the information needed to access and use the file: location, physical identification, labels, record size, blocking factor, recording mode, and approximate volume in bytes.

6. PROCESSING OF FILE. Indicate which programs modify or use the file after it is created and how it is updated.

7. CROSS REFERENCES. Give the identification number of all programs which interact with this file.

8. APPENDICES. Include record layouts and a glossary of terms.

All Data Specifications will be updated for inclusion in the SEAS Programmers Manual after completion of system testing.

Users Guide (UG). Users Guides will be prepared for each SEAS prototype model after all its associated components have been tested. These guides will be maintained in a common notebook, which will become the SEAS Users Manual on completion of acceptance testing. A SEAS system overview, written from the user's viewpoint, will be included in the front of the manual.

Each Users Guide will clearly describe all system options available to the user. These will be expressed in non-technical terms so that users other than data processing personnel may exercise the system. The form of each guide will be as follows:

1. INTRODUCTION. Describe the purpose of the model and the functions it performs.

2. OPTIONS. List the input and output options available to the user at time of operation.

3.   INPUT.   Give the name of any files which must be called in by this model for processing. Present and describe the run deck setups, including all JCL, program directives, and data cards.

4.   PROCEDURE.   Give any information which might be helpful to the user in submitting his job to the computation center.

5.   OUTPUT.   Present and describe sample outputs which can be expected for each option chosen.

6.   ERROR MESSAGES.   Present and interpret all program error messages and major system return codes which may be encountered by the user.

7.   RESTART PROCEDURES.   If provided by the program clearly describe procedures to be followed for restart.

8.   CROSS REFERENCE.   Identify all Program and Data Specifications applicable to the model.

9.   APPENDICES.   Provide a glossary of unique terms.

Test Documentation. Working Papers will be prepared by the programming support contractor to document the procedures followed for each component and system test. These Papers will describe the scenario used and the output produced in response to each set of input stimuli. The procedures followed for output data validation, error condition response, and input/output option demonstration will be included. Test decks and a set of test output listings will be maintained on file following each test.

Run Books. Master listings of data files, program compilations and output reports will be maintained in run books at the support contractor's facility. Reduced 8½ by 11 inch copies of all formatted reports will be periodically supplied to the Project Officer for inclusion in a central file accessible to the SEAS project.

8.11   Lee on Modeling Sins and Guidelines (Lee, 1973)

8.11.1   *"Seven Sins of Large-Scale Models":*

Hypercomprehensiveness. Excessive comprehensiveness has been partly the result of historical accident. The dominant pattern in city planning emphasized the need for comprehensive thinking and a comprehensive master plan in order to guide metropolitan growth, prevent large-scale inefficiencies and negative neighborhood effects, and preserve open space. Comprehensive models were an inadvertent way to continue this school of thought while at the same time making planning less the province of architects.

Another historical accident was the expansion in scope of the field. Everything seemed to be an urban problem, and everything seemed interrelated; the whole world was a jumble of secondary and iterative side effects. Some way of integrating it all was needed without giving up anything (having just discovered the interrelationships existed, we did not want them to ignore them intentionally), and computers and models held out this promise.

The overly comprehensive structure of existing large-scale models has two aspects: (1) the models were designed to replicate too complex a system in a single shot, and (2) they were expected to serve too many purposes at the same time. . . .

Grossness. Ironically, while the models often sank under the weight of excessive data that were required to provide microscopic detail, the actual level of detail was much too coarse to be of use to most policymakers . . .

Hungriness. Data requirements of any model that purports to realistically replicate a specific city are enormous. . . .

Wrongheadedness. Perhaps the least discussed problem in modeling is the deviation between claimed model behavior and the equations or statements that actually govern model behavior. The impression is often given that the structure used in a given model is adaptable to any kind of system performance that might be encountered, but in fact, a specific model may absolutely preclude some alternatives and combinations, and it may substantially distort many others. The deeper problem is that relationships between variables other than the specified ones are implicit in the model and often difficult to perceive . . .

Complicatedness. As the number of components (e.g., variables) increases in a model, the number of potential interactions between them increases as the square of the number of components . . .

Mechanicalness. All large-scale models must be implemented on a digital computer, and the machine may be simply a fast device for carrying out the required calculations and decisions trees or it may introduce additional problems. Aside from the difficulties of preparing and debugging a program which will represent the model correctly (no small feat), the computer has two characteristics that must be explicitly dealt with: (1) a solution which is "exact" is effectively impossible, because there is always some amount of rounding error; and (2) all solutions are achieved iteratively, i.e., one step at a time.

Expensiveness. The cost of most of the modeling efforts can run into the millions of dollars. While it is difficult to identify the specific costs of any particular model, a rule-of-thumb estimate for a full-scale land-use model is probably at least $500,000.

8.11.2 Guidelines for Model Building

From the inspection and evaluation of previous large-scale models and their flaws, a few rough guidelines can be derived for designing future modeling efforts.

Balance. A balance should be obtained between theory, objectivity, and intuition. Excessive concern for theory results in a loss of contact with the policy problem, but policy cannot be formulated well without a strong theoretical foundation. Overemphasis on objectivity is one of the major mistakes of the large models, and results in an empty-headed empiricism; on the other hand, most social questions have a quantitative component and require quantitative information to resolve. Some kind of wisdom or judgment is also essential, but intuition in

the absence of theory and methodology is useless for dealing with urban problems. Both traditional comprehensive planning and large-scale modeling have
been significantly lacking in theory.

Purpose. Start with a particular policy problem that needs solving, not a
methodology that needs applying (master planning is a methodology, in this
sense). Work backward from the problem, matching specific methods with specific purposes and obtaining just enough information to be able to provide
adequate policy guidance. Over kill is not only wasteful, it is almost always too
late. Long-range planning means evaluating immediate decisions with regard to
long-run consequences, rather than constructing grand plans or big models.

Simplicity. Build only very simple models. Complicated models do not work
very well if at all, they do not fit reality very well, and they should not be used in
any case because they will not be understood. The skill and discipline of the
modeler is in figuring out what to disregard in building his model.

8.12   Pack on The Use of Urban Models (Pack, 1974)

This paper reports the results of a mail survey sent to nearly 1500 planning
agencies to determine the extent to which urban models are being used.
The survey was undertaken as part of a larger research effort aimed at
identifying and analyzing the use of urban models in urban policymaking.

Urban models have been defined as those models which comprehend the basic
activities of the urban area, i.e., business activity and jobs, households, and
housing, government and public policy. Models which deal with only a single
major part of the scenario may also be included. We do wish to exclude, however,
operations research type models of specific activities or operations, e.g., bus
scheduling models, etc. The area may be either a city or a metropolitan area,
including any of the comprehensive or major subsector models which have been
developed for urban areas. Included are those models which attempt to explain/
predict the aggregate level of an activity for an urban area, and those which
attempt to distribute these activities to sub-parts of the urban area.

8.12.1   Scope of a Survey

While the overall research effort will be concerned with determining the extent to
which models have been used to guide policy, the conditions under which they are
most likely to be used, and their impact on the quality of policy, the primary
purpose of the mail survey was to identify the universe of model users and the
types of models in use; to determine how widespread model use is. Thus, the first
survey question concerned model use. Agencies were asked to describe their
activity in this regard as follows:

currently using models
currently developing models for use
currently considering the use of models

not now considering the use of models
considered models in the past, but rejected the idea
have been unsuccessful in an attempt to develop a model
developed a model, but abandoned its use
have never considered using models

Since it is possible that a response could fall into more than one of the categories, we summarize the responses as follows (see Table 8.12-1).

1. All agencies "currently using a model"—This group could include any combination of responses including this one, e.g., currently *using* a model *and* currently developing a model;
2. All agencies "currently *developing* a model" *but not* "currently using a model"—This group might include combinations of this response with, e.g., "considered a model in the past, but rejected the idea";
3. All agencies "currently considering the use of a model," but not using or developing one; and
4. All agencies not included in the first three groups, those who "have never considered using a model," "developed a model, but abandoned its use," etc.

8.12.2 User and Non-User Agencies

Table 8.12-2 shows the distribution of agencies within each of the model use categories (read across, rather than down; it also shows the distribution of model use categories for each type of agency). The major model *user* is the regional agency, particularly the Council of Governments (COG). Although city agencies are somewhat more numerous among the survey respondents, they comprise only 21% of users compared with regional agencies which comprise 35% of users. Special purpose agencies, on the other hand, although only a very small proportion of total respondents, also make up 21% of the total model user group.

Cities do make up, however, a larger proportion of the agencies with models in development or considering model use: cities make up 32% of the agencies with models in development and 40% of the agencies considering the use of models. The major difference between the users, on the one hand, and the agencies developing or considering the development of models on the other, is the increased relative importance of the cities in the latter two groups and the decreased importance of the special purpose agencies.

Table 8.12-1. *Current Model Use*

Description of Use	Number	Percent
a. Currently using, etc.	146	19%
b. Currently developing, etc.	63	8
c. Considering use, etc.	95	12
d. All other	478	61
Total respondents	782	100%

Table 8.12-2. Use of Models, by Type of Agency

Type of Agency	Total	Using			Developing			Considering Use			Other		
		#	%	%AG	#	%	%AG	#	%	%AG	#	%	%AG
City	283	30	21	11	20	32	7	38	40	13	195	41	69
County	142	26	18	18	12	19	8	12	13	9	92	19	65
City-County	25	4	3	16	2	3	8	5	5	20	14	3	56
Region-SMSA	265	51	35	19	23	37	9	31	33	12	160	33	60
COG	(230)	(48)	(33)	(21)	(21)	(33)	(9)	(26)	(27)	(11)	(135)	(28)	(59)
Special Purpose	51	31	21	61	4	6	8	5	5	10	11	2	22
State Hway.	(33)	(22)	(15)	(67)	(1)	(1)	(3)	(3)	(3)	(9)	(7)	(1)	(21)
Urban Trans.	(15)	(8)	(5)	(53)	(3)	(5)	(20)	(2)	(2)	(13)	(2)	(<1)	(13)
Other	(3)	(1)	(1)	(33)	0	0	0	0	0	0	(2)	(<1)	(67)
State	(16)	4	3	25	2	3	12	4	4	25	6	1	38
Total	782	146	100%		63	100%		95	100%		478	98%	

%AG is the percentage of the total agencies of that type, e.g., 11% of cities are model users, as are 18% of counties and 13% of cities are considering model use, as are 9% of counties, etc.
The % column indicates the percentage of the model use category comprised by each agency, e.g., 21% of all users are cities, and 18% are counties: 40% of agencies considering use are cities and 13 are counties, etc.

If we look at the residual group, "other"—those not now using or considering the use of models, the city agencies are the largest single component.

If we look at the agencies, rather than at the use categories, we find that the heaviest model use occurs among special purpose agencies, in particular the state highway boards, while the agencies least likely to be using models are the cities. Only 11% of all the city respondents were using models, but 61% of special purpose agencies were users. All the other agencies—counties, regions, states— make up 15% to 25% of the total. Looking at it another way, the largest proportion of non-users, i.e., not now using, nor planning to use models, occurs in the city agencies (69%) closely followed by the county agencies (65%). Only 22% of the special purpose agencies, however, fall in the non-user group.

The relatively small representation of cities and the greater representation of regional and special purpose agencies among current model users is not startling in view of the sources of simulation for model construction and the subject emphasis of most models. The U.S. Department of Transportation has been one of the major funders of modeling efforts and has encouraged the development of comprehensive transportation and land use models on a regional basis. That is, of course, not a complete explanation of the differences observed and it remains to be determined why those agencies providing the planning funds for cities did not provide such stimulus and why the cities themselves were not more active.

8.12.3   Uses of Urban Models

The alleged or potential uses of urban models are very broad indeed. Our questionnaire included as use choices the two most prevalent in the literature: projection and plan evaluation. In addition, we include an "other uses" category, but relatively few agencies checked it. Table 8.12-3 shows actual uses to which models are being put by the user agencies and the planned uses of those agencies with models in development.

For both groups projection is substantially more important than plan evaluation. Nearly 80% of the models in use are used for projection (includes models used for both projection *and* plan evaluation), while only 52% are being used for plan

Table 8.12-3.   *Actual or Planned Uses of Urban Models*

	In User Agencies		In Developer Agencies	
Use	Number of Models	Pct. of Models Reported (335)	Number of Models	Pct. of Models Reported (88)
Projection only	141	42.1	25	28.4
Plan evaluation only	48	14.3	16	18.2
Proj. and plan. eval.	126	37.6	29	33.0
Other	16	4.8	12	13.6
Not reported	4	1.2	6	6.8
Total	335	100.0	88	100.0

evaluation (also includes models being used for plan evaluation and projection). Although it is true among agencies developing models that a greater percentage of the models will be used for projection than for plan evaluation, the proportion used for projection is far less than for the models already in use. But it should be noted that since relatively more agencies in the development stage do not report intended use, the figures are not directly comparable. The observed difference is so large, however, that it is certainly not totally attributable to the differences in the "not reported" category.

This finding is certainly consistent with earlier evidence on the use of models. (Boyce et al., 1970) Whereas major emphasis in the model literature is on the potential usefulness of the model in evaluating alternative plans and policies, the principal use appears to be a kind of impact analysis—which could certainly be interpreted as a projection—of a particular plan. However, this emphasis on projection is not obvious from the types of models in use or development. Our survey results show that land use and transportation models are far more numerous than straight population or employment projection models.

8.12.4   Usefulness of Urban Models

The questionnaire asked two questions about the usefulness of the models. The first concerned the absolute usefulness and the second the relative usefulness,

Table 8.12-4.   *Evaluations of Urban Models*

	User Agencies		Developer Agencies	
Absolute Evaluation	Number of Models	Pct. of Models Reported (335)	Number of Models	Pct. of Models Reported (88)
Very useful	184	54.9	27	30.7
Moderately useful	83	24.8	9	10.4
Not useful	3	0.9	2	2.3
Not reported	65	19.4	50	56.8
Total	335	100.0	88	100.2
Relative Evaluation				
More useful than alternatives	180	53.7	30	34.1
About as useful as alternatives	34	10.1	3	3.4
Not as useful as alternatives	7	2.1	2	2.3
Not reported	114	34.0	53	60.2
Total	335	99.9	88	100.0

i.e., relative to alternative modes of analysis or projection. The responses to these questions are shown in Table 8.12-4.

Our impression from the published literature is that models have not been very useful (the general feeling might even be that models have been useless; see Lee, 1973; Brewer, 1973). Table 8.12-4 gives a very different picture indeed. Among the current model users, we find that more than half of the models are rated as very useful. Moreover, they are also rated as more useful than available alternatives. On the other hand, fewer than 1% of these models are indicated as not useful and only 2% as not as useful as alternatives. The difference, however, may well be temporal. The comments of Lee and Brewer were cogent and for the most part valid at the time. Hopefully their criticism contributed to a better understanding and wiser use of simulation which was reflected at the later date.

We have indicated earlier that many model using agencies also have models in the development state. The 19% of models for which no absolute evaluation as to usefulness is reported is precisely this group of models in development. Thus, a more accurate appraisal of the usefulness of models in use is obtained by removing this group. When this is done we find that of the 270 models actually in use,

> 184 or 68% are very useful,
> 83 or 31% are moderately useful,
> and 3 or 1% are not useful.

Similarly, if we remove the 65 models in development from the relative usefulness table, we find

> 180 or 67% more useful than alternatives,
> 34 or 12% about as useful as alternatives,
> 7 or 3% not as useful as alternatives,
> and 49 or 18% no comparison reported.

Thus, about two-thirds of the models in use are judged by the agencies using them to be very useful—nearly all the others are moderately useful. Moreover, about two-thirds are also judged to be more useful tools than available alternatives.

8.12.5 Summary

These findings suggest that additional inquiry is warranted. It is clear from their titles that most of the persons who filled out the questionnaires belong in the technical-research category. It might be very useful to follow up this survey with one addressed to other types of users, that is, policymakers, elected officials, and the heads of operation agencies.

Afterthoughts

The format for this book, which placed the summary and conclusions at the beginning, was adopted for the benefit of those who might wish to determine the essence of the contents before plunging into details. Although that format precludes a summary and conclusion here, where either or both might normally appear, some sort of recapitulation nevertheless seems in order.

The intent of the book has been to document ways in which problems attendant on the development and use of large-scale models can be addressed. Obviously, we could not present solutions to all such problems. In fact, the examples given and the solutions suggested can only be expected to point the way for future progress.

This book indicates that there is an increasing number of large-scale policy models in use. This is not solely because our ability to build and apply such models has improved; a more important factor is that in the United States, and other nations as well, there is an increasing realization that problems of policy are too complex and too interrelated to be solved by existing organizations using traditional methods. Short-term, quick fix solutions are too likely to aggravate, or even create, worse problems in the future. Perceiving the difficulties this creates for the policymaker, several funding agencies are operating, or are developing, large-scale policy models to explore possible conditions for from a decade in the future to beyond the year 2000. We are pleased that these agencies claim that such models are actually being used for decision making.

This recent development and use of large-scale policy models is the result of the environmental, economic, and energy crises of the early seventies. Now the Departments of Agriculture, Interior, Commerce, and Labor, as well as the Federal Energy Administration, the Energy Research and Development Agency, and the Environmental Protection Agency, are all said to posses operating models and the analytic capability to make use of them (Library of Congress, 1975; Chestnut, 1975).

This change, of course, required that the perceived need for large-scale policy models be accompanied by concomitant improvements in theory, hardware, software, and data. It is also interesting to note that the failure of some early models to meet the overenthusiastic claims of their protagonists illuminated problem areas and directed work toward solutions. As a result, the art and science of modeling have progressed to the point that many of those extravagant claims can now be met, and the large sums

183

of money required for the gestation, care, and feeding of large models can be openly discussed and competitively sought by potential users.

However, the use of large models for policy studies and as aids to decision making is just beginning. Although great progress has been made, such models are still a long way from being what they need to be.

Large-scale policy models have survived years of political carping and professional cynicism; if they survive a few more—and are not oversold by their supporters—our policymakers should have available a tool capable of giving them greatly improved insight concerning the possible impacts of their policies well before those impacts are reported in the newspapers—or used against them by their political opponents.

Appendix I

Brief Descriptions of Selected Models

We have two purposes in presenting the short descriptions of selected models in this Appendix. Obviously the primary one is to give examples of the kind of models with which this book is concerned. The secondary one is to illustrate different ways models have been documented (see Chapter 6). This latter purpose is accomplished by presenting descriptions of SEAS taken from three different sources. For details of the SEAS project see Appendix II-4.

AI-1 SEAS (Strategic Environmental Assessment System)

AI-1.1 SEAS according to House

This is a brief natural-language description of SEAS prepared by the senior author of this book, who was in charge of the SEAS development project.

The SEAS represents a combination of three approaches that will be described in more detail in Appendix II-4. It has the unweighted display output of the SD/Rand model, the use of existing partial models as in HPMP, and the top-down systems analysis of GEM. It is designed to be relatively flexible and to forecast the results of variations in assumptions (around a described base case) to produce a number of alternative futures.

The original conceptual structure of the system is relatively straightforward. Various assumptions as to the population level and economy are fed into the model. The "Process" section of the model includes all the activities that go into the extraction, production, distribution, consumption, and disposal of goods and services. These activities use "Stocks," which consist of raw materials, land, energy, and the like, and at the same time, they produce "Residuals." These residuals have an "Effect" on the human and natural system and produce a "Reaction" that feeds back to the "Process" sector and becomes part of the next

185

iteration of the model. This system is relatively self-contained and, once the original set of assumptions is specified, will iterate to 1985 (or further if desired) without human intervention. However, the input procedure allows timed assumptions so that certain actions do not take place until specified years of the model run (e.g., the timing of abatement strategies). Of course, the model could be interrupted and interfaced with new policy inputs, but generally it is not designed to operate in this fashion. It is clearly comprehensive, in an economic-physical fashion, because it includes a broad range of topics of the total system.

AI-1.2 SEAS according to Chestnut and Sheridan

Another brief description of SEAS is taken from a report entitled "Modeling Large Scale Systems at National and Regional Levels" (Chestnut, 1975). This author supports a short natural-language description with a flow diagram.

In late 1972, the Washington Environmental Research Center of EPA began work on [SEAS] for use in forecasting the state of the U.S. environment. Design goals for the system included the projection of preexisting demographic, economic and technological estimates to forecast environmental conditions on a national scale, with the capability of handling smaller jurisdictions, if necessary, to 1985. Another design objective was to predict the secondary effects and reactions which might result from the impact of enforcement of various environmental quality levels on economic, social, and ecological conditions.

House described the Strategic Environmental Assessment System (SEAS) Model, shown in Figure AI-1 in a general overview, as providing a capability for testing the impacts of alternative scenarios on the environment with a time horizon of 10 to 20 years. The geometric figures represent assessment modules; the arrows and dotted lines represent the connective links between the modules.

Change agents include population, economic, technologic demand, and other factors which are subject to change with time, as well as with feedback from the process. *Processes* include production of goods and services and use is made of the INFORUM relationships here. *Stocks* are the supply of natural or man-produced resources which are effectively available for use by the processes. *Residuals* include outputs from the processes of a sociopolitical, economic, or environmental character that have an impact on the population. *Effects* are the results of the final discharge of the residuals; and *Reactions* are subsequent responses to the effects of recycled residuals which may cause feedbacks that may result in future alterations to the change agents.

Although SEAS has not yet been fully completed, it has provided useful responses for various specific "what-if" questions for numerous governmental agencies concerned with air and water quality. It was due to become operational in mid 1975.

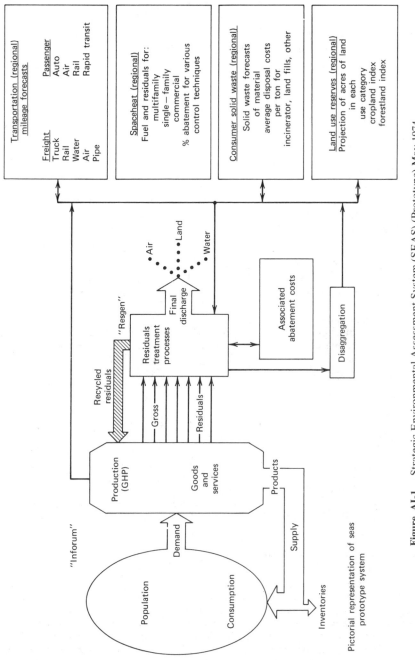

Figure AI-1. Strategic Environmental Assessment System (SEAS) (Prototype) May 1974.

AI-1.3   SEAS According to the Library of Congress

A quite different method of documenting models was employed in another report (Library of Congress, 1975). SEAS was documented in that publication as follows.

Strategic Environmental Assessment System (SEAS) Distinguishing Characteristics

Major purposes. To provide a comprehensive means for evaluating the longrange impact of trends, processes, activities and policies on the environment including: national and regional levels; multimedia (air, water, and solid wastes) pollution generators and effects; costs for abatement, raw materials constraints, materials flow and energy budgets. In phase IV, extension is being made to include energy, economic and environmental trade-offs.

Scope. Environmental and national.

Principal investigator. Dr. Peter House, Assistant Director, Office of R&D U.S. Environmental Protection Agency, Washington, D.C. 20460.

Status. First three phases completed and operational. Phase four, which updates and adds new capabilities to the model, now being worked on.

Major funding source. Environmental Protection Agency internal funds.

Time horizon. 10–15 years (1975 to 1990).

Major data sources. Same as INFORUM (See INFORUM Model); also regional economic data Bureau of Census, Department of Commerce; emission data from EPA; engineering cost data from EPA; resources data from Bureau of Mines, U.S. Geologic Survey; energy data from Federal Energy Administration; technological and process data from a variety of sources.

Major hardware/software features. SEAS runs on an IBM 370/158 and is programmed in FORTRAN IV. It can be run from a remote terminal.

Major references:

1. Unpublished documentation from SEAS are Phase II and Phase III Final Reports, EPA, 1974 and 1975.
2. House, Peter W. and Gene R. Tyndall. *Models and Policymaking*. Chapter 2. Appendix *In* A Guide to Models in Government Planning and Operations. U.S. Environmental Protection Agency. Office of Research and Development, Washington, D.C. (Contract No. 68-01-0788).
3. Operating Manuals: SEAS User Manuals, SEAS Data Specifications Manual, E.P.A., Office of Research & Development.

Description of the SEAS Model

SEAS is a system of special-purpose models linked to a macroeconometric model and an interindustry input-output of the United States economy. The other models in the system use the economic forecasts to estimate pollutant levels and associated abatement costs, pollution abatement benefits, energy demands, solid waste generation and associated recycling, land use requirements, mineral use and virgin stock status, processed ore inventories, transportation demand, and relative commodity price changes. The model is presently used to simulate forecasts of other government agencies in order to predict pollution loadings, costs of clean-up and associated economic impacts.

1. The Economic Models

The SEAS economic forecasts are at three levels. The first, the macro-economic forecast, provides the general parameter projection on an annual basis through 1985. These general values include employment, general production sector output volumes, personal consumption, disposable income, capital investment, etc. and allow projections of the general subaccounts of the GNP. These assumptions come from Bureau of Labor Statistics and the Commerce Department. The macro-economic model used in SEAS was developed and is maintained by Chase Econometric Associates (CEA).

The second level of forecast is the calculation of interactions among industries in order to meet the levels of output in the demand forecast of the macro model. This economic input/output model provides the economic projections for each year for 185 sectors of the economy, and statistics for each sector such as employment, output sold for final demand, total output, durable goods and construction expenditures, export, imports and inventories. The model form, input/output, is a rigorous system that provides great detail and balanced accounting of values that can act as physical goods flow among the sectors and to the final consumers. The specific model in SEAS is the INFORUM model maintained by a staff at the University of Maryland and linked to the macroeconometric model by CEA.

A third level of forecast detail of economic activity is produced by the SEAS design and systems teams and deals with procedures that break the specific (185) industry forecasts into richer information where required for specific analysis questions; it uses official estimates of the Departments of Commerce, Agriculture and Interior for more detailed economic activity levels. This last level of detail in SEAS is easily expanded and now represents three times the detail available from the INFORUM sectors.

2. ABATE, The Abatement Cost Feedback Model

ABATE estimates the investment, operating and maintenance costs associated with abating the emissions of air and water pollutants by each economic sector. It also feeds back to INFORUM the increased monetary and goods demands placed by pollution control investment and operating purchases on the industrial sectors which supply construction materials and labor, abatement equipment, chemicals for abatement, energy sources, and operating manpower requirements. INFORUM uses this information to rebalance its forecasts of sector economic activity. Non-industrial consumption and disposal processes, such as utilities, sewage treatment plants, and commercial and residential spaceheating consumption, are handled by INFORUM, RESGEN, and ABATE in concert, in the same manner as the industrial sectors.

3. SOLIDWASTE, The Solid Waste-Recycling Model

SOLIDWASTE estimates the amounts of solid wastes from nonindustrial sources, the expected method of disposal, and the costs associated with each method. For incineration and open burning disposal methods, it also estimates the annual levels of air pollutant emissions. Recycling levels are applied to the product classes which comprise significant elements of the solid waste stream to calculate total amounts of materials available for recycling and the levels actually recycled.

4. STOCKS, The Material Reserves Model

After the economic models have derived the annual total demand for a number of fuels and mineral ores, and the recycling model has forecast the degree to which demand for some materials can be met by reprocessed materials, SEAS applies the STOCKS model to provide detail on raw material sources, levels of economic reserves depletion, and relative production cost increases under a wide range of possible inventory/export/import assumptions. It uses official estimates of the Department of the Interior for reserves.

5. ENERGY, The Energy Use Model

ENERGY estimates energy use by fuel category based on the INFORUM forecasts of economic activity for 185 sectors of the economy. For each fuel category, it also indicates whether the fuel is used for combustion or as a raw material in six user categories—industrial, commercial, residential, transportation, electric utility consumption, and electricity generation. The model provides detailed accounting of all fuel usage (and implicit fuel losses) in a consistent measure (quadrillions of BTU's) based strictly on the values developed in the economic forecast model, INFORUM.

6. RESGEN, The Residual Generation Model

RESGEN estimates annual emissions of air and water pollutants and of solid wastes for the most significant polluting industries. It estimates first the potential environmental emissions before abatement, and then the emissions actually reaching the environment; the latter depends on the degree of pollution abatement in each sector and its subprocesses. The released emissions include not only the untreated primary pollutants, but also the significant secondary pollutants produced by the pollution treatment processes themselves (e.g., sludges).

7. TRANSPORT, The Transportation Model

TRANSPORT forecasts the demand for automobiles, buses, trucks, railroads, and airplanes in terms of miles traveled for both passenger and freight transportation purposes using the Department of Transportation forecasted totals of miles traveled. It estimates the annual volume of controlled emissions produced by mobile sources.

8. LAND USE, The Land Use Model

LAND USE forecasts amounts of land used in broad categories as a function of forecasts of economic activity. For non-point sources of pollution, such as agriculture, construction, forestry, mining and drilling, and urban runoff plus naturally occurring pollution sources, it forecasts levels of air, water and solid waste pollutant emissions.

9. REGION, *The Assignment of Processes and Associated Activities to Subnational Regions Model*

In order to enrich the forecast of economic and environmental impacts, this model provides a forecast of distributions of industry outputs and the associated environmental emissions to a number of geographical subdivisions. The subdivisions include states, SMSA (Standard Metropolitan Statistical Areas), river basins, air quality control areas and "basic economic areas." The OBERS projections developed by the Department of Commerce and the USDA are employed in this model.

A most important element is the analyses that are performed outside the computer system. These are made up of two elements; (1) the analysis used to make the experimental design of alternate scenarios to modify the specific input data for each scenario and (2) the analysis of the computer outputs to show impacts of scenario changes, and hence insight as to probable effects of specific national policies and regulations plus public and institutional reactions.

Major Conclusions and Recommendations

The model has been used inside and outside the Environmental Protection Agency. Within EPA, its key use has been for developing the 1975 cost of clean air and clean water for Congress.

Within EPA:

1. If the nation continues to pursue the time-table for air and water clean-up the investment in public control devices will add a positive stimulus to the economy and improve unemployment situations.

2. Measures of water quality of 99 river basins in the nation have been developed. These measures have been compared with water quality measures for 1975 and 1985 (with full legislative clean-up assumed for 1985). On the average, the results show a dramatic improvement in water quality. However, a number of river basins have been identified where the improvement is minimal.

3. EPA has used the model to estimate primary and secondary industrial sludge emanating from various industrial sources. A larger industrial sludge estimate than originally anticipated was obtained. In return, EPA was able to check some of the parametric values in the SEAS model and consequently modify some of these values.

Outside EPA:

1. The Council on Environmental Quality used the SEAS system to project pollution in their 1974 report to the President. One major conclusion reached indicated that the four western regions of the United States (out of the ten federal regions in the nation) had a disproportionate share of water pollution in 1971 but by 1985 their share of water pollutants is expected to be closer to their share of the population.

2. Thirteen stringent energy conservation measures thought to be the ones most likely to substantially reduce the recent growth rate in energy consumption

were selected for analysis. These included such items as insulation, increased public transit uses, lighter autos, changes in freight handling patterns, etc. A 15% reduction in energy consumption in 1985 was attained with these measures. Concurrently, air pollution decreases ranged from 12 to 26 percent (depending on the type of pollutant), and water pollutants remained the same.

Summary of Major Limitations

1.   It has been argued that the energy component of the model needs to have a better interaction between supply and demand; the role of price is not sufficiently taken into account in the supply-demand process.

2.   For most changes in technology that affect other modules in the total system, hand adjustments must be made. This can significantly increase the analysis time and effort of model users and can create a risk that some effects of technological change may fail to be incorporated in these other modules.

3.   Policy options are now phrased in terms of tons of pollution emissions, costs of control and associated economic impacts rather than in terms of human health and property values, esthetics, and recreation.

AI-2   STAR (Short-Haul Transportation Analysis for Research and Development)

This and the next three models are described by our senior author.

Soon after the formation of EPA it became evident that much of the battle against pollution would have to be fought at the local level. To reduce and prevent pollution while carrying out their numerous other responsibilities, local governments needed a rather sophisticated trade-off methodology. The RAND Corporation had developed, for the Department of Transportation, a technique it called STAR, the core of which was a "scorecard" of alternatives from which the decision maker could choose. The philosophy behind this approach is relatively simple. The designers of the system believed that most of the transfer functions between segments of the system were unknown, making any kind of comprehensive analysis impossible. At the same time, most policy decisions were complex and required taking into consideration a large number of disparate factors. Consequently the decision display is seen as a matrix (or scorecard) of information; the rows are strategies and the columns are effects. No standardized methodology is utilized to obtain the data to fill a particular cell as long as the method is consistent across strategies. The policy maker is presented with a completed matrix in which each strategy sector is a complete analysis of the information he requires to make a decision. This technique, therefore, allows the user to specify the weights between the various rows and between the cells in specific columns. In this way each policy maker can derive his own "best" strategy based on his personal assessment of that portion of the situation with which he is most familiar. Its comprehensiveness is present solely in the display technique but satisfies our present analysis in that it can be used to analyze strategies that are quite broad in scope.

AI-3   HPMP (Harris–Putman Model Package)

Several years ago Britton Harris suggested that the only proper way to construct a large-scale urban development model was to build the various submodels carefully and then combine them into a comprehensive whole. A project was launched to take some of the better-known and used partial models of land use and transportation, wed these to environmental models, and convert them so that they could be easily transferred throughout the country. The system was not, however, designed with an overall system in mind.

From a theoretical point of view, the methodology is fairly standard. An exogenous model or source is used to project the regional or local share of such factors as population, industrial growth, GNP, and the like. At this stage the various submodels that have been designed to be spatially sensitive are called into play; they distribute people and land uses throughout the study area. This distribution, based on the public and private activities carried out in these areas, produces, in addition to the needs of the area, a certain amount of residuals, or pollutants. These residuals are then considered in the light of the natural assimilative capacity of the area, resulting in calculated ambient environmental levels. For details see Appendix II-2.

AI-4   GEM (General Environmental Model)

Of all the models discussed in this book, GEM is one of the most complex and has demanded considerable conceptual work in the last several years. GEM is an attempt to construct a truly comprehensive and general model of the social system at a level of aggregation roughly equivalent to the SMSA (Standard Metropolitan Statistical Area). It is meant to be largely a parametric model that can be loaded with data to simulate specific areas, but with national averages provided as default values where new data is not specified. The system includes economic, social, environmental, and political factors, with specified functional relationships between many of the individual sectors.

The model was designed to be used as a game, a man-machine simulation, or (in all but the public sector) an all-machine simulation. It functions as a computer program that relates the effects of various decisions in discrete portions of the simulated region to each other and reports these outcomes in various bookkeeping and indicator formats. On the basis of these outcomes for each iteration, new decisions can be made to drive the total system (or portions thereof) in a direction judged most desirable by the user.

The sector theory is a description of the subject matter input of the model. It does not specify the numerous interrelations extant in the algorithms, but does show the system as a series of possible decision points for the allocation of power, money, and time. The algorithms (embedded in the system) and the human inputs of the user allocate these resources based on specified criteria, implicitly or explicitly determined.

For illustrative purposes, let us trace one branch of one sector. The total system is divided into the man-made and natural systems. The man-made is further divided into economic, social, and public sectors. The economic sector has available to it the resources of time, power, and capital. In the case of capital, it can be used to invest, save, transfer to other sectors, or expand. If it is expanded, it can be used to purchase goods and services, to buy land, buildings, materials, and equipment or to hire people. If it is used in the area of land, it can be used to purchase, sell, or rent developed or undeveloped land.

This accounting paradigm of the total system is a useful first step in building a taxonomy of human and man-environment relationships. It catalogs the various algorithms required in the GEM system. (GEM is described in more detail in Appendix II-5).

AI-5   SOS (State of the System)

This model, described at some length in Appendix II-7, attempts to replicate a self-adjusting system that predicts the ability of a group to accomplish a planned goal, given a level of resources and their desired life style. The model only requires specification of the desired or anticipated growth rates of the study area and the value of the quality-of-life (QOL) sector.

The public and private sectors in this model are disaggregated and each subsector, as well as the population of the locale, is assigned an expected growth rate. The growth rates are tied to specified drains on the resources available to the area, and the outputs produced are compared to a defined QOL sector. If the desired goals have not been met, the model self-adjusts after each iteration.

AI-6   PIES (Project Independence Evaluation System)

The report (Library of Congress, 1975) quoted in Section A-1.3 documented 20 models in all. However, as this book is intended to cover only models developed by government agencies, only SEAS, PIES and two other of those models BLS and NIRAP, will be covered here.

Project Independence Evaluation System (PIES) Distinguishing Characteristics

Major purposes: To assess the effect of alternative policies on the supply, demand, and price of all forms of energy in the United States.
   Scope: Energy and national (on a regionalized basis).
   Principal investigator: William W. Hogan, Office of Quantitative Methods, Federal Energy Administration, 12th and Pennsylvania Ave., N.W., Washington, D.C. 20461, (202) 961-8462.
   Status: Completed and operational. Major updating effort begun.
   Major funding source: Federal Energy Administration budget appropriations.
   Time horizon: 1977–1985.
   Major data sources: Data was obtained from task force collaborators from the U.S. Dept. of Commerce, U.S. Dept. of Transportation, U.S. Dept. of Labor, U.S. Dept. of the Interior, Federal Power Commission, U.S. Environmental Protection Agency, Atomic Energy Commission, Water Resources Council and National Petroleum Council. Contract support and data were also provided by: American Management Systems; Data Resources, Inc.; LaRue, Moore & Schafer; Bechtel Corp.; Battelle Memorial Institute; Denver Research Institute; Mathematica, Inc.; Engineering Sciences Institute; General Electric Company Inc.; Gas Development Corporation; and PACE Company.
   Major hardware/software features: PIES is operated on CDC 6600 and IBM 370/168 computers. Supply and demand models are primarily in Fortran. The Intergrating Model (IM) makes use of a standard matrix generator, and mathematical programming and report-writer software packages.
   Major references:
Project Independence Report, Federal Energy Administration, Washington, D.C., GPO No. 4118-00028, November 1974.
"Emergency Energy Capacity Model," Users Manual, Bonner and Moore Associates Inc., April 22, 1974.
Hogan, William E., Energy Policy Models for Project Independence. Federal Energy Administration. Office of the Deputy Assistant Administrator for Analysis. June 18, 1975. (Discussion paper.)

Description of the Project Independence Evaluation System (PIES) Model

Project Independence is the generic title describing the activities organized through the Federal Energy Administration in the continuing development and implementation of a national energy policy for the United States. The system generates planning estimates depicting possible states of the energy system with explicit recognition of the effect of relative prices, the potential for fuel substitution, and the technological constraints which inhibit the increase of energy supply.

The national energy system is highly interdependent. A variety of energy forms are employed to accomplish many ultimate requirements. Alternative production modes compete for many of the same resources, physical and technological limitations restrict the supply or potential uses of energy, environmental effects or other externalities alter the permissible production and use patterns, and new technologies rapidly transform the available options. Relative prices guide and determine the options that are selected from the many alternatives. The evaluation of alternatives must be done within the framework of a flexible system. The FEA quantitative analysis system considered several objectives in analyzing alternative strategies including:

1. *Price sensitivity*—the impact of relative prices.
2. *Fuel competition*—the substitution of one energy source for another.
3. *Technology*—the variation of the production and conversion technologies within the energy system.
4. *Resource limitations*—the physical capacities and other resource limitations.
5. *Externalities*—the by-products or side-effects of energy production and consumption.
6. *Economic impact*—the interaction with the total energy production and consumption.
7. *Regional variations*—the uneven geographic distribution of energy production and consumption.
8. *Dynamics*—the lead times, capacity in previous periods, and other time-dependent conditions.
9. *Modularity*—the possibility of expansion of major components of the energy system or the introduction of new components.
10. *Judgment*—the capability of incorporating information and making approximations and estimates.

The energy system is depicted as a sort of network wherein production, processing, conversion, distribution, transportation and consumption activities take place. The prices and capacities for these activities are described in a manner consistent with the dual objectives of preserving price sensitivity and providing explicit recognition of potential constraints on the system. The structure of this framework is developed by separating the supply and demand sectors.

The supply system which produces, processes, and converts activities is represented as nodes within an energy network. These nodes are connected with links depicting the transportation and distribution system.

Potential activities in the energy production system are described by a set of supply curves that identify the prices that must be paid and the non-energy resources that will be consumed at each possible level of operation.

The important physical or technological limitations which affect the production of energy are described within the transportation and distribution network. The refining and conversion sectors are included as the intermediate nodes of the network, each with a description of its capacities and conversion technologies. The refining and conversion activities are joined with the demand or consumption sectors through an additional set of transportation and distribution links. These links are subject to capacity restrictions which can be modified if sufficient key resources are available (when compared with alternative uses in the production or distribution of energy). The supply curves, conversion technologies, transportation possibilities, costs and resource requirements are produced by supply sub-models of the Evaluation System and linked within this framework.

The estimates of the demand for energy are produced by a demand model. The demand for energy products takes place in different geographical regions and varies with energy prices. The choice of the activities to be described as demand is somewhat arbitrary, but can be thought of as the final demands for energy. Fuel substitution is simulated by the demand model through the empirical development of the relationships between demands and relative prices.

Given the prices, resource requirements, and capacity constraints, an integration model constructs a feasible set of energy flows that satisfies the final demands for energy. The energy supply activities and the demand prices are adjusted during this market simulation to obtain a balanced solution which is in equilibrium. This equilibrium balance is a point where no consuming sector would be willing to pay more for an additional unit of any energy product and no supplier would provide an additional unit of any energy product for less than the prevailing market price.

For an arbitrary selection of prices and demands, the least cost balancing solution may not be an equilibrium solution: there is no means of guaranteeing that an arbitrary price for estimating product demand will be equal to the price at which the product is supplied. However, the necessary adjustments in the prices are identified and these adjustments are repeated until the equilibrium solution is obtained.

The supply demand and equilibrium balancing components describing the energy system are combined with models of the economy, assessments of non-energy resource availability, and report writers that evaluate energy solutions in terms of the environmental, economic or resource impacts. Econometric, simulation, accounting, and optimization models are included in this system, each exploiting special capabilities for the relevant components of the problem. The model of macroeconomic activity is a well known system developed by Data Resources, Inc.[2] and is one of several major econometric models of the United States economy.

The resource constraint elements consist of a large data base which records the coefficients of demand for non-energy resources for the alternative energy activities included in the system. These coefficients are employed to construct constraints for the equilibrium solution if capacities are known, or to prepare ex-post summaries for off-line evaluation of potential bottlenecks. The supply model component consists of a variety of procedures used to construct stepwise approximations to the energy supply curves. These range from non-automated engineering analysis in the case of coal to the complex software of the National Petroleum Council for the estimation of the supply of oil and gas.

The demand model is a behavioral econometric model. The demand for energy is not represented in terms of its final use as energy but as the demand for the variety of energy products in the using sectors. The structure of demand and

[2] Data Resources, Inc. The Data Resources Quarterly Model, Econometric Forecasting System. Equation Specifications, 1974.

substitution is postulated in terms of relative prices and the parameters of these relationships are estimated using econometric techniques. The resulting system consists of over 800 behavioral relationships governing the demand for energy in 40 product and sectoral combinations.

The demand, supply, and resource assessment models are combined through the series of programs which constitute the integrating model. This constructs and solves the network description of the energy system to obtain a partial equilibrium by balancing prices and quantities for all energy products. The quantity flows and prices of the equilibrium energy sector solution provide the input to a series of evaluation or report writing programs that relate the solution to particular problems under consideration. These reports, over 20 in total, range from an executive summary of the energy balance to detailed classification and compilation of associated environmental residuals, water requirements, or implied non-energy resource usage for those inputs which have not been considered directly in the energy system network.

Computer runs were made and results recorded under three scenarios, namely (1) business as usual; (2) accelerating domestic supply; (3) energy conservation and demand management.

Major Conclusions and Recommendations

In the Project Independence report it was stated that the Project Independence Evaluation System (PIES) model was developed only to evaluate alternative energy initiatives and was not intended to be used to make recommendations per se.

Some of the conclusions reached under the business-as-usual scenario were:

1. At $11 per barrel world oil prices, domestic energy demand will grow at substantially lower rates than it has in the past.
2. Petroleum production is severely constrained in the short run and is greatly affected by world oil prices in the long run.
3. Coal production will increase significantly by 1985, but is limited by the lack of markets.
4. Potential increases in natural gas production are limited, but continued regulation could result in significant declines.
5. Synthetic fuels from coal will not play a major role between 1975 and 1985.
6. Geothermal, solar and other advanced technologies are large potential sources of energy but will not significantly contribute to our energy requirements before 1985.

Some of the conclusions reached under the accelerating domestic supply scenario were:

1. Federal policies to lease the Atlantic Outer Continental Shelf, reopen the Pacific OCS and tap the Naval Petroleum Reserves can dramatically increase domestic oil production. At $11 prices, production could reach as high as 17 million barrels per day, although less is needed to achieve zero imports.
2. Accelerating nuclear power plant construction does not reduce imports much; in general, it replaces new coal-fired power plants.

Some of the conclusions reached under the energy conservation and demand scenario were:

   1.   Energy conservation actions can reduce demand growth to about 2 percent per year between 1972 and 1985.
   2.   Demand management can further reduce dependence on limited oil and gas supplies by actions that involve switching from petroleum and natural gas consumption to coal or coal-fired electric power. However, implementation may be limited by environmental restrictions and financial inability of the electric utility industry to support a large electrification strategy.

   Other stated conclusions were:

   1.   Domestic supply and demand actions can greatly reduce U.S. vulnerability to import disruptions by 1985. At $11 per barrel for imported oil (1973 dollars), either all the demand actions or only a portion of the supply strategy would completely eliminate our vulnerability.
   2.   Increased domestic supply may result in wider regional price disparities than if no action were taken.

Summary of Major Limitations

   1.   The determination of a supply/demand balance is viewed as a static problem without a time dimension. This tends to cause the equilibrium solutions to be falsely consistent over time.
   2.   Under the assumed price conditions, there is a tendency to overstate the likely level of net imports of oil in 1985.
   3.   The deregulation assumptions and the material availability assumptions may be too stringent and not hold over time.
   4.   The approach used in the oil and natural gas supply models may be deficient. The most important factors are taken as exogeneous to the models and the responsiveness of supply to price changes may be underestimated.
   5.   The assumptions of sufficient financing being available and the removal of obstructions to the construction of nuclear and coal electricity generating capacity are questionable.
   6.   There appear to be downward biases in the estimates of consumption of natural gas and perhaps coal.

A1-7   Bureau of Labor Statistics: Economic Growth Model (1975 Revision). Distinguishing Characteristics*

   Major Purposes: (1) To project the U.S. economy under a set of assumed conditions and obtain official benchmarks against which to measure the actual performance of the economy; (2) to assess the impacts of alternative government policies, especially on employment.
   Scope: Economic and national.
   Principal investigators: Jack Alterman (now retired), Ronald Kutscher, Bureau of Labor Statistics, 431 G Street, NW, Washington, D.C. (202) 961-2450.
   Status: Completed and Updated.

---

* BLS (Bureau of Labor Statistics/Economic Growth Model). The above is taken from the previously referenced report (Library of Congress, 1975).

Major funding source: Bureau of Labor Statistics.

Time horizon: 1968–1980 and 1980–1985.

Major data sources: Consumption data from National Income and Product Accounts; investment, trade and interindustry data from Department of Commerce, Bureau of Economic Analysis; population data, Census Bureau; labor force, employment and price data from BLS; production data from Federal Reserve Board (for updating); fuel/energy consumption data from Federal Energy Administration (for updating); government expenditure data from OMB, DOD.

Major hardware/software features: IBM 370/165 used with Fortran IV and can operate over a remote terminal.

Major references:

U.S. Dept. of Labor, Bureau of Labor Statistics, The Structure of the U.S. Economy in 1980 and 1985, Bulletin 1831.

H. S. Houthakker and L. D. Taylor, "Consumer Demand in the United States: Analysis and Projections," Cambridge, Mass., Harvard University Press 1970.

Lester C. Thurow, "A Fiscal Policy Model of the United States," Survey of Current Business, June 1959.

Dennis C. Johnston, "Population and Labor Force Projections," Monthly Labor Review, December 1973.

Richard C. Barth, "The Development of Wage and Price Relationships for a Long-Term Economic Model," Survey of Current Business, August 1972.

GENERAL DESCRIPTION OF BLS ECONOMIC GROWTH MODEL

The BLS Economic Growth Projection System formally combines a macro-econometric forecasting model and an input-output model. It consists of two basic parts which work iteratively together. First, there is a supply (or production) side concerned with projecting the potential absolute size of the economy in terms of various constraints on production (labor force, employment and productivity). This leads to a "supply-side" projection of gross national product (GNP). In this part of the model, population and labor force projections are derived independently based on census and other survey data and age-sex mix in the population. At this stage, employment and output per man-hour are assumed, although they are subsequently derived by calculations later in the sequence.

Second, there is a demand (or consumption) side in which GNP is viewed in its alternative but equivalent guise as gross national expenditure. The two sides are linked by incomes: production creates incomes (through wages) and incomes create demand leading to expenditures. GNP together with a number of independent supplementary projections about taxation, government expenditures and export demand thus permits a determination of national income and a set of explicit forecasts of expenditure divided into investment (producer durables, housing) and final consumption expenditure. The latter is divided into government consumption and private consumption expenditure (PCE), again by gross category (automobiles, other consumer durables, and non-durables).

The link between the GNP projection via incomes to expenditures by category is by means of a long-range macro-econometric model designed by L. Thurow of Harvard University. The Thurow model projects employment, wages, GNP, personal incomes, corporate and government revenues (taxes), transfer payments, gross private consumption expenditure, housing expenditure, non-residential structures investment and investment in producers durable equipment. Wages and price indices (deflators) have recently been introduced to the model. This set of projections, in turn, is linked to a second econometric model, designed by H. A. Houthakker and L. D. Taylor, also at Harvard. This model starts from PCE projections, by gross category, plus wage-price projections provided by the Thurow model together with historical consumption data from 1929 to 1964 broken down to 82 detailed categories, and projects consumption demand to the same degree of detail. Personal income, prices, unemployment and existing stocks (of durables) are taken into account in these projections. Unfortunately these forecasting equations have only been partially updated to reflect more recent experience since 1964.

The 82 consumption categories are allocated to the 134 industrial sectors of the BLS input-output table on pro-rata basis. The 134 sector input-output table was aggregated by BLS from a 367 sector "benchmark" I-O table compiled by the Bureau of Economic Analysis, based on 1963 Census of Manufactures data, and 1963 base-year prices. The 1963 table has been approximately updated to 1970 by BLS, using the latest available census data. The I-O table itself must be projected forward however, to take account of technological product mix and price changes at the industry level which alter the basic pattern of purchases and sales. For instance, the substitution of natural gas for coal as an industrial fuel by a third industry causes two coefficients to change in value; as one coefficient rises the other declines in proportion. The method of forecasting used depends on the circumstances of each case; in some cases explicit (non-extrapolative) technological forecasts have been utilized where "reversals" or dramatic changes are expected.

Having developed 1980 and 1985 I-O tables, output by industry can be calculated directly. From this set of results employment (i.e., man hours) and capital requirements by industrial sector can be estimated using output per man-hour (productivity) coefficients by sector and capital/output coefficients, by sector, respectively. The former permits a revision of the original labor input estimate, while the latter permits a revision of the demand-by-sector (since capital goods are a component of demand). This re-estimation procedure is ad hoc; it is not yet integrated into the model. Labor requirements associated with a given level of economic activities are computed in considerable detail by specific occupational categories. Where requirements appear to exceed available labor supply, for some occupations, demand can be correspondingly adjusted downward.

Summary of Major Conclusions and Recommendations

As with all large-scale models, all actual forecasts are contingent on the particular assumptions made. They are not predictions about the real future but, rather, "if . . . then" statements. The model is only a tool for analysis, not an analysis as such. Only a particular study that uses the model can be said to have meaningful conclusions.

The study reported in Bulletin 1831 concludes that real GNP growth from 1968 –1980 will be 4.1 percent per year, compared to 3.8 percent per year in the period 1955–1968, but that it will slow down after 1980 to 3.3 percent per year due to lower growth rate of the labor force.

It is noteworthy that the macro-model assumed 4 percent unemployment and projected a 3 percent inflation rate after 1975. The oil-price rise of 1974 was not taken into account in this project.

Summary of Major Limitations

1. The econometric forecasting model (Thurow) is highly aggregated as regards elements of demand. It ignores monetary variables, though it is quite detailed on the fiscal side.

2. BLS uses a 134 sector table derived from the 1963 "benchmark" I-O table of the Bureau of Economic Analysis (formerly OBE). The table is partially updated to 1970 by BLS. (The 1967 "benchmark" table was not available at the time.)

3. BLS uses the Houthakker-Taylor demand equations, based on consumption expenditure data over the period 1929–1964. More recent experience since 1964 has been taken into account only marginally in the equations.

4. BLS treatment of demand for capital equipment is not truly internal to the model, but rather is used for external consistency checking and ad hoc revisions. (The procedure is not fully reduced to mathematical algorithms and programs.)

AI-8 NIRAP (National Interregional Agricultural Projections System). Distinguishing Characteristics*

Major purposes: (1) To define scenarios of potential alternative futures for U.S. agriculture. (2) To analyze trade-offs between possible conflicting policy goals and suggest possible solutions. (3) To provide projections of the major facets of U.S. agriculture in meeting future demands for selected commodities, natural resources, and energy use. (4) To analyze the resulting projections and scenarios and anticipate future problems with respect to food and fibers and to provide an "early warning" potential (for unprecedented or "shock" events).

Scope: Agricultural, national and regional.

Principal investigator: Leroy Quance, Program Leader, National Economics Analysis Division, Department of Agriculture, 500 12th Street, S. W., Washington, D.C. 20250. (202-447-7681).

Status: Completed—the system is constantly being updated each year as new inputs are formulated and new conclusions are drawn.

Major funding source: Funded completely from the Economic Research Service budget of the Department of Agriculture.

Time horizon: Projections have been made from 1975 to 1985 and in some instances to the year 2000.

Major data sources: Department of Agriculture statistics on annual figures of production, land availability, crop patterns; and Census Bureau Service statistics on population growth. "Coordinated projection teams" from the Economic Research Service of the Department of Agriculture, other government agencies, and universities originated and reviewed the input data.

Major hardware/software features: The IBM 370/168 computer was used with the Fortran programming language.

Major references:

Introduction to the Economic Projections Program No. LQ 2.75, compiled by

* NIRAP (National Interregional Agricultural Projections System) The above is also from the aforementioned report (Library of Congress, 1975).

Leroy Quance, February 19, 1975. Economic Projections and Analytical Systems Programs, National Economic Analysis Division. Economic Research Service, Washington, D.C. 20250.

Scenario for Change: First Annual Report to the Administrator, No. LQ 1.74. Economic Projections and Analytical Systems Program, NEAD, ERS, Department of Agriculture, Washington, D.C. 20250.

Brief on the ERS Economic Projections Program, May 11, 1975, 6 p., Economic Projections Program.

Regional Agricultural Production, 1985 and Beyond, U.S. Department of Agriculture, Economic Research Service, ERS 564, Reprinted from the Farm Index; March, April, June and July 1974.

Description of NIRAP System

The NIRAP system is concerned with the analysis of the food and fiber system of U.S. agriculture. The food and fiber system contains major facets of U.S. agriculture such as production, consumption (e.g. export demand and market demand), and the distribution and processing of commodities such as cotton and tobacco (fiber), livestock and grain (food).

The NIRAP system currently contains eleven component models or sectors. It is planned to add more models as the need arises. In order to prime the system, scenarios of expected future demand for U.S. food and fiber are developed. These baseline, high, and low demand scenarios are constructed in terms of three analytical variables:

1. Population Growth (Census Bureau figures)
2. Economic Growth (in terms of total disposable income)
3. International Trade (U.S. farm exports)

Different values are assigned to each of these variables according to the type of scenario used. For example, if a high demand scenario is being developed, each variable is assigned a greater value than for baseline or low scenarios. The exception to this is the export variable which utilizes only high and moderate projections, whereas population and economic growth consider high, moderate and low projections.

These scenarios provide assumptions which set attributes and values as inputs to prime the models and initiate the interactions between the sectors. Four of the sectors are supply-demand oriented and interact with the other seven sectors to constitute the structure of the system. The models, their descriptors, and their interactions are:

1. Aggregate Farm Output Model provides the shifts in the aggregate supply of products, the prices received and paid by farmers, the aggregate farm output, and projections of gross and net income for farmers. The model receives inputs from a technological change model, a general economy model, a world trade model, and a supply utilization model. As in all of the supply-demand models, the scenarios interact directly with the models.

2. The Commodity Model projects the United States' domestic and foreign demand, and exports for 21 farm commodities. The interactions for the commodity model are the same as for the aggregate farm output model.

3. The Non-Farm Produced Input Models are based on derived projected demands for inputs not produced on the farm (e.g. fertilizer and fuel). Inputs from

the commodity model and the state distribution of production model (which distributes national commodity projections to states and regions based upon productive resources, crop yields, land availability and historical production data) provide the major interactions of the models.

4. The Land Use Model projects land use by irrigated and nonirrigated practice on state, region, and national levels based on projected crop yields, land availability, and past land use data. The state distribution of production model, a cropland availability model, and a crop yield simulator model interact with the land use supply-demand model to formulate projections.

Eight types of projections of the food and fiber system are formulated as a result of the interactions of the supply and demand models. These projections were "normalized" in the sense that short run phenomena such as weather production cycles and short-run market conditions were not considered. These projections are:

Northeast, South, and North Central States, and to the year 2000 for the West. Two assumptions were utilized in making these projections:

1. A slow rate of increase in agricultural R&D, and
2. A high level of net farm exports.

Major Conclusions and Recommendations

Projections were derived on regional and national levels as follows:

1. Northeast—there would not be a shortage of cropland in 1985, even if high export demand were to occur. Crop yields are projected to increase for six commodities—wheat, rye, oats, barley, soybeans, and potatoes.

2. South—less cropland will be needed in the South due to increased crop yields and shifting of crops previously grown in the South to other regions. The South's share of the national production of certain commodities including soybeans, wheat, grain, sorghum, barley, sugar cane and chickens is expected to increase. Like the Northeast there will be no cropland shortage even if high export demand were to occur.

3. North Central States—projected to have a limited supply of cropland to 1985. The region will fall short of meeting its cropland requirements under normal demand conditions, and under high export demand, the shortage may require a shift in crop production to other regions. The North Central States are projected to produce a larger share of the Nation's corn, turkeys, and hogs by 1985. Production of wheat, rye, oats, dry beans, sheep, chickens, and eggs will be reduced, but more acres of corn and soybeans are projected for 1985 than were cultivated in 1970.

4. West—expected to have an increasing role in U.S. agriculture due to a projected increase in irrigated cropland. Expected to utilize fewer acres in food and fiber production due to the increase of irrigation and higher crop yield. Peanut production is projected to double, and grain sorghum, cattle and calves, and chicken and eggs production will increase. Oats, barley, rye, sweet potatoes, sheep and lambs and milk production are expected to decrease. The West is not likely to be affected by higher export demand.

5. United States—projected to meet high export demand with the shifting of some commodities produced by the regions. For instance, the South may have to

devote new cropland to produce dry beans the North Central region cannot supply because of its dearth of cropland.

6. There is great uncertainty in the agricultural system because of the potential movement toward freer world trade and the role of the Soviet Union and the People's Republic of China as regular buyers of grain in the world markets.

7. Purchased input requirements for crop yields (e.g. fuel to 1985 and fertilizer to 1980) will not substantially increase.

Summary of Major Limitations

1. Model inputs may have been based on invalid estimating procedures, insufficient research (e.g. commodity production and prices and grain reserves), and inadequate coordination of the efforts of independent sources.

2. The model seems too inflexible. It does not allow for structural and functional modifications in the food and fiber system to take place over time.

3. The model did not take into account the concept of the management of resources because the degree of aggregation precluded detailed analysis at this level.

4. It would appear that the model is more valid at the national level than the regional level.

5. Most of the incorporation of technological and economic factors are alleged to lack analytical depth.

AI-9 Quantifying the Quality of Life*

Conferences have been held and books have been written on this extremely subjective subject. The problem is obvious: The meaning of quality of life (QOL) is different for every culture and for every individual in each culture. Furthermore, it changes with circumstances. One who aspires to a certain QOL will change his aspirations if he attains it. Thus quantifying QOL seems an impossible task. Yet it is one that apparently must be done. Policymakers, whether they use simulation or not, must have some measure by which they can determine whether a proposed course of action will improve matters. For policymakers in the public domain this usually amounts to whether the change will improve (or at least be perceived to improve) the QOL of their constituents.

Thus we must devise a means for assigning a number to it. However, before we can measure anything we must know—and others must be informed of—what it is that we are measuring; we must define QOL before we can even attempt to measure it in quantifiable terms.

---

* Throughout most of the models discussed above, there appears the issue of quantifying the quality of life. Although most of the schemes developed to construct these measures are not as complex or as sophisticated as other models presented in this chapter, the discussion is presented here because of the utility of having such indexing capabilities.

Some have said that the definition must consider the relationships between the actual (objective) conditions of life and the perceived (subjective) conditions. Campbell has written that "the QOL must be in the eye of the beholder and it is only through an evaluation of the experience of life as our people perceive it that we will understand the human meaning of the great social and institutional changes which dramatize our time" (Campbell, 1972).

Of the two views we feel compelled to accept the position dictated by the latter. For the policymaker it matters little what conditions are, if they are not perceived to be so by those with whom he is concerned.

One does not ordinarily speak of the quality of life without implying a comparison of what exists to some more or less explicit standard of what ought to exist. Thus, in thinking about enhancing one's quality of life, one thinks about how things ought to be. There should be less pollution and better housing; people should have less sickness and more education. But these very assumptions introduce subjectivity into objective measures. Thus it appears that what the policymaker really needs is a measure of QOL that is based on the status of his constituents as they perceive it, as compared to their aspirations.

AI-9.1   A Definition

For the purpose of this book, then, we shall define QOL as some function of perceived conditions and conditions that are aspired to.

Thus by fiat we have a definition of QOL; it is now necessary only that we measure and quantify it!

AI-9.2   An Equation

Symbolically our definition states

$$QOL = f(S, A)$$

where

$$S = \text{Status} \quad \text{and} \quad A = \text{Aspirations.}$$

Going a step further, let us assume that the function is a simple proportionality. Then

$$QOL = S/A$$

However, both S and A are the sum of many factors (which, for consistency, must have the same dimensions for each). Furthermore, the factors differ in importance. Thus,

$$S = \sum_{i=1}^{n} (w_i s_i)$$

where the w is the relative importance of the individual factors, s, that make up S. Similarly,

$$A = \sum_{i=1}^{n} (w_i a_i).$$

Now the problem has been changed from one of evaluating QOL in terms of two difficult-to-measure parameters, S and A, to that of measuring $3n$ parameters (all the s, all the a, and all the w). A mitigating factor, however, is that because all such measurements must of necessity be estimates and will, therefore, contain errors, there is a much greater chance that the errors will offset each other than that they will be cumulative.

In any case, the policymaker is not dealing with a subjective/objective relationship, but a subjective/subjective ratio, all factors of which depend on the attitude of the population of concern.

AI-9.3   Satisfaction/Dissatisfaction

Attitude is a person's reaction to a *perceived* stimulus which, it is said, can be qualitatively assessed from verbal disclosures with regard to direction (polarity of effect) and magnitude (strength, degree or favorability of disclosure). Social psychologists include three dimensions in the definition of attitude: (1) the affective dimension including feelings, satisfaction and so on; (2) the cognitive dimension, which includes judgments, beliefs, and evaluations; and (3) the behavioral dimension, which involves a complex interaction of the other two dimensions. Our concern with attitude involves the first dimension, and is especially focused on satisfaction because some have implied that perceived satisfactions can be equated in a simplistic way with QOL. Satisfactions and frustrations depend jointly upon objective reality on the one side and aspirations and expectations on the other. Unfortunately, our concern over QOL must include the possibility of personal development beyond the individual's present limits. This implies that any measure of QOL will change with time.

We must also recognize that society is divided into subpopulations that differ greatly in the degree to which they find their worlds satisfying; furthermore, the profile of satisfaction that we might find for one segment of the population may have quite a different contour from that of another.

Furthermore, it is evident that satisfaction and deprivation or dissatisfaction are completely psychological concepts and that we cannot assume that levels of living which are objectively equal or similar will have the same meaning for everyone. People evaluate their achievements in relation to their levels of aspiration, and what may be entirely gratifying to one person may be intolerably frustrating to another. And, as noted above, levels of aspiration change through time and what may be satisfying at one point in time may be dissatisfying at another.

Measuring satisfaction. For the foregoing reasons, the quantification or measurement of personal satisfaction has raised doubts as to whether it can ever be successfully assessed directly. Can it be said that the satisfaction of a college student who has been elected president of his class is equal to that of a candidate who has been elected to the United States Senate? In some sense, it cannot; for example, the one achievement may be thought to represent a more important goal than the other. But in the sense that specific aspirations are fulfilled, they are equally fulfilled. The satisfactions are equal in the same sense that two bottles may be equally full even though one holds more than the other.

Indeed, one's satisfaction is so intricately complex and dynamic that even the attempt to measure it has highly questionable validity. The satisfaction scalar is so open ended that once one threshold is reached and satisfied for the moment a new threshold is established. Therefore, it has been suggested that some of these problems can be avoided by looking at measures of the effects of dissatisfaction instead of attempting to measure satisfaction. These effects measures would include such things as the number of people leaving the system or part of it, job changes, mental and physical health, measures of income, and the like.

Furthermore, it has been suggested that regulations governing many aspects of our lives are a result of, and therefore a means of measuring dissatisfaction.

Federal Laws as Dissatisfaction Indices. One possibly fruitful avenue of research for determining dissatisfaction levels is investigation of the Federal laws related to the QOL sector. Such an approach is appealing and justifiable for two principal reasons: (1) The laws get on the books and stay there with the approval of the people, in that they are established by the people's elected representatives; and (2) the laws, or the regulations promulgated pursuant to their provisions, often express the goals and priorities of the people in terms of minimum thresholds.

Our first attempts at research using this approach have uncovered a number of laws that set important minimum thresholds for the quality of American life. As examples salary, environmental quality, and education will be discussed.

The Fair Labor Standards Act (29 USC, Chapter 8, Secs. 201–219), first enacted in 1938 and amended many times since, established the typical 40-hour week by providing that overtime must be paid for hours worked beyond that threshold. The minimum wage that it sets for most manufacturing and retail jobs is, in practice, accepted as a standard by employers and employees of a far wider spectrum.

Depending on a person's background, inclinations, and aspirations, the minimum wage might, of course, be wholly unacceptable. However, by using some scale based on an individual's education, training, and years of experience, we could determine that a different set of thresholds is applicable. In this case, the U.S. Civil Service Commission's Government Service ratings and pay levels could be employed. From them we can obtain minimum thresholds for clerical, secretarial, semiprofessional, professional, and executive salaries. Because the GS rating system itself factors in education, training, and years of experience, this would provide fairly specific threshold levels.

Another major area in which the laws provide basic thresholds is in the massive new block of regulations governing environmental quality. The National Environmental Policy Act of 1969 (PL 91-190) sets a broad role for the Federal Government in establishing and promoting environmental quality so that "man and nature can exist in productive harmony, and fulfill the social, economic, and other requirements of present and future generations of Americans." Based on that Act, regulations have been promulgated to establish specific standards for the quality of the environment. These standards provide, for example, laws governing the threshold of water quality needed both for safe human consumption and for recreational purposes, as well as with the maximum thresholds of particulates in the air for safe human habitation. The possible uses of these laws in constituting our dissatisfaction index are numerous, but it will take a great deal of research to factor in all such uses.

A study of Federal laws as an aid to arriving at a dissatisfaction index has its drawbacks. The most important is that the basic thresholds formulated in the laws are probably created in response to what is envisioned as average minimums for the entire country, and do not necessarily apply to specific areas or individuals. What is considered a low salary in one place may be a high salary in another.

In addition to the extensive research that this type of study entails, the question of how and what to factor into the dissatisfaction index represents a major potential stumbling block. However, until a valid nationwide survey is conducted, Federal laws may well represent the best approach to establishing a measure of dissatisfaction index.

AI-9.4   Assigning Numbers

Our previous discussion of both the equation and the dissatisfaction index stop short of recommendations for assigning the numerical values required by computer models. One approach to this problem is the "self-anchoring striving scale" described in *The Hopes and Fears of the American People* (Cantril and Roll, 1971) and republished in *Quality of Life Indicators: a review of state-of-the-art and guidelines derived to assist in developing environmental indicators* (EPA, 1972), from which the following excerpt was taken.

In the striving scale technique, the respondent is first asked to describe what life would be like if he were to imagine his future in the best possible light. This question is open-ended and the respondent's comments are recorded verbatim by the interviewer. The respondent is then asked the opposite: "What his future would be like in the worst possible light." Again, his comments are recorded verbatim. The actual wording of the question follows:
All of us want certain things out of life.
When you think about what really matters in your own life, what are your wishes and hopes for the future? In other words, if you imagine your future in the *best* possible light, what would your life look like then, if you are to be happy? Take your time in answering; such things aren't easy to put into words.
Now taking the other side of the picture, what are your fears and worries about the future? In other words, if you imagine your future in the *worst* possible light, what would your life look like then? Again, take your time in answering.
The substance of the hopes and fears mentioned is subsequently coded by major categories of concern.
The respondent is next shown a picture of a ladder, symbolic of the ladder of life. The top rung of the ladder, he is told, represents the entire complex of hopes he has just described as the ideal state of affairs, and the bottom rung represents the worst state of affairs. He is then asked to indicate where he feels he stands on the ladder at the present time in relation to his aspirations, where he believes he stood five years ago, and where he thinks he will be five years hence.
The respondent's ladder ratings are self-anchored in that the top and bottom of the ladder are defined in his own terms. Thus a present ladder rating of "6" rating for an upper-middle class housewife in the New York suburbs is the psychological equivalent of a "6" rating for a sharecropper in the Southwest even though the substance of their hopes and fears may differ markedly. Further, the respondent's three ladder ratings can be compared, giving a measure of his personal sense of accomplishment (as indicated by the ladder rating shift from past to present) and personal sense of optimism (as indicated by the shift from present to future). The same series of interrelated questions is then asked about the United States to determine the respondent's hopes and fears for the nation.
The respondent is asked to describe the best and worst possible states of affairs for the United States and to indicate national ladder ratings for past, present, and future. One result of their study is indicated in Figure AI-2.

Figure AI-2.   *Personal Hopes and Fears in Percentages*

	Personal Hopes		
	1959	1964	1971
Good health for self	40	29	29
Better standard of living	38	40	27
Peace in the world	9	17	19
Achievement of aspirations for children	29	35	17
Happy family life	18	18	14
Good health for family	16	25	13
Own house or live in better one	24	12	11
Peace of mind; emotional maturity	5	9	8
Having wealth	2	5	7
Having leisure time	11	5	6
Happy old age	10	8	6
Good job; congenial work	7	9	6
Employment	5	8	6
Freedom from inflation	1	2	6
Other general concerns for family	7	4	5

	Personal Fears		
	1959	1964	1971
Ill health for self	40	25	28
Lower standard of living	23	19	18
War	21	29	17
Ill health for family	25	27	16
Unemployment	10	14	13
Inflation	1	3	11
Unhappy children	12	10	8
Drug problem in family	—	—	7
Pollution	—	—	7
Political instability	1	2	5
No fears at all	12	10	5
Crime	—	—	5

AI-9.5   Next Steps in QOL Research

Although it is possible to theorize extensively about the relative benefits of a dissatisfaction measure versus a satisfaction one, both concepts will have to be field tested for numerous reasons. First, we will have to test the sensitivity of the various surrogates that must be used to develop these indicators from secondary sources (we will assume that original data gathering will be too costly, at least in the short run). Second, we will have to compare the relative merits in terms of ease of data collection, interpretation of indices, and system reaction over time for both satisfaction as a measure of QOL, and dissatisfaction as an inverse measure. Finally, there is a reasonably well-developed body of scientific literature, both theoretical and empirical, from the psychological disciplines that discusses these concepts as they apply to individuals. Although reading the various works on development of these measures from a sociological point of view reveals considerable direct transference, there has been no research done, to our knowledge, to test the efficiency of such assumptions and hypotheses with respect to selected populations.

Certainly, we do not expect that the results of the study will give us all the answers to all our questions, or even that we will really be able to use the results in the ways we hope. Such measures are, however, desperately needed. The almost glib statement, "when one is concerned with the environment, one is concerned with everything," is becoming ever less glib as we make our global policies. We need to know where we are and how we are doing now in order to create the policies that we might use to correct those situations with which we are concerned. We also need to tie such measures to comprehensive models, in order to see if the policy choices we would make will really make life better for our people and our land. It is only with knowledge that we can make correct policy; all else is guesswork. There are those who say that our period of surplus is over, and that questions of scarcity, poverty, and pollution will have to be addressed. It is clear that whatever next steps are taken should be done with knowledge, because guesswork in times of little margin for error could be disastrous.

AI-10 Conclusion

An analysis of these comprehensive models suggests that each could be considered comprehensive and large scale. They by no means cover the very wide range of models available, nor are they necessarily representative of all models. On the other hand, each is currently operative, and, like all models, they are continually being updated and improved. They are consistent, in the main, with what one group or another would see as a description of how some portion of the world operates. These constructs certainly adhere to a formal definition of the term theory, i.e., "a formulation of apparent relationships or underlying principles of certain observed phenomena which has been verified to some degree" (Webster, 1972). In sum, since models discussed thus represent large-scale theories successfully programmed for a computer, it is demonstrable that theories do exist to explain our social system, or at least portions of it. It remains only to prove that the theories actually explain something of importance.

Appendix II

Examples in Detail

In previous sections of this book we saw that there are several sources and methods available to those who wish to gather or synthesize data for computer models. The feasibility and cost effectiveness of the selected alternatives depends, however, on the use to which the analyst will put the model.

So that there can be no misunderstanding concerning the content of this Appendix, let us declare at the outset that because the range of approaches to model building is large, this section by no means attempts to exhaust all possible alternatives. To be specific, we assume that our goal is to build a general, comprehensive, man-machine model that will be useful to the policymaker. We discuss several exemplary approaches to constructing such a model. Since the approaches discussed differ in their treatment of man, machine, and interface, any attempts to compare them are heroic, to say the least.

A recent article entitled "Selective Adaptation" (Millar, 1972) contends that the algorithms most models incorporate are surrogates for social-political decision making and are usually attempts to replicate and extrapolate the "natural laws of social science."

In keeping with our attempt to build general, comprehensive man-machine models for policy makers, the models discussed here have numerous factors in common. To be specific, they are all comprehensive in that they are designed to take cognizance of a broad range of issues across several variables. They are general in that they were not really designed to handle a specific policy issue nor a single locale but are amendable to several policy analysis questions. They are all more or less capable of being run with a human interface, although this interaction is simpler for some than others. Finally, most are not goal-seeking in the traditional optimization sense, although some form of mathematical programming (optimizing and satisficing) is included in two of the larger models.

The most readily discerned difference among the models is the extent to which the decision makers' tradeoffs among policy impacts (as well as the interactions among policy variables) is internalized. These range from the San Diego model, which assumed that most of the tradeoffs among policy impacts will be made externally by the decision maker who will exogenously specify any alterations to the model system, to SOS (State of the System Model), which, unless there is deliberate intervention, sets its feedback loops that determine the tradeoffs endogenously. Rather than continue a discussion of these methodologies in the abstract, several model research projects are now discussed.

AII-1   The San Diego-Rand Methodology Package

The most disaggregate approach to the comprehensive model—and also the most responsive to public attitudes—was expected to occur in an actual region confronting an actual environmental policy problem. In the San Diego Clean Air Project, a sophisticated new analytical methodology was to be wedded to an existing local government structure (which already had appreciable planning capabilities) on an experimental basis. The project's purposes were to (1) develop a comprehensive methodology, based upon a certain approach and premises for analyzing policies in terms of their many impacts on a region, and (2) to apply the methodology to analyze alternative policies in a particular region, thereby helping actual regional decision makers identify the policy preferred for implementation.

From the standpoint of the region, the Clean Air Project was viewed primarily as a policy study. From the standpoint of the EPA sponsors of the project (the Environmental Studies Division, Office of Research and Development), it was viewed primarily as a case-study in large-scale policy modeling—an experiment with a certain approach to comprehensive modeling.

The San Diego Clean Air Project produced a number of interesting methodological and policy results. From the standpoint of this report, however, the most germane features of that project are reflected in its general approach to the development of a comprehensive model.

The general approach of the San Diego-Rand Methodology Package can best be described by certain premises that motivated and guided its development. (Indeed, we title it a "methodology package" rather than a "model" because, as a consequence of several premises, it includes some items that do not fit traditional definitions of a model.)

AII-1.1   Premises

The first, and most basic, premise* holds that it is impossible for a comprehensive model to realistically internalize the policymaking process, that is, to individually weigh and trade off the numerous factors involved in making a policy decision and to select the preferred alternatives. Past attempts to do so were not considered credible to either the researcher or the policymaker.

To overcome this deficiency, the policy analyst is viewed as a person who constructs and maintains a toolkit of models and analytical techniques that can be brought to bear on specific policy issues; the specific mix of these tools is variable and determined by the specific problem.

The many impacts—environmental, economic, transportation service, social (i.e., distributional)—are estimated by the tools and then presented to the policymakers for the comparison of alternatives. The usual approach combines the different impacts into a single measure of effectiveness. But this loses information and substitutes the analyst's values for those of the decision makers. In the system impact assessment approach, as applied in San Diego, the various impacts are displayed on a "scorecard," a table that also shows, by color code, each alternative's ranking for a particular impact. The policymakers can then add to this factual knowledge their value judgments about the relative importance of the different impacts, thereby weighing and trading off the impacts to select a preferred alternative. (These value judgments can, of course, reflect the policymaker's perceptions about how the impacts will influence the attainment of both societal objectives and his individual organizational objectives). The interaction between analysts and policymakers is viewed as an iterative one; in response to questions and concerns of the policymaker, the analysts will modify the menu of alternatives or enrich the menu of impacts by which they are compared.

The second premise is that the methodological approach of policy analysis models should often differ from that of planning (implementation analysis) models because their purposes differ. *Policy analysis*, in our view, is primarily concerned with deciding *what* to do; that is, what are the multiple consequences of alternative policies and which policy is preferred. Implementation analysis is concerned with deciding *how* to do something; that is, what actions by what institutions will bring a particular preferred policy into being. Since they must evaluate many possible policies in terms of many possible impacts, policy analysis models should

---

* The following premises are based on a personal communication from Bruce Goeller, who served as Rand project leader.

strive for flexibility, inexpensive operation (both in terms of computer and human costs), and relatively fast response; moreover, they should allow policies to be described at a relatively gross and conceptual level. Implementation analysis models, in contrast, can, and generally do, operate at a considerably more detailed and concrete level, since they will be used to evaluate only a few alternatives.

As an example of the distinction between implementation analysis and policy analysis, suppose the decision problem is how to improve a regional bus system. During implementation analysis, one is concerned with such questions as whether the buses should run on First and Third Streets rather than Second and Fourth Streets. During policy analysis, in contrast, one is concerned with such questions as whether the route-spacing should be two blocks rather than four or six blocks, or whether the fare should be reduced instead, and how many people will ride on the buses.

The hypothesis has been advanced that large-scale models have a poor record of transfer and use because of their transfer cost and documentation problems. We feel that there is an alternative, complementary hypothesis that is at least as plausible: The existing models were generally implementation analysis models, not policy analysis models; as such, they lacked sufficient flexibility, responsiveness, and economical operation to be perceived as really useful for policy analysis. Thus, they were not transferred and used because they did not seem useful.

The third premise is that a policy model's primary purpose is to improve decision making rather than to improve forecasting per se. For example, a relatively crude model that can clearly demonstrate that alternative *A* performs better than alternative *B* under both favorable and unfavorable assumptions will probably lead to a better decision than a complex model that can perform only a highly detailed expected value extrapolation. Policy models generally need the capability easily to perform various kinds of sensitivity analyses, not only on the policies themselves, but on the basic technical and scenario assumptions as well.

Because such assumptions can strongly influence, and may even dominate, the potential impact of different policies, their uncertainties should be explicitly considered and their tradeoffs explicitly weighed in policy selection. As an illustration of the importance of such assumptions, imagine the shifts in national energy policy that might become appropriate if a major change for the worse obtained in the technical assumptions about the cost or safety of breeder reactors or in the scenario assumptions about the long-run price or availability of foreign oil, regardless of the internal composition of whatever model was being employed.

The fourth premise is that our *Tinker-Toy* approach to a comprehensive model (where a kit of tools exists that may be used in different combinations) is better suited to many kinds of policy problems than the *monolithic* model approach. With the Tinker-Toy approach, the component models, which relate to different parts of the problem, may be used separately to analyze a particular part of the problem in many different ways, with a minimum of data inertia or housekeeping problems, thereby increasing the analyst's understanding of that part of the problem and his ability to design effective policies for it. When the component models are used in combination, the output data set from one model is generally part of the input data set of a subsequent model. Although the analyst could submit a combination of models as one computer run, he often gains advantages from making separate serial runs. This enables him to see various intermediate results, to check the output data from one model for reasonableness and, if necessary, to modify them before they are input to the next step. He can adaptively intervene in the interaction process between the models to reflect the effect of factors that the models do not explicitly treat or to heuristically increase the efficiency of search or convergence (Paxson, 1971).

Different types of problems generally require different analytic strategies, and hence different modeling approaches. A stimulating paper (Cartwright, 1973) presents a problem typology that is helpful. In Cartwright's terms, *simple problems* have a specified number of calculable variables, *compound problems* have an unspecified (i.e., open-ended) number of calculable variables, *complex problems* have a specified number of incalculable variables, and *metaproblems* have an unspecified number of incalculable variables. A truly comprehensive and rational analysis is possible only for simple problems, according to Cartwright; for these we believe the monolithic approach is preferred. The other types require an analysis that is either disjointed or incremental or both simultaneously; for those we believe the flexible and partitionable approach of Tinker-Toy models is advantageous.

The fifth premise is that the design of a comprehensive policy model should be decision-maker-oriented from the start. Initially, the model should be considered as a black box (toolkit!) and the question should be what knobs, representing policy variables (and the scenario), and what dials, representing impacts, should be put on the front of the box to make it useful to the decision makers. Only after this exercise should attention be given to designing the algorithmic contents of the box.

The sixth premise is that there might be synergistic complementarities from developing comprehensive policy models, using the Tinker Toy approach in a region that already has a fairly well-developed system of planning models. First, and most obvious, the planning models could be used as part of the detailed implementation planning process after the preferred policy is chosen. Second, they could be used as a pump-primer for the policy analysis methodology: By generating detailed forecasts of numerous regional characteristics (population and land use by small areas, etc.) in machine-readable form, planning models provide a voluminous but internally consistent and systematic data base that may be aggregated, incorporated, and used in various ways by the policy models. This approach can be particularly effective for studying the near-term effects of near-term policies since it is common to treat land use and other slowly varying regional quantities as exogenous in such studies. In this context, we use the planning methodology to provide a detailed forecast of the region in the near term assuming that the "do nothing" or "existing trends" policies prevail, and then use the policy model to predict the impacts of changes in policy. We call this a perturbation approach.

The final premise is that the practicality and usefulness of a particular policy model for other (related) policy problems is strongly determined by the concreteness of the original policy problem for which it was developed.

The San Diego methodology was transferred and adapted to an entirely different region, Los Angeles, in a space of a few weeks, where it was used in two major but different policy studies in a space of a few months: One, for EPA, was an analysis of the sensitivity to assumptions of optimal strategies for oxidant control and their impacts (Goeller, 1973), while the other, done for the Southern California Association of Governments, became the basis for the SCAG short-range transportation plan for dealing with transportation and related air-pollution and energy problems in Los Angeles (Mikolowsky, 1974; Southern California Association of Governments, 1974).

It was decided that this conceptualization of comprehensive policy modeling could best be demonstrated by testing it on a crucial environmental issue in the San Diego region, which already had considerable planning methodology, and seeing how this issue might be handled in the context of San Diego County's comprehensive planning process. The environmental issue chosen was the analysis of alternative strategies for San Diego to use in meeting the 1975 ambient air quality standards.

The San Diego Rand methodology package has been used in at least three policy environments First, as stated above, it was used in the San Diego policy environment; indeed, it produced a strategy that was formally adopted by the San Diego supervisors and presented formally in public hearings as a counterproposal to the EPA plan. (Although that strategy was not implemented because the primary authority was shifted from the San Diego Office of Environment Management to CALTRANS by action of Governor Reagan, this should not obscure the fact that the

San Diego methodology was used in a policy context, and, indeed, the outputs were presented to the San Diego key policymakers and a policy decision resulted.) Second, the methodology was applied to support the EPA headquarters Task Force studying Los Angeles, the results were briefed to the Deputy and three Assistant Administrators, and produced R-1368-EPA, *Strategy Alternatives for Oxidant Control in the Los Angeles Air Quality Control Region.* Third, the San Diego methodology was applied in a study done by Rand for SCAG of near-term transportation strategies, from which one strategy became the short-range transportation plan formally adopted by the Southern California Association of Governments (Mikolowsky, 1974).

AII-1.2   Ancillary Models

The following San Diego models, taken from *Regional Model System— San Diego County* (McLeod, July 1972), were used in the project, primarily as pump-primers for the policy models. Their interrelation is shown in Figure AII-1.

Computer models, as developed and used in the regional planning program, perform a basic and vital set of functions—they are the principal tools used to translate alternative sets of policies into patterns for future land use and transportation.

Each of the models developed addresses a particular aspect of the regional environment. They can be used independently to analyze a particular situation or

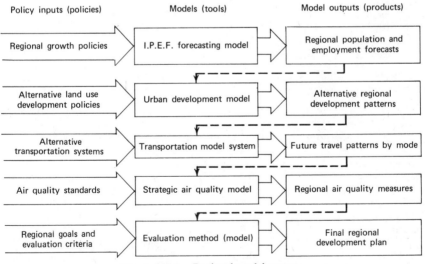

Figure AII-1.   Regional model system.

problem, or because of built-in linkages among the models, can be viewed as a system. When viewed in this manner, the regional models constitute a sequence which allows information produced by one model to flow to the next.

The following discussion of the major simulations currently in use or under development will describe how each model relates to the overall model system and to the regional planning program.

IPEF (Interactive Population/Employment Forecasting) Model. The IPEF produces long-range forecasts of total regional population and employment based upon regional policy decisions. It provides a detailed age, race, and sex breakdown of the forecasted population, and a breakdown of employment by detailed industry categories. The IPEF model, as developed by the Research and Information Systems staff, was designed to be a versatile forecasting tool and has been applied in a variety of ways to the question of determining future population levels for the San Diego region. As a result of this initial application it has been found that population in 1995 could range from 1.9 to 2.7 million people. The IPEF has shown that local decision-makers, through adoption of a regional growth policy, can have considerable influence on the quality and quantity of growth in the San Diego region.

In preparing the IPEF primary consideration was given to the notion that certain policies made on the regional or local level have a significant effect on the rate of population and economic growth. The model, therefore, was designed to respond to a variety of alternative policies. It has been used to test the impact of policies relating to such factors as unemployment rate, family planning, health care, and industrial expansion. In addition it recognizes certain factors which are beyond the influence of local policy decisions. These include such factors as the number of military personnel stationed in the region and growth of the national economy.

IPEF population forecasts are based on five components of regional growth:

1. Births
2. Deaths
3. Employment-related migration
4. Military-related migration
5. Retirement-related migration

Each component is simulated according to specified assumptions and policy alternatives. The output consists of forecasts of population by age, race, sex, and employment by industry for each five-year interval in the forecast period.

UDM (Urban Development Model). The UDM, most important model in the regional planning program, is also the most complex. It is actually a system of submodels designed to simulate development patterns in the San Diego region. The role of the UDM is to distribute a specific amount of future growth throughout the region, given specific sets of growth policies and development constraints. Forecasting population and employment growth is the function of the IPEF model; these regional population and employment forecasts are then fed into the UDM to be distributed geographically. The UDM focuses on incremental growth and identifies where, within the region, growth is likely to occur.

The UDM involves a rather complex set of calculations, but the basic notions upon which it operates are quite simple. The model assumes that three overriding factors determine where development will occur within the region:

1. Accessibility to employment opportunities
2. Availability of developable land in which residents may locate
3. Attractiveness of any given area

Accessibility represents the time it takes to get to and from various activities throughout the region (e.g. work, shopping, recreation). Obviously different individuals place varying degrees of importance on the desirability of living close to work or recreation areas. But these different attitudes toward commuting are, to a degree, predictable in an overall regional context. For example, it might be observed that 30% of the population may desire to live within 15 minutes of work while 10% are willing to endure a 35-minute commute. Both commuting patterns and the travel times possible on the transportation system are considered by the Urban Development Model.

Availability of vacant developable land in any particular area is also considered; residential densities and open space policies are important in determining the location and amount of vacant developable land.

Attractiveness of an area is also a factor considered by the UDM. Certain locations have uniquely desirable characteristics which attract development; proximity to the seacoast, natural beauty, prestige neighborhoods, and the like. These factors are usually taken into account in existing housing values, which become a proxy for attractiveness.

The foregoing elements—accessibility, availability of vacant land, and attractiveness—are combined in the *allocation function*, a mathematical equation expressing the relationship between these elements and future development within the region.

The Urban Development Model is primarily a tool for testing alternative policy choices with respect to (1) transportation system, (2) urban governmental services, and (3) land use constraints.

Transportation System—It is widely agreed that the transportation system is the single most important factor influencing an urban environment; policies concerning the nature and routine of the transportation system will shape development in years to come. A new freeway, for example, is likely to attract development, unless other factors such as land use constraints intervene. Relevant factors are travel times which can be achieved on the transportation system and costs associated with alternative modes of travel.

Urban Governmental Services—Within the UDM framework, governmental services refer specifically to the availability of municipal water and sewer services. If these are not available, development will normally be limited to low residential densities. On the other hand, public decisions to provide these services usually constitute a green light for development to proceed.

Land Use Constraints—The most commonly used control on development has been land use constraints. A variety of land use constraints are considered in the UDM, including land withheld from development because of unsuitable soil conditions or topographical features, such as excessive slope; and land earmarked for particular uses such as that designated as public open space, agricultural preserves, or military reservations and therefore unavailable for residential development. In addition the UDM takes account of density constraints imposed by local government through zoning.

Primary function of the UDM is to indicate how the region is likely to develop under a variety of alternative policies. The following information is provided, as output from the Urban Development Model, by small geographic units:

1. Total population and dwelling units
2. Employment by place of work and at place of residence
3. Total land use acreage by type of use
4. Household income
5. Housing values
6. Property, sales, and income tax revenues

The above information forms the economic and land use profile for each geographic unit throughout the region. Depending on the level of detail required, the UDM will forecast future growth for a variety of geographic units, with Traffic Zones forming the smallest unit for which forecasts are produced. (There are 663 Traffic Zones in the San Diego County region.) The UDM will also produce forecasts for Census Tracts (315) and Regional Traffic Zones (85).

TM (Transportation Models). The Transportation Models are designed to simulate traffic patterns on each major segment of the transportation network. This is done by using a detailed description of the transportation system, including speeds, distances, costs and travel times, and the economic, social, and land use characteristics derived from the Urban Development Model. There are four individual models in the Transportation Model system:

1. Trip generation
2. Trip distribution
3. Mode split
4. Assignment

The *Trip Generation Model* involves estimating the number of trips originating or ending in any given location (Traffic Zone). This is done by considering the number and characteristics of the residents and employees at each location. (This model is already in use by the State Division of Highways.)

Trip Distribution is the process by which the trips generated by the trip generation model are connected or linked together. Whereas the generation model identifies only the number of trips beginning or ending at any location, the distribution model identifies where the trips are coming from or going to. (This model is also in use by the State Division of Highways.)

Mode Split identifies the transportation modes (*e.g.* automobiles, bus, rapid transit) used to make the trips. The modes used depend upon the trip purpose (*e.g.* work trip, shopping trip), characteristics of the transportation system (*i.e.* costs, travel times, convenience), and the characteristics of users (income, age, occupation).

Trip Assignment is the process of identifying the route on the transportation system by which each trip will be made. Assignments to the transportation network are based on the assumption that people will choose the fastest available route to their destination. (This model is in use at the State Division of Highways.)

The information obtained from the transportation models indicates how major transportation facilities will be used in the future. It shows, for example, how much traffic can be expected on a proposed freeway, or how much use a proposed rapid transit system will receive under each land use concept. It indicates whether existing or proposed transportation facilities will be operating above or below capacity. An analysis of the output from the transportation models will allow the system to be redesigned to accommodate expected future travel demands.

SAQ (Strategic Air Quality) Model. The SAQ Model (being developed under the auspices of the County's Integrated Regional Environmental Management Project (IREM), will describe future air quality based on stationary and mobile sources of pollution and the meteorological characteristics of the region. The Urban Development Model will provide much of the information concerning location of stationary sources of pollution (primarily industrial facilities and power generating plants) and the transportation models will identify location of mobile sources (cars, trucks, buses, for example). The manner in which these pollutants are dispersed throughout the region, and the expected quality of air, will be described by the SAQ Model.

PEM (Plan Evaluation Method). The model system developed for the CPO program activity is designed to simulate alternative futures for the San Diego region under a variety of alternative policies. The models will provide detailed information concerning population, housing, employment, land use, transportation and environmental quality. Outputs from the models will in turn serve as the basis for identifying policies which should lead to the most desirable situation in the future. The Plan Evaluation Method will relate data developed by the model system to various criteria to determine how well each plan or choice fits in with goals for the San Diego region.

Criteria for evaluation, to be related to key issues and problems of the region, will be supplied by the Regional Goals Committee and the CPO standing committees, and will include a full range of technical, social, economic, environmental, land use, developmental, and other impacts, both positive and negative. The Plan Evaluation Method will describe the ability of each alternative plan to meet the criteria, and express that evaluation in terms of a common denominator, an overall score, so that plans can be compared.

"It should be pointed out," say the San Diego County Comprehensive Planning Organization, "that planning models are not without limitations. In any forecasting system, assumptions must be made in order to forecast future events. For example, in forecasting future regional population and employment levels via the IPEF model, it was assumed that the national economy would not experience any drastic changes from historical patterns. If, for example, the national economy were to experience a significant and unforeseen increase in productivity and growth, the IPEF model forecast would require adjustments to account for this trend.

"The forecasts derived from the regional model system are also predicated upon various policy assumptions. The UDM, for example, is specifically used to test the effects of alternative regional policies on land use and transportation patterns. If these implied policies in any one of these alternative forecasts were not adopted and carried out, the projected land use and transportation patterns provided by the model would not be achieved.

". . . planning models, like any other forecasting technique, are highly dependent upon accurate and reliable information. If significant errors are inherent in the data base upon which forecasts are being made, these errors will be reflected in the final projections.

"Moreover, if relationships between various dynamic forces within the urban growth environment are not properly defined, the resultant forecasts will not be entirely reliable.

"The limitations mentioned above are inherent in any method of projecting alternative future events or situations. Through the use of models, many of these difficulties can be overcome or minimized. In order to achieve a truly viable forecasting system in the San Diego County Region, a great deal of reliance has been placed upon the use of reliable and well tested methods. Moreover, every effort has been made to assemble a highly specialized and technically competent staff with the ability to develop and employ these models in the appropriate manner."

AII-2 HPMP (Harris–Putman Model Package)

Britton Harris, in a now classic article entitled "Quantitative Models of Urban Development: Their Role in Metropolitan Policy-Making" (Harris, 1968), stated that the only way to build models was by testing and validating partial models and then linking them to form a pseudocomprehensive model. We refer to this as the bottom-up approach.

With the considerable amount of research done on partial models that are in fairly widespread use throughout the country—the Lowry and EMPIRIC type land use models, and the Urban Transportation Program System put out in 1970 by the Bureau of Public Roads, FHWA (Federal Highway Administration)—linking of such models would appear to be a natural next step and, possibly, provide a readily acceptable tool for those who have already made use of some of these partial models. The following is an early description of such a linkage attempt that was undertaken by Britton Harris and Stephen Putman at the University of Pennsylvania (EPA, 1973).

AII-2.1   The Need

To examine the environmental impacts of a very large number of decisions having to do with policy implementation and facility location at the national, state, and local level, the Agency needs a capability for developing forecasts or predictions of urban-metropolitan and regional development. The prediction mechanism which is needed has at its input end some statement regarding national and possibly local growth, policies to be pursued, and the current state of the system. At the output end, the mechanism should produce a predicted future state of the system, together with conclusions as to the effects on environmental indices and measurements of quality which follow from this state.

The location of activities and the utilization of services (including, for example, water, power, and transportation) are important parts of these predictions. They are characterized by four aspects which make this prediction difficult and complex in terms of evaluating the impact on the environment. First, the activities in the metropolitan area are diverse and their development responds in diverse ways to a number of stimuli. Second, the location and interaction of activities must be examined on the basis of small areas, since the environmental impacts are, in the first instance, largely local. Third, the effects of decisions are propagated in many ways over space and time, and the cumulative remote effects may be more important than the immediate effects. Finally, these developments are influenced by a very large number of public decisions, and the predictions should be able to discriminate between the effects of different decisions.

There is substantial agreement that this complexity can effectively be dealt with principally by the use of large-scale simulation models of urban growth, development, and equilibrium. There is no definitive agreement as to the appropriate models for different purposes and different scales of analysis, as to the ways in which the models can be jointly utilized, or as to the appropriate definition of data requirements and means for satisfying them. In this context, we have undertaken a three-stage investigation, as follows:

(1) We have conducted a limited, detailed, and mission-oriented review of existing models and their potential utilization in meeting this generalized need. This review was not a general survey of the literature, but rather a practical assessment of what can be done in developing a total system.

(2) We developed a prototype system using selected alternative building blocks. We will have this prototype system operational, if only at a low level, so that the EPA and other interested parties can make experimental use of it with a view to delineating further modifications and improvements of this existing system, or specifying alternative systems.

(3) It hardly need be said that a third stage of the project specifies further research needs. In this case, however, the specification is based on detailed experience in building the prototype system and on the development of knowledge of the needs of the EPA and other agencies as the work proceeds. The first stage of the study is discussed in more detail below.

AII-2.2   Review of Models and System Design

The first stage of the study pursued an intensive review of existing models in relation to their cogency, reliability, data requirements, and capacity for conversion to the needs of a general models system. Different portions of the modeling procedure require different degrees of emphasis. In outlining here the various aspects of the total effort which had to be reviewed, we simultaneously present a preliminary sketch of the general effort. This effort was to a considerable extent organized around the land uses which occur in the organized habitation of large regions, but only as a convenient handle for the development of a schema. We also recognize the importance of other forms of organization of the material. These include the actors (such as governments, households, and firms), academic disciplines (such as economics, sociology, and engineering), functional systems (such as transportation and education), and steps in the decision-making process. These represent a selection of the most important ways in which this problem may be viewed, and the art of system design consists in harmonizing all different views and ensuring that no aspect of any is neglected.

AII-2.3   Submodels

Regional projections. The analysis of any local area requires regional projections. In principle, these projections should be made in a national framework, but this recourse may not be fully capable of being implemented at this time. We reviewed the status of nationally generated regional projections and determined the appropriate method for such projections, given data availability and the requirements of later phases of the model. We chose the OBERS projections and made use of them as exogenous inputs to the system. Ideally, regional projections themselves should ultimately be endogenous to one or more models. Such projections can be made for a single region if national conditions can be taken as given. It would then be possible to generate some feedback in which environmental conditions and environmental policies influence the growth of the region, both positively and negatively. More generally, these environmental feedbacks should be fed into a national projection system, which we did not propose to develop in this study. [What follows are brief descriptions of what Harris-Putman proposed as the key elements of their total Urban Development Package. Those with an asterisk in front of the name are the components which had actually been totally completed for EPA at the time of this writing.]

Migration. Migration is treated in this system as a reflex of regional growth or decline. An analysis of migration is needed, however, for projections of over-all household composition. Migration figures are ordinarily available in very gross aggregates. Methods for disaggregating these flows should be part of the models rather than part of the preparation for using the models.

Household Projections. Other portions of this model system require a projection of household composition by size and income. Such a model, which permits taking into account migration, changes in fertility patterns, and changes in income levels, had been designed and programmed at the Institute for Environmental Studies. Linkages with the other models had to be defined, as did the data needs for this particular application.

The foregoing elements deal with regional or metropolitan control totals; the following elements deal principally with internal regional distribution patterns and their interconnections.

Basic Industry Location. This factor in regional development patterns is critical to the analysis for two reasons. First, certain basic industries are primary sources of pollution, and means for studying and projecting their location had to be provided. Second, site-oriented basic industries are the locational anchor for a considerable portion of metropolitan development, and operation of many models, particularly those of the Lowry type, depends on a prior determination of their location pattern. Unfortunately, definitive studies and modeling methods for dealing with this problem are not available, and considerable attention had to be addressed to it.

Intermediate Industries. A number of industries, both basic and non-basic, but not site-oriented, are slow to relocate either because of building requirements or because of economies and diseconomies of agglomeration. Some of these industries are more tractable and better understood and modeled than the site-oriented basic industries.

Retail Trade. Retail trade location is quite well understood, and numerous models are available relating it to the location of purchasing power, the state of the transportation system, and economies of agglomeration. A particularly flexible model had been programmed and was used in the Penn-Jersey Transportation Study. This model was the one chosen for integration into the larger system of models.

Residential Location. Several models of residential location existed and were operational at different levels of aggregation and accuracy. In the context of the system being described here, we chose between one of the incremental descendants of the Lowry model (PLUM, TOMM, or BASS) and some version of the Herbert-Stevens model. All of these models, except BASS, have been acquired by the Institute for Environmental Studies Planning Sciences Simulation Laboratory, and are operational. Some consideration was given to other dynamic models of the Forrester and EMPIRIC type, but there are reasons to believe that these are not so useful. Consideration was given to the provision of a housing supply model, since although supply is implicit in a number of the models discussed, they did not adequately reflect actual changes in the housing stock.

Transportation. Transportation enters into these discussions and in the model in two distinct ways. First, the state of the transportation system and the distance or separation between activities which it measures is a prime factor in all locational decisions. Second, transportation itself, spatially distributed, is a prime source of pollution. For both of these reasons, a capability is provided for simulating the loading on transportation systems. This is the end product of a series of land use interaction and network simulations. It had to be closely integrated into the entire model structure. The Simulation Laboratory had on hand two complete sets of models dealing with these phenomena, and integrated them into the larger system.

Recreational Facilities. The location and utilization of recreational facilities (which are largely but not exclusively provided in the public sector) has many implications for other locational patterns, for the use of transportation facilities, and for the generation of certain types of pollution. It also has implications for the joint use of facilities with pollution control and other aspects of environmental planning. In view of the increasing orientation of the society toward leisure-time activities, the inclusion of recreational system modeling was an important part of this work. A small difficulty arose in that many recreational areas are jointly used by more than one metropolitan area.

Other Public Services. Many public services are users of land, generators of traffic, and independent sources of pollution. The necessity and feasibility of modeling their locational patterns was reviewed. Public services in this category include schools, fire departments, police stations, libraries, and hospitals. In addition, consideration was given to those public facilities which dealt with the amelioration or control of polluting activities such as incinerators, landfill, water treatment plants, and the like. In the whole spectrum of these activities, decisions had to be made in the design of the model system package as to which portions of the public activity sector were considered endogenous to the model and which require specific inputs.

Other Public Policy Inputs. Many public policy inputs which are not in the nature of the location of facilities entered into this modeling effort in a different way. These include taxes, subsidies, and exercises of police power such as zoning or the prohibition of emissions. Most of these public policy decisions serve either as constraints or as parameters for locational models, and consideration of them is thus implicit in all of the modeling efforts discussed above. Once again, an important point for exploration was the manner in which they are entered into the models and the system. In certain cases, the response of government can be regarded as an endogenous or pseudo-market response. In other cases, it can be regarded as a programmed response, the program being entered in advance, but the implementation of that program being endogenous to the system. Finally, discrete policies can be entered not only in advance but at various points in time in the development of the modeled system.

Models of Pollution and the Ecosystem. To date, modeling efforts of the development of metropolitan areas and other regions have considered the natural system and the system of human occupancy quite separately. As a first step in remedying this defect, we included in the model system readily available models of air pollution, water pollution, and ecological responses to human occupancy of the natural environment. This meant that by coupling the models in a forward direction, the user of the system is able to predict ecological responses to changes in the pattern of human occupancy in response to public policy. These predictions naturally depend on the accuracy and completeness of the models employed. The acquisition, assimilation, and use of air-shed, water-shed, and ecological models depended very heavily upon the cooperation of the EPA, since we did not profess a large-scale ability to initiate original work in this field. A more difficult question arose as to whether the ecological models should be so integrated into the system as to provide feedback influencing the operation of the earlier models. Thus, for example, air pollution might differentially discourage residential location in various parts of the region and thus affect the performance of a residential location model. We have already indicated that a higher order of feedback between environmental conditions and regional growth is probably not appropriate for attention in this study. The system finally chosen was IMMP, to be described in detail later in this chapter.

The principal models described relate, of course, to the principal activities and connectors in the metropolitan region—implicitly define a type of over-all system structure. The interconnections between parts of the system are expressed by the fact that the outputs of one model become a part of the environment for other models. If certain models are dynamic in character, as was proposed for the residential and industry location models, then the entire system becomes dynamic in precisely the sense of the Forrester model, but with substantially greater areal and industry detail, and of course with much higher operating costs.

Substantial review effort was devoted to the selection of computer methods for linking various models efficiently and flexibly. There has been a substantial proliferation of computer methods in this area since the linked models systems were first developed in the Penn-Jersey and other transportation studies. A usable system had many characteristics which are difficult to define and more difficult to reconcile, and which hence present substantial design problems.

AII-2.4 Data Requirements

Special mention must be made of the difficulties which were anticipated in the review stage of this study in arriving at an appropriate definition of the data requirements and data sources for these systems. Several aspects of this vexatious problem will be noted. The use of a model system in a specific novel locality for which the package was not originally designed requires new data inputs for two reasons. First, the model must be calibrated or fitted to local conditions so that it may be anticipated to make reliable predictions. Second, the data provides an initial state or base from which projections can take off.

Fundamentally, a system of models of this type, therefore, requires data regarding the location of all the locators discussed in the previous section. Such data are readily available for population in the Census of 1970. Almost all of the other data are very difficult to acquire in the form needed. Particular difficulty should be mentioned in attempting to establish an adequate description of the transportation system and an adequate description of the location of activities and their employment.

In the extreme case, transportation network information could be simulated by using some form of a so-called spider network and airline distances. Such distances can be computed from centroids which are available in digitized Census data.

The acquisition of employment data from public sources presents some problems as to confidentiality and many problems as to data processing. Such information may be available in selected metropolitan areas through a tabulation of Census returns coded by place of work.

Both network and employment information are apt to be available from a fairly recent transportation study in almost any large metropolitan area. Problems arise in making use of these data as to the coincidence of dates, the level of detail of coding of information, and most particularly, the definition of sub-areas. Most of these difficulties can be overcome by some form of approximation, but we did not anticipate that our review would uncover any easily automatable system of local data acquisition.

A particular design difficulty arises out of the fact that the calibration of a dynamic model ordinarily requires data for more than one point in time. The econometric approach implicit in this requirement has not ordinarily been followed in the construction of planning models because time series data in fine area and activity detail has not usually been available. The development of the EMPIRIC model was delayed for several years on account of precisely this difficulty. Very special design efforts will have to be devoted to minimizing the necessity for establishing a local data base at two or more points in time.

A larger problem which is, however, related to data arises both on input and output for any large model system. It would appear desirable to enter a minimal amount of data into the system and to provide means by which these data would be expanded endogenously to meet the needs of various models. At the small scale, this implies that many distributions are characterized by a few summary measures, and in the larger scale it implies that the entire status and performance of large urban and regional complexes can be specified with relatively few and relatively simple parameters. Such simplicity must be a very long-term aim, but it will be examined in the course of this study. Similarly, the usual model system provides far more information than can adequately be used by most decision makers. At the output end of the model system, there was serious need for condensing, summarizing, and filtering the characterization of the performance of the system which will be examined by decision makers. A special aspect of expanding, condensing, and presenting information of this type is the transition from one area system to another—e.g., from Census tracts to grid squares. The mechanisms of these transitions were examined in relation to model linkages, but at this level of effort all such problems were not solved. Finally, it may be suggested that if a compact set of measures can specify its performance under the influence of time and of a compactly specified set of policies, then there ought to be a compact transformation under which a given state is transformed by time and policy into a new state and a new set of outcomes. Such a compact transformation represents the goal of an extremely simple yet very rich model which will animate some of the investigations, but which we do not expect fully to achieve.

AII-3 IMMP (The Integrated Multi-Media Pollution Model)

A research group at Georgetown University developed a multipollution model which is self-contained enough to be used alone as a tool for environmental resource management, but is flexible enough to allow it to be linked with other urban system models, such as the Harris-Putman Model Package or GEM. A description of the model (Paik, 1973), IMMP, follows.

AII-3.1 Scope and Purpose

The primary objective of the project has been to develop a prototype multi-pollution model for a typical metropolitan region. The IMMP model embodies the trade-offs among different forms of residuals dispersed finally in the environment that are affected by alternative production processes—including possibilities of input substitution—and alternative control strategies and methods. These trade-offs are ignored in most of the currently existing environmental pollution models but are clearly of critical importance for rational environmental quality management.

The IMMP model differs from most of the currently existing environmental pollution models in several important respects. The distinguishing feature of the IMMP is its explicit recognition and representation of all of the significant elements of metropolitan environmental pollution and their interrelationships. In contrast to other models which focus their attention on only a part of the total environmental system, the IMMP views environmental pollution as an integral set of interrelated problems—the solution of which requires examination of all types of pollution jointly and simultaneously—and attempts to seek an overall solution, while others offer partial solutions based on partial analyses.

The analysts and policymakers often find that existing models—even when they are designed to deal with multiple pollutants and thus are quite comprehensive in scope—do not readily render themselves as a practical tool for analyzing and evaluating alternative programs and policies in the real world. This is commonly due to the rigid structure to which the model is "locked-in," as in the case of input-output models and linear programming models. Flexibility in addition to "comprehensiveness" and "integrality" is another distinguishing feature of IMMP. Specifically, the IMMP model is designed in modular form so that any part of the model—e.g., an activity—can be added or deleted freely with no structural change in the model; and it can be linked with other urban models to form a more comprehensive model. With such built-in flexibility it can easily be adapted to different metropolitan regions faced with their own sets of environmental problems.

Finally, another main feature of the IMMP is a data bank developed and maintained to provide the user of the model with up-to-date information on alternative production processes of major industries, alternative abatement technologies, etc. The data bank is a necessity for the practical use to which the model is to be put.

In short, the IMMP is a multi-media pollution model which synthesizes the currently available information on all important aspects of the environmental degradation problem and is intended as a comprehensive, flexible and practical tool for analyzing and evaluating alternative strategies for managing the environmental resources of metropolitan areas.

AII-3.2 Structure

Programs to protect environmental quality can be classified into three broad categories: (1) programs to regulate land-use patterns, (2) programs to regulate economic and non-economic activities which create the residuals initially, and programs to regulate on-site and central residuals treatment activities which alter the forms of residuals, and (3) programs to alter the residual dispersion processes. The IMMP model is structured with respect to these categories. The actions that affect the configuration of the metropolitan region and locations of pollutant generating and altering activities determine the distribution of pollutants within the region and belong to the first category. The actions determining the levels of pollution generating activities, of production processes and of pollution treatment processes, all of which in turn determine the magnitudes and types of pollutants produced, belong to the second category. The actions which determine the disposal-dispersion of pollutants belong to the third category. These components of the model are shown in flowchart form in Figure AII-2.

Each rectangular entry represents a controllable variable or structural relation on which the user of the model is allowed to exercise his option, while each circled entry denotes a non-controllable variable or relation which is determined within the model, given the specifications of the controllable variables and relations and the parameters.

With the aid of the data bank, the user of the model can test and make a wide range of decisions from those involving land-use to those concerning the choice of an appropriate set of activities (and locations thereof), through the knowledge of the quantities of pollutants generated therefrom and their ultimate impact on the ambient pollution levels throughout the region. Conversely, the model provides a framework for evaluating the impact of alternative pollutant emission standards or ambient quality standards on various activities within the region.

In anticipation of a more detailed discussion in the subsequent chapters, a brief overview of the basic nature and concepts of the model is given below with reference to the flowchart.

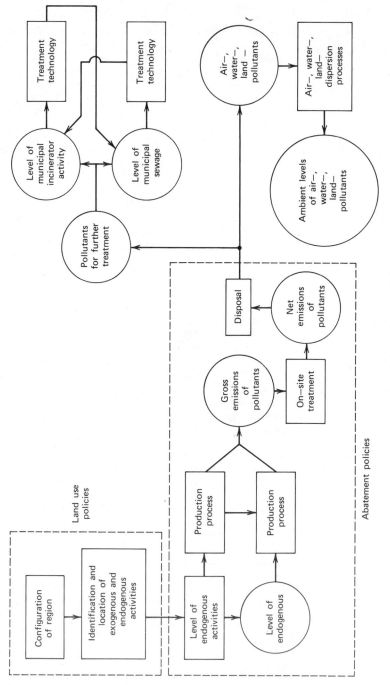

Figure AII-2. A flow diagram of the model.

AII-3.3 Configuration of the Region

For the model, a metropolitan region is considered a rectangular space with a number of rows and columns that divide the space into a set of square grids.

In addition to defining the size of the region, the user can exercise a considerable degree of discretion in specifying the land-use pattern. If a new city is being planned and designed from scratch, the option over the land-use available to the user of the model is rather complete, but even with an existing metropolitan region with more or less fixed spatial structure, the managers may be able to relocate activities, especially in the long run, through zoning classification, taxation and other means. The model can evaluate the environmental impact of these alternative configurations of the region.

AII-3.4 Identification and Location of Activities

The activities in the model as sources of pollution consist of a set of endogenous activities and a set of exogenous activities. Exogenous activities are those with levels of operation determined outside the model, i.e., by the user of the model. For IMMP, the agricultural, industrial, commercial, and residential activities are included as exogenous variables. For endogenous activities, the levels of operation are determined within the model as the result of the exogenous activities. For the purpose of IMMP, the endogenous activities are classified into two categories: those representing residuals-treatment activities such as municipal incinerators and waste water treatment plants, and those other than treatment activities such as transportation and power plants.

Whether for a new or existing metropolitan region, the user of the model has the option of choosing which of these exogenous and endogenous activities are to be included in the model and of deciding where to locate them. Through exercise of this option, the managers can evaluate the environmental impact of alternative mixes of industries, etc., and of alternative land uses.

AII-3.5 Levels of Exogenous Activities and Nontreatment Endogenous Activities

Upon stipulating a set of activities, the user is required to specify for each exogenous activity its level of operation, e.g., output per day or year in dollars or tons for a steel mill. Once this is done, the levels of non-treatment endogenous activities, i.e., of transportation and power plant activities, are determined automatically by applying transformation coefficients (or functions). Through varying the levels of various activities and evaluating the resulting variation in the levels of pollutant emissions and of ambient quality, the user enhances his understanding of the effect of economic (and other) policies on the environment and vice versa.

AII-3.6 Production Processes

The magnitude and type of pollutants arising from an activity—be it exogenous or endogenous—are the functions not only of the level of operation but also of production processes and inputs used, including fuel types. Thus, each of the alternative production processes can be represented by a matrix with an appropriate set of residual coefficients which transforms a sector of inputs into an output sector of pollutants.

The user of the model is allowed to evaluate the pollution effects of using alternative inputs, especially in reference to high-sulfur vs. low-sulfur fuels, as well as the effects of using alternative production processes. The data bank contains polluted transformation coefficients for various production processes of each industry both in current use and in development, and the possibilities of input substitution.

Since different inputs and production processes involve different costs of investment and maintenance, the data bank includes data for these costs, enabling the user to compare the differential pollution effects of alternatives with their differential cost effects.

AII-3.7 Gross Emissions of Pollutants

As shown in the flowchart (Figure AII-2), the result of the decisions made by the model user up to this point is the gross emissions of all pollutants in the various subareas of the region where the pollution-generating activities are located. In bare skeleton, the structural relations involved are as follows.

Where: X = a vector of exogenous activities, each element of which represents an activity in a particular subarea.

Y = a vector of endogenous activities such as transportation and power plants. Each element of Y represents an endogenous activity in a particular subarea.

E_g = a vector of gross pollutants emitted prior to any treatment, on-site or otherwise.

Then: $Y = F_1(X)$

$$E_g = F_2(X) + F_2(Y) = F_2(X) + F_3[F_1(X)]$$

The decision maker has no policy control over the transformation of X into Y, i.e., over the relation F_1, but he can specify alternative levels of X as well as alternative residual transformations of X and Y into E_g, i.e., alternative relations, F_2 and F_3, on order to observe their effects on E_g. Since all the relations involved are "one-to-one," the processes of transformation may be reversed, that is, the decision maker may stipulate alternative levels of E_g—alternative emission standards—and observe their effects on X and Y, the activities.

AII-3.8 On-Site Treatment

Prior to being dispersed into environmental receptors (air, water and land) or being transported to other facilities for further treatment, the pollutants arising from the activities are often treated at the source.

In the model, a treatment process is represented by an array of coefficients whereby given (untreated) residuals are transformed into a set of treated residuals.

The data bank supplies the user of the model a list of treatment technologies for each of the activities that correspond to known alternatives. If the user does not specify what treatment technology is applied in a given activity at a given location, the model will assume that no treatment is applied in that instance. In addition to the transformation matrix of coefficients, the data bank contains the information on the costs of investment and maintenance for alternative on-site treatments.

The quantities of net emissions after on-site treatment are the final emissions at the source and may serve as the basis for pollution regulation by setting standards. The user therefore is supplied with the printout of these net emissions.

AII-3.9   Disposal

The next decision to be made by the user is what part of these initially treated pollutants is to be "shipped" to the municipal sewage treatment plants and incinerators, E_f, and to which environmental medium and at which location (subarea) the remainder of pollutants are to be disposed, E_d. For each iteration, the user has complete freedom in specifying these proportions. Again the data bank supplies cost information on alternative disposal decisions.

AII-3.10   Municipal Water Treatment and Incinerator Activities

Municipal waste water treatment and incinerator activities are endogenous in that the levels of these operations are determined as the result of exogenous activities. Thus, given the disposal decision and E_f, the resulting quantities of pollutants designated to be treated at the municipal facilities, the levels of these treatment activities are determined within the model. This is accomplished by solving a matrix equation reminiscent of the solution to an input-output problem.

The reason that E_f (the result of the disposal decision) cannot be directly used as the levels of these "central" or "collective" treatment operations is the interdependence that exists between the treatment activities themselves. Sludge and suspended solids produced by the water treatment plan may be shipped to the incinerator, and the residues from the incinerator may be discharged into the sewer or a river to end up as an added load to the water treatment plant.

Thus, ultimately the levels of central treatment activities E_f, determine the increases in the loads of the treatment activities necessitated from the treatment activities themselves; that is $E_t = E_f + E_e$. Now since E_e can be obtained as $E_c = SE_t$, where S is the matrix of coefficients each column of which represents the changes in the levels of all the treatment activities induced by a particular treatment activity, $E_t = E_f + SE_t$. Therefore, $E_t - SE_t = E_f$; $(I - S)E_t = E_f$; $E_t = (I - S) - {}^IE_f$.

AII-3.11   Summary

In summary, the steps in determining the endogenous treatment activities are: (1) The user specifies a particular treatment technology for each and every treatment activity. This means in effect the specification of how much of what pollutant is discharged into air, water and land, and of how much of what pollutant requires further treatment at other treatment activities per unit activity of the treatment plant in question. (2) The computer forms a particular matrix based on the decision in the first step. Each column of this matrix pertains to a particular treatment activity. The (row) entries of a column are the changes in the levels of all the treatment activities induced by an additional unit of a particular treatment activity that is represented by the column. (3) The computer forms the matrix $(I-S)$

and then inverts it. (4) When E_f, the pollutant loads resulting from the disposal decision, are read in, the ultimate levels of treatment activities E_t are computed by the matrix multiplication $(I-S)$ -1 E_f.

Now that the levels of central treatment activities E_t have been computed, the next step is to determine E_m, the quantities of pollutants which are discharged from the treatment plants to the environmental media. In order to obtain E_m, another matrix multiplication, similar to the earlier transformation for production processes and on-site treatments, is performed on E_t. That is, $E_m = RE_t$, where the matrix R depends on the choice of treatment technologies made by the user in connection with the determination of the levels of treatment activities.

Again, the data bank stores descriptions of alternative treatment technologies together with the associated residual transformation matrices and costs so as to enable the user to evaluate their impact.

The sum of the quantities of pollutants discharged by the central treatment plants E_m and that part of pollutants emerging from on-site treatments which is discharged directly to the environmental media as the result of the disposal decision E_d, namely $E = E_m + E_d$, is the final quantities of emissions the environment receives initially at various subareas (i.e., square grids). As a practical matter, these quantities often serve as the basis for pollution regulations, and accordingly, their printout is supplied to the user of the model.

AII-4   SEAS (Strategic Environmental Assessment System)

Another logical method for designing and constructing a comprehensive model would be to formulate a general design that one wished to achieve, to find which partial models already exist to satisfy some portions of that design, to improve these models where necessary, and then to build missing portions from scratch. SEAS was conceived to be such a system. A description of this model as it was initially designed and reported (EPA, 1973) follows.

Development of SEAS began in the fall of 1972. The system was to have a forecasting capability that would detect changes in pollutant levels and the effects that would result from economic and demographic changes. Also required was the ability to project the impacts of environmental controls on the economy, on the natural environment, and on society.

Fulfillment of this mandate was approached in an evolutionary fashion. In the beginning, the concepts were cloaked in the builders' jargon and much time was spent trying to arrive at consensus among the developers on exactly what these terms meant and how they would be measured. In order to cut short much armchair debate, a three-stage plan was formulated and the project moved from conception to construction. The three stages were a test model, a prototype model, and full-scale operating system. Each of these stages was to be a decision point in the development of SEAS. At the end of a stage, the cost of the development of the next stage and the availability of data and theory were examined in light of the system operation.

From one point of view, the test model was the most ambitious plan of the three. During a 3-month period, we attempted to construct a system that forecasted the results of extraction, production, distribution, consumption, and disposal activities on the total natural resource base and on the amount of residuals produced. The residuals were to be tested for their effects on human and other ecological sectors. The results would then predict the impact of these effects back on the growth sectors of the model.

Although the test model was completed on time, its principal utility was to the developers; they received an intensive lesson in the availability of various data and the relative state of the art of the various areas of relevant theory. On the basis of this information, the overall design of the prototype phase was developed.

On the positive side, there was no need to develop a model from scratch to predict the productive activities of the nation. One of the working papers developed for the test model was concerned with reporting on the availability, documentation, and relative utility of the existing macroeconomic and input-output (I/O) models. For many reasons, it seemed wasteful for us to build models from scratch since quite acceptable models of national forecasting already existed. To the extent that these models were readily available and could be used for our analysis needs, time and money would be better utilized by adding to a present model. The national economic model finally chosen was the Interindustry Forecasting Model of the University of Maryland (INFORUM). This model remains a basic part of the system today. It is the only portion of the test model to survive.

On the other hand, the research of the test model led to several disappointing findings. There was very little information on the national ecological system's reaction to environmental effects. Further, because of the paucity of information and the difficulty of analysis, the ecological portion of the model was dropped. Finally, because of the small amount of time available to build the prototype, as well as the demonstrated need for detailed depth, a relatively narrow scope was chosen over a broad-based, less detailed one. Consequently, most of the effort was in the direction of production and consumption activities and in the resultant creation of various emissions in the areas of air, water, solid waste, noise, and radiation.

The prototype itself was easier to discuss than the test model because its design was more straightforward. The next level model just completed is somewhat less straightforward and significantly larger. Figure AII-3 shows a rather complex flowchart of macroparts of SEAS Phase III. Rather than go into a great deal of discussion about the individual boxes, we discuss the major segments of this figure.

AII-4.1   Economic Models: An Assessment System

The SEAS economic forecasts are at three levels. The first, the macroeconomic forecast, provides the general parameter projections on an annual basis through 1985. These general values include employment, general production sector output volumes, personal consumption, disposable income, and capital investment. They allow projections of the general GNP subaccounts. The macroeconomic model used in SEAS was developed and maintained by Chase Econometric Associates.

The second level of forecast is the calculation of interactions among industries to meet the levels of output in the demand forecast of the macro model. This economic I/O model provides the economic projections for each year for 185 sectors of the economy as well as statistics for each sector such as employment, output sold for final demand, total output, durable goods and construction expenditures, export, imports, and inventories. The model form, I/O, is a rigorous system that provides great detail and balanced accounting of values that can act as physical goods flow among the sectors and to the final consumers. The specific model in SEAS is the INFORUM model, maintained by a staff at the University of Maryland and linked to the macroeconometric model by Chase.

A third level of forecast detail for economic activity is produced by the SEAS design and systems teams and deals with procedures that break the specific (185) industry forecasts into richer information required for particular analysis questions. As an example, the INFORUM model provides a single set of values to forecast the diverse activities of the Industrial Chemicals sector of our economy. Since many of the subcategories of this sector are of interest to study groups performing resources and environmental analyses, the third level of economic forecasting details this sector into about 20 subcategories that show projected subproduct outputs as well as time trends of production process (technological) changes. This last level of detail in SEAS is easily expanded and now represents three times the details available from the INFORUM sector. Following are other modules tied to the system.

AII-4.2   ABATE, The Abatement Cost Feedback Model

ABATE estimates the investment and operating and maintenance costs associated with abating the emissions of air and water pollutants by each economic sector. It also feeds back to INFORUM the increased monetary and goods demands placed by pollution control investment and operating purchases on the industrial sectors that apply construction materials and labor, abatement equipment, chemicals for abatement, energy sources, and operating manpower requirements. INFORUM uses this information to rebalance its forecasts of sector economic activity. Nonindustrial consumption and disposal processes, such as utilities, sewage treatment plants, and commercial and residential space-heating consumptions, are handled by INFORUM, RESGEN, and ABATE in concert, in the same manner as the industrial sectors.

AII-4.3 SOLID WASTE, The Solid Waste-Recycling Model

SOLID WASTE estimates the amounts of solid wastes from nonindustrial sources, the expected method of disposal, and the costs associated with each method. For incineration and open-burning disposal methods, it estimates the annual levels of air pollutant emissions. Recycling levels are applied to the product classes that comprise significant elements of the solid-waste stream to calculate total amounts of materials available for recycling and the levels actually recycled. These amounts are transferred to the Stocks Model, which may alter them depending on the available quantities and relative unit prices of virgin ores and recycled materials. The recycling levels are also used to adjust technological ore splits of input materials used by an industry, such as primary versus secondary metals production ratios.

AII-4.4 STOCKS, The Material Reserves Model

After the economic models have derived the annual total demand for a number of fuels and mineral ores, and the recycling model has forecast the degree to which demand for some materials can be met by reprocessed materials, SEAS applies the STOCKS Model to provide detail on raw material sources, levels of economic reserves depletion, and relative production cost increases under a wide range of possible inventory/export/import assumptions. Accounts are maintained on U.S. reserves and on rest-of-world reserves as functions of the relative production price presently for 28 stock categories, of which 6 are fuels and 18 are nonfuel minerals. To properly maintain the needed information on ore status, the model must forecast price changes, modify recycling levels, estimate new investment requirements for mining and refining capacity, project mixes of domestic/import patterns for each ore, assign domestic production to subnational regions, and allow for increasing environmental effects as ore sources are depleted. The major outputs of the model are provided for each ore; these are annual demand levels for each ore and the relative price change for the ore. The first statistic provides material flow impact if demand is not modified; the second, coupled with the next model, provides the mechanism for modifying demand in INFORUM projections.

AII-4.5 *RELPRICES, The Commodity Relative Prices Forecast Model*

In the economic forecast of industrial outputs by INFORUM, the annual calculations require an estimate for each of the industries of the cost of the output relative to the Consumer Price Index. Like all basic I/O models, INFORUM includes the assumption that the total outputs are not supply constrained, but are set by the consumer's final demands. To add the obviously needed supply constraints to this pure-demand system requires the addition of elasticities of output demand as a function of relative prices so that, as one price rises relative to the others, there is a relative decrease in the amount demanded. Since the SEAS system has several elements that can affect the supply–demand balance (STOCKS, SOLID WASTE, ABATE), there is a need to provide a module to dynamically calculate a new set of relative price of goods; this is provided by the model RELPRICES. The model can accept any combination of relative price adjustments for any goods, say, a monthly price increase of coal in 1974–1975 of 3%, or an additional annualized capital investment by the steel industry of 1% for abatement equipment, and will calculate the expected changes in all goods, prices, and wages for all industries. This information is transferred to the relative price tables of INFORUM so that INFORUM can provide an updated forecast based on these dynamic economic reactions to the demand/supply balance. Thus, requirement is met by making the economic forecasts in a supply-constrained system.

AII-4.6 *ENERGY, The Energy Use Model*

ENERGY estimates the energy use by fuel category based on the INFORUM forecasts of economic activity for 185 sectors of the economy. For each fuel category, it also indicates whether the fuel is used for combustion or for raw material in six user categories: industrial, commercial, residential transportation, electric utility consumption, and electricity generation. The model provides detailed accounting of all fuel usage (and implicit fuel losses) in a consistent measure (quadrillions of BTUs) based strictly on the values developed in the economic forecast model, INFORUM. Additionally, rates of increase are provided in use of each fuel category by each user category or by each industrial sector. Because the energy forecasts are based on INFORUM, the following are dramatically introduced: (1) supply constraints (through the mechanism of price modifications by solid waste burning), (2) fuel stock levels, and (3) relative price adjustments. Also, since final consumer demands and consumer purchase elasticities are easily modified before the INFORUM calculations, it is possible to enter a wide range of material conservation policies and see the annual effect on fuel consumption.

AII-4.7   RESGEN, The Residual Generation Model

RESGEN estimates annual emissions of air pollutants, water pollutants, and solid wastes for the most significant polluting industries. It does not estimate transportation emissions or emissions from a nonpoint source. These are associated with land use activities such as agriculture, forestry, mining and drilling, construction, and urban runoff. With these exceptions, it estimates, first, the potential environmental emissions before abatement and then the emissions actually reaching the environment. The latter depends on the degree of pollution abatement in each sector and its subprocesses. The released emissions include the untreated primary pollutants as well as the significant secondary pollutants produced by the pollution treatment process themselves (sludges).

AII-4.8   TRANSPORT, The Transportation Model

TRANSPORT forecasts the demand for automobiles, buses, trucks, railroads, and airplanes in terms of miles traveled for both passenger and freight transportation purposes. It estimates the annual volume of controlled emissions produced by mobile sources. For passenger automobiles, the model calculates nonrecurring and recurring costs of controlling air pollutant emissions according to specified abatement strategies (as given in urban transportation control plans) based on scheduled use of pollution control devices on new cars and on the projected metropolitan transportation control plans.

AII-4.9   LAND USE, The Land-Use Model

LAND USE forecasts the amounts of land used in broad categories as a function for forecasting economic activity. For nonprofit sources of pollution (agriculture, construction, forestry, mining and drilling, and urban runoff, plus naturally occurring pollution sources), it forecasts levels of air, water, and solid waste pollutant emissions. Currently, the model does not estimate associated costs of abatement.

AII-4.10   REGION, The Assignment of Processes and Associated Activities to Subnational Regions Model

Many of the models discussed thus far perform their forecasts at the national level; exceptions to this are STOCKS, LAND USE, and TRANSPORT. In order to enrich the forecast of economic and environmental impacts, this model provides a forecast of distribution in industry outputs and the associated environmental emissions to a number of geographical subdivisions. The subdivisions include states, SMSAs (Standard Metropolitan Statistical Areas), river basins, air-quality control areas and "basic economic areas." To subdivide the national data, a number of procedures are used to properly represent statistical differentials due to known modifiers (sulfur content of coal burned by utilities is a function of area). Historical trends in plant relocations are reflected. As the various environmental emissions are assigned to regions, an experimental routine is used to calculate total emissions of criteria pollutants and, where appropriate, to modify growth in regions to reflect the deviation from historical trends due to environmental regulations and control plans.

AII-4.11   AMBIAIR and AMBIWATER, The Emissions to Ambient Quality Models

AMBIAIR and AMBIWATER are the links between air emissions levels and ambient air quality. They are also the links between water effluent discharge levels and ambient water quality, respectively. These simple rollback models estimate regional average air and water concentrations and represent a major effect of pollution control efforts.

AII-4.12   BENEFITS, The Relative Damages and Benefits Model

The BENEFITS model forecasts benefits of pollution abatement by first forecasting the damages to the environment that would have occurred without the impacts of federal legislation. It then subtracts the damages to the environment forecast, using the assumed level of pollution abatement for a scenario. The resulting differences are benefits, defined as the reductions in damages to the environment for some future year.

Finally, the upper right-hand corner of Figure AII-3 describes the spatial allocation portion of the model. All of the outputs of SEAS are projected at the national level and are then disaggregated into the various political and statistical subareas. The disaggregation is concerned principally with levels of economic activity and pollution. One of the subareas chosen is the Standard Metropolitan Statistical Area (SMSA).

The 253 SMSAs in the country are then to be divided into ten "modal" areas using principal component analyses. These areas are considered representative and thus indicative of the type of response such locales might have to national policy decisions. The spatial portion of the model then takes these national forecasts and distributes them into a spatial arrangement. The module has land use and transportation subroutines coupled to various pollution modules and is used to forecast variables of interest to the local decision maker.

AII-4.13 Summary

In sum, we have presented SEAS as a system that is a tool for use at the policy level of EPA. Its scope accommodates the interests of people working at this level and it is being designed so as to provide maximum flexibility. The forms in which the output can be presented and the attention being paid to ensuring that potential users understand the assumptions in the system, should help mitigate against, on the one hand, unwarranted expectations of the capability of the system, and on the other, a lack of appreciation of its real worth. Finally, the uses of SEAS in policymaking are expected to be broad in scope and, by designing for maximum flexibility, hopefully diverse in nature. There are also difficulties in developing guidelines for policymakers' application of SEAS to environmental pollution problems at the national level. However, policymakers (in EPA, in CEQ, and in the state and local governments across the country) must make decisions that have effects across all areas every day. Consequently, this research project is a first attempt to see just how much help the modeler and the analytical scientist can offer the policymaker in his quest for information about the total impact of his decisions.

We hope that SEAS will evolve into a comprehensive system capable of forecasting potential future environmental pollution problems with their concomitant effects and reactions. At this point it is useful to reemphasize another realistic decision that is part of the SEAS design. It was never contemplated that the total model would be machine-oriented. Consequently, a great deal of work has gone into designing SEAS so that each parameter in the model can be easily accessed by the user. The "users" of the model could be defined, for the moment, as a group of people who would do the policy analysis of the questions posed by the decision makers. Policy analysis consists of two types: (1) the restructuring of the policymaker's questions into a form acceptable to the model and (2) an analysis of the output of simulation runs to put the information in a form most useful and meaningful to the policymaker.

The SEAS experiment is an attempt to develop a state-of-the-art policy

model to enable managers who are making policy in the environment area
to consider the effects of their decisions not only on all media, but also on
the rest of the local system. Furthermore, it enables them to see the
consequences of their decisions as time passes, and as numerous and
unexpected exogenous events exert their influence.

SEAS has moved in the direction of a full-scale, comprehensive model.
It is, however, flexible, influenced by its component partial models.
Naturally, then, the final stage in building it and other comprehensive
models is the planned design of such a system from scratch so that each
module is conceived of (and thereby both enriched and constrained) by
the others. Following are two examples of such models: The General
Environmental Model (GEM) and EIC's Regional Growth/Land Use
Model (RG/LU).

AII-5 GEM (General Environmental Model)

(Much of the material in this section was taken from House, June 1973,
and House, October 1974).

Most models have been designed to be used not by policymakers, but by
aficionados of the modeling field who created them to inform or impress
their peers. However, the models described here were designed with an
eye toward the users, and their designs address many of the user's needs.
GEM is particularly strong in this regard. The following discussion shows
it to be a framework within which models can be used to advantage by
the policymaker.

AII-5.1   Overview

GEM was developed to provide decision makers at local and national
levels with a useful tool for policy analysis. Using GEM, the different
impacts of a wide variety of resource utilization policies and alternatives
can be tested on characteristic types of urban areas. The system can be
used with any of the modal data bases being designed that represent the
253 SMSAs (nearly two-thirds of the U.S. population). Alternatively, a
data-base generator is being designed for simulating local areas using a
minimum number of data inputs. (See Appendix III on data sources.)

The model itself structurally defines urban areas in terms of three basic
sectors—The Social Sector, The Economic Sector, and The Government
Sector—and considers the control and usage of system resources
(natural, human, physical, and monetary) accordingly. The subsystem
processes (migration, transportation, employment, etc.) in the model
programs describe the behavioral mechanisms by which the sectors trade,

utilize, and consume resources. There are no dynamically changing functional relationships within the model's program. Change is introduced only through a modification in either the amount of resources, the control of resources, or the utilization of resources as the program processes the effects brought about through user inputs.

The operation of GEM provides a representation of the immediate status of an urban area, given an adequate description of the system resources and the policies attached to the use of those resources. Through successive iterations of the model (which cycles on a one-year basis), trends in the changing status of the urban area can be examined in view of the policies in effect and the methods being used to meet or adjust to those policies. Returning to the original starting configuration, the user can cycle the model again with different policies or implementation procedures to examine the potential consequences of proposed alternatives. The model then is best considered as an impact model concerned with resource allocation problems which, when cycled through 5–20 iterations, portrays the possible changing status of the system resources.

AII-5.2   DAS (Decision-Analysis System)

Figure AII-4 represents schematically a software system that has as its purpose the linking of numerous modeling substructures to allow a decision maker to experiment with and investigate the effects of various alternative decisions. The DAS framework consists of five parts: constrictor models, the data base, GEM, the output, and the specific decision analysis modules.

AII-5.3   Constrictor Models

Most models operate in a sequence in which several system-defining decisions are made to serve as exogenous variables. These high-level decisions are then used to make the model predict changes at a world or national level. The predicted changes are then allocated to the local levels on the basis of predetermined functions. There is nothing intrinsically wrong with this procedure if the purpose of the model is strictly national forecasting to be disaggregated to regional levels. There is some room for question, however, as to whether the methodology is useful for decision analysis at the regional level. At this level the decision maker is presented with a *fait accompli* that has been generated by the high-level models and in which all of the primary decisions, as well as many of the forcing ones, have been determined and are beyond his control. However, a model need not be built so that this is the case.

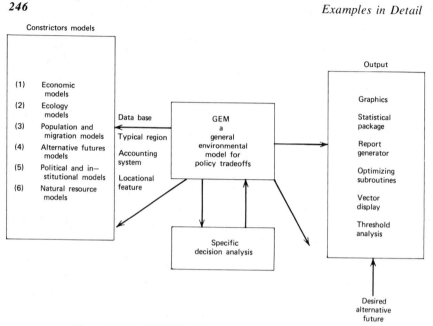

Figure AII-4. (DAS) Decision Analysis System framework.

If the purpose of developing a model is to build a system in which the local or regional policymaker is able to test the effects of his own "what if" types of decisions, he should have even more flexibility available to him than he has in the real world. Consequently, the models that are constructed to represent the workings of the metasystems (which are, as noted, outside the purview and control of local policymakers) must operate in such a way as to reflect the effects of policy choices, rather than to mandate a particular outcome. In this respect, the models representing the outside system are "constrictor" models because they act to restrict the freedom of choices of the local decision makers, although not to actually dictate them. This is a major difference from the deterministic choices typically encountered in land use, transportation, and other current models.

As such, macroprojection models like GEM can be used not only to determine change, but to set probabilistic limits on the effects of decisions made internally in GEM. This feature means that the Econometric Models determine such things as the production functions, the price and wage structure, and other economic parameters for the subsystem. The Ecology Models are used to interrelate the decision structure to multimedia models, which show the effects of residuals and the concomitant feedback. The Population and Migration Models are used to allocate people to a region on the basis of its shifting share of an extrapolated national growth trend. This populace is differentiated on the basis of age, sex, and skills to give work characteristics, and by family size for education and other purposes. Like the multimedia models, the Natural Resources Models reflect the carrying capacity of the region in terms of such things as pollution, land use, and local raw materials.

The Alternate Future models are projection models that are used to adjust such things as the production cost coefficients of goods and services and consumption rates. Political and Institutional model routines represent the underlying values and operating principles of the system and adjust the transfer functions between the various sectors in the model. Like the future models, they also can readjust the exchange values of an area's resources without new decisions.

In sum, all of these models are exogenous with respect to the regional decision maker who interacts with the larger system, generally in a reactive fashion (i.e., the larger system helps to define and limit the issues that will be of prime interest to the policymaker at the regional level).

The formal theory behind GEM evolved over several years. In continuing to trace the model's development and construction, we extract from a work (House, 1974) that is based in part on the GEM experience.

AII-5.4   Model Inputs

The decision inputs for GEM allow the user to exert complete control over the local system if he so desires. They permit him to determine everything from the maintenance operations of an individual industrial activity to the distribution of tax revenues. This means there is an extensive set of options at the user's disposal.

These decision inputs also represent the driving force that introduces change into the system. To minimize the necessary user inputs and to prevent an artificial type of control over the system by the user, decision-making simulators are developed to model the decision making phenomena in the Economic and Government Sectors. (Only EDS is operational; see Section AII-5.5.) These simulators will limit the number of required user inputs. The simulated decisions are based upon system characteristics and on the past performance of previous similar decisions. Thus decisions made by the Economic and Government simulators are based on information about the system. They are based also on a changing probability that a particular course of action on a decision will be taken, including in this calculation a positive weighting for past behavior, given the past success of that course of action.

The simulators operate in a separate fashion from the other GEM programs; they print out a card for each decision. This sequence allows the user opportunity to modify or substitute decisions before submitting the cards for processing. Through this mechanism, the user can expand his control over the model to whatever point is needed or desired.

The computer programs in GEM simulate the processes that utilize and manipulate the system resources distributed among the four modules. Through these processes, the relationships between the modules are demonstrated, and the effects of decisions are used in determining system behavior.

- Migration. This computer routine calculates dissatisfaction (based on a series of indices) and determines population shifts accordingly.
- Depreciation. This routine depreciates all developments and calculations requiring maintenance expenditures.
- Employment. The employment routine assigns full-time or part-time workers to jobs on the basis of best education first and on the assumption that workers will attempt to maximize their net salary (salary received minus transportation costs).
- Transportation. This assigns workers to transportation mode and routes in an effort to minimize total transportation costs, subject to the constraints imposed by public transit capacity, road congestion, and transportation boycotts.
- School Allocation. This routine assigns students to public or private schools based upon school quality criteria and capacity of the school serving their district.
- Time Allocation. For each population unit, time spent in various activities (transportation, part-time employment, adult education, politics, recreation) is computed. A resultant measure of "Involuntary Time" is used with other factors to determine level of dissatisfaction.
- Commercial. In the commercial routine, purchases (normal and recreation-related) of the population groups of a parcel, and residential maintenance expenditures are allocated to personal goods and personal services establishments based on minimizing total costs (sale price plus transportation charges). Similar methods apply to the purchase of business goods and business services.
- Bookkeeping. This routine makes all the final calculations of incomes and expenditures and of indicators for use in the computer output.

AII-5.5 EDS (Economic Decision-Making Simulation)

EDS, a GEM submodel, gives the system a nearly closed simulation of all Economic Sector activities. It plans all actions to be taken in old and new

AII-5 GEM (General Environmental Model)

economic activities and provides information to decision makers in other sectors concerning the likely patterns of economic expansion, plus major expansion constraints under control of the Government Sector.

Subroutines. Six major EDS subroutines are used after the user enters the extra-region data projections: percentage growth estimated in heavy industry, light industry, and national services for the next five years as well as a general economic change ratio comparing this year's prices to last year's real prices.

The first subroutine, EDS-I (EDS-Initialize), performs two major functions. First, the output of the last round is summarized and reassembled in the forms needed in later steps of EDS. Second, the preferences of each of the planning units of the Economic Sector (EU) to develop types of new businesses are modified, based on a set of factors including rates of return of the existing similar businesses, both owned by the EU or by other EU, and the sites presently owned by the EU that can be used for that type business.

The second initialization routine is the LUA-T (Land Use Allocation) subroutine that projects likely economic growth patterns as five-year plans and develops indices of tracts as candidate areas for new construction for each of the five primary economic activities.

The third subroutine, EDS-P (present business), provides a review for each currently operating business to adjust operating factors such as salaries, rents, or unit prices. Then a calculation of cash position of each EU is made to determine:

- if the EU must generate more operating funds by short-term borrowing, deferring maintenance, or selling properties.
- if the EU has sufficient operating funds, then it will upgrade some facilities if this improvement is likely to increase income.

After these steps are completed, a final check is made to determine if any EU is in a position during this round to begin expansion of present operating levels or construction of new business sites.

If any EU have sufficient capital funds, the fourth subroutine, EDS-N (new developments) is initiated. For all EU, depending on their preferences to develop new activities (developed on EDS-I) and their capital funds position, the expected levels of new development in each activity are developed. Then the search for a location for each type of new development is done as a four-step process. After locations are found, various projections are made for the business and if the estimates are appropriate, the new land purchases, construction and long-term loans are scheduled.

The final subroutine of EDS-E (editor) performs certain data housekeeping chores to set up information to be used in other programs of the GEM system. It also processes several output forms to be provided to the decision makers of the Government and Social Sectors. These outputs include:

- publication of the five year expected economic growth,
- distribution by tract,
- indication of sites for all new or expanded EU activities,
- indication of tracts and parcels that were not chosen for new development, and the reasons for the constraint.

AII-5.6   Simulation of Other Sectors

The next major development effort for the GEM system would be to design and implement decision-making simulations within the Government Sector, and, as required, the Social Sector. The primary efforts to be simulated are the operating funds and the capital funds budgeting function, including the allocations to departments and the establishment of tax rates, plus the development of priorities for scheduling new public facilities in each jurisdiction.

The land use allocation routine would be integrated with the EDS procedure, primarily developing general levels of activities and selecting locations for new sites. From this routine the priority list for public capital projects could be developed.

The next routine would be the development of salary adjustments and departmental operating budgets. An estimate of new capital projects that can be initiated this round and the associated subsidies is produced next. A major factor here is the influence of the Social Sector decision makers.

Estimated assessment rates and tax rates are then developed and checked to ensure that they are within realistic bounds. This is followed by the detailed planning of new public projects and the checking of all with respect to operating factors for present public activities.

As has been stated earlier, GEM evolved from a complex decision game. The concept behind gaming of this sort (used widely in the military and in business) is that the computer programs can be made sufficiently realistic to allow the gaming portion to be merely an extension of the policy desires of a particular area. In this way, the model is similar to the "scorecard" concept discussed in connection with STAR (Appendix I).

To the extent that the machine portions of the model are valid, the next logical step is to begin to investigate the simulation of the decision makers themselves. This, too, has a familiar ring to modelers, who are often called upon to stochastically produce decision values for their simulations. In essence, EDS does a similar service, although it attempts to operationalize the heuristic decision maker (Newell et al., 1959).

AII-6 RGLU (Regional Growth/Land Use Model)

Another approach to comprehensive modeling is lucidly and impressively discussed by Alexander L. Pugh II and his colleagues at the Environmental Impact Center (EIC), Cambridge. Although rather lengthy, it is sufficiently impressive to quote at length from their report (Environmental Impact Center, 1973). The overview follows:

AII-6.1 An Overview of the System

A "region," as we use the term in the context of this project, is a geographical area inside which the vast majority of the population remains to work, shop, and sleep. In the case of a city, regional boundaries should encompass the greater metropolitan area (perhaps the SMSA for data purposes). If the region does not involve a major city, boundaries may be chosen more arbitrarily (with data structure, again, being a predominant practical criterion).

The dynamics of regional change depend on the locational decisions of people and businesses. Such decisions occur on two levels: the regional and the intraregional. These two levels are largely separate and hierarchical. The regional location decision precedes the intraregional decision, with little interaction between the two. The former determines aggregate levels of activities in the region, while the latter determines the spatial distribution of those activities, that is, the land use pattern within the region. Thus, in order to analyze regional dynamics, the region must be subdivided into smaller geographical units, which we call "zones." Regional location decisions depend upon the characteristics of the region as a whole, relative to other regions, while intra-regional or zonal location decisions depend on the characteristics of each zone relative to other zones (including their proximity to one another) within the region.

AII-6.2 Regional Versus Zonal Levels

The number of variables involved in the interaction between regional and zonal levels is small. However, extensive feedback takes place within each level. The characteristics which make regions or zones either attractive or unattractive to people and businesses are highly interdependent. The availability of employment is a critical factor in regional attractiveness to people, while businesses require an adequate labor force in the region where they are considering new facilities. The same factors enter into zonal attractiveness, but emphasis shifts from "availability" to "access." Workers desire easy access to their jobs, while businesses are aware of the benefits of an accessible site. Figure AII-5 depicts these simplified interactions.

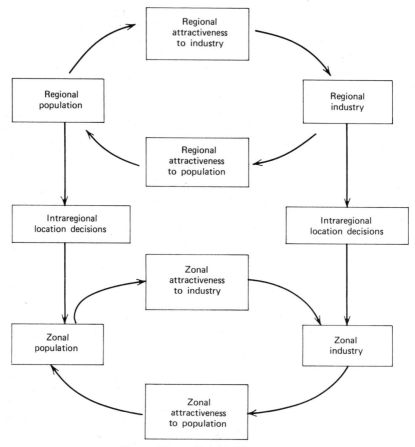

Figure AII-5. Simplified interactions.

Because the regional and zonal levels are largely separate, we can consider them individually. We will begin with the regional level, since that is higher or "prior" in the hierarchy. At this level, land use per se is not in question and no attempt is made to specify where, *within* a region, activities are located. Our only considerations, therefore, are demographic and industrial.

AII-6.3 Population

Figure AII-6 shows the major parameters and relationships for regional population and industry. The population level depends upon births, deaths, and net migration. In actuality, these three factors vary widely for different combinations of age, skill, and income within the population. These variations are more thoroughly discussed in our description of the demographic sector. For simplicity, they are omitted in the figure.

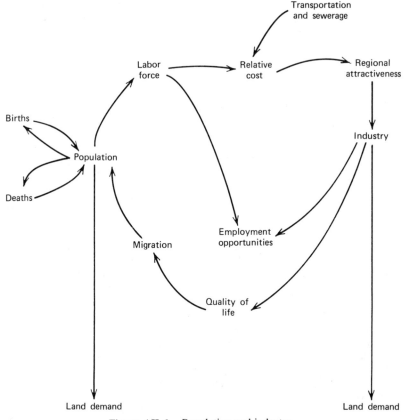

Figure AII-6. Population and industry.

Migration into or out of the region depends primarily on perceived relative employment opportunities. This reflects the fact that an individual, in deciding among alternative regions, will weight their relative advantages rather than judge them in some absolute fashion. However, many other factors also influence migration. The term "quality of life" is perhaps the most adequate to summarize these factors, which include regional climate, life style, cultural activities, general standard of living, etc.

Employment and quality of life provide major links between the population and industrial sector. Both are partially determined by the number and types of jobs in the region. The number and types of jobs in turn depend on the region's economic base. Thus, in order to adequately describe population dynamics, we must turn to regional economic theory.

Figure AII-6 indicates that industrial growth depends on relative costs within the region. As for migration, this representation takes the point of view of the individual business comparing regions to each other in order to choose a location. Another similarity is that the importance of different costs varies widely among industries: hence labor-intensive industries and capital-intensive industries might disagree about which regions are most attractive. Our simplified figure does not show these differences.

AII-6.4   Costs

A number of relative costs are important for industrial location decisions. A complete list need not be given here. However, two costs that are indicated individually are transportation and sewerage. This is the point at which they influence regional behavior. As the diagram implies, they are not significant factors at this level. The third cost shown explicitly is labor costs. We have included it separately because it completes a feedback loop to the population sector through labor force participation. Thus, as the population increases, so does the labor force, making the region more attractive to industry and bringing in more jobs. At the same time, however, an increased labor force tightens the job market and lowers employment opportunities, which can reduce population levels through out-migration. Thus, two feedback loops, one positive and one negative, tend to counterbalance each other.

Population and industry are linked to the second hierarchical level, the zonal, through generation of land use demands. These demands, or preferences, are based on socio-economic and industrial characteristics, and when matched to land supply characteristics, determine specific land usage throughout the region.

As we mentioned before, a number of structural similarities exist between zonal and regional location decisions. Relative attractiveness at both levels is based on socio-economic and industrial characteristics. Strong interactions between population and industry exist at both levels. However, there are important differences. The nature and importance of cost factors influencing relative attractiveness change at the zonal level. Interactions of population and industry at the zonal level are in terms of "co-location" and access rather than more general availability or opportunity influences. Furthermore, zonal location decisions are made in a real economic market area, the urban land market, where supply must be compared to demand, buyers must find sellers, and subjective factors may dominate more objective, measurable factors in any given transaction.

AII-6.5   Land Use

Figure AII-7 depicts land use for a single zone in simplified fashion. Land use demand based on housing and site preferences of regional population and industry are compared to the actual characteristics of the zone's housing stock, industrial sites, and access to public and private services. In addition to the zone's own characteristics, the characteristics of all other zones in the region are examined by households and businesses with respect to their accessibility to the zone in question. Thus a zone which does not contain some positive characteristics but has access to them in nearby zones may still be judged very attractive. Theoretically, each zone in the region will be examined in this fashion, and location decisions based on their relative attractiveness. Over time, location decisions change zonal characteristics and, therefore, relative attractiveness.

Obviously, changes in zonal accessibility through transportation investment play a key role in this process. The term, "opening up" an area for developments

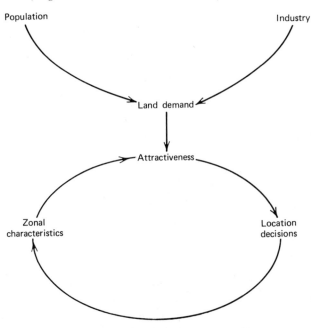

Figure AII-7.   Intraregional location decisions.

means literally making it accessible enough to be attractive for households and industry. However, changes in accessibility do not occur solely through transportation investments. As areas build up, travel increases, congestion increases travel times and costs, and accessibility decreases. This is the familiar "highway spiral" in which new investments are induced by their predecessors.

Development, whether on open land or previously developed land, depends largely on the entrepreneurial decisions of private enterprise. Because such decision makers are interested in profits, their actions depend on the market for different types of buildings, on costs, on possible intensities of development, and ultimately on their expectations of resulting profit. Here, local policies such as zoning and tax structure importantly influence the process. In addition, sewerage investments can affect development costs by acting as a subsidy. They can also affect local tax and zoning policies by encouraging zoning variances, increased taxes, and unfair distribution of tax burdens depending on the financial structure and location of the investments.

As shown in Figure AII-8, developers depend upon available information, in the form of vacancy rates, to determine market strength. The actual density of new construction starts depends in turn on costs, developmental controls, and type of construction. Land costs, an important component of total developmental costs, depend upon the amount of land available for development and the demand for different uses. The other important component from our point of view, sewerage costs, depends upon previous investments and local service charges.

Viewed as a whole, this land use system does much to explain secondary effects

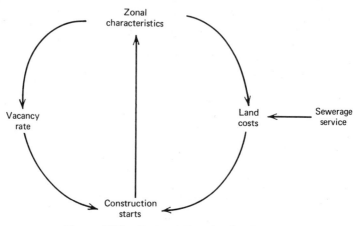

Figure AII-8. Factors influencing development.

of infrastructure investments. Transportation investments can dramatically alter accessibility characteristics—and, therefore, the relative attractiveness of all areas—within a region. Once this change occurs, all the major impacts cited, including social, demographic, economic, etc., follow through the normal workings of the system. As these changes occur, new transportation demands evolve requiring new investment. Sewerage investments, on the other hand, have a similar effect but on a smaller scale. New sewers and treatment plants, through the mechanisms described above, not only allow but also stimulate development, particularly in previously undeveloped areas where sewerage costs are a relatively major component of total developmental costs. It is by following chains of cause-and-effect from the original mechanisms through the system that multiple kinds of secondary effects are generated.

The literature's emphasis of secondary effects on the intra-regional level seems to suggest that regional-level interactions should be treated either exogenously or in a highly simplified fashion, with intra-regional dynamics receiving a detailed analysis. While the latter approach is clearly necessary, there are two major difficulties involved in taking a simplified approach at the regional level.

The first major difficulty is the fact that in a relatively small but still significant number of cases, transportation investments can be the dominant factor in future development. In a region that is largely undeveloped, for example, but which has good recreational potential, a new highway link to major urban areas may strongly stimulate resort developments, construction of "second" or "summer" homes, etc. Further, this sort of developmental impact, with its accompanying reduction of natural open space and degradation of environmentally sensitive areas, has proven to be one of the most controversial kinds of secondary effects. Thus, despite the fact that this combination of conditions is not common, it is vital both to recognize and to analyze such regions.

The second major difficulty is the fact that intra-regional changes—those most important for secondary impacts—depend on regional changes. The accuracy of regional forecasts is therefore critical to the accuracy of intra-regional forecasts. For this reason, the use of highly simplified or exogenous regional projections, because they are subject to rather gross errors in prediction, often can invalidate intra-regional projections.

Our efforts in this project need not emphasize development of the regional level of the model. The bulk of our previous work, as well as other successful modeling efforts has been aimed at such development. We will limit our attention to a few small improvements which will require little time but may significantly improve the projective accuracy previously obtained. Most of our research effort will be concerned with intra-regional, or zonal, impacts and their interactions with the regional level. Although we devote a considerable amount of time to describing regional parameters and relationships in the following section, this is intended primarily to provide a balanced view of the model rather than our research effort.

AII-7 SOS (State of the System) Model

The final model discussed makes great use of the concept of Quality of Life (QOL); in fact, it makes the concept one of its principal driving forces. This model, like the IMMP model discussed earlier, began as an attempt to conceptualize the constrictor models described in GEM. Although during its building, SOS also took on a life of its own, in the final form of its evolution it could serve the original purpose quite well. The following material describing the SOS Model is based on *The Carrying Capacity of a Nation* (House, 1976).

AII-7.1 Ecological Carrying Capacity

The book, *Limits to Growth* (Meadows, 1972), has attracted widespread attention. While some of its critics feel that the book lacks scientific accuracy, it does call attention to the shortcomings of many of our fondest assumptions. For years planning, both public and private, has been based on the basic assumption of an ever "fruitful" earth. Few of the plans ever questioned the possibility of continued social and economic growth under conditions of available resources and with minimal environmental damage. The following sections describe the technique the SOS model offers to assist in this analysis. While the model's supportive algorithms have been defined mathematically elsewhere, the following discussion eschews mathematics in favor of conceptual descriptions.

In the past few decades, the unfettered development of our cities, responding primarily to economic considerations, has faltered in its purpose of providing maximum benefit to the majority of the inhabitants. Now we are beginning to question the very possibility of unlimited growth. Thus, the comprehensive plans of localities need to be tested for practicality under situations of limited resources and established environmental qualities: they must be related to the "carrying capacity" of the region. The population growth of a species has been shown generally to have one of the forms shown in Figure AII-9. The earliest use of the carrying capacity concept was in the ecological sciences, where it was conceived as a measure relating population to resources.

In an environment supporting an organism or a collection of ecosystem components, limiting factors are always present. These include food, climate, space (e.g., land), cover (habitat and protection), the extent of the ecological "niche," and water. Such factors determine the carrying capacity of the ecosystem.In the absence of limiting factors, population would grow exponentially as shown in the graph by the lower portion of curve 1 and the dashed extension. Such an increasing trend cannot continue indefinitely; it levels off as it approaches the carrying capacity of the system as shown in curve 2. However, if the rate of increase is too great as the carrying capacity is approached, an overshoot and subsequent decline might occur as shown by curve 3.

AII-7.2 Purpose and Applications

The state-of-the-system (SOS) model is an attempt to reconcile the growth desires of a population with the limitations of the locale. The

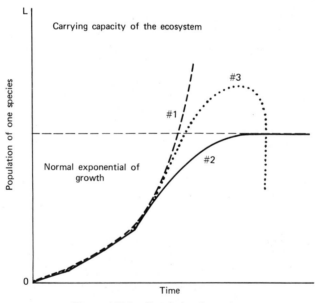

Figure AII-9. Population dynamics.

model has been designed to test various assumptions about the desired growth of an area under a selected set of side conditions (boundaries, constraints, or thresholds). Feasibility is demonstrated if the desired growth can be achieved without violating the conditions imposed.

As examples of conditions that might be imposed, the model would translate higher-level laws (federal and state, for example, if the model is of a local government), health thresholds, natural boundaries, and the local desires of the inhabitants into quantitative side-conditions. Specifically, one could set values such as a minimum level of subsistence per family, a maximum unemployment rate, various environmental standards, housing and other industrial/commercial codes, density, and minimum education levels.

The SOS model can then be used to analyze at least three types of system characteristics: (1) the compatibility of existing growth trends with the goals of the locale, (2) the probable life of the system and the most viable and critical linkages and constraints, (3) and the effect of different policy alternatives.

AII-7.3   Structure

The SOS model includes four major elements:

1. *Growth of a Sector*. This consists of three components: the population (quantified in terms of physical needs), private production, and public services. (The two latter are quantified in terms of expenditures for production and maintenance per year). Both the private production sector and the public services sector can be subdivided into component categories (e.g., heavy industry and education). While the population growth is not divided into components, it can be partitioned into special-need groupings in response to the relative levels of output by the components of the private and public sectors.

2. *Regional System Outputs*. This is the output of regional economic systems which is available for regional consumption plus net export.

3. *Ecosystem Limiting Factors*. These include the input limiters of resource availability and requirements for environmental quality.

4. *Societal Demands*. These are the demands placed on private and public sector output to maintain an acceptable (or desired) QOL.

The interaction of these model elements is illustrated in Figure AII-10. Using growth projections and estimates of output for each regional production component, the model provides an analysis of limiters on the

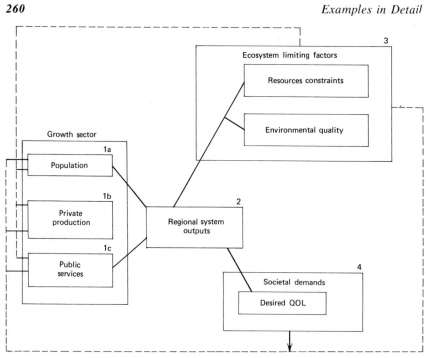

Figure AII-10.   Conceptual form of SOS model.

production output, determining apparent shortages in resources or deficient quality in ecosystem indicators. The model also determines short-run failures in meeting QOL demands.

AII-7.4   Model Formulation

System Inputs. These inputs include total regional funds and allocation of expenditures to the private and public sector, and the population size and age distribution.

System Outputs. The model translates the inputs to an overall demographic and economic picture of the region for the year considered.

State of the System. These relationships are associated with the system limiters or constraints. They define the resource utilization and QOL.

System Adjustments. The relationships associated with the long-term goals provide the necessary adjustments and feedbacks when the state of the system is found to be incompatible with goals.

Total Production. The model takes its impetus for cyclic iteration from yearly development rates. The efficacy with which the development rates are changed by the feedback loops is the key to the success of the allocative portions of the model. However, while the rates can change, the exogenous inputs to the regional system cannot.

This level of regional funds sets an upper constraint on input to the production sectors and components for each current cycle. The process of funds allocation to production components is done subject to the condition that the total of the funds of the components is equal to the total regional funds. The allocation process has two major steps. First, an expected allocation of funds is provided such that the relative growth rates, set and adjusted for each component in the past cycle, are followed. Additional changes in rates are introduced as functions of net exogenous funds available and the population preference for goods or services.

Production Sectors. The sectors of regional growth, other than population, are the production and services components of the private production and the public services sectors. The dimension of both sectors, and hence their input to the system, is the level of funds used annually to procure and transform resources into capital, ecosystem maintenance, and sector outputs.

For the private sector, production components are established: e.g., heavy-polluting industry, light-polluting industry, commercial goods and services, agriculture, and household-related industries.

The Public Sector. Components include safety, defense and administrative services, health, and transportation/communication. In the model, each of these components has a yearly rate of change related with it.

Population Sector. Population growth, as such, is not seen as significant in the sense of regional limits until it is related to territory: the larger the physical space in which the population is accommodated, the less pressure is exerted on the group as a result of food and living space demands. The population is divided into two age groups to represent labor resources and to determine the expected consumption rates. Included in this partitioning process are a number of factors that can be correlated to the regional outputs to represent the present socioeconomic level of the society. Typical partition characteristics include:

- length of immaturity/educational time;
- rates of short-term and long-term infirmity;
- ratio of educational units to work units achieved in each age grouping;
- death rates by age grouping;

- birth rates by age grouping;
- size of work force, further partitioned as:
  employed, paid workers,
  unemployed, paid workers,
  workers not in paid status (housewives, volunteers).

The population characteristics are assumed to change directly with the production and services levels of the private and public sectors (e.g., shifting population elements from unemployed to employed).

System Outputs. The major measures to be used for system output are the expenditures of the various production components to produce the output. Expenditures for maintenance include capital investment required. The maintenance components are obviously not constant over time.

Resources. A key element in the SOS model is the treatment of resources. SOS attempts to anticipate adaptive changes through substitution of resources of similar types (or strata), and to account for the discovery and (delayed) development of new areas of resources as a function of resource prices.

Ecological accessibility as a limiter has meaning with respect to resource constraints; the availability of resources at any particular time is the result of the interactions among the kind and size of man's requirements, the physical occurrence of the resource, and the means of producing it. Estimates of the future availability of resources, therefore, require the assessment of economic and technological conditions, the level of production that would take place under different economic or technological conditions, and the kind and quantity of the total physical stock of both "renewable" and "nonrenewable" resources.

The model follows the accepted definitions of resources used in manufacturing and services and considers eight groups: energy sources, natural resources (durable ores), agricultural resources (food and fibers), land, labor, capital (including R&D funds), air, and water. These eight groups are divided into nonrenewable (energy and natural resources) and renewable resources.

The following general rules can be associated with all resources represented in the SOS model:

- The available resources at any point in time can be associated with a unit procurement cost.
- At any period the stockpile of a given resource in absolute terms is unknown. However, the quantities available as resource reserves at any unit procurement cost can be known.

- For any source, the indication of a perceived resource crisis occurs when the present resource stocks can no longer produce a unit of the resource at the current unit price.
- The resources of ores, foods, fibers, and land have resource strata within the general resource category. Energy can be viewed as a single stratum. Within any strata the mix of associated resources used to make up a single unit of that resource stratum is maintained without change unless a stock depletion signal occurs for a resource in that stratum.
- If a stock depletion signal for a resource or a stratum occurs, a check of allowable overcost substitutions is made to determine if another acceptable resource mix or replacement can be made.
- For any substitution process, the full change may require several time periods. The appropriate resource mix is automatically used in production processes for each time period.
- In addition to the expansion of a critical resource base by substitution (which is not only nonlinear but asymptotic to some unknown upper limit), the availability of resource total stocks is checked to determine if the unit cost will cause a greater stockpile of the resource to be transferred to the reserve status. Such increments are carried out using a time delay function for activating the new reserve sources.
- The natural resources and subcategories of other resources can include a recycling expansion of available materials. The rate of recycling is based on maintenance of a minimum unit cost of material from the complementary sources of extraction and recycling.
- Currently, the location of the original source of transportable resources (ores, energy, foods, and fibers) is not considered.

A key feature of the model's consideration of resources is that the "available" reserve level is the amount of that resource that can be extracted (or otherwise obtained) at a relatively fixed unit cost. Thus, resource levels can be increased by accepting a higher unit cost as well as by improved processing techniques.

- At any time, the total energy stock available to a region is the sum of the amount of the various energy sources.
- Natural resources, like energy, are normally viewed as a nonrenewable category. However, there are two important hedges in considering the actual stock reserve at any one time. First, for many of the ores, a high level of substitution of other resources in the production process is possible. A second hedge available is the ability to recycle debris from processed and consumed goods to regain material in the form of salvage. This procedure sets a resource reserve that is once again

influenced by cost (i.e., recycling costs will determine the level of salvage from the system debris).

- Methods for expanding reserves of a land use category are similar to other resources. The maximum potential for transformation at various costs levels is defined and, if added to the existent stock of land, represents the total stock level for a region at a given land cost. From this data, a resource reserve generation procedure is possible (as used in nonrenewable resources). In this procedure, land use succession is activated for a given land use type as the unused reserve reaches a stock depletion warning level. At that time, additional reserves in one land use category require its removal from others.
- With depletion of natural resource availability, a greater emphasis will be placed on the agricultural portion of the resource base and on its output, food and fibers.
- Capital is also an important renewable resource used as an intermediate step between raw materials and final consumption.
- Labor as a resource is measured in work units. The partition for paid workers into employed and unemployed provides at any time the instantaneous maximum labor supply level. The labor cost is a function of this level and the demand for workers. Additional labor units can be generated as a function of this cost by transferring, in later time periods, work units from the population in training or in unpaid work activities.
- The model is not concerned with the "level" of air or water, but with the level of pollution.

Quality of Life. Major elements of the state of the system are measured in terms of societal perceptions—a set of judgments dealing with various components of quality of life. Our particular system must be area-specific and represent the planning system responsible for the adjustment of growth and output to achieve an acceptable state in that area. Hence, only a general formulation of measures can be provided here.

In planning systems intended for the achievement of the comprehensive goals, the procedure is reasonably straightforward. Each goal by itself is a specific threshold to be realized. The relative importance assigned the goals in the plan provides a set of weighting coefficients to determine priorities in establishing tradeoffs, given that total achievement of all goals cannot be accomplished. Thus, the only requirement in setting the goals is to restate the goals in terms of parameters developed in the model operations.

Another alternative is a planning system that requires attainment of certain minimum values to achieve an acceptable state. It involves supplementary measures relating to the resilience of the system in remaining above the minima. Each of the collection of measures is generated directly from the comprehensive goals, a set of measures selected in terms of the area-specific needs and desires of the society in the region. Minimum acceptable values are set rather than a goal of achievement. The setting of relative weights to combine the measures is more difficult. Instead, an iterative process can be carried out that measures the state of the system and then adjusts fund levels among the production components until all thresholds are met.

AII-7.5 System Adjustments

If a given state of the system is found unacceptable, a set of adjustments must be made to improve the situation. The adjustments are performed in the following order:

Short-term adjustments
(a) short-term deferral of capital maintenance.

Long-term adjustments
(a) changing I/O production functions to achieve the minimum cost mix for components contributing to unacceptable values;

(b) reallocating the total projected funds level within a sector to better balance projected growth rates and needed outputs of deficient components;

(c) scheduling on a permanent basis the annual transfer of funds from one sector to the other, and then repeating the procedure;

(d) adjusting the rates and direction of net migration to reduce per-capita consumption needs if significant unemployment exists in the region.

If none of the long-term adjustments produces a satisfactory correction of the projected state of the system, the system goals are modified to lower levels. This will allow a possibility of maintaining the regional growth projections at the cost of a less acceptable QOL.

Reaching its carrying capacity, the system may suggest merely a short-run imbalance of the demand and supply of a specific resource. This imbalance can be corrected by changing the rate of extraction and distribution of the resource in question. On the other hand, if reaching a depletion warning at a particular point in time heralds the beginning of a serious shortage of a particular resource, then there are numerous possible responses, such as:

- increase the rate of extraction, despite increasing costs,
- supply from other regional systems at higher costs,
- change the population's demand function,
- change the growth rate of specific sectors in the system.

AII-7.6 Summary

The model allows iteration through time until one or another of the system resources is exhausted. This means that the system can be thought of as having several limits or thresholds that will prevent its further growth. As one, or all, of the system resources begin to be scarce and relatively expensive, there is a tendency first to skimp on maintenance to a given level and then to curtail growth.

This form of the model is of limited use to local regions and to the policymaker who must make day-to-day decisions based on limited information, but it can be used to test the operating or comprehensive plan for a specific region. The assumption is that the region will make whatever adjustments are necessary to implement the plan. Whenever a specific value (or series of values) is out of phase with the desired plan, the model will adjust itself to refocus the iterations toward the end goal. In this manner, the possible limitations on the comprehensive plan can be discovered and the required adjustments considered. In this way the model helps determine if the region can achieve the goals of the comprehensive plan.

AII-8   Conclusion

Inasmuch as these models/systems have so far had little use as policy models, what can be said on their behalf? Both the San Diego-Rand Methodology Package and SEAS models have been used in policy environments. The GEM and SOS models are still very much in the research stage and there is considerable development work yet to be done on them before they can be seriously considered for policy use. The Harris-Putman Package stands somewhat closer to such testing.

At this stage, however, at least one conclusion can be drawn. Although it is possible to conceive of numerous ways to build general, comprehensive models, there is a near-zero chance that the results of the models, regardless of the amount of care and imagination that went into their construction, can be proved "valid" in a technical, mathematical sense. This assessment may seem harsh, but it should be noted that few of the policies that are actually made in the real world by other means could stand such analysis. Moreover, there is a real question of the utility of formal validity versus "reasonableness" in the field of policy analysis. This is considered more closely in the section in Chapter 5 on Validation.

The only really unique characteristic of the approaches reported in this section is that each is an attempt to go beyond the early tendency to design around a particular theoretical or practical problem that "useful" models have historically had. If these attempts are successful—and introduce no new problems—then the time may be near when the technical feasibility of building a general, comprehensive, man-machine model for policymakers is realized.

Appendix III

Data Source Details

AIII-1 SEAS Data Sources

Two general caveats are in order concerning the following. The first is that the information, although extensive, is limited to the Federal Government. It does not include similar data available from private corporations such as Dun & Bradstreet or organizations such as ICMA (International City Managers Association), which produces a City-County Data Book. These sources and others like them would have to be added to surveys available on a regular basis at the state government level, supplemented by regularly collected local and regional information. Second, even the Federal listing is by no means exhaustive but was, as noted, constrained by the more limited needs of a specific project.

What follows is based on a report (EPA-IBM, February 1973) on the SEAS Information System.

The initial effort in identifying data-base requirements was to define the classes of information that should be included and the potential sources of such information. This was accomplished by performing a "topdown" analysis, with the choice between a disciplinary and operational approach in performing the analysis.

The operational approach was selected on the basis of the test that the data sources are operationally oriented. This analysis involved the definition of the major information areas of interest (e.g., population, the potential sources of such information, and a preliminary definition of the parameters that could be used to quantify the information of interest).

The federal agencies covered in this data-base investigation appear to be the principal sources of information appropriate for inclusion in the data bases. In those instances in which nonfederal agencies are primarily responsible for the development of information, the federal agency with corresponding responsiblities was found to make use of the nonfederal information in preparing its reports; thus the Construction Statistics Division of the Bureau of Census uses the F.W. Dodge division, McGraw-

Hill, monthly "Dodge Construction Contract Statistics Service" reports.

The information available is, in general, available at the state or county level of detail, together with a national summary. In some cases such as the Water Resources Council reports, the geographic areas are naturally defined and do not follow state or county political boundaries. Mineral resources data, except for the fossil fuels, is available only at the national level. The confidentiality of data may severely restrict the distribution of information to other federal agencies. Another problem arises in that statistical reports do not have the same base year. The principal emphasis in this initial screening of data sources was on the identification of machine readable information suitable for inclusion in the profile or stock data bases. The data sources investigated are described briefly below.

AIII-1.1   Department of Agriculture

The agricultural commodity data, as reported annually in "Agricultural Statistics," is developed manually, with no plans of developing an automatic data processing system because of difficulties in maintaining a data base. The Economic Research Service, in conjunction with the OBERS (Bureau of Economic Analysis, Department of Commerce), has developed the system's historical and projection data that is available in machine-readable form. The historical data includes information from the 1969 Agricultural Census.

The Farm Labor report summary tape has very limited distribution, even within the Department of Agriculture. Agriculture income, historical, and projection information are available in the OBERS machine-readable data. Internal Revenue Service data would also provide farm income information for both corporate and noncorporate agricultural, forestry, and fisheries tax returns.

The Economic Research Service has machine-readable output for the agricultural tables available in Vol. 5 of the OBERS report. These tables provide historical (through 1969) and projection (through 2020) information about production, value of production, use of land in farms, and the amount of irrigated land. Commodity production and value information are restricted to those commodities for which a state's projected (1980, 2000, or 2020) production is 1% or more of the projected U.S. production or value. The next Agricultural Census will probably be conducted in 1977. The OBERS Vol. 5 data relative to agricultural production, crop value, and land use, available through the Economic Research Service, Department of Agriculture, appears to be the best currently available source of this kind of information.

AIII-1.2   Forestry Service

Forestry production and land use information are available in machine-readable form through the U.S. Forest Service.

AIII-1.3   Civil Aeronautics Board

CAB has available machine-readable information on airport activity, passenger and freight enplanement, origin-destination and route segment enplanement of passengers and freight for commercial aviation, except for intrastate carriers. The Federal Aviation Agency, Department of Transportation, publishes similar reports for airport activity, air traffic hubs, airport facilities, and aircraft population information.

AIII-1.4   Department of Commerce

The Bureau of Census—County and City Data Book—1967 provides coverage of economic and demographic information at the national, regional, state, county, SMSA (Standard Metropolitan Statistical Area), and city level on a single magnetic tape.

The 1970 census data relative to population, households, and housing is available in machine-readable format at various levels of detail. The Fifth Count (ZIP Code)—File A, provides a summary, in a single reel, at three-digit ZIP code level. This information may be updated annually using the Current Population Survey—March Supplement. SMSA data is available on the Fifth Count tape, using the ZIP Code. Selected SMSA data is available in the Current Population Survey—March Supplement.

The Agricultural Census data for 1969 is available in a total of 18 tapes, providing information at county level. The Economic Research Service, Department of Agriculture, is currently abstracting information from these 1969 tapes to generate a single tape containing information for use in the OBERS system. The next Agricultural Census will probably be conducted in 1977, rather than the previously scheduled 1974 census.

The Government Division has several of their reports available in machine-readable format. These include the 1967 Census of Governments, 1971 Annual Sample Based Finance Survey, 1971 Annual Sample Based Employment Survey, and 1971 Assessed Valuation Data—Survey of Taxable Property Values.

The Transportation Division has machine-readable output available for the national truck inventory, passenger miles, and ton miles by commodity for 25 production areas. Much of this information is based upon data provided by the Federal Highway Administration, Department of Transportation, and is updated annually. It appears that the cargo movement data being developed by the Maritime Administration will be more complete, covering all modes of transportation.

The Bureau of Census reports on construction, business, manufacturing, and minerals are derived from ADP output reports. The final reports include, however, a number of changes based upon the need to protect proprietary information, analyses, and the correction of errors. Corresponding changes are not made in the data bases or any output machine-readable data.

The Foreign Trade Division can supply machine-readable data for both imports and exports. This information is extremely detailed, but does not provide information as to the point of manufacture of exports, or the final destination of imports. This division prepares a summary report for internal use at the two-digit SIC level. It would be necessary to manually prepare input data from this report if it is to be used in any model.

AIII-1.5 The Bureau of Economic Analysis

As previously mentioned, this Bureau has, in cooperation with the Economic Research Service of the Department of Agriculture, developed the OBERS system. BEA has machine readable output available for OBERS Table 1 covering population and income. Information contained in OBERS Table 2, Indexes of Production, can also be provided in machine-readable form, if desired.

Other data sources within BEA, including the data provided for use in the damage assessment systems operated by the Office of Civil Defense, Department of Defense, and the Office of Emergency Preparedness, Executive Office of the President, are based upon precise geographic locations.

AIII-1.6 Maritime Administration

The Office of Domestic Shipping has developed an analysis of freight movement between the 173 BEA Economic areas by the mode of transportation. Machine-readable information from this report can be provided.

The division of Trade Studies and Statistics is not allowed to provide detailed information to other agencies without legislative approval, because of the proprietary nature of most of this information. Import and export information may be obtained from Foreign Trade Division, Bureau of Census.

AIII-1.7   National Technical Information Service

This agency does not produce information, but is the designated repository for data-base documentation and tapes developed by any federal agency. They have data bases for a number of agencies, including some no longer in existence or in process of phasing out of operation.

AIII-1.8   Environmental Protection Agency

A recently completed EPA contract identifies the various information systems that are currently operational or under development. The major information systems that could provide data to the profile and stock data bases include the National Emissions Data System (NEDS) and Storage and Retrieval of Aerometric Data (SAROAD) for air, and Storage and Retrieval of Water Quality Data (STORET) for water. There are also a number of specialized information systems used by the various National Environmental Research Centers and the EPA Regional offices.

AIII-1.9   Executive Office of the President

The Council on Environmental Quality relies on other agencies, such as the Environmental Protection Agency, to develop information for their use.

The Office of Emergency Preparedness used the National Resource Data Base in its defense and damage assessment activities; this data is defined in terms of precise geographic locations. Resource reserves, such as mineral reserves, are based upon the criticality of these materials for defense purposes. The data now resides in GSA (the General Services Administration).

AIII-1.10   Federal Power Commission

Annual statistics for both privately and publicly owned utilities are available in machine-readable form. Electric utility annual statements, collected by regional power pools, are available at FPC, but are not available in reduced form. The annual reports provide data on power distribution facilities and the ten-year plan for facility development.

AIII-1.11   Department of Health, Education and Welfare

There are a number of data files in report and machine-readable form available from the Office of Education, Health Services and Mental Health Administration, National Institutes of Health, Social and Rehabilitation Services Administration, Food and Drug Administration, and the

Social Security Administration. The data files on state school statistics and health facilities could provide information for both the profile and the stock data bases. The natality and mortality data files could provide more precise information for use in population estimates and projections.

AIII-1.12   Department of Interior

The three principal Bureau of Mines reports on minerals are produced manually. The Commodity Data Summaries include reserve information at the national level, with no current plan to use ADP (automatic data processing). The MERIT (Mines Energy Resources Information and Transportation) system, located at the ADP facility in Denver, Colorado covers the mineral fuels (coal, petroleum, natural gas, and natural gas liquids). Machine-readable information can be obtained for these minerals, including stocks at the state level.

The mineral production information, as presented in the annual Minerals Yearbook, is developed manually.

The Office of Economic Analysis is considering developing an information system for the Department of Interior. If this is done, the system will probably not be built upon existing Department of Interior data bases. The RALI (Resource and Land Information) program, being developed by the U.S. Geological Survey, is currently in the concept-definition phase, and did not enter the initial implementation phase until February 1976 according to a report on the conceptual phase of the RALI program.

Some of the analyses formerly performed by the Interstate Commerce Commission, such as the 1% railroad waybill sample, are now carried out by the Department of Transportation, Federal Railroad Administration. Information contained in the annual "Transport Economics" is not available in machine-readable form.

AIII-1.13   Department of Justice

Summary criminal justice data from the Law Enforcement Assistance Administration (LEAA) reports is included in reports prepared by the Government Division, Bureau of Census. The National Criminal Justice Information and Statistics Service (NCISS) of LEAA operates several information systems in detail.

AIII-1.14   Department of Labor

Machine-readable information covering the Employment and Earnings annual report of the Bureau of Labor Statistics is available at SMSA, state, and national level. Information at the four-digit SIC (Standard Industrial Category) level would be available for employment, weekly earnings, and hourly rates. The May issue each year includes the end-of-year information for the preceding calendar year.

AIII-1.15   Department of Transportation

Much of the data presented in the Federal Aviation Administration reports is based on information developed by the Civil Aeronautics Board. No data is available for intrastate carrier traffic. Selected machine-readable data could be provided by FAA on the basis of detailed specifications provided by potential users. Such selected information covers FAA reports such as airport activity, air traffic hubs (which coincide with SMSA's to a considerable degree) airport facilities, aircraft population, licensed airmen, etc.

No machine-readable information is available for the annual "Highway Statistics" report by the Federal Highway Administration (FHWA), a major source of highway motor vehicle, traffic, and vehicle population information. Most of the information contained in this and other FHWA reports is based on state reports prepared in accordance with FHWA specifications, with some special studies conducted by FHWA. The states also use FHWA-developed computer programs for modeling and gaming activities in such areas as traffic assignment, population transportation patterns, etc.

The Federal Railroad Administration is now responsible for conducting the 1% railroad waybill sample analysis, formerly the responsibility of the Interstate Commerce Commission. This study is conducted on a three-year cycle, rather than on an annual basis, beginning in 1969. The waybill report covers carload traffic that originates and terminates in the United States; ICC reports cover Canadian, Mexican, and Seatrain traffic. A machine-readable summary tape is available for the 1969 analysis. Passenger statistics, based on reports prepared by the conductor, may be available soon.

The Office of Systems Analysis and Information is responsible for preparing the National Transportation Statistics report through a contract with the Urban Systems Laboratory, MIT, based on information provided by the Interstate Commerce Commission, Civil Aeronautics Board, U.S. Army Corps of Engineers, Maritime Administration, Federal Aviation Agency, Federal Highway Administration, and the Federal Railroad Administration. No machine-readable information is available. Railroad and trucking transport statistics for 1971, based upon ICC data, are available in machine-readable form.

AIII-1.16   Department of Treasury

The Statistics Division of the Internal Revenue Service performs an annual analysis of income of corporate and noncorporate businesses. It will be possible for them to develop machine-readable information, at the two-digit SIC level, of gross and net income of corporations, proprietorships, and partnerships. The net income information may be among the best available approximation of value added at the two-digit SIC level.

AIII-2   Simulating A Data Base

A previously referenced report (Voorhees, 1973) describes a methodology devised to synthesize much of the data required to simulate a city. The following is based on that report.

It is apparent that any realization of such a model will be influenced significantly by the analytical model or family of models to which it will be providing input. It is necessary to accommodate the input requirements of the policy planning model while producing an acceptable representation of the real city to synthesize the required data.

AIII-2.1   Components of the Simulation

There were two types of information required for Simulation City: aggregate parameters that are representative of the overall socioeconomic system of the city, and descriptors of detail, which give a sketchy picture of the city's spatial distribution of activity. The simulation is intended to imply a good deal more detail about the socioeconomic system, given some knowledge of what cities in general have in common, and to postulate how the socioeconomic activity is distributed over the skeleton of pattern provided by the sketchy descriptions. A picture of the level and distribution of activities that comprise the basic structure of the city is thus developed.

Observations of how cities in general operate and grow permit some aspects of the city's character to be inferred from this description of basic structure. For example, population density and median income are found to be negatively correlated in residential areas (Voorhees, 1968). Provision of adequate road access must generally precede development of an area, so that information indicating that an area has been developed justifies an assumption that such access exists.

Finally, schools and other municipal services will be provided, but their quality is quite variable, and it is dependent on the individual community.

Simulation thus requires some judgment or measure of the community's character.

AIII-2.2   *Basis for Simulating a City*

In considering the body of theory and observation that is available as a basis for development of the Simulation City approach, it is important to recognize that the Simulation City model is not intended to be predictive, in the sense of most planning models. There is no consideration given to future conditions, and hence no debate regarding whether the model is in any sense normative. A Simulation City model is intended to be purely descriptive—descriptive of the present conditions in a given city. It is then not unrealistic to expect that wherever theory is inadequate to explain the patterns of urban development, statistics may fill the void.

With these points in mind, a search may be made to find what theories and facts are available, and whether what is available is adequate to make development of the Simulation City approach a practical undertaking. In this chapter, the findings of such a search are reviewed.

AIII-2.3   *Types of Urban Areas*

Attempts to classify urban areas—cities—into typical categories has been a relatively popular area of research among geographers and planners. Work by Harris (Harris, 1943) was among the earliest to attract attention, while that of Berry (Berry, 1972) reflects the recent trend toward applications of advanced statistical methods. While it has been felt by many observers that in the conduct of such research there has been inadequate thought given to why one should classify cities and what is thereby accomplished, such work represents a resource for the Simulation City Approach; it is apparent that the statistics that identify groups and distinguish them from one another are better predictors of the characteristics of an individual city with the group than are the statistics for all groups combined.

Recent work (Pidot, 1973), for example, tested variables of population, education, social character, housing quality, labor base, and industrial character for standard metropolitan statistical areas in the United States and found what they considered to be a rational grouping into nine categories. One group was characterized, for instance, as heavily oriented to recreational activity, while another had high components of elderly population. These categories suggest a way to predict more accurately certain characteristics of a metropolitan area.

Classifications of city type are typically most dependent upon population and industry characteristics for these comprise the basis of the city's existence. But there is reason to suppose that there are other categories that could be applied at a lower level of detail to give other types of useful relationships.

For example, there has been substantial literature produced by studies of the theory and process of agglomeration among businesses. According to the theory (Weber, 1929), industries tend to cluster, spatially, to take advantage of economies of scale in minimizing transportation costs for intermediate goods. Explorations of the theory have led to the concept of industrial clusters, groups of industries that are found in many urban areas. One researcher (Bergsman, 1972) found four widespread clusters in their preliminary analysis, which they termed market center, low-wage apparel, labor intensive, and southern textile. Such work suggests that indication of the major industry or cluster type in an area might prove sufficient to simulate the industrial composition of the area, in terms of economic importance (such as sales, value added labor proportion, or other measures). Other findings (Morrissett, 1958) on minimum employment levels as a function of city size support this concept.

However, a number of unique economic systems were noted in this work. New York, Los Angeles, and Chicago are not surprising in this category, but cities such as Philadelphia and Akron are perhaps less expected as singularities. An investigator (Bryce, 1973) suggested that roughly 30% of metropolitan areas have demographic profiles that could best be termed atypical. Such findings indicate that it may not be reasonable to carry the stratification of cities into type categories of too detailed a level.

Somewhat related to the concept of distinct types, based on industry and demography, is that of the economic base. Drawing from international trade theory, regional economists postulate (Blumenfeld, 1959) that industries that export the bulk of their production from the region, thus drawing cash into the region, comprise the base of the region's economy. The employees associated with these businesses have a need for services—retail outlets, building trades, etc.—which stimulates the flow of goods and services in an urban economy.

There are generally 15–30% or more of all workers employed in these service industries, with the percentage rising as city size grows. This latter observation stems from the larger city's importance as a center of a larger region of activity. It would seem then that one might predict the number of workers in a city of given population, and the likely split of these workers between basic and service businesses, without reference to more detailed categories.

AIII-2.4   Infrastructure of the Urban Economy

While attempts at stratification of urban areas focus on differences among types, there has been considerable theoretical and historical support for the idea that there are certain consistencies of structure underlying the economies of all cities. Location theory suggests that the initial formulation of a settlement in an area (Isard, 1956) is highly dependent on its physical site. The site therefore may reveal a good bit about the city. For example, location on a river suggests a transport orientation, and shipping in or out of heavy raw materials. Location at a source of natural resources indicates information about the probable mix of labor.

More interesting, from the standpoint of the Simulation City Approach, are observations about supplies of services in urban areas. Another aspect of the agglomeration process mentioned above is that urbanization supports economies of scale, relative to provision of such infrastructure services as sewer, water, electricity, and schools. One researcher (Borcherding, 1972), for example, was able to develop regression equations to predict with fair accuracy the dollar expenditures on such services. Other investigations have reported sufficient consistency among urban areas to lend support to the idea that there may be an optimum city size, relative to minimization of per capita service costs.

Similar consistencies are found in the provision of transportation services. Highway-lane miles or percentage of land in highway use are approximated by a function of population and urbanized land area. Although public transit service is not so well defined, perhaps largely because of the lack of consistent data, predictive regression equations for route-miles of supply can be developed (Wells, 1972).

AIII-2.5   Simulation of the Socioeconomic System

The above discussion has been concerned with general characteristics of urban demography and economy. Such information may provide the basis for simulating the basic structure of the socioeconomic system of an urban area. At the extreme, simulation might proceed on the basis of only an estimate of total population and a city-type designator or the industry/ service ratio.

From these two bits of data, the size of the work force might be estimated and a split of this work force into industry categories made. The split might be simply basic industry versus service, or it might deal with major activities such as manufacturing, retail, and wholesale. Some reference about the distribution of income might be drawn.

Given a value for the median income, an income distribution is derived and utilized to infer a distribution of land values and rental costs for the area. Total supply levels of services and transportation facilities are then estimated.

In this fashion, a general, aggregated picture of the city is developed. Simulation of these aspects of the city might be considered analogous to the reconstruction of a set of accounts for a company in which the records have been lost.

AIII-2.6 Historical Patterns and Location Theory

The analysis of why certain activities are located in certain places, and of how individual locations combine into the pattern of a metropolitan region, has focused upon a tradeoff between attractive features of a piece of land and the problems of gaining physical access to that land. In these terms, the location of a city at the site of a good harbor, rail terminus, or concentration of mineral wealth is analogous to the location of higher-income residence within the metropolitan areas on sites with high ground, good vegetation, and highway service.

Emphasis on attractions of particular areas within a region is reflected in the work of some earlier analysts (Weimer, 1966) to devise a coherent explanation of the patterns of activity within an area. The sector theory, which addresses residential location and urban growth, postulated that similar activities would tend to grow outward from the center city in wedge-shaped land sections. The initial location of a sector was determined by factors attractive to the activity, for example, higher ground for residential development.

More recent work (Timms, 1971) has extended the earlier work into social analysis. Here, social rank as a whole, rather than simply income, is said to be distributed along sectoral lines, while status within a social class generally increases toward the center—until a reversal occurs as one enters the central core area.

The extent to which the sector concept represents a contribution to urban theory rather than a restatement of historical development, is uncertain.

The radial patterns of highway and the street railways in the past several decades certainly have encouraged such segregation of activities, and have given characteristic forms to many cities. The fact that the sector concept was useful in guiding decision making in real estate investment was adequate to justify its widespread acceptance.

An alternative focus is provided by the attempts to explore variations in the level of activity within an urban area. Density of development is the measure generally used, stated as people or jobs per unit area. Viewing the urban region as a whole, reasonably good success has been achieved with statistical fitting of an exponential function to patterns of density. One of the more recent and extensive efforts in this area (Mills, 1972) uses a model of the form

$$D(x) = D_o e^{-Yx}$$

where $D(x)$ is the density of activity at a distance x from the center of the city, D is a central density measure, and Y is a gradient measure. Some geographers have attempted to use this type of approach to define the limits of urbanized areas, instead of using the artificial legal boundary as a limit for analysis. However, the model seems most useful in replicating activity in the more stable sections of the urban region rather than in the often decaying central core or newly growing fringes. On a regional level, the fitted function has been shown to provide a reasonable measure of the degree to which a city is centralized or dispersed.

Microscale attempts have been made to explain density on the basis of particular factors of a site or subarea in a region. One study (Chapin, 1962) listed five factors which influenced density of development:

1. Poor drainage discourages development.
2. Major transportation encourages development.
3. Large employment potential intensifies development.
4. Availability of services intensifies development.
5. Proximity of blight discourages development.

Knowledge about the location of any of these factors could be useful in predicting the overall urban pattern.

AIII-2.7 Transport Orientation

Something of a contrast to the above empirical studies is provided by the analyses undertaken with a strong transport point of view. Typically there has been a model or theoretical approach to which data has then been fitted. Some work (Hansen, 1959), an example of one of the early efforts to formalize the role of distances among activities within an urban region as a locational factor, draws upon earlier work in transportation where trip patterns were being predicted on this basis.

The Lowry model of land use (Goldner, 1971) is perhaps the foremost representative of the approach in which the level of activity in a subarea is dependent on the travel distance from that site to all other activities in the region. The case for this type of model was strengthened (Wilson, 1969) by demonstrating that it provides a maximum likelihood estimator of the area's pattern of development, given limited information on personnel travel characteristics and the attractive features of a site, and there is a quite extensive literature in this area. Linked with models to predict (1) attractive subareas and (2) mean trip length characteristics (Voorhees, 1968), the Lowry type model provides a useful predictor of density of activity.

A significant problem in these transport-oriented models (one present also, to a lesser degree, in the other work reviewed) is that they start from a knowledge of the locations of the principal, or basic, industries in an urban area. The factors determining the historical location of industries and thus their current patterns of spatial distribution, within a metropolitan region, have received little attention, although it might be expected, for example, that industrial concentrations would occur close to harbors and railheads. Relative to current knowledge in this area, location of basic industries might be judged a random process. This situation obviously presents a potential problem for the Simulation City concept, for it cannot be said with any certainty that it would be possible to develop empirical predictors of industrial location primarily as a function of natural features. Greater user input would then be required.

AIII-2.8 Distribution of Socioeconomic Factors

Beyond the simple description of what activities occur in which areas of a metropolitan region, and with what intensity, there are a range of factors describing socioeconomic qualities of these activities that must also be distributed spatially throughout the region. Rents, income, taxes, auto ownership, racial character, and many other such factors are of interest in various planning models. It has been found (Bellomo, 1970), for example, that median income within subareas of a city was highly correlated with residential density. Rent levels and auto ownership would then be expected to be correlated with density, via their relationship to income.

Land values have been found (Wieand, 1972; Downing, 1973) to be inversely correlated with distance from the central business district. And as might be expected, commercial land value is higher along streets having higher traffic levels. A similar increased value in vacant land and residential areas, attributable to parkland having significant bodies of water, has also been identified (Darling, 1973).

The likely level of commercial sales at shopping centers was found (Lakshmanan, 1965) to be related to accessibility as well as size. The accessibility of the center was computed as a function of the income of population surrounding the center weighted by the distance of the population of given income from the center.

AIII-2.9 Simulation of the Spatial Pattern

The above paragraphs have been concerned primarily with simulation of the spatial pattern of the city, and to a lesser degree, with what is termed descriptive structure. Starting only with a few major features of the urban area—major highways, rivers, lake or ocean frontage, location of city center—it would appear to be feasible to simulate the locations of basic structural features: land use types and levels of activity.

First, estimates are made of the overall pattern of activity intensity, based upon city size and type. In general, intensity decreases exponentially as distance from center increases. More specific information on intensity levels could then be inferred from the location of major features. Activity intensity concentrates along highways, for example.

The greater the amount of information that is input to the simulation, the greater will be the possible level of detail or accuracy. For example, if it is possible to indicate, prior to simulation, which subareas within an urban region are heavily developed, and which of these subareas are older, it will be more reasonable to attempt to simulate the locations of services of all types, sewer, utility, school, hospital. These activities are typically located as a function of political factors and land availability, and less often through consideration of access to users of most desirable building sites. It is then rather difficult to estimate location through information other than historical observation. This difficulty is also a reflection of the problems inherent in any simulation effort as the level of detail to be simulated increases.

The preceding discussion has attempted, through a brief review of a selection of theoretical and empirical studies in urban economics and geography, to illustrate that the concept of simulating a city—or rather a detailed description of the city—is perhaps a reasonable undertaking. Information such as that reviewed here provides a basis for using the Simulation City Approach.

As has been pointed out, the appeal of the Simulation City Approach stems from the possible tradeoff between cost and accuracy in preparing a data base. It has also been pointed out that accuracy is, in this case, judged by how effectively the simulated data base reproduces the results that would be obtained by using a very detailed, custom-built data base for input to a given planning model. It is this strong, and quite necessary, tie between a Simulation City model and the planning model for which it will be used that makes it impossible to judge with certainty how accurate, in general, data synthesized by a Simulation City model might be. The quantity of work reported in the literature suggests that the concept is feasible, although the concept should not be carried too far.

If cost can be reduced sufficiently to make planning tools more accessible to decision makers, without reducing accuracy so much as to render the model results useless, then the Simulation City Approach will be a success.

AIII-3 Typical Cities

The following is based on "Modal Cities," a report prepared at Dartmouth College as part of Project SUPERB (Simulation of Urban Pressures on the Environment of a River Basin) (Pidot, 1973).

The central problem for the SUPERB classification is simply to discover a technique for creating "average cities" that are typical of the American urban system. This has been done, and the results are sound. It is not clear to us that any one Modal City typology will necessarily lead directly to greater insights into fundamental socioeconomic structures of our cities but, apart from the creation of modal cities data bases, it does seem that some intriguing speculation may be achieved when the maps of each class of Modal City distribution are examined. The following comments (Arnold 1967) on city classification come close to the aims of the Modal City classification effort:

Classification serves as a framework, rather than as a developer of alternatives or a predictor for management decision-making . . . . Classification is no more nor less than an attempt to group items (physical objects, biological characteristics, economic and social data, words, etc.) on the basis of similarities or differences as measured by data. It begins with the assembly of information in the form of data.

AIII-3.1 Aims

The purpose of the SUPERB study is to show how to classify urban areas of the United States into a relatively small set of types based on their economic, social, and demographic characteristics.

The ultimate application of any of these classifications is to define types of urban areas to generate data for loading a simulation model. Both for diversified modeling use and intellectual interest, it is desirable to have a relatively small set of scenarios that typify the wide variety of conditions found in different urban areas of the United States. On the one hand, massive information requirements dictate the use of a small number of areas; on the other, it is attractive to represent as broad a spectrum of places as possible. The task has been to arrive at a rational selection procedure.

The approach used in this work is to derive modal groups and then to select actual areas that most nearly represent the range of conditions encountered in that group at a particular time. While the simplifications inherent in any model require some abstraction and simplification from the real-world data, the use of actual areas allows a fineness of calibration and testing that entirely synthetic cities would not permit. It should be emphasized that the cities selected as Modal Cities are truly representative of their class.

Fundamentally, the test model chosen to illustrate our technique, EPA's River Basin Simulation (EPA-Envirometrics, 1973), is designed to represent an urban region with a limited portion of supporting hinterland. The most readily available statistical construct that genuinely conforms to such a region is the Census-defined SMSA (Standard Metropolitan Statistical Area). Its use of the county as a building block (outside New England) results in poor delineation of the areas for some parts of the country where counties are large and urban areas compact. However, SMSAs do represent reasonably well-defined socioeconomic functional entities that are widely accepted for analytic purposes.

We began with all 224 of the SMSAs defined by the Census as of the time our data were collected (1960). Three had to be deleted because of lack of data availability, but we judged their omission to have minimal effect on the succeeding analysis. We prefer not to delete any areas on a priori grounds of "distorting" the results as we feel this approach introduces and narrows the base of the resulting typology. Our selection includes roughly two-thirds of the entire United States population as of 1960.

AIII-3.2 Variable Selection

Our choice of variables to describe the SMSAs for purpose of classification was guided by a combination of a priori reasoning applied to the needs of the chosen test model and the logic of urban structure, and a pragmatic appreciation of data availability. We sought to include measures of the major demographic labor force, housing income, and business characteristics of the SMSAs with particular detail for manufacturing because of the emphasis of the model. We utilized principal-components analysis to reduce the carefully selected original set of 48 variables for 221 SMSAs to seven indices. On the basis of these summary measures, nine classes are delineated using a grouping algorithm. Finally, representative areas are chosen for each class. Other test models would demand different variables and derive different sets of modal cities.

More detailed variables might have been interesting, particularly for services, in understanding the internal structure of urban areas, but it is doubtful that the ultimate classification would have been altered substantially (see Table AIII-3-1). Similarly, more contemporary data would be desirable, but we believe that our typology is sufficiently generalized to withstand developments over time. It is possible that particular areas may have sufficiently altered characteristics that they would now fall into a different class, but we feel that the broad groupings would be maintained.

Studies of almost every facet of urban life include population, size, density, and growth as the major variables describing the extent and nature of urban development. They reflect the scale economies, critical mass, proximity, stage of growth, and dynamics of the public and private economies. Given the SMSA as an analytic unit, the degree of urbanization adds further useful information about the extent of development in the particular area. Race and age variables are important in describing the political dynamics as well as potential demands on the public sector. Educational achievement reflects the general quality of the labor force and may also be related to attitudes and tastes. The broad employment variables outline the distribution among types of economic activity. Income and its distribution are both the outcome of economic activity and determinants of its future direction. Housing type and quality are important physical characteristics as well as reflecting age and affluence of the area. Value added is the most comprehensive measure of manufacturing activity, and we have attempted to estimate it at the two-digit SIC (Standard Industrial Category) level for SMSAs. Capital expenditure rate indicates rate of expansion for this activity. The retailing, wholesaling, and service variables similarly indicate the scale, extent, development, and composition of the other major private economic activities.

Table AIII-3-1.   *Variables Used for SMSA Classification*

Number	Variable	Number	Variable
1	Population, 1960	7	Median year of education of population aged over 24, 1960
2	Population per square mile, 1960		
3	Population increase, 1950–1960	8	Percent population aged over 24 with less than 5 years of school, 1960
4	Percent urban population, 1960	9	Percent population aged over 24 with high school or more, 1960
5	Percent Negro population, 1960		
6	Percent population aged over 65, 1960	10	Percent employment in manufacturing, 1960

Table AIII-3-1. *(Continued)*

Num-ber	Variable	Num-ber	Variable
11	Percent white collar employment, 1960	30	Retail sales increase, 1958
12	Percent families with income under $3000, 1960	31	Wholesale sales per establishment, 1963
13	Percent families with income $10,000 and up, 1960	32	Wholesale sales per capita, 1963
14	Percent single family housing units, 1960	33	Percent employment in wholesaling, 1963
15	Percent housing units sound with all plumbing, 1960	34	Increase in wholesale sales, 1958–1963
16	Percent owner occupied housing units, 1960	35	Selected service receipts per establishment, 1963
17	Percent population aged 5 to 34 in school, 1960	36	Selected service receipts per capita, 1963
18	Income per capita, 1960	37	Percent employment in selected services, 1963
19	Unemployment rate, 1960	38	Increase in selected service receipts, 1958–1963
20	Percent employment in local government, 1962		Estimated value added per capita, 1963 in:
21	Value added by manufacturing per capita 1963	39	Food and tobacco products
22	Capital expenditures percent of value added, 1963	40	Textile, apparel, and leather products
23	Value added increase, 1958–1963	41	Paper and printing
24	Retail sales per establishment, 1963	42	Chemicals, petroleum, rubber, and plastic products
25	Percent employment in retailing, 1963	43	Lumber, wood products, and furniture
26	Other retail sales per capita, 1963	44	Stone, clay, and glass products
27	General merchandise retail sales per capita, 1963	45	Primary and intermediate metal products
28	Retail food sales per capita, 1963	46	Electrical and nonelectrical machinery
29	Retail auto sales per capita, 1963	47	Transportation and ordinance
		48	Instruments and miscellaneous products

We believe that our selection of variables, while limited, reflects the panoply of conditions observed in urban areas. The number is already such as to make classification an almost impossible task without reducing the dimensions of the problem. Furthermore, it may be argued that the variables are not independent measures but reflect closely related aspects of the urban complex. Underlying them is an enormously complicated set of economic, political, and demographic relationships that we cannot specify explicitly. We may hope to capture one view of these interactions while reducing the dimensionality of our analysis through application of the principal-components technique. This will also reduce the problem of overweighting aspects of the urban setting in our subsequent classification, which happen to be reflected in a large number of our variables.

AIII-3.3 Principal-Components Technique

Briefly, the technique creates a smaller set of artificial measures from the original collection of variables. The new indices explain as large a portion of the original variance as possible, but are uncorrelated with each other. The principal components may be analyzed per se to gain insights into the urban structures we are working with as well as being used for classification purposes.

Formally, we wish to specify our variables $V_{ij}(i=1, \ldots, n$ SMSAs; $j = 1, \ldots, m$ variables) in terms of a set of underlying components F_{ik} $(k=1, \ldots;$ components) and residuals e_i,

$$V_{ij} = \sum_{k=1}^{P} W_{jk} F_{ik} + e_1$$

where W_{jk} are the weights used in combining the components with the original variables. If the residual terms reflect errors of measurement and sampling, then, under the usual assumptions, they "disappear" from the covariance matrix. We assume that the components account for all the variance of the variables, and we are trying to attribute a portion of the variance to each of the components. If there are unique elements of variance in some of the original variables or if we omit some of the components, then the error terms do not vanish. Ideally, we should know a priori these specific variances, or alternatively the commonalties, and perform our analysis only on the latter. Here we assume that all of the variance is to be analyzed. Since we standardized our original variables, i.e., they have zero mean and unit variance, we are in effect examining the correlation matrix with unity on the diagonal. It should be noted that this standardization affects the results analysis in a complex fashion. The resulting weights cannot be readily converted into those that would arise from nonstandardized data.

In principal components, we know the resulting variables and wish to estimate both the underlying components F_{ik} and the weights W_{jkl}. This introduces a degree of indeterminacy in the results, which we eliminate by constraining the components to have zero mean and unit variance. We wish to choose a set of coefficients a_{jk} for

$$F_{ik} = \sum_{j=1}^{m} a_{jk} V_{ij}$$

that minimize the residual variance, i.e., the sum of squared residuals between the original variables and their estimates based on the first component. This is equivalent to explaining as much of the original variance as possible with the first component. Having done so, we might then eliminate the effects of the first component from the original variables and estimate a second component such that it explained as much of the remaining variance as possible. This interactive procedure can be followed up to a limit of m components. We hope to find a set of r components, $r \leq m$, that will account for most of the observed variance (see Table AIII-3-2).

It turns out that our problem is equivalent to finding the successive roots of the correlation matrix by solving its characteristic equation $R - \alpha I = \phi$. The solution for the largest root corresponds to that set of weights explaining the greater portion of the variance. The eigenvalue is the portion of the variance explained and the accompanying eigenvector contains the weights. Successively smaller roots and their vectors correspond to subsequent components. It can also be shown that these vectors are orthogonal, or uncorrelated with each other.

Table AIII-3-2. *Proportion of Total Variance Accounted for by Principal Components*

Principal Component	Eigenvalue	Percent of Pooled Variance	Cumulative Percent
1	10.52	21.9	21.9
2	7.49	15.6	37.5
3	4.11	8.6	46.1
4	3.26	6.8	52.9
5	2.67	5.6	58.5
6	2.12	4.4	62.9
7	1.73	3.6	66.5

The table refers to an analysis of 48 variables for 221 SMSAs.

We may also view the analysis in geometric terms as a rotation of the axes on which the variables are measured. The weights are, in fact, the direction cosines used to transform the variable into the components of the new metric.

In interpreting the components we examine the correlation of each with the original set of variates. We also compute the component scores (F_{ik}) for each SMSA.

We attempt to verify our understanding of the components by examining areas that rank very high or low in the metric of the new variables (see Table AIII-3-3). Recall that the component variables were standardized with zero mean and unit variance, so we may view an area's score directly in terms of a distribution.

Results. Our analysis retains seven components for examination, based on their explanation of the pooled variance. They account for two-thirds of the original variation. A substantial portion of the variance is included from each of the original variables although less so for school enrollment, capital expenditure in manufacturing, value added, growth, and lumber and wood products.

It should be noted that the arithmetic signs on components are not unique; that is, multiplying all the coefficients for a component by a minus one does not affect the statistical properties. Thus for interpretation one may think of a component with many large negative weights in terms of its inverse. Since the component scores are standardized about a zero mean, one might view an area with a large negative score as ranking high on those variables with large negative weights.

COMPONENT I.   The first component is linked with high levels of income and growth and their associated phenomena. The growth includes retailing, wholesaling, and services as well as population. The labor force is highly educated and concentrated in white collar jobs. Housing quality is high. All measures of retailing and selected services are strong. Wholesaling is important to a somewhat lesser degree.

COMPONENT II.   The second component reflects a dominance of manufacturing in employment and value added. The linkage is strong with paper and printing, metals, machinery, instruments, and miscellaneous, and less so with chemicals, petroleum, rubber and plastics, and transportation and ordnance. The people are moderately well-to-do with a notable absence of poor and those with poor education. They live in generally good quality multifamily dwellings.

COMPONENT III.   The third component is the antithesis of metropolitanism. It is negatively linked to size, density, and urbanization.

Table AIII-3-3. **SMSAs with Extreme Principal Component Scores**

1		2		3		4		5	
Anaheim – Santa Ana – Garden Grove, Cal.	3.07	Jersey City, N.J.	2.49	Anaheim–Santa Ana–Garden Grove, Cal.	3.32	Anaheim–Santa Ana–Garden Grove, Cal.	-2.36	Atlanta, Ga.	2.40
Las Vegas, Nev.	5.51	Kenosha, Wisc.	2.57	Anderson, Ind.	2.42	Atlantic City, N.J.	-2.18	Charleston, W. Va.	2.70
Reno, Nev.	3.58	New Britain, Conn.	2.07	Ann Arbor, Mich.	2.63	Fall River, Mass.	-2.25	Charlotte, N.C.	3.00
San Jose, Cal.	2.24	Waterbury, Conn.	2.20	Flint, Mich.	2.20	Huntsville, Ala.	-2.78	Durham, N.C.	2.36
Santa Barbara, Cal.	2.02	Brownsville–Harlingen–San Benito, Tex.	-2.11	Kenosha, Wisc.	2.34	Jersey City, N.J.	-3.66	Memphis, Tenn.	2.65
Stamford, Conn.	2.11	Fayetteville, N.C.	-2.24	Las Vegas, Nev.	2.14	Las Vegas, Nev.	-6.44	Richmond, Va.	2.06
Washington, D.C.	2.37	Laredo, Tex.	-2.81	Boston, Mass.	-2.00	New Bedford, Mass.	-2.13	Winston–Salem, N.C.	3.24
Brownsville–Harlingen–San Benito, Tex.	-2.31			Chicago, Ill.	-2.47	New York, N.Y.	-2.64	Colorado Springs, Col.	-2.05
Gadsden, Al.	-2.07			Jersey City, N.J.	-4.08	Reno, Nev.	-3.12	Meriden, Conn.	-2.05
Johnstown, Pa.	-2.10			New York, N.Y.	-5.05				

6		7	
Las Vegas, Nev.	2.06	Anaheim–Santa Ana–Garden Grove, Cal.	3.11
St. Joseph, Mo.	2.47	Huntsville, Ala.	3.13
Ann Arbor, Mich.	-2.21	Huntington–Ashland, W. Va.	-2.73
Beaumont–Pt. Arthur, Tex.	-2.05	Las Vegas, Nev.	-4.98
Galveston–Texas C., Tex.	-2.39	Reno, Nev.	-3.78
Jersey City, N.J.	-2.00	Steubenville–Weirton, Ohio	-3.15
Lake Charles, La.	-2.21	Wheeling, W. Va.	-2.22
Midland, Tex.	-2.11		
Provo–Orem, Utah	-2.06		
Waterbury, Conn.	-2.52		

Growth is fairly important, for retailing and manufacturing as well as population. People live in their own, single-family homes. Wholesaling is notably absent, being a function of the heavily urbanized area. There is some concentration of stone, clay, and glass industry, also of metals, transportation, and ordnance; there is an absence of textile and apparel manufacturing.

COMPONENT IV.   The fourth component is negatively associated with all measures of services and the textile and apparel industry. On the other hand, it is linked to high educational attainment. Economic growth is poor for manufacturing, retailing, services, and wholesaling. People tend to live in owner-occupied, single-family homes.

COMPONENT V.   The fifth component stresses the presence of a black population and the absence of older people. There is emphasis on various measures of wholesaling. Manufacturing is growing and is important in food and tobacco, less so for chemical-petroleum-rubber and plastics, stone, clay and glass, and lumber and wood products.

COMPONENT VI.   The sixth component is strongly representative of the aged population and consequent lower school enrollments. There is also an absence of local government employment.

COMPONENT VII.   The seventh component is clearly linked to full employment, and modestly linked to growth in retailing, services, and wholesaling, although the levels of service employment and receipts are low. It is, however, related to a low level of manufacturing capital outlays and an absence of the stone-clay-glass industry.

Grouping Procedure.   Having derived a set of measures describing the multiplicity of conditions existing in urban areas, we must now categorize the SMSAs on these bases into a workable set of classes. Given our goal of a small group of representative types, we want to create these classes in such a way that the members of a class are as nearly like each other as possible.

Formally, we want to define a small number of groups (g) such that the intragroup variance of the principal component measures, F_{ik}, is minimized.

$$\min V = \sum_{g=1}^{t} \left(\sum_{k=1}^{p} \left(\sum_{i-1}^{ng} (F_{ik} - \sqrt{\bar{F}_{gk}})^2 \right) \right)$$

where ng is the number of members in group g and $\bar{F}_{gk}$ is the mean of factor k in group g (see Table AIII-3-4). Equivalently, the intragroup differences are maximized. Optimal solutions to such grouping problems

Table AIII-3-4.   *Mean Component Value by Type of SMSA*

SMSA Type	Number of SMSA's in Type	Mean Value of Component						
		1	2	3	4	5	6	7
A	20	0.72	1.07	−1.45	−0.45	0.06	−0.77	−0.23
B	2	4.54	−1.35	1.32	−4.78	0.41	1.72	−4.38
C	20	0.61	−0.02	−0.92	0.92	1.14	0.67	−0.05
D	12	1.28	−0.70	1.52	−0.93	−0.25	0.05	1.00
E	33	−0.63	−0.24	0.20	−0.19	0.40	1.06	0.45
F	22	−0.69	0.68	−0.54	−0.85	−1.28	0.63	0.12
G	30	−0.84	−1.09	−0.24	−0.25	0.53	−0.96	−0.14
H	43	−0.22	0.96	0.92	0.37	0.10	−0.19	−0.24
I	39	0.51	−0.67	−0.02	0.73	−0.72	−0.31	0.02

with more than trivial dimensions are intractable from a practical viewpoint. The solution we choose here is Ward's grouping algorithm, which builds up groups in a nonrecursive stepwise procedure that minimizes the increased error at each stage (Veldman, 1967).

This approach begins with each observation placed in a separate group. That pair of groups is combined which will cause the smallest increase in the error function. This function is simply the pooled intragroup variance for the measures we are using. At each subsequent step, the potential error resulting from any further combination of the remaining groups is computed, and then a new error-minimizing combination is selected. The procedure does not backtrack or select groups simultaneously, so it does not result in a true optimum combination. However, if the associations among types of items being grouped are fairly strong, the resulting groupings are likely to be near optimal in terms of the error variance.

There is no statistical test to determine how many classes should be defined. The selection is based on the rough number of types one wishes to have. However, examination of the error function does not indicate the cost of a particular choice; the increased cost due to a further reduction in the number of classes helps to delineate the appropriate stopping point. Because the grouping algorithm gives equal weight to the measures used as a basis for selection, one needs to consider the number of indices related to particular facets of the items and their variance. By definition, our principal components are orthogonal and maximally efficient in describing the underlying variables. Furthermore, they are standardized to zero mean and unit variance, so no further manipulation is necessary.

Ward's algorithm was applied to our seven principal-component measures for 221 SMSAs. The accompanying table indicates the behavior of the error function over the range of classes we were concerned with. However, it might be noted that increases in the error function were very small over the entire range up to this point. The very large jump in the cumulative error reducing the number of classes from nine to eight (approximately a 50% increase) led us to select that as the desirable level of aggregation. Subsequent examination of class membership confirmed the feeling that further combinations would submerge distinctive types. It might also be added that the class which contains only Las Vegas and Reno remains distinct with further combination until the last step.

The complete listing of SMSAs by type is given in Table AIII-3-5. The geographic clustering in the resulting typology is clear, although there is no bias in our procedures to produce it. Aside from the obvious, Type B being solely Nevada, D is California and Florida, E is South and Central U.S., F is Northeast, especially New England, G is Deep South, H is Midwest, and I is South Central United States.

Type A clearly consists of very large, highly developed urban areas across the country with important manufacturing sectors. Category B is highly specialized in recreation, with rapid growth and high income. Category C contains the medium-size areas with a relatively smaller service sector, emphasizing distribution and some manufacturing. Class D areas are affluent and growing, but less highly urbanized. Class E represents less well-to-do areas with elderly populations. F types are traditional New England with relative stagnation, lack of wholesaling, and an absence of blacks. G areas are nonmanufacturing with rather high levels of poverty and many blacks. The H class areas are archetypal Midwestern, stressing manufacturing, somewhat smaller but growing. Finally, the I group are reasonably affluent, medium-size regional centers, individually specializing in a variety of functions.

Modal Cities Selection. The final stage of our analysis was to rank the areas within their types and select representative SMSAs for each class. This was done on the basis of the sum of square deviations of each SMSA from its class means for the seven principal components,

$$D_i = \sum_{k=1}^{7} (F_{ik} - \bar{F}_{gk})^2$$

where F_{gk} is the mean value of component k for group g.

An area with zero deviation would have precisely the mean characteristics for its type. In examining the deviations for specific types or areas, it should be remembered that the components from which the deviations are computed were standardized with zero mean and unit variance.

Table AIII-3-5. *Ranking the SMSAs by Type*

Census Number	Name	Deviation Score*	Census Number	Name	Deviation Score*
	Type A			Type C	
136	Newark, N.J.	0.42	93	Kansas City, Mo.	0.42
149	Philadelphia, Pa.	0.94	143	Omaha, Neb.	0.53
122	Milwaukee, Wisc.	0.97	47	Dallas, Tex.	0.69
41	Cleveland, Ohio	1.37	163	Richmond, Va.	0.99
27	Boston, Mass.	1.65	52	Des Moines, Iowa	1.18
40	Cincinnati, Ohio	1.83	86	Indianapolis, Ind.	1.22
177	San Francisco–Oakland, Calif.	1.86	155	Portland, Ore.	1.37
110	Los Angeles–Long Beach, Calif.	1.92	123	Minneapolis–St. Paul, Minn.	1.59
18	Baltimore, Md.	2.18	89	Jacksonville, Fla.	1.79
31	Buffalo, N.Y.	2.19	185	Sioux Falls, S. Dak.	2.11
170	St. Louis, Mo.	2.22	219	Wilmington, Del.	2.54
39	Chicago, Ill.	3.08	83	Houston, Tex.	2.89
146	Paterson–Clifton–Passaic, N.J.	3.08	154	Portland, Me.	2.97
53	Detroit, Mich.	3.65	184	Sioux City, Iowa	2.98
152	Pittsburgh, Pa.	4.29	13	Atlanta, Ga.	3.14
132	New Haven, Conn.	4.95	62	Fargo–Moorhead, N. Dak.	3.45
211	Washington, D.C.	7.18	111	Louisville, Ky.	3.75
192	Stamford, Conn.	8.35	37	Charlotte, N.C.	5.25
135	New York, N.Y.	19.59	118	Memphis, Tenn.	5.38
90	Jersey City, N.J.	26.02	169	St. Joseph, Mo.	5.53
	Type B			Type D	
101	Las Vegas, Nev.	5.52	145	Oxnard–Ventura, Calif.	1.13
162	Reno, Nev.	5.52	150	Phoenix, Ariz.	1.37

Table AIII-3-5. (Continued)

Census Number	Name	Deviation Score*	Census Number	Name	Deviation Score*
	Type D (Continued)		54	Dubuque, Iowa	1.88
			80	Harrisburg, Pa.	2.02
144	Orlando, Fla.	1.74	200	Texarkana, Tex.	2.04
179	Santa Barbara, Calif.	2.09	223	York, Pa.	2.17
214	W. Palm Beach, Fla.	2.23	105	Lexington, Ky.	2.34
167	Sacramento, Calif.	2.83	7	Altoona, Pa.	2.36
66	Ft. Lauderdale–Hollywood, Fla.	3.76	67	Ft. Smith, Ark.	2.37
175	San Bernadino–Riverside–ario Ontario, Calif.	3.76	108	Little Rock, Ark.	2.45
178	San Jose, Calif.	4.00	114	Lynchburg, Va.	2.61
59	Eugene, Ore.	5.18	78	Greensville, S.C.	2.67
85	Huntsville, Ala.	11.10	98	Lancaster, Pa.	2.97
9	Anaheim–Santa Ana–Garden Grove, Calif.	14.66	6	Allentown–Bethlehem–Easton, Pa.	3.17
			188	Springfield, Ill.	3.34
	Type E		25	Bloomington–Normal, Ind.	3.50
			161	Reading, Pa.	3.54
95	Knoxville, Tenn.	0.91	171	Salem, Ore.	3.62
12	Ashville, N.C.	1.29	77	Greensboro–High Point, N.C.	3.82
164	Roanoke, Va.	1.32	198	Tampa–St. Petersburg, Fla.	3.99
207	Tyler, Tex.	1.37	160	Raleigh, N.C.	4.25
129	Nashville, Tenn.	1.64	199	Terre Haute, Ind.	4.46
210	Waco, Tex.	1.70	15	Augusta, Ga.	5.13
189	Springfield, Mo.	1.72	56	Durham, N.C.	5.34
38	Chattanooga, Tenn.	1.73	151	Pine Bluffs, Ark.	8.42
60	Evansville, Ind.	1.84	221	Winston–Salem, N.C.	13.82

Table AIII-3-5. (*Continued*)

Census Number	Name	Deviation Score*	Census Number	Name	Deviation Score*
	Type F		91	Johnstown, Pa.	8.27
208	Utica-Rome, N.Y.	0.68	14	Atlantic City, N.J.	8.32
222	Worcester, Mass.	0.93			
112	Lowell, Mass.	1.11		Type G	
191	Springfield–Chicopee–Holyoke, Mass.	1.24	124	Mobile, Ala.	0.19
			180	Savannah, Ga.	1.13
4	Albany–Schenectady–Troy, N.Y.	1.38	43	Columbia, S.C.	1.23
			125	Monroe, La.	1.29
23	Binghamton, N.Y.	1.44	88	Jackson, Miss.	1.29
156	Pawtucket–Providence–Warwick, R.I.	1.55	115	Macon, Ga.	1.43
			44	Columbus, Ga.	1.43
104	Lewiston–Auburn, Me.	1.70	174	San Antonio, Tex.	1.43
29	Brockton, Mass.	1.99	138	Norfolk–Portsmouth, Va.	1.45
181	Scranton, Pa.	2.11	206	Tuscaloosa, Ala.	1.49
218	Wilkes Barre–Hazelton, Pa.	2.81	96	Lafayette, La.	1.66
64	Fitchburg–Leominster, Mass.	2.98	35	Charleston, S.C.	1.92
119	Meriden, Conn.	3.07	147	Pensacola, Fla.	2.08
117	Manchester, N.H.	3.08	126	Montgomery, Ala.	2.29
130	New Bedford, Mass.	3.40	57	El Paso, Tex.	2.34
102	Lawrence–Haverhill, Mass.	4.44	24	Birmingham, Ala.	2.56
28	Bridgeport, Conn.	4.93	183	Shreveport, La.	2.64
61	Fall River, Mass.	5.39	3	Albany, Ga.	2.69
131	New Britain, Conn.	5.77	220	Wilmington, N.C.	3.15
215	Wheeling, W. Va.	8.02	134	New Orleans, La.	3.59

Table AIII-3-5. (*Continued*)

Census Number	Name	Deviation Score*	Census Number	Name	Deviation Score*
	Type G (*Continued*)		201	Toledo, Ohio	0.99
			128	Muskegon, Mich.	1.04
63	Fayetteville, N.C.	4.23	106	Akron, Ohio	1.07
30	Brownsville–Harlingen–San Benito, Tex.	4.78	2	Lima, Ohio	1.25
			203	Trenton, N.J.	1.43
19	Baton Rouge, La.	4.91	186	South Bend, Ind.	1.51
97	Lake Charles, La.	5.38	159	Racine, Wisc.	1.58
71	Gadsden, Ala.	5.46	99	Lansing, Mich.	1.59
21	Beaumont–Port Arthur, Tex.	6.74	224	Youngstown–Warren, Ohio	1.65
100	Laredo, Tex.	8.22	195	Syracuse, N.Y.	1.73
72	Galveston–Texas City, Tex.	8.24	165	Rochester, N.Y.	1.74
141	Ogden, Utah	9.28	87	Jackson, Mich.	1.86
84	Huntington–Ashland, W. Va.	9.69	50	Decatur, Ill.	2.04
			48	Davenport–Rock Island–Moline, Ill.	2.10
	Type H		190	Springfield, Ohio	2.29
79	Hamilton–Middletown, Ohio	0.58	68	Fort Wayne, Ind.	2.33
168	Saginaw, Mich.	0.61	20	Bay City, Mich.	2.46
92	Kalamazoo, Mich.	0.62	58	Erie, Pa.	2.51
127	Muncie, Ind.	0.66	148	Peoria, Ill.	2.68
166	Rockford, Ill.	0.74	158	Pueblo, Colo.	3.06
49	Dayton, Ohio	0.79	81	Hartford, Conn.	3.58
213	Waterloo, Iowa	0.85	33	Cedar Rapids, Iowa	3.67
74	Grand Rapids, Mich.	0.87	65	Flint, Mich.	3.89
32	Canton, Ohio	0.93			

Table AIII-3-5. *(Continued)*

Census Number	Name	Deviation Score*	Census Number	Name	Deviation Score*
	Type H *(Continued)*		172	Salt Lake City, Utah	1.76
			16	Austin, Tex.	1.86
10	Anderson, Ind.	4.34	8	Amarillo, Tex.	1.89
109	Lorain–Elyria, Ohio	4.43	116	Madison, Wisc.	1.91
76	Green Bay, Wisc.	5.08	45	Columbus, Ohio	1.94
73	Gary–Hammond–E. Chicago, Ind.	6.12	176	San Diego, Calif.	2.03
157	Provo–Orem, Utah	6.86	142	Oklahoma City	2.10
153	Pittsfield, Mass.	7.14	216	Wichita, Kan.	2.14
94	Kenosha, Wisc.	7.20	26	Boise City, Idaho	2.21
36	Charleston, W. Va.	10.62	113	Lubbock, Texas	2.29
11	Ann Arbor, Mich.	11.18	34	Champaign–Urbana, Ill.	2.33
212	Waterbury, Conn.	13.83	209	Vallejo–Napa, Calif.	2.37
193	Steubenville–Weirton, Ohio	15.01	51	Denver, Calif.	2.44
	Type I		22	Billings, Mont.	2.80
			182	Seattle–Everett, Wash.	2.85
205	Tulsa, Okla.	0.57	187	Spokane, Wash.	2.94
196	Tacoma, Wash.	0.62	42	Colorado Springs, Colo.	3.04
75	Great Falls, Mont.	0.69	103	Lawton, Okla.	3.09
202	Topeka, Kans.	0.91	17	Bakersfield, Calif.	3.16
217	Wichita Falls, Tex.	0.98	194	Stockton, Calif.	3.26
1	Abilene, Tex.	1.21	70	Fresno, Calif.	3.27
69	Fort Worth, Tex.	1.23	82	Honolulu, Hawaii	4.59
141	Ogden, Utah	1.23	120	Miami, Fla.	4.71
5	Albuquerque, N. Mex.	1.49	121	Midland, Tex.	4.88
107	Lincoln, Nebr.	1.54	55	Duluth–Superior, Minn.	5.38
173	San Angelo, Tex.	1.62	137	Newport News–Hampton, Va.	5.80
204	Tucson, Ariz.	1.73	197	Tallahassee, Fla.	6.31

*Sum of squared deviations from type means for seven grouping components.

While the choice of representative cities for each modal group is determined by the grouping algorithm in an absolute sense, it is worthwhile to consider some other factors not included in the statistical analysis that can lead one to alternative selections. As shown in Table AIII-3-5, Newark, New Jersey, Las Vegas or Reno, Nevada, Kansas City, Missouri, Oxnard—Ventura, California, Knoxville, Tennessee, Utica—Rome, New York, Mobile, Alabama, Hamilton—Middletown, Ohio, and Tulsa, Oklahoma are the least deviant from the mean characteristics of their respective groups in a statistical sense, but there are some spatial considerations that temper the actual choice of the "typical" city of several of the classes.

The chief consideration that arises is that of "independence" of the city as a unit. Notwithstanding the obvious fact that the whole urban system is intensely interrelated, particularly within the megalopian concentrations, it does appear that Newark (Type A) and Oxnard—Ventura (Type D) are heavily influenced by their relationships to New York City and Los Angeles, respectively. Therefore, we must submit that Philadelphia and Phoenix are "more typical" representatives of their categories: both are spatially separated units next on the list of deviancy from their class means. For the purposes of the SUPERB project there are also good substitutions from the point of view of water-related issues.

Similarly, the substitution of Lowell, Massachusetts (Type F) for Utica—Rome is attractive because of spatial discreteness and classic New England manufacturing city water pollution problems. Worcester, Massachusetts, ranking directly behind Utica—Rome and above Lowell, would have been our choice if Lowell's position were not in the Merrimack River Basin, where pollution issues are nearly two centuries old.

Whether one chooses Las Vegas or Reno (Type B) is a toss-up, and while there is no question about this being a distinct class, its sparseness of representative cities, and its lack of clear-cut pollution issues makes it a candidate for exclusion.

Type H, the small northern manufacturing centers, presents a luxuriant set of choices for a data base. The first ten cities in this modal group are less than a standard deviation from the mean, and less than half a standard deviation separates them. For that matter, the next ten are barely more than a standard deviation away from Hamilton—Middletown, the leader. On inspection it seemed to us that Saginaw, Michigan or Rockford, Illinois might be the best choices on the basis of "independence" and water quality kinds of questions. The point is that convenience for the user of the typology should play a role in the choice here (as of course it should for each modal type).

For the other modalities (Type E, Kansas City, Type F, Knoxville,

Type G, Mobile, and Type I, Tulsa) there appeared to us to be no compelling reason to seek alternative representatives.

Our summary suggestion for a list of modal cities is shown in Table AIII-3-5. We have chosen the cities in pairs by class, listing primary selection first.

In all of the cases where we have suggested alternatives we believe that the suggestions are in accord with the classification principle enunciated (Smith, 1965) and quoted earlier in this report.

Conclusions. As we have proceeded with this classification effort we have become aware of the richness and vitality of the existing literature and current research, and we are pleased to discover that others have found the kind of effort pursued in this study to be rewarding. We are also happy to see that our effort is unique in the sense of employing data from, and ultimately classifying, virtually all of the SMSAs in the United States using a large number of carefully selected variables. Other studies have used more variables on fewer urban areas, but none, to our knowledge, has spanned the whole United States urban system in the same way as that presented in this report. Furthermore, our research has been set up in such a way that this study may be replicated for any period when new (or old) data is available. There are also possibilities for extending empirical research of this kind in accord with the sound assertions of Johnston concerning theory-building from regionalization techniques. He points out that it is only after a classification procedure has been undertaken that the question of spatial contiguity should be considered and hypotheses formed and tested (Arnold, 1967). While the purpose of SUPERB has been entirely in the realm of empirical methodology—devising a modal city typology—there may be some attractive realms of *theorizing* that result from our analysis.

AIII-3.4 *Another Way of Describing a Typical City*

The second description of "typical" cities is a pollution-sensitive typology of urban regions, based on a different report (Berry, 1973).

The purpose of the study was to isolate key relationships between urban form and land use on the one hand, and environmental pollution on the other, so that insights might be provided into the consequences of alternative land use policies. To accomplish this, a two-stage research process was initiated:

(a) A "sorting table" with urban regions in the rows and environmental variables in the columns was to be developed to assess the availability and quality of pollutant surveillance systems on a nationwide basis, to evaluate the status of environmental quality indexes, and to study the relationships between urban characteristics and environmental pollution across the set of urban regions.

(b)   For a sample of the urban regions representative of the universe in the sorting table, equivalent intraurban data systems were to be developed as a basis for studying detailed local relationships between environmental pollution and land use.

[Note: Berry's analysis methodology is similar to Pidot and Sommers'. The development of his typology is, therefore, omitted from this discussion.]

Data and Results. The methods [used in developing the typology] were applied to a data matrix that included the information on types of air, water, and land pollution, including solid wastes, pesticides, radiation, and noise, recorded in the overall sorting table. Seventy-six urban regions were included in the investigation. Where problems of missing data existed, correlations were computed only across the available data set, however.

A six-factor solution was able to reproduce a very high proportion of the variance, as indicated by the vector of eigenvalues presented in Table AIII-3-6 and the communities of each of the 76 urban regions listed in Table AIII-3-7. Moreover, the optimum oblique rotation of the factors showed the factor solution to be naturally near-orthogonal (Table AIII-3-8).

The taxonomy was then derived using the 76 × 6 matrices of factor loadings for the principal axis, varimax rotated and oblimin rotated solutions in the following manner:

1.   The group (factor) on which each urban region loaded most highly was identified in the varimax and oblimin solutions, as were all other larger loadings lying beyond the range −0.50 to +0.50.

2.   "Core" groupings were developed by identifying those urban regions with their highest loadings on the same factor in both the varimax and oblimin solutions.

3.   The mirror-image couplets comprising centers with high positive loadings at one extreme and high negative loadings at the other extreme were separated on the first five factors (factor six had only strong positive loadings.)

4.   Residual cases were allocated to the core groups on the basis of the overall pattern of correlations with the set of core-group members.

Table AIII-3-9 shows the resulting 11 groups into which the urban regions naturally cluster with respect to similarities in environmental pollution.

Table AIII-3-6. *Urban Regions Included in the Analysis, With Proportions of Variance Accounted for by a Six-Factor Model*

Akron	0.95909
Albuquerque	0.81815
Allentown-Bethlehem	0.93993
Atlanta	0.76499
Baltimore	0.96484
Birmingham	0.86774
Boston	0.98037
Bridgeport	0.89217
Buffalo	0.98062
Canton	0.95253
Charleston	0.97332
Chattanooga	0.97332
Chicago	0.97160
Cincinnati	0.70762
Cleveland	0.72660
Columbus	0.95821
Dallas	0.76780
Dayton	0.50343
Denver	0.89343
Des Moines	0.96685
Detroit	0.94162
El Paso	0.94084
Flint	0.94585
Fort Worth	0.96728
Gary-Hammond	0.93011
Grand Rapids	0.84280
Hartford	0.94653
Honolulu	0.96685
Houston	0.87825
Indianapolis	0.85657
Jacksonville	0.99271
Jersey City	0.86763
Johnstown	0.89400
Kansas City	0.73713
Los Angeles	0.98062
Louisville	0.84280
Memphis	0.95988
Miami	0.94084
Milwaukee	0.91401
Minneapolis	0.92985
Nashville	0.90461
New Haven	0.95253
New Orleans	0.96087
New York	0.89816

Newark	0.84179
Norfolk	0.84829
Oklahoma City	0.91310
Omaha	0.99271
Paterson	0.84542
Philadelphia	0.92983
Phoenix	0.73365
Pittsburgh	0.92983
Portland	0.98725
Providence	0.88076
Reading	0.93785
Richmond	0.91761
Rochester	0.74876
St. Louis	0.91297
Salt Lake City	0.83433
San Antonio	0.87332
San Bernadino	0.70782
San Diego	0.92773
San Francisco	0.94891
San Jose	0.95909
Seattle	0.85793
Syracuse	0.84113
Tampa-St. Petersburg	0.98544
Toledo	0.94585
Tulsa	0.91310
Utica-Rome	0.83283
Washington, D.C.	0.98725
Wichita	0.86774
Wilmington	0.89230
Worcester	0.97160
York	0.91572
Youngstown	0.94207

Table AIII-3-7. *Variance Extracted by the Six-Factor Solution*

Factor	Eigenvalue	Percentage of Variance	Cumulative Percentage
1	21.81287	28.7	28.7
2	14.91827	19.6	48.3
3	13.12157	17.3	65.6
4	9.77722	12.9	78.5
5	9.05012	11.9	90.4
6	7.20181	9.5	99.8

Table AIII-3-8. Correlations Among Factors in Optimum Oblimin Solution

	FACTOR 1	FACTOR 2	FACTOR 3	FACTOR 4	FACTOR 5	FACTOR 6
FACTOR 1	1.00000	0.05051	−0.00492	−0.14781	−0.01018	0.09101
FACTOR 2	0.05051	1.00000	0.08361	0.04017	−0.05146	−0.04503
FACTOR 3	−0.00492	0.08361	1.00000	0.02517	−0.06304	0.09662
FACTOR 4	−0.14781	0.04017	0.02517	1.00000	−0.08579	−0.02097
FACTOR 5	−0.01018	−0.05146	−0.06304	−0.08579	1.00000	0.02331
FACTOR 6	0.09101	−0.04503	0.09662	−0.02097	0.02331	1.00000

Table AIII-3-9. *Core Groups Common to the Orthogonal and Oblique Q-Mode Factor Structures*

Factor	Group of Metropolitan Areas	
1+	Atlanta	New Orleans
	Boston	New York
	Columbus	San Antonio
	Dallas	San Diego
	Detroit	San Francisco
	Fort Worth	San Jose
	Houston	*Seattle*
	Miami	Tampa-St. Petersburg
1−	*Birmingham*	Johnstown
	Charleston	Nashville
	Chattanooga	Omaha
	Dayton	Reading
	Des Moines	Utica-Rome
	Gary-Hammond	Worcester
2+	*Chicago*	Pittsburgh
	Milwaukee	Portland
	Minneapolis	St. Louis
	Philadelphia	
2−	Albuquerque	Phoenix
	El Paso	Tulsa
	Oklahoma City	Wichita
3+	Bridgeport	New Haven
	Cleveland	Newark
	Hartford	*Providence*
3−	*Cincinnati*	San Bernardino
	Jersey City	Syracuse
	Kansas City	Wilmington
4+	Baltimore	*Los Angeles*
	Buffalo	*Washington, D.C.*
	Indianapolis	
4−	*Denver*	Salt Lake City
5+	*Akron*	Rochester
	Allentown-Bethlehem	Youngstown
	Canton	York
5−	Honolulu	Memphis
6+	Flint	Norfolk
	Grand Rapids	Paterson
	Jacksonville	Richmond
	Louisville	Toledo

Factors 1–6 near-orthogonal.
Bipolar + and − categories on a given factor have reverse-image pollution characteristics.
Cities italicized are cases for which more detailed intraurban investigations will be undertaken.

The cases selected for detailed study are italicized. Rather than choosing sample cases on a randomized basis, the selection was made on the basis of adequacy of basic information on internal variations in environmental quality and the prospect of deriving metropolitan-scale land use data.

Discussion. On inspection, many of the groups appear, intuitively, to make good common sense; for example Group 2+ containing such industrial cities as Chicago, Milwaukee, Minneapolis, Philadelphia, Pittsburgh, Portland, and St. Louis certainly contrasts with the mirror-image set comprising Group 2-members Albuquerque, El Paso, Oklahoma City, Phoenix, Tulsa, and Wichita. But intuition is not enough. The questions that arise in terms of the initial "sorting table" approach to the research effort described earlier are these:

(a)   How are the groups differentiated in terms of the pollution characteristics of their members?

(b)   What characteristics of urban form and function discriminate among the groups?

(c)   How do the pollution difference and urban variables covary, and what do the covariances imply?

Tables AIII-3-10 and AIII-3-11 provide an initial insight into these questions. The groups are arranged in mirror-image sequence in Table AIII-3-10 from the cities in groups 4+, 2+, 5+, and 1−, most heavily afflicted by air pollution, through groups 3− and 1+, with the greatest water pollution, to the least-polluted cities in groups 5−, 2−, and 4−. Where the pollution level exceeds the national average, the number in the table is underlined. Table AIII-3-11 records related city characteristics in the same progression from group 4+ to group 4−.

What is indicated is the following: high-density, core-oriented metropolitan areas with the most pronounced radial highway nets and average-to-high levels of manufacturing employment are afflicted by the highest levels of air pollution, and some of these cities are afflicted with water pollution problems, too. At the other extreme small, low-density, highly dispersed western metropolitan areas with low levels of manufacturing employment have the lowest levels of environmental pollution. Between these extremes are, for example, the large regional capitals of the West and South, plus New York, Boston, and Detroit, seen as suffering in particular from severe problems of water pollution. Enough covariance is indicated between city characteristics and pollution levels to proceed with more detailed modeling of those relationships.

Table AIII-3-10. Pollution—Variations Across the Groups

	Grand Mean	S.D.	4+	2+	5+	1-	3+	6+	3-	1+	5-	2-	4-
WQI 1 (drinking)	3.3	2.7	7.6	1.7	4.7	2.1	5.2	4.0	5.4	4.7	n.a.	2.3	2.0
WQI 2 (recreation)	2.2	2.3	6.3	1.2	2.2	1.5	0.7	1.5	4.3	3.0	n.a.	2.2	0.4
WQI 3 (industry)	1.8	1.8	1.4	0.6	1.4	1.2	0.5	1.0	3.3	2.0	n.a.	2.4	1.4
WQI 4 (average)	2.5	2.0	5.1	1.2	2.8	1.6	2.1	2.2	4.5	3.3	n.a.	2.3	1.3
Temperature	61	9	58	59	63	58	57	58	61	69	n.a.	62	51
Color	15	13	10	14	10	6	n.a.	20	24	20	n.a.	12	n.a.
PH	7.3	0.9	7.4	7.4	6.8	6.9	6.7	7.7	7.1	7.3	n.a.	8.0	7.7
Tot. dissolved solids	1945	5467	865	211	820	353	95	407	4765	4448	n.a.	1894	445
Tot. nitrates	11	13	3	5	16	7	4	3	8	19	n.a.	16	11
Hardness	483	947	335	148	333	226	42	234	874	886	n.a.	561	264
Color	1146	619	39	33	323	30	16	30	4885	2337	n.a.	666	264
Tot. iron and manganese	1.0	2.5	n.a.	0.5	0.9	2.1	0.2	n.a.	0.6	0.3	n.a.	0.2	n.a.
Sulfate	235	435	n.a.	54	96	160	15	76	474	369	n.a.	424	113
Dissolved oxygen	6.9	2.1	7.2	8.0	5.3	7.8	7.1	7.9	7.0	6.9	n.a.	4.9	n.a.
Tot. MAQI	2.7	0.8	3.2	3.4	2.7	3.2	2.7	2.1	2.9	2.3	2.3	2.1	2.2
Tot. FUI	6.0	5.0	9.7	8.4	5.9	10.6	4.2	2.2	5.0	3.5	2.3	3.4	1.1
SO2 AVE	27	21	34	49	38	25	51	20	22	19	16	9	13
SO2 MAX	117	93	127	191	149	117	241	74	87	80	208	40	37
SO2 MAQI	0.5	0.1	0.6	0.8	0.6	0.5	0.9	.3	0.4	0.4	0.3	0.1	0.1
NO2 MAQI	1.4	0.4	1.2	1.6	1.4	1.2	1.6	1.6	1.6	1.4	1.4	1.0	1.3
TSP AVE	97	25	115	117	106	119	84	82	104	85	61	84	82
TSP MAX	231	95	325	317	229	310	168	184	238	179	145	197	159
TSP MAQI	2.2	0.8	2.9	2.8	2.4	2.9	1.7	1.7	2.4	1.7	1.9	1.9	1.7
TSP EVI	6.1	5.0	9.7	8.4	5.9	10.6	4.4	2.2	5.0	3.5	2.3	3.4	1.1
AUTO. TRV.	342	362	803	705	155	120	278	193	239	515	183	154	263
AIR. TRV.	104	123	170	228	194	36	99	34	66	152	114	46	110
G.B.R. MAX	2.7	2.1	2.0	2.2	2.0	2.4	1.7	1.0	3.0	2.1	2.0	6.0	1.5
G.B.R. AVE	1.3	0.7	1.0	1.0	n.a.	1.0	1.0	1.0	1.5	1.3	n.a.	1.8	.231

Table AIII-3-10 (Continued)

	Grand Mean	S.D.	4+	2+	5+	1-	3+	6+	3-	1+	5-	2-	4-
Rainfall	.641	.395	.548	.893	.121	1.030	.675	.648	.568	.624	.448	.095	.231
B.R. DEP	99	92	4	88	28	223	129	132	133	19	n.a.	79	92
S.W.G.F. 1	4.89	1.43	5.09	4.49	4.39	5.04	3.98	4.66	5.98	4.75	5.72	5.30	5.72
S.W.G.F. 4	n.a.	n.a.	5987	6737	1440	999	2482	1434	1940	4527	1174	984	1564
S.W.G.F. 5	n.a.	n.a.	3811	3858	741	579	1287	914	1198	2938	882	712	1178
No. Cases	76		5	7	6	12	6	8	6	16	2	6	2

Table AIII-3-11. Some Characteristics of Cities in the 11 Groups (Group Averages)

	4+	2+	5+	1-	3+	6+	3-	1+	5-	2-	4-
Population of central city	1209	1185	186	209	321	327	329	1152	475	354	346
Population of SMSA	2285	2969	557	448	1040	705	921	2267	700	525	893
Density of central city	10669	10111	6966	4711	9630	8774	7553	7569	4285	3958	5380
Density of SMSA	6396	5911	3413	2048				6302	3586	637	2891
Growth rate, central city	1.7	-6.5	-5.8	-5.8	-6.1	3.9	0.8	14.2	17.9	19.7	-1.5
Growth rate, SMSA	31.9	30.1	23.6	21.5	25.3	24.9	24.5	48.2	15.2	19.5	55.8
Md. age of central city residents	29.5	31.3	30.8	31.0	29.1	28.1	29.8	29.4	27.2	26.9	28.8
Md. age of SMSA residents	27.4	27.7	28.5	28.0	30.4	26.4	26.2	28.1	22.4	24.8	23.2
Md. family income	11.1	10.9	10.6	9.7	11.4	10.3	10.2	10.4	10.3	9.1	10.4
Percent employed in manufacturing	24.2	29.8	43.9	32.5	34.0	29.4	30.3	22.0	14.7	19.9	15.4
Area of central city	215	108	30	89	36	144	107	180	151	224	77
Area of SMSA	2670	3093	1225	1400	668	1027	5973	2519	980	3306	2361
Degrees of arc: SMSA	264	291	330	330	210	285	250	225	240	280	270
Radial highways: central city	9.8	8.6	3.0	3.6	5.3	4.6	6.0	7.3	4.0	3.7	5.0
Radial highways: SMSA	10.6	10.9	5.0	5.4	7.5	6.6	7.5	8.3	5.5	4.0	7.0
Circumferential highways	3.0	2.7	2.5	1.5	1.6	1.7	1.8	2.4	2.0	3.0	1.5
Total land + property values in SMSA	25.2	18.5	3.4	3.1	10.3	4.7	8.5	18.8	4.1	3.4	6.6

AIII-3.5   Conclusion

It will not be possible to give a completely satisfactory answer to the relative utility of each of the three methodologies described in this Appendix. There are still numerous comparative questions to be asked in terms of relative accuracy versus intended usage, fixed versus variable cost of use, production time, and the like. Years of research and effort will probably be needed before definitive answers can be given.

Nonetheless, it is possible, even at this stage, to suggest that data for large-scale or comprehensive models may *not* really be the key problem. This is more assuredly so if the need for the model is of a broadly based, strategic nature; specific and detailed accuracy may in that case be less important. This is not to say that the data for all models is lying around somewhere waiting to be retrieved or massaged into shape, or that it will be useful or cost-effective to approximate data bases for all models. However, there do appear, at least for some applications, to be promising adjuncts or even alternatives to the oftimes crippling restriction of customized data bases.

With this admittedly tentative, although hopeful note, we close our discussion of data sources and of Large-Scale Models for Policy Evaluation.

BIBLIOGRAPHY

Aagesen, A. "The Population." In N. Nielsen (Ed.), *Atlas of Denmark*. Copenhagen: C.A. Reitzels Forlag, 1961, pp. 89–92. In Berry and Horton, p. 108.

Abelson, P.H. "Discovery and Evaluation of Resources." *Science*, 2 February 1973, p. 431.

Ackoff, R.L. *Scientific Method: Applied Research Decisions*. New York: Wiley, 1972.

Air Pollution Task Force of the County of San Diego, California. "Evaluation of EPA's Proposed Air Pollution Control Plan with Alternatives." 1 August 1973.

Alford, R.R. "Critical Evaluation of the Principles of City Classification." In Berry and Horton, p. 337.

Allison, J.S. In Proceedings of the Third Australian Comprehensive Conference. Canberra, May 1966, p.13.

Almon, C., Jr. et al. "1985 Interindustry Forecasts of the American Economy." College Park, Maryland: Bureau of Business and Economic Research, University of Maryland, 1974.

Alonso, W. "Predicting Best with Imperfect Data." *American Institute of Planners Journal*, July 1968, pp. 248–252.

Alonso, W. "The Quality of Data and the Choice and Design of Predictive Models." In *Urban Development Models*. Highway Research Board, Washington, D.C. Special Report 97, 1968.

Apri, D.W. "An Interim Study of the TRANS Model." State University of New York at Stony Brook. Office of Systems Analysis and Information, Office of the U.S. Secretary of Transportation, pp. 7–17.

Arnold, D.S. "Classification as Part of Urban Management." In Berry, 1967, p. 326.

Beller, M. "Energy Systems Analysis and Technology Assessment Program." Energy Research and Development Administration, Office of Planning and Analysis. Annual Report, Fiscal Year 1975. September 1975.

Bellomo, S.J., R.B. Dial, and A.M. Voorhees. "Factors, Trends and Guidelines Related to Trip Lengths." Highway Research Board, Washington, D.C. NCHRP 89, 1970.

Benyon, P.R. "Computer Modelling and Interdisciplinary Teams." *Search*, July 1972, pp. 250–256.

Bergsman, J.P., P. Greenston, and R. Healy. "The Agglomeration Process In Urban Growth." *Urban Studies*, October 1972.

Berry, B.J.L. *City Classification Handbook: Methods and Applications*. New York: Wiley-Interscience, 1972.

Berry, B.J.L. "Grouping and Regionalizing: An Approach to the Problem Using Multivariate Analysis." In Garrison and Marble (Eds.), *Quantitative Geography, Part I: Economic and Cultural Topics*. Evanston: Northwestern University, 1967, p. 245.

Berry, B.J.L., D.B. Cargo, D.C. Dahmann, P.G. Goheen, C.C. Kaplan, R.E. Lamb, M.W. Mikesell, and J.P. Mrowka. "Land Use Forms and the Environment." Department of Geography, University of Chicago. WERC, ORD, U.S. Environmental Protection Agency, Washington, D.C. EPA Project No. R-801419. November 1973 (draft).

Berry, B.J.L. and F.E. Horton. *Geographic Perspectives on Urban Systems*. Englewood Cliffs: Prentice-Hall, 1970, p. 107.

Biggs, A.G. and A.R. Cawthorne. "Bloodhound Missile Evaluation." *Royal Aeronautical Society Journal*, September 1962, p. 571.

Bisselle, C.A. et al. "Strategic Environmental Assessment System: Initial Analysis of Environmental Residuals." Mitre Corporation, McLean, Virginia. WERC, ORD, U.S. Environmental Protection Agency, Washington, D.C. Contract No. 68-01-0784. Report MTR No. 6362. February 1973.

Blumenfeld, H. "Are Land Use Patterns Predictable?" *American Institute of Planners Journal*, May 1959.

Borcherding, T.E. and R.T. Deacon. "The Demand for Services of Non-Federal Governments." *American Economic Review*, December 1972.

Boulding, K.E. "General Systems Theory—The Skeleton Science." In W. Buckley (Ed.), *Modern Systems Research for the Behavioral Scientist: A Sourcebook*. Chicago: Aldine Publishing Co., 1968, p. 3.

Boyce, D.E., N.D. Day, and C. McDonald. *Metropolitan Plan Making: An Analysis of Experience with the Preparation and Evaluation of Alternative Land Use and Transportation Plans*. Philadelphia: Regional Science Research Institute, 1970, p. 203.

Brewer, G.D. *The Politician, The Bureaucrat, and the Consultant: A Critique of Urban Problem Solving*. New York: Basic Books, 1973.

Bryce, H.J. "Identifying Socio-Economic Differences Between High and Low Income Metropolitan Areas." *Socio-Economic Planning Sciences*, April 1973.

Campbell, A. and P.E. Converse. *The Human Meaning of Social Change*. New York: Russell Sage Foundation, 1972.

Cantril, A.H. and C.W. Roll Jr. *The Hopes and Fears of the American People*. New York: Universe Books, 1971.

Cartwright, T.J. "Problems, Solutions and Strategies: A Contribution to the Theory and Practice of Planning." *American Institute of Planners Journal*, May 1973.

Catanese, A.J. and A.W. Steiss. "The Search for a Systems Approach to the Planning of Complex Urban Systems." *Plan 10* (1), 1969.

Chapin, F.S. "Patterns of Urban Development." In Chapin and Weiss (Eds.), *Urban Growth Dynamics*. New York: Wiley, 1962.

Charpentier, J.P. "A Review of Energy Models: No. 1—May 1974." International Institute for Applied Systems Analysis, RR-74-10. Schloss Laxenburg A-2361, Austria, July 1974.

Charpentier, J.P. "A Review of Energy Models: No. 2—July 1975." International Institute for Applied Systems Analysis, RR-75-35. Schloss Laxenburg A-2361, Austria, October 1975.

Chase, S. *Men at Work*. New York: Harcourt Brace, 1941.

Cherrington, Paul W. Remarks before the Transportation Research Forum while he was Assistant Secretary for Policy and International Affairs of the U.S. Department of Transportation, October 1969.

Chestnut, H. and T.B. Sheridan. "Modeling Large Scale Systems at National and Regional Levels." Report of a workshop held at Brookings Institute, Washington, D.C., 10–12 February 1975.

Clymer, A.B. "The Modeling and Simulation of Big Systems." In *Proceedings of Simulation and Modeling Conference*. Pittsburgh, April 1969, p. 107.

Commoner, B. "The Ecological Facts of Life (No Deposit–No Return)." In R.F. Kohn (Ed.), *Environmental "Education": The Last Measure of Man*. United States National Commission for UNESCO, Washington, D.C., 1971.

Commoner, B. "The Environmental Costs of Economic Growth." In R. and N.S. Dorfman (Eds.), *Economics of the Environment: Selected Readings*. New York: Norton, 1972, pp. 262–263.

Creighton, Hamburg, Planning Consultants. "Data Requirements in Metropolitan Transportation Planning." Highway Research Board, Washington, D.C. NCHRP 120, 1971.

Dalkey, Norman C. et al. *Studies in the Quality of Life: Delphi and Decision-Making.* Lexington, Massachusetts: Lexington Books, 1972.

Dansereau, P. *An Ecological Perspective*, New York: Ronald Press, 1957, pp. 54, 122, 203–204, 293.

Darling, A.H. "Measuring the Benefits Generated by Urban Water Parks." *Land Economics*, February 1973.

Dasmann, R.F. *Wildlife Biology.* London: John Wiley & Sons, 1964, pp. 75, 154.

"DATA" (Report of the Working Committee on Data). In D.M. McAllister (Ed.), *Environment: A New Focus for Land-Use Planning.* Report on an NSF-RANN-Sponsored Workshop/Conference held in the summer of 1972 at Boulder, Colorado, p. 456.

Downing, P.B. "Factors Affecting Land Values: An Empirical Study of Milwaukee, Wisconsin." *Land Economics*, February 1973.

Drake, J.W. *The Administration of Transportation Modeling Projects.* Lexington Books Studies in Transportation and Regional Science. Lexington, Massachusetts: Heath, 1973, pp. 243–246.

Engle, R., III, F. Fisher, J. Harris, and J. Rothenberg. "An Econometric Simulation of Intra-Metropolitan Housing Location: Housing, Business, Transportation, and Local Government." *American Economic Review*, May 1972, pp. 87–97.

Environmental Impact Center Inc. "A Methodology for Assessing Environmental Impact of Water Resources Development." Quarterly reports for the Office of Water Resources Research, Cambridge, Massachusetts. December 1972, March 1973, June 1973.

Environmental Impact Center Inc. "Secondary Impacts of Federal Infrastructure Investments—Task I Final Report" Council on Environmental Quality, Washington, D.C. Contract No. EQC 317, 15 July 1973.

Environmental Protection Agency. "EPA Proposal #801225." From the Environmental Development Agency, County of San Diego, California to Environmental Studies Division, ORD, U.S. Environmental Protection Agency, March 1972.

Environmental Protection Agency. "EPA Proposal #P312022." From the Institute for Environmental Studies and the Department of City and Regional Planning, Graduate School of Fine Arts, University of Pennsylvania to Environmental Studies Division, ORD, U.S. Environmental Protection Agency, 1 March 1973.

Environmental Protection Agency. *The Quality of Life Concept: A Potential New Tool for Decision-Makers.* ESD, ORD, U.S. Environmental Protection Agency, Washington, D.C., Government Printing Office No. 5500-3088, 1973, pp. I-1 through I-85.

Environmental Protection Agency. "Quality of Life Indicators: A Review of State-of-the-Art and Guidelines Derived to Assist in Developing Environmental Indicators." Environmental Studies Division, Office of Research and Monitoring, Environmental Protection Agency, December 1972. 83 pp.

Environmental Protection Agency. *River Basin Simulation.* Washington, D.C.: Envirometrics, 1973.

Environmental Protection Agency. *SEAS Task IV Information System* (Vol. I—IBM Technical Proposal). Federal Systems Center, IBM, Gaithersburg, Maryland, WERC, ORD, U.S. Environmental Protection Agency, 26 February 1973, pp. 3-4a, 3-4b.

Environmental Protection Agency. *SEAS National and Regional Profiles.* Federal Systems Center, IBM, Gaithersburg, Maryland. WERC, ORD, U.S. Environmental Protection Agency, Contract No. EPA 68-01-1824, June 1973. 128 pp.

Environmental Protection Agency. *SEAS Phase I Stocks.* Federal Systems Center, IBM, Gaithersburg, Maryland, WERC, ORD, U.S. Environmental Protection Agency, Contract No. EPA 68-01-1824, August 1973. 18 pp.

Environmental Protection Agency. *SEAS Phase I Final Report*. WERC, ORD, Environmental Protection Agency, in-house report, October 1973.

Environmental Protection Agency. *Strategic Environmental Assessment System* (SEAS). ESD, ORD, U.S. Environmental Protection Agency, February 1973. 56 pp.

Environmental Protection Agency. *Strategic Environmental Assessment System (SEAS): Part II*. U.S. Environmental Protection Agency, in-house publication, Spring 1974.

Environmental Protection Agency. *Working Papers in Alternative Futures and Environmental Quality*. Office of Research and Development, Washington Environmental Research Center, Environmental Studies Division. May 1973.

EROS Mini-Manual. EROS Program, U.S. Department of the Interior, EROS reprint No. 171, pp. 1, 2.

Forecasting, Planning, Resource Allocation Source Book. Washington, D.C.: International Research and Technology, 1973.

Forrester, J.W. "Counterintuitive Behavior of Social Systems." *Simulation*, February 1971, reprinted from *Technology Review*, January 1971.

Forrester, J.W. *Principles of Systems*. Cambridge, Massachusetts: Wright-Allen Press, 1968.

Forrester, J.W. *Urban Dynamics*. Cambridge, Massachusetts: MIT Press, 1969.

Forrester, J.W. *World Dynamics*. Cambridge, Massachusetts: Wright-Allen Press, 1971.

Fri, R.W. "Beyond the Brushfires." In *National Conference on Managing the Environment: Final Conference Report*. Washington, D.C.: International City Management Association, WERC, ORD, U.S. Environmental Protection Agency, 1973, pp. 1–4.

Fromm, G., W.L. Hamilton, and D.E. Hamilton. *Federally Supported Mathematical Models: Survey and Analysis*. Washington, D.C.: Data Resources Inc. and Abt Associates Inc., National Science Foundation, June 1975.

Galbraith, J.K. *The New Industrial State*. Boston: Houghton Mifflin, 1967.

Geisler, M.A. and W.A. Steger. "The Combination of Alternative Research Techniques in Logistics Systems Analysis." Rand Corporation. Presented at the annual meeting of the American Association for the Advancement of Science, Philadelphia, December 1962.

Gilmore, J. et al. "Defense Systems Research in the Civil Sector." Washington, D.C.: Arms Control and Disarmament Agency, 1967.

Ginn, J. "The NBER Prototype Urban Simulation Model." Preliminary Draft. New York: National Bureau of Economic Research, March 1973.

Gitter, A.G. and D.I. Mostofsky. "The Social Indicator: An Index of the Quality of Life." *Social Biology*, September 1973.

Goeller, B.F. et al. "San Diego Clean Air Project: Summary Report." Rand Corporation, R-1362-SD, December 1973.

Goeller, B.F. "Strategy Alternatives for Oxidant Control in the Los Angeles Air Quality Control Region." Rand Corporation, R-1368-EPA. December 1973.

Goldner, W. "The Lowry Model Heritage." *American Institute of Planners Journal*, March 1971.

Golob, T.F., E.T. Canty, and R.L. Gustafson. "Classification of Metropolitan Areas for the Study of New Systems of Arterial Transportation." General Motors Research Laboratory, Publication No. GMR-1225, 1 August 1972, pp. 37–43.

Goodman, M.R. "Conceptualization of System Structure." In *Simulation in the Service of Society*, February 1971, p. 1.

Gross, B. "Management Strategy for Economic and Social Development: Part II." *Policy Sciences*, March 1972, pp. 9–20.

Hamilton, H.R., S.E. Goldstone, J.W. Milliman, A.L. Pugh III, E.B. Roberts, and A. Zellner. "The Management of a Multidisciplinary Research Project (Appendix A)." In *Systems Simulation for Regional Analysis—An Application to River Basin Planning*. Cambridge, Massachusetts: MIT Press, 1969, pp. 289–305.

Hansen, W.G. "How Accessibility Shapes Land Use." *American Institute of Planners Journal*, May 1959.

Harris, B. "Quantitative Models of Urban Development: Their Role in Metropolitan Policy-Making." In H.S. Perloff and L. Wingo, Jr. (Eds.), *Issues in Urban Economics*. Baltimore: Johns Hopkins University Press, 1968, pp. 371–372.

Harris, C.D. "A Functional Classification of Cities in the United States." *Geographical Review*, January 1943.

Hemmens, G.C. "Survey of Planning Agency Experience with Urban Development Models, Data Processing and Computers." In G.C. Hemmens (Ed.), *Urban Development Models*. Washington, D.C.: Highway Research Board, Special Report 97, 1968.

Hermann, C. "Validation Problems in Games and Simulations with Special Reference to Models of International Politics." *Behavioral Science*, May 1967.

Hillegass, T.J. "Urban Transportation Planning—A Question of Emphasis." *Traffic Engineering*, June 1969.

Hoos, I.R. "A Critical Review of Systems Analysis: The California Experience." Working Paper No. 89. Berkeley: Space Sciences Laboratory, December 1968.

Hoos, I.R. "Systems Techniques for Managing Society: A Critique." *Public Administration Review*. March/April 1972.

House, P.W. "Building Games: Retrospection." *Simulation and Games Journal*, September 1972, pp. 271–289.

House, P.W. "Diogenes Revisited—The Search for a Valid Model." *Simulation*, October 1974.

House, P.W. "Environmental Modeling Versus the 'Chicken Soup' Approach: Work in Progress." *Simulation*, June 1973, pp. 181–191.

House, P.W. *The Urban Environmental System: Modeling for Research, Policymaking and Education*. Beverly Hills, California: Sage Publications, 1974.

House, P.W., R.L. Livingston, and C.D. Swinburn. "Monitoring Mankind: The Search for Quality." U.S. Environmental Protection Agency. Presented at the 9th World Congress of the International Political Science Association, Montreal, August 1973.

House, P.W. and G.R. Tyndall. "Models and Policy-Making." In *A Guide to Models in Governmental Planning and Operations*. Bethesda, Maryland: Mathematica, Inc., WERC, ORD, U.S. Environmental Protection Agency, 1974, pp. 39–69.

House, P.W., and E.R. Williams, *The Carrying Capacity of a Nation*. Lexington, Massachusetts: Lexington Books, 1976.

House, P.W. and E.R. Williams. The State of the System (SOS) Model: Measuring Growth Limitations Using Ecological Concepts. Chase, Rosen, and Wallace (Williams). Washington, D.C.: WERC, ORD, U.S. Environmental Protection Agency, Government Printing Office No. EPA-600-5-73-013, February 1974, 324 pp.

Hummon, N.P. "On The Evaluation of Simulation Models." Program in Environmental Systems Engineering and Department of Sociology, University of Pittsburgh, Pittsburgh, Pennsylvania, 1973.

Humphrey, H.H. "The Balanced National Growth and Development Act." S. 3050, 93/2. Introduced by Senator Humphrey in March 1974; referred to Senate Committee on Government Operations.

Isard, W. *Location and Space Economy*. Cambridge, Massachusetts: MIT Press, 1956.

Johnston, R.J. "Grouping and Regionalizing: Some Methodological and Technical Observations." *Economic Geography*, June 1970, pp. 293–305.

Kain, J. and G. Ingram. "The Urban Simulation Model as a Theory of Urban Spatial Structure." New York: National Bureau of Economic Research, Inc., October 1972.

Kelvin, William Thomson, Baron. *Popular Lectures and Addresses*. 1891–1894.

Knisely, R.A. Statement before the Subcommittee on Foreign Operations and Government Information of the Committee on Government Operations, U.S. House of Representatives, 19 June 1973, by the Director, Division of Community Management Programs, U.S. Department of Housing and Urban Development.

Lakshmanan, T.R. "A Theoretical and Empirical Analysis of Intra-urban Retail Location." Ph.D. Thesis, Department of Geography, Ohio State University, 1965.

Lamson, Robert. Statement in *Congressional Record*, 16 December 1974.

Lapp, R.E. *The New Priesthood*. New York: Harper & Row, 1965, pp. 63–70.

Lee, D.B., Jr. "Requiem for Large-Scale Models." *American Institute of Planners Journal*, May 1973.

Levin, M.R. and N.A. Abend. *Bureaucrats in Collision: Case Studies in Transportation Planning*. Cambridge, Massachusetts: MIT Press, 1971.

Library of Congress—Congressional Research Service. *Computer Simulation Methods to Aid National Growth Policy*. Committee Print, 94th Congress, 1st session. Prepared for the Subcommittee on Fisheries and Wildlife Conservation and the Environment of the Committee on Merchant Marine and Fisheries. Serial No. 94-B. Washington, D.C.: U.S. Government Printing Office, 1975.

Linstone, H.A. and M. Turoff. *The Delphi Method: Techniques and Applications*. Reading, Massachusetts: Addison-Wesley, 1975.

Machlup, F. *The Production and Distribution of Knowledge in the United States*. Princeton, New Jersey: Princeton University Press, 1962.

McLeod, J. "How to Simulate." *Simulation in the Service of Society*, September 1974.

McLeod, J. "The Other Side of the Coin." *Simulation in the Service of Society*, April 1975.

McLeod, J. "Regional Model System—San Diego County." *Simulation in the Service of Society*, July 1972.

McLeod, J. "Simulation: from Art to Science for Society." *Simulation*, December 1973.

McLeod, J. "Simulation Today—from Fuzz to Fact." *Simulation*, March 1973.

Mar, B.W. and W.T. Newell. "Assessment of Selected RANN Environmental Modeling Efforts." Environmental Systems and Resources Division, Research Applied to National Needs, National Science Foundation, June 1973.

Mathematica, Inc. "A Guide to Models in Governmental Planning and Operations." WERC, ORD, U.S. Environmental Protection Agency, 1974.

Maugh, T.H. II. "ERTS: Surveying Earth's Resources from Space." *Science*, 6 April 1973, p. 49.

Meadows, D.H. et al. *The Limits to Growth*. Washington: Potomac Associates, 1972.

Mihram, G.A. "Simulation Models." *Operational Research Quarterly*, March 1972.

Mihram, G.A. *Simulation: Statistical Foundations and Methodology*. New York: Academic Press, 1971.

Mikolowsky, W.T. et al. "The Regional Impacts of Near-term Transportation Alternatives: A Case Study of Los Angeles." Rand Corporation, R-1524-SCAG, June 1974.

Millar, J.A. "Selective Adaptation." *Policy Sciences*, July 1972, p. 126.

Mills, E.S. *Studies in the Structure of the Urban Economy. Resources for the Future*. Baltimore: Johns Hopkins University Press, 1972.

Moder, J.J. in *Engineering News-Record*, 14 March 1963.

Moore, W.T., F.J. Ridel, and C.G. Rodriguez. "An Introduction to Urban Development Models and Guidelines for Their Use in Urban Transportation Planning." U.S. Department of Transportation, October 1975.

Morrissett, I. "The Economic Structure of American Cities." *Papers and Proceedings of the Regional Science Association 4*, 1958.

Moser, C.A. and W. Scott. *British Towns: A Statistical Study of Their Social and Economic Differences*. Edinburgh: Oliver & Boyd, 1961.

National Science Foundation. "The Need for Documentation Standards for Computerized Mathematical Modeling Activity in the Federal Government." Washington, D.C.: National Science Foundation.

Naylor, T.H. *The Design of Computer Simulation Experiments*. Durham, North Carolina: Duke University Press, 1969.

Nelson, H.J. "A Service Classification of American Cities." *Economic Geography*, July 1955, pp. 189–210.

Newell, A., J.C. Shaw, and H.A. Simon. "A Variety of Intelligent Learning in a General Problem Solver." Rand Corporation, Publication P-1742, July 1959.

Pack, J.R. "The Use of Urban Models: Report on a Survey of Planning Organizations." In *The Use of Urban Models in Urban Policy Making: Report on Research to Refine the Relevant Questions and to Provide an Appropriate Research Design, Vol. 1*. Fels Center of Government, University of Pennsylvania. RANN, National Science Foundation, NSF No. GI-37789, January 1974.

Paik, I.K., F.W. McElroy, and J. Harrington. "The Integrated Multimedia Pollution Simulation Model." Washington, D.C.: Georgetown University, 13 August 1973.

Paxson, E.W. "XRAY Game." In G.H. Fisher (ed.), *Cost Considerations in Systems Analysis*. New York: American Elsevier, 1971.

Perloff, H. and L. Wingo. *Issues in Urban Economics*. Washington, D.C.: Resources for the Future Inc., 1969.

Pidot, G.B. and J.W. Sommer. "Modal Cities (Final Report), Project SUPERB (Simulation of Urban Pressures on the Environment of a River Basin)." Hanover, New Hampshire: Dartmouth College. WERC, ORD, U.S. Environmental Protection Agency. EPA Grant No. R-801226, December 1973.

Quinn, J.A. *Human Ecology*. Hamden, Connecticut: Anchor Books, 1971, pp. 282–289.

Ramo, S. *Cure for Chaos*. New York: David McKay, 1969, pp. 33–34.

Regional Environment Management Conference, held in San Diego, California 26–27 February 1973.

"Report on National Growth 1972." President's Report to Congress.

Richards, J.A., F.W. Sears, M.R. Wehr, and M.W. Zemansky. *Modern College Physics*. Reading, Massachusetts: Addison-Wesley, 1962, p. 850.

Roberts, E.B. In *Simulation in the Service of Society*, January 1975, pp. 6–7.

Roethlisberger, F.J. and W.J. Dickson. *Management and the Worker*. Cambridge, Massachusetts: Harvard University Press, 1939.

Sackman, H. *Delphi Critique, Expert Opinion, Forecasting, and Group Process*. (A Rand Corporation Research Study). Lexington, Massachusetts: Lexington Books, 1975.

Saxe, J.G. "The Blind Men and the Elephant." In L. Untermeyer (Ed.), *Story Poems: An Anthology of Narrative Verse*. New York: Washington Square Press, 1969.

Schalow, R.D. and V.W. Everleigh. In *Proceedings of the Hawaii International Conference on System Sciences*. Honolulu: University of Hawaii Press, 1968.

Schneider, J.B. and J.R. Beck. "Reducing the Travel Requirements of the American City: An Investigation of Alternative Urban Spatial Structures." PB-232 317/8GA, University of Washington, Seattle, Urban Transportation Program, August 1973, 44 pp.

Schultz, R.L. "The Edge of the Coin." *Simulation in the Service of Society*, March 1976.

Schultz, R.L. "The Use of Simulation for Decision Making." *Behavioral Science*, September 1974, pp. 344–349.

Schultz, R.L. and D.P. Slevin (Eds.), *Implementing Operations Research/Management Science*. New York: American Elsevier, 1975.

Shubik, M. and G.D. Brewer. "Models, Simulations and Games: A Survey." Rand Corporation, 1972.

Smith, R.H.T. "Method and Purpose in Functional Town Classification." *Annals of the Association of American Geographers*, September 1965, pp. 539–548. Cited in Berry and Horton, p. 108.

Society for Computer Simulation. "Terms and Definitions—Report of the Standards Committee." *Simulation*, March 1976, pp. 79–87.

Southern California Association of Governments. *SCAG Short Range Transportation Plan*. 11 April 1974.

Stöber, G.J. and D. Schumacher. *Technology Assessment and Quality of Life*. Proceedings of the 4th general conference of SAINT (Salzburg Assembly: Impact of the New Technology) 24–28 September 1972. Amsterdam: Elsevier, 1973.

Timms, D.W.G. *The Urban Mosaic: Towards a Theory of Residential Differentiation*. Cambridge, England: Cambridge University Press, 1971.

Toffler, A. *Future Shock*. New York: Random House, 1970.

Tukey, J.W. "The Propagation of Errors, Fluctuations, and Tolerances: Basic Generalized Formulas." Statistical Techniques Research Group, Department of Mathematics, Princeton University, Technical Report No. 10.

Turk, A. et al. *Ecology, Pollution, Environment*. Philadelphia: W.B. Saunders, 1972, p. 15.

Ubico, R.E. "Documentation Standards for the Strategic Environmental Assessment System (SEAS)." Control Data Corporation, Rockville, Maryland. WERC, ORD, U.S. Environmental Protection Agency, 24 August 1973, 30 pp.

Van Horn, R. "Validation." In T.H. Naylor (Ed.), *The Design of Computer Simulation Experiments*. Durham, North Carolina: Duke University Press, 1969.

Veldman, D.J. *Fortran Programming for the Behavioral Sciences*. New York: Holt, Rinehart & Winston, 1967.

Voelker, A.H. "Some Pitfalls of Land-use Model Building." Regional Environmental Systems Analysis Program, Regional and Urban Studies Department, Oak Ridge National Laboratory, Oak Ridge, Tennessee, June 1975.

Voorhees, A.M. & Associates, Inc. "Factors and Trends in Trip Length." Highway Research Board, Washington, D.C. NCHRP 48, 1968.

Voorhees, A.M. & Associates, Inc. "A Simulation City Approach for Preparation of Urban Area Data Bases." WERC, ORD, U.S. Environmental Protection Agency, Washington, D.C. Contract No. 68-01-1805, November 1973.

Weber, A. *Theory of the Location of Industries*. Translated by C.J. Friedrich. Chicago: University of Chicago Press, 1929.

Webster's New World Dictionary of the American Language (Second College Edition). New York: World Publishing Co., 1972, p. 1475.

Weimer, A.M. and H. Hoyt. *Real Estate*. New York: Ronald Press, 1966.

Wells, J.D. et al. "Economic Characteristics of the Urban Public Transportation Industry." Institute for Defense Analysis, Arlington, Virginia. U.S. Department of Transportation, Washington, D.C., 1972.

Wieand, K., and R.F. Muth. "A Note on the Variation of Land Values with Distance from the CBD in St. Louis." *Journal of Regional Science*, December 1972.

Wilson, A.G. "The Use of Entropy Maximizing Models." *Journal of Transport Economics and Policy*, January 1969.

Wilson, E.B. *An Introduction to Scientific Research*. New York: McGraw-Hill, 1952.

Wright, J.W. "City Hall's Approaching Revolution in Service Delivery." *Nation's Cities*, January 1972, pp. 10–31.

Yamaguschi, T. "Japanese Cities: Their Functions and Characteristics." In *Papers and Proceedings of the Third Far East Conference of the Regional Science Association 3*, 1969, pp. 141–156.

Zimmerman, S. and T. Hillegass. "Community Aggregate Planning Model (CAPM I)." 1973, pp. 6–7.

Index

Abatement cost feedback model (ABATE),
 189, 238, 239, 240
Abelson, P. H., 35
Aggregation, 25, 159
"Agricultural Statistics," 269
Agriculture, Department of (USDA), as data
 source, 35, 51, 191, 269
 models, 189, 202
Allison, J. S., 74
Alonso, W., 113-116
Alterman, J., 199
AMBIAIR, 242
AMBIWATER, 242
American Management Systems, 195
Army Corps of Engineers, U. S., 274
Arnold, D. S., 283, 300
Atomic Energy Commission, 195

Battelle Memorial Institute, 195
Bechtel Corporation, 195
Beller, M., 29
Bellomo, S. J., 281
BENEFITS, 242-243
Benyon, P. R., 43, 44-45
Bergsman, J. P., 277
Berry, B. J. L., 39, 276, 300, 301
Bias, 25
Biggs, A. G., 73
"Blind Men and the Elephant," 113
BLS; see Labor Statistics, Bureau of
Blumenfeld, H., 277
Bogdan, Mary, xi
Bonner & Moore Associates, 195
Borcherding, T. E., 278
Brewer, G. D., 11, 12, 29, 107

Bryce, H. J., 277
"Building Games: Retrospection," 145

CAB (Civil Aeronautics Board), 270,
 274
Campbell, A., 206
CAPM (Community Aggregate Planning
 Model), 32
Carpenter, Hal, xi
Carrying capacity, ecological, 257-258
Carrying Capacity of a Nation, 257
Cartwright, T. J., 217
Cawthorne, A. R., 73
CBD (Central Business District), 32
CEA (Chase Econometric Associates),
 189, 238
Census, Bureau of, 33, 202, 229, 268,
 270-271, 284
Central Business District (CBD), 32
Chapin, F. S., 280
Charpentier, J. P., 102
Chase Econometric Associates (CEA),
 189, 238
Cherrington, P. W., 9
Chestnut, H., 29, 183, 186
Cities, modal, 293-300
 typical, 38, 283-310
CITY I, 145-146
CITY II, 146-147
CITY III, 146-147
CITY IV, 147
City, simulating, 276
Civil Aeronautics Board (CAB), 270,
 274
Civil Defense, Office of, 271

319